RECONCILIATION, LAW, & RIGHTEOUSNESS

PETER STUHLMACHER

RECONCILIATION, LAW, & RIGHTEOUSNESS

ESSAYS IN BIBLICAL THEOLOGY

FORTRESS PRESS   PHILADELPHIA

Translated from the German *Versöhnung, Gesetz und Gerechtigkeit: Aufsätze zur biblischen Theologie* (Göttingen: Vandenhoeck & Ruprecht, 1981).

Library of Congress Cataloging-in-Publication Data

Stuhlmacher, Peter.
  Reconciliation, law, and righteousness.

  Translation of: Versöhnung, Gesetz und Gerechtigkeit.
  1. Bible. N.T.—Theology—Addresses, essays,
lectures. I. Title.
  BS2397.S8813 1986   230   85-45482
  ISBN 0-8006-0770-8

1805H85 Printed in the United States of America 1–770

For Hartmut Gese,
with gratitude

Contents

Foreword to
the English Edition

Thanks to the friendly endeavors of Fortress Press and to the efforts of Professor Everett Kalin of Christ Seminary—Seminex and Pacific Lutheran Seminary, it is now possible for some of my biblical-theological essays on the New Testament to appear in English. I would like to thank Fortress Press for its accommodating spirit and Everett Kalin for his precise translation!

That the New Testament can be examined and interpreted historically according to all the rules of the discipline is a fact which has by now become well-known. This research has given us not just many hypotheses, but, even more, genuine insights as well. All those who want to know what the writings of the New Testament meant when they were written are interested in scholarly, historical investigation of these documents. The churches which define themselves in terms of the Holy Scriptures have all the more a vital theological interest in understanding the original witness of the Bible, which is for them authoritative.

Hermeneutically, however, historical-critical investigation of the New Testament dare under no circumstances conceal or forget that the New Testament has been handed down to us as the book of the Church, that ever since early Christian times it could be detached from the Old Testament only to its own harm, and that the Bible, both Old and New Testament, is read and interpreted in the churches as Holy Scripture up to this very day. An interpretation of the New Testament which takes these facts into consideration has to be—in the interest of and in service to the church(es)—in the same measure historically precise and the product of careful theological reflection. My biblical-theological studies attempt to do justice to this two-fold task.

In the school of Rudolf Bultmann (in which I myself, through my teacher Ernst Käsemann, was trained), the New Testament was interpreted to a large extent without reference to the Old Testament. Bultmann and his students furthermore proceeded from the view that in the New Testament a sharp distinction had to be drawn between Palestinian and Hellenistic churches, and also that Hellenistic Christianity, before and parallel to Paul, the Apostle himself, as well as the Gospel of John and its traditions were already exposed to the influences of pre-Christian and Christian Gnosticism. We have now learned to judge matters differently. All New Testament books were written and read in Christian churches which themselves read and interpreted the "Holy Scriptures" (of the Old Testament) in their worship services as witnesses of God's revelation in and through Christ; furthermore, the canon of the Old Testament was at the turn of the first century C.E. still not closed. From this perspective, the Old and New Testaments stand in a very close traditio-historical and kerygmatic relationship to one another. The differences between Palestinian and Hellenistic churches now appear to us to be far less substantive. On the basis of original gnostic texts (including those from Nag Hammadi), it has not been possible to demonstrate the existence of an oriental, pre-Christian gnostic redeemer-myth, which Bultmann conceived. The primary history-of-religions frame of reference for the New Testament is for us today (an itself multi-layered) early Judaism. It is therefore necessary to search for a different paradigm of interpretation than the one handed down to us from Bultmann. Biblical theology, to which in the United States especially Ulrich Mauser (Pittsburgh Theological Seminary) and the authors of the journal that he edits, *Horizons in Biblical Theology*, see themselves dedicated, is searching for just such a new paradigm.

When one begins this search from a New Testament perspective, it is methodologically possible to approach biblical-theological studies in a number of different ways. One can search for traditio-historical connections between Old and New Testament themes or writings; one can investigate how the Old Testament is quoted and interpreted in the New Testament; one can pursue the question regarding the testimony concerning the saving activity of the one God which connects the Old and New Testaments and so forth. The predominant line of investigation in my essays involves the traditio-historical approach; it should neither replace or displace, but rather only complement, the question of the interpretation of the Old Testament in the New and the question concerning the testimony of God's revelation which joins the two Testaments. That these traditio-historical, hermeneutical and kerygmatic approaches complement each other biblical-theologically and are not mutually exclusive is demonstrated, for example, by a dialogue between the Old Testament scholar Horst Seebass and myself, which will be published (in German) in the *Jahrbuch für Biblische Theologie* (Neukirchen-Vluyn: Neukirchener Verlag) in 1986.

Occasionally my essays cross over from the descriptive dimension of historical-exegetical research and proceed to a biblical-theological evaluation. The reason for this lies in the simple fact that the development of a biblical theology (of the New or also of the Old Testament) is not a purely descriptive task; it also involves systematic classification and evaluation. Since exegetical research should not simply serve the pursuit of academic knowledge, but also and above all help the Church to testify to the Gospel of Jesus Christ in today's world, the crossing over from historical description to theological classification and evaluation is, in my view, neither a mistake nor a makeshift solution, but rather the task of every exegete who is as such a teacher of theology and a servant of his or her Church.

PETER STUHLMACHER
Tübingen, November 1, 1985

Preface

The essays in biblical theology that have emanated from Tübingen in recent years have been received with appreciation, but they have also encountered severe criticism. In part this criticism has intended to unmask the pietistic evil spirit hostile to scholarly research alleged to be at work in these essays. The passion with which these critical objections have been offered shows that the solutions to theological problems proposed in the essays have been seen as threatening for the most varied reasons. The critics fear for historical criticism, seen as a necessary and dependable tool of scholarly research; for the New Testament's own distinctive message, which in their view emerges clearly only in contrast to the Old Testament and early Judaism; for exegetical argumentation that is free of being patronized by those who press dogmatic concerns; for a distinction between scholarly discussion and preaching; they fear a withdrawal from the theology of the word of God to a salvation-history perspective, and so on and so forth. Criticism of this kind gives one pause. But it also shows that in a number of places the Tübingen position needs to endure the criticism in order to solve its own unanswered questions through polemical attention to the outside.

To the degree to which others are able to speak with greater historical clarity and theological persuasiveness than I about Jesus and his proclamation, about the resurrection, the law, reconciliation and righteousness, I shall gladly surrender the field to them. But I do not consider it wise, because of the criticism directed against us, to give up at this time using tradition history to carry out biblical-theological investigations or indeed to drop the theme biblical theology entirely. As I have done exegesis I have found that precisely the central biblical traditions about Jesus' proclamation and his sovereign claims, about the resurrection of the dead, atonement and reconciliation, the law and righteousness, acquire an unanticipated historical profile through an approach that takes the whole Bible into consideration and in this way become a genuine theological challenge. If my observation is correct, then the efforts to achieve a

biblical theology of the New Testament that is open to the Old Testament need
to be continued for a while. The perplexities and problems attendant to a theology of this kind are in my opinion no greater or smaller than those faced
by exegetical theology as a whole.

For this reason I dare to offer this collection of older and newer essays for
discussion. My plea is that one does not deal with the above-mentioned
themes without carefully tracing these themes back from the New Testament
into the Old Testament and early Judaism, from there finding the way back
to what the New Testament says. If without traditional or dogmatic bias a
person views the Old Testament as a collection of "Scriptures" among which
we are to make distinctions in the same way New Testament authors themselves did, then it will be seen that the Old and New Testaments join one
another directly and that it is historically incorrect to make a fundamental
separation between the Old and New Testaments by means of the chasm of
early Judaism. Moving from the New Testament back into the Old by way of
early Judaism means that one must reconstruct the verbal and experiential
context from which the principal themes of New Testament theology and
proclamation arose. If this complex context is kept in mind, it becomes clear
that it is by no means accidental that the New Testament speaks of God's righteousness and justification before God, of atonement and reconciliation, of
faith and law, of the resurrection of the dead and of Jesus' exalted status as
the messianic Son of man. Rather, in the light of Jesus' appearance, the New
Testament takes up the basic religious questions that were and are of fundamental importance in the history of the faith of Israel. The theological significance of this observation needs further discussion despite all the exegetical
and theological habits that hold us back.

I would like to thank all those who contributed to the appearance of this collection of essays. Frau Gisela Kienle patiently typed the entire manuscript
which Karl Theodor Kleinknecht and Ulrich Mack read through with care.
Heinz-Peter Hempelmann prepared the index and bore the principal burden
of proofreading. Dr. Arndt Ruprecht and his colleagues provided cordial and
willing assistance in preparing the book for publication. Since an earlier form
of the essay "The New Righteousness in the Proclamation of Jesus" was part
of a private Festschrift for Hartmut Gese's fiftieth birthday, I would like to
dedicate the whole collection of essays to him. For many years I have profited
from Gese's counsel.

PETER STUHLMACHER
Tübingen, March 20, 1981

Abbreviations

AGJU	Arbeiten zur Geschichte des antiken Judentums und des Urchristentums
AnBib	Analecta biblica
BDF	F. Blass, A. Debrunner, and R. W. Funk, *A Greek Grammar of the NT*
BEvT	Beiträge zur evangelischen Theologie
BHT	Beiträge zur historischen Theologie
BibS(N)	Biblische Studien (Neukirchen, 1951–)
BWANT	Beiträge zur Wissenschaft vom Alten und Neuen Testament
EKKNT	Evangelisch-katholischer Kommentar zum Neuen Testament
ET	English Translation
EvK	*Evangelische Kommentare*
EvT	*Evangelische Theologie*
EWNT	H. Balz and G. Schneider (eds.), *Exegetisches Wörterbuch zum Neuen Testament*
FRLANT	Forschungen zur Religion and Literatur des Alten und Neuen Testaments
HKNT	Handkommentar zum Neuen Testament
HNT	Handbuch zum Neuen Testament
HTKNT	Herders theologischer Kommentar zum Neuen Testament
HTS	Harvard Theological Studies
IEJ	*Israel Exploration Journal*
JSJ	*Journal for the Study of Judaism in the Persian, Hellenistic and Roman Period*
JTS	*Journal of Theological Studies*
KD	*Kerygma und Dogma*
KlT	Kleine Texte
LR	*Lutherische Rundschau*
MTZ	*Münchener theologische Zeitschrift*

NTAbh	Neutestamentliche Abhandlungen
NTD	Das Neue Testament Deutsch
NTS	*New Testament Studies*
RAC	*Reallexikon für Antike und Christentum*
OTL	The Old Testament Library
QD	Quaestiones Disputatae
RB	*Revue biblique*
RGG	*Religion in Geschichte und Gegenwart*
SANT	Studien zum Alten und Neuen Testament
SBM	Stuttgarter biblische Monographien
SBS	Stuttgarter Bibelstudien
SBT	Studies in Biblical Theology
SEÅ	*Svensk exegetisk årsbok*
SNT	Studien zum Neuen Testament
SPB	Studia postbiblica
ST	*Studia theologica*
Str-B	[H. Strack and] P. Billerbeck, *Kommentar zum Neuen Testament*
SUNT	Studien zur Umwelt des Neuen Testaments
TBü	Theologische Bücherei
TDNT	G. Kittel and G. Friedrich (eds.), *Theological Dictionary of the New Testament*
TGl	*Theologie und Glaube*
THAT	E. Jenni (ed.), *Theologisches Handwörterbuch zum Alten Testament*
TLZ	*Theologische Literaturzeitung*
TP	*Theologie und Philosophie*
TRu	*Theologische Rundschau*
TU	Texte und Untersuchungen
TZ	*Theologische Zeitschrift*
WMANT	Wissenschaftliche Monographien zum Alten und Neuen Testament
WUNT	Wissenschaftliche Untersuchungen zum Neuen Testament
ZNW	*Zeitschrift für die neutestamentliche Wissenschaft*
ZTK	*Zeitschrift für Theologie und Kirche*

CHAPTER 1

Jesus as Reconciler. Reflections on the Problem of Portraying Jesus Within the Framework of a Biblical Theology of the New Testament

There are theological problems that dare not be neglected even if it will take generations to solve them. One such problem is the question how and to what extent Jesus' proclamation and fate ought to be included in the presentation of a theology of the New Testament.

I

This is precisely the question Hans Conzelmann asked us to consider. It is true that already in his important article "Jesus Christus," which appeared in 1959 in the third edition of *Die Religion in Geschichte and Gegenwart* [an article that has now been translated into English and published as a small book entitled *Jesus*—trans.], he made a comprehensive presentation of Jesus' work and proclamation, but at the end he stressed that such a historical reconstruction possessed theological relevance only as an illustration and concretization of the preaching of Christ, that is, as a reminder of and exercise in the historicality of revelation.[1] Then, in *An Outline of the Theology of the New Testament*, published in 1967, he insisted, "not for arbitrary reasons, but out of methodological consistency and as a result of the exegetical basis to my approach . . . that the 'historical Jesus' is not a theme of New Testament theology,"[2] because it is the particular task of New Testament theology to present and make comprehensible the kerygma contained in the New Testament texts. But since this very kerygma, above all in the Synoptic Gospels, insists that the exalted Christ is identical with the earthly Jesus, Conzelmann not only expressly incorporated the Synoptic kerygma into his theological plan but also offered a sketch of Jesus' proclamation in the second principal division of his book, which is devoted to this kerygma. By proceeding in this way Conzelmann took account of the question, "Why did faith maintain the identity of the Exalted One with Jesus of Nazareth after the resurrection appearances?"[3] Thus, going beyond the approach of his teacher Rudolf Bultmann, Conzelmann incorporated the proclamation of the earthly Jesus, as the essence of the Synoptic kerygma, into his presentation of New Testament theology, and he did this in such a way that, beginning with the kerygma, that is, the proclamation about the crucified and risen Christ as Lord, he pushed back to investigate the word and work of the earthly Jesus.

Particularly within the framework of the development of a theology of the New Testament this decision of Conzelmann's is both a step forward and an incomplete program. It is a step forward in that the New Testament's faith-evoking proclamation about Christ is preserved from being spiritualized out of existence and at the same time protected against being swallowed up or reduced to a hypothetical reconstruction, taking on various appearances as times and methods change, something that the so-called historical Jesus has represented from the beginning and still represents today. It is also a step for-ward in that the kerygma of the Synoptic Gospels is restored to its rightful the-ological place, something it no longer had in Rudolf Bultmann's famous *Theology of the New Testament* even though the church's proclamation about Christ has for two thousand years found its support precisely in the evan-gelists' narratives about Jesus, and that is true even when this preaching is and wants to be preaching about justification *sola fide propter Christum*.

There are two principal reasons that Conzelmann's decision presents an incomplete program. In his placement of the proclamation of Jesus as the foundation and concretization of the Synoptic kerygma, it does not yet become sufficiently clear that the Synoptic Gospels are not the first to stake their case on the identity of the crucified and risen Christ with Jesus and therefore to speak about Jesus kerygmatically, but that this is already done in the kerygma of the primitive community and of the earliest Christian missionaries. In both their confessional formulas and their proclamation about Christ, their starting point is that Jesus of Nazareth was and came to be the messianic deliverer sent by God (cf. 1 Cor. 15:3–5; Acts 10:36ff.; Rom. 1:3f.). If in a theology of the New Testament that is structured along history-of-traditions lines—a theology that attempts to lay bare the origin and claims of the New Testament kerygma—one wishes to get back to Jesus himself, then it is advisable to raise this issue right at the outset in order to be able to establish how and why from the beginning, from Easter on, faith staked its claim on Jesus, took up his work, and understood itself as faith in Jesus Christ. Only recently Ferdinand Hahn brilliantly discussed the possibilities and problems of such an analysis,[4] and Eduard Lohse helped open up this way of thinking in his *Grundriss der neutestamentlichen Theologie*. After two introductory paragraphs on "The Task and Method of New Testament Theology" and "The Gospel as Church-establishing Preaching," Lohse begins at once with a presentation of the proclamation of Jesus, using this governing principle:

> The gospels do not contain accounts of the course of Jesus' life, but, in concert with the early Christian kerygma, they are testimonies to Jesus as the Christ, whom the community confesses by faith. Since Christian preaching is related to the beginning of the gospel, New Testament theology has to show the indissoluble

connection between the kerygma and the story of Jesus that was at hand for its use.[5]

Conzelmann's approach is also incomplete in that it does not include sufficient reflection on the extent to which the Old Testament makes the problems about Jesus the very place at which it is necessary to begin. It is not only that the biblical canon forces on us the theological question of how and for what reasons the New Testament, which begins with the gospels' narrative about Jesus, remains dependent on the Old Testament. It is also that even initial formulations of the kerygma implicitly and explicitly refer to the Old Testament, in order that, starting there, they can make it possible to understand and hear who Jesus was and what he became for faith. Therefore, proceeding from the kerygma to an inquiry about Jesus also means proceeding from the kerygma to ask why from the beginning Jesus was proclaimed as the fulfiller and embodiment of the saving will of God proclaimed in the Old Testament. The insight, gaining more and more acceptance today, that at the beginning of the New Testament era the Old Testament represented a tradition process that was still open and incomplete[6] likewise presses us not to defer the question about Jesus within the framework of a New Testament theology until after the treatment of the Synoptics but to put it right at the start, that is, to let it follow reflections on the early Christian kerygma and on the relationship between the Old and New Testaments which this kerygma establishes. As far as this second issue is concerned, we point once again to Lohse's *Grundriss,* which already in the paragraph about the gospel that preceded his discussion of the proclamation of Jesus emphasized that the Christ event from the beginning "was proclaimed as God's eschatological act of salvation in which the promises of the scripture found their fulfillment,"[7] and from the beginning the Christian community assumed that "the meaning of the suffering and death of Jesus Christ [can] be comprehended and understood as God's will [only with the help of the scripture]."[8] But above all we can appeal to Leonhard Goppelt's *Theology of the New Testament.* Its first part, on "The Ministry of Jesus in Its Theological Significance," proceeds from the hermeneutical principle that it is fundamental to the message of the New Testament that it "wishes to attest to a fulfillment event coming from the God of the Old Testament and having Jesus as its center,"[9] and that this message moves, therefore, from the community's faith- and church-producing Easter kerygma back to an inquiry into the work of the earthly Jesus as such a fulfillment event.

If people do not see themselves forced for theological and historical or methodological reasons to persist in Bultmann's original position, according to which the proclamation of Jesus belongs only to the presuppositions of New Testament theology and is no part of this theology itself;[10] and if, despite all the theological insights of dialectical theology, they do not wish to bind or surrender faith to a reconstruction—whether positive or critical—of the figure of Jesus,[11] it is theologically and historically imperative today to include the proclamation of Jesus in a presentation of New Testament theology, to place it here at the beginning—after a consideration of the task and goal of a New

Testament theology and of the form and dimension of early Christian preaching about Christ, with its Old Testament orientation—and then to attempt to sketch a picture of how the New Testament kerygma identified and explained itself as the message about Jesus Christ. To proceed in this way is to keep on working in the direction in which Conzelmann pointed.

II

If one asks for specific kerygmatic passages that can provide support and criteria for our historical return to Jesus, we turn, on the one hand, to the pre-Pauline (Jerusalem) creed in 1 Cor. 15:3b–5 that Paul himself expressly designates as "gospel" and, on the other hand, to the sermon about Christ in Acts 10:34ff., which succinctly describes Jesus' mission, work, and fate. Whereas current research is almost unanimous today in speaking of 1 Cor. 15:3ff. as very early traditional material, the understanding of the traditional character of the kerygmatic narrative in Acts 10:34ff. is only beginning to gain acceptance again.[12] The two texts certainly do not belong to unrelated areas of tradition, but together give a general impression of how at first (in Jerusalem and in missionary activity) one spoke of Jesus in catechesis, preaching, and confession.

The succinct confession in 1 Cor. 15:3b–5—which, in contrast to two-part formulations like Rom. 4:25 or Luke 24:34, is already intended as a well-balanced whole—concentrates its attention on the substitutionary death and the resurrection of Jesus as the Christ (that is, as the Messiah) declaring both events to be in accord with God's saving will revealed in the Scriptures. It merely alludes to Jesus' burial and to his appearance to Peter (the founder of the primitive Christian community in Jerusalem) after his resurrection on the third day. The "sermon" in Acts 10:34ff. sets forth the mission of Jesus in the light of Isa. 52:7 and Nah. 2:1;[13] has Jesus set out from Galilee, after his baptism by John, as the messianic Savior and helper; experience in Jerusalem death on a cross, in accord with Deut. 21:22; be raised by God on the third day; and subsequently appear to a particular group of chosen witnesses so that they proclaim him as the one appointed by God to judge the world and as the messianic Savior inaugurating for all believers the forgiveness of their sins and, one may add, thereby also inaugurating the community of the endtime. Whereas in the creed in 1 Cor. 15:3b–5 Jesus' whole existence is embodied in his atoning death and his resurrection, Acts 10:34ff., which almost appears to be an outline of the tradition that is found in the Gospel of Mark, depicts the work of Jesus as a whole as a saving work that inaugurates the eschatological peace promised by God, that ends with the crucifixion, but that by virtue of the resurrection is made by God the basis of the faith that experiences the forgiveness of sins and thereby can have a part in eschatological salvation as communion with God.

This is not the place to investigate in detail the similarities and differences in the two texts. It is sufficient if agreement and a common kerygmatic intention can be maintained in the following respect: both texts speak of Jesus as the promised Messiah. According to Acts 10:34ff., it is his mission to accomplish and inaugurate salvation in the form of "peace" between God and humanity, enabling people to share in eschatological communion with God. It is asserted of such salvation that the prophets of the Old Testament promised it. Second, both texts agree in assuming that Jesus' work climaxed in his death. In both cases this death is said to have occurred in accordance with the Scriptures, that is, in accord with God's intention. Whereas Acts 10:39–40 works with a contrast pattern that in my opinion was part of the arsenal of the earliest Christian apologetics: you (Jews) put Jesus (in accord with Deut. 21:22) on the cross (and assumed that he was under God's curse)—but God raised him (that is, identified with the crucified and thus made this evil the basis of salvation);[14] the summary in 1 Cor. 15:3b–5 does not explicitly mention the crucifixion but immediately stresses that as the Messiah Jesus "died for our sins" and grounds this assertion in all probability not in a general reference to the Old Testament as a whole but directly to the atonement and substitution traditions of Isaiah 53. The combination of Jesus' atoning death and his resurrection in our creed may be understood as in Rom. 4:25. The resurrection, as the work of God identifying with the Christ who had been given over to death, ratifies the sacrifice of his life and elevates Jesus' death to become the basis for the forgiveness of sins, or, as Rom. 4:25 puts it, to become the basis for life-creating justification (in such a way that our sins are forgiven). If in this way one correctly describes the thoughts of the credal text and observes that Acts 10 also speaks of a forgiveness of sins made available to "everyone who believes" in the name of Jesus, the crucified and risen one (v. 43), one sees that also with respect to their soteriology the two texts dare not be separated too far from one another.[15] This is true, finally, also of the references to Jesus' appearances. In Acts 10:40–41 the kerygma about Jesus as the messianic reconciler is inaugurated by the epiphany of the risen one before chosen witnesses and the meal he ate with them, and the brief statement in 1 Cor. 15:5 about the appearance of the Christ who was given into death for us and raised on the third day might, beyond its role of simply attesting the resurrection, serve to express a similar idea.

To summarize, the pre-Pauline primitive missionary community already proclaimed and confessed Jesus as the Messiah whose mission and work, culminating in his vicarious death on the cross, was understood as the inauguration of the "peace" between God and humanity that God had promised, the eternal communion with God; in the resurrection of the crucified one God acknowledged this work once and for all, made Jesus' atoning death the basis of the forgiveness of sins for those who believe, and in the appearance of the risen one to certain chosen (apostolic) witnesses put into operation the salvation-bringing kerygma about Jesus as the Christ of God.

III

If from this kerygma and its fundamental assertion defining Jesus' work as messianic reconciliation one looks back at Jesus himself, there is an astonishing congruity with the picture reconstructed by historical criticism. As little as the kerygma's eschatological "definition" of the significance of Jesus' mission can be gained by a historical reconstruction, it is still encouraging to see the striking precision with which our historical reconstruction leads us to the kerygma of which we have spoken. Moving backward historically thus accomplishes precisely what F. Hahn wishes it to achieve: it allows us to reveal and reconstruct the process by which events occurred and were received, the process that led to the biblical kerygma:

> We no longer need to rely solely on an analysis of the final stage of this early Christian reception of the tradition about Jesus in its various forms, but we are also able to show in detail the way this reception process occurred.[16]

Or, to restate the substance of that ourselves: The reconstructive inquiry helps us to see that the early Christian kerygma was correct in proclaiming Jesus as the messianic reconciler.

To support this thesis I shall first of all refer to a series of contemporary portrayals of Jesus, without regard for completeness. If Günther Bornkamm, in the fourth chapter of his book about Jesus, first published in 1956, had already spoken emphatically about Jesus' proclamation of the approaching reign of God as salvation for the poor and wretched and at the same time shown that table fellowship with Jesus was an actualization of this call to salvation, a symbol of the closest kind of communion between God and humanity and a foretaste of the feast to come, the joyous messianic banquet,[17] Conzelmann in his article on Jesus Christ also impressed it upon us that the primary element in the proclamation of Jesus and of his work, which is fully incorporated into the proclamation, is "the absoluteness of the promise of salvation *(Heilszusage)*. It takes shape in the presentation of God as Father, that is, in the recovery of immediacy to him through the proclamation of forgiveness," and he adds that the connection of this promise of salvation to Jesus' person lies "simply in the fact that *he* offers this salvation as present, final possibility, that he now comforts the poor, and calls sinners to himself. Indirect Christology and theo-logy [i.e., the concept of God] are brought into congruence."[18] Along with Bornkamm and Conzelmann, Joachim Jeremias also designates the proclamation of salvation for the poor as "the heart of Jesus' proclamation,"[19] calls the "inclusion of sinners in the community of salvation, achieved in table-fellowship, . . . the most meaningful expression of the message of the redeeming love of God,"[20] and stresses that the opposition to Jesus erupted over precisely this unconditional proclamation of salvation. Similarly, Norman Perrin presents the message about the forgiveness of sins as the fundamental experience in which, according to the message of Jesus, the reign of God is met, and Perrin designates table fellowship with tax collectors and sinners as "the aspect of Jesus' ministry which must have been most meaningful to his followers and most offensive to his critics."[21] Finally, in the two most recent theologies of the New Testament, Lohse's *Grundriss* and Goppelt's presentation of the work of Jesus, the paragraphs about the compassion of God proclaimed by Jesus and demonstrated by his signs are undeniably the center of the respective constructions. If Lohse begins with the principle,

> Jesus calls God "Father" and bears witness to the nearness of the compassionate God who receives sinners and makes them his children, who are free to call on him with total confidence, and imparts to them the new life they are to live in trust to him,[22]

then Goppelt begins with the thesis that the reception of sinners by Jesus was the primary significance of his earthly work:

> in the person of Jesus it was God who was involving himself with people and was now establishing his eschatological reign. That was the foundation for New Testament Christology.[23]

We are able to state as a finding of this overview that made no pretense at completeness and that cut across the various schools of thought that a substantial segment of current New Testament scholarship sees in the work of Jesus historically the precise symbolic actualization of eschatological salvation as communion with God of which the kerygma speaks. What was essentially new historically in Jesus' coming and work was his endeavor to establish eschatological peace between God and humanity.

The result of this survey of scholarly opinion can be confirmed precisely by looking directly at exegetical material that can be regarded as characteristic of Jesus even if one looks upon the Synoptic tradition with the greatest historical skepticism (a point of view, conditioned by previous research, whose appropriateness or inappropriateness need not be decided here). Even if one merely begins with Jesus' comprehensive proclamation of God as the Father in the Lord's Prayer, if one sees how this proclamation about God gains new, independent expression in his striking parables of the lost sheep (Luke 15:1ff.), the laborers in the vineyard (Matt. 20:1ff.), the good Samaritan (Luke 10:30ff.), the Pharisee and the publican (Luke 18:10ff.), or even the unmerciful servant (Matt. 18:23ff.); if one further sees how precisely this new proclamation is accompanied by the incredible audacity to pronounce the forgiveness of sins by his own authority (Mark 2:5; Luke 18:10ff.), to actualize such forgiveness in the symbolic action of table fellowship with sinners in anticipation of the Son of man's eschatological meal with those who are his (1 Enoch 62:14), to put the healing of the sick, who because of their sickness are considered unfit for worship, above the Sabbath command, indeed to transgress the cultic law as a whole for the sake of direct contact with those considered lost and lawless (Mark 1:21ff.; 3:1ff.; 7:14–15), to go behind the wording of the law, together with its Pharisaic interpretation, and to declare love, as expressed in love of the enemy, to be the original will of God (Matt. 5:43ff.); if one sees all this the picture emerges of a proclaimer of God's reign "who breaks every mold" (E. Schweizer). What results is the picture of a prophetic witness for God who had to come into conflict with all significant

Jewish groups of his time over his deeds testifying to God's nearness, to God's willingness to forgive even the outcasts and his love's incessant summons to humanity. This conflict did not arise from some drive on Jesus' part to be provocative but because of the very thing he was there for, the proclamation and manifestation of the messianic reconciliation God opened to humanity through him.

IV

We now stand directly before the problem of the passion and death of Jesus, about which the kerygma of the pre-Pauline community said that Jesus' work led to it directly and that in his dying his messianic mission reached its goal.

As is known, the stratification the (Synoptic) passion tradition underwent during its transmission, its historical reliability, and its theological value are still very much in dispute. It is astounding that despite this a historical judgment like Lohse's can be ventured:

> Jesus' preaching and his actions, through which the universally binding character of the law was called into question, brought him into sharp conflict with the leading representatives of contemporary Judaism. Not only the Pharisees and scribes but also the Sadducees and priests were thus one in their opposition to him. The authority he claimed was either acknowledged or decisively opposed, so that his cross was inseparable from his message. Jesus was condemned to death on the charge that he claimed to be *basileus tōn Ioudaiōn* (Mark 15:26 par.). Thus, in order to secure his condemnation by the Romans, his message about the coming reign of God was distorted into the charge that he was a messianic pretender.[24]

If even this judgment alone, supported, for example, by M. Hengel[25] and F. Hahn,[26] holds true, it can be said that also in respect to Jesus' death the kerygma and historical reconstruction converge.

It appears to me, in fact, that everything speaks for the view we have presented. Consider the fact that none of the influential Jewish groups at that time could in the long run tolerate Jesus' work. Jesus' freedom over against the law and his indifference to the ideal of levitical purity was bound to be intolerable to the Pharisees. For the Zealots the command to love one's enemies, including religious opponents; Jesus' lack of prejudice against even the Roman military (Luke 7:1ff. par.); and his approval of paying taxes to Caesar (Mark 12:13ff.) were more than a provocation. The Sadducees and the high-priestly nobility must have felt themselves challenged to the limit by Jesus' forgiveness of sins apart from expiatory ritual, his (somber) word about the destruction of the temple (Mark 14:58 par.; John 2:18ff.), and then, naturally, by his stand against the trade in sacrificial animals and money changing when he cleansed the temple (an event that many, it's true, consider unhistorical). The popularity Jesus experienced with the people for a time might also have finally filled with suspicion the political powers in the land, the Herodians, the Sanhedrin, and then, of course, the Romans. That under these circumstances a catastrophe occurred as Jesus decided to go up to Jerusalem "in order to place before his people in their very center, at the place of the temple and of the highest authorities, a final decision"[27] is both historically unavoidable and easily understandable. Thus Jesus' death came as a result of his mission and his messianic activity. It is clear that Jesus accepted his death with open eyes and with no attempt to flee or defend himself.

If up to this point historical reconstruction and kerygmatic assertion about Jesus' activity as messianic reconciler coalesce, with the kerygma's two theses that Jesus died in fulfillment of his messianic mission and, indeed, to atone for the sins of humanity, we reach the realm in which the historical reality we can attain interweaves with the Easter perception of faith to declare a new eschatological reality. Interestingly, however, even here there is no reason to speak of a substantial divergence between the kerygma and historical reality. Rather, it is possible to reconstruct with understanding the origin of the kerygmatic proclamation.

First of all, with reference to Jesus' messianic claim, the following is worthy of note: First, there is hardly any doubt that Jesus' words and actions, such as his authoritative interpretation of the law, his disclosure about the destruction of the temple, his choice of the twelve, his entry into Jerusalem, and, by all odds, his prophetic act of cleansing the temple, were subject to being interpreted messianically and presented an unparalleled authority claim. What's more, from Mark 8:27–30, which is clearly older and more original than the parallel passage in Matt. 16:13–20, it can be seen that Jesus himself was confronted with messianic expectations from his own circle of disciples. If in that context Jesus tries to turn aside such expectations, it must be remembered that in the New Testament era there were all sorts of messianic expectations. They extended from the idea of a messiah who would come to free Israel from the yoke of foreign domination, to the concept, based on Zech. 13:7ff.,[28] of a martyr-messiah, all the way to that apocalyptic dimension now opened up by the publication of the Aramaic Qumran fragment 4Q243, with its formulations that parallel Luke 1:32, 35 to an astonishing degree,[29] forcing us as interpreters to confess that we are still far from seeing Jewish eschatology and messianology with sufficient clarity. Thus we can only draw from Mark 8:27ff. that Jesus would not allow himself to be made into a political liberationist-king and that as much as possible he avoided the ambiguous title of Messiah. The current state of research has brought us to the point where it no longer seems advisable to understand as merely a product of the community's theology the reproach that runs "like a scarlet thread"[30] through the trial of Jesus until it becomes the Roman title on the cross, namely, that Jesus set himself up as messiah. The very multiplicity of the messianic image could, as we have seen, make it possible for the Sanhedrin, provoked by Jesus' actions, to expose Jesus as "a false messiah," to deliver him to the Romans as a messianic pretender, and thus to hand him over to certain execution. The community, on the other hand, in the light of the Easter events and with the support of Zech. 13:7ff., could give full form to its view of the martyr-messiah and in this way come to their soteriological messianic proclamation. Even if this is only one of several ways things could have happened at that time, it can be seen with some

degree of certainty that the question of how Jesus was the Messiah followed
the Nazarene all the way to his death. As the synoptic temptation narrative,
Luke 24:21, and Acts 1:6 show, this very question bothered the community
even after Easter. In addition, the question of Jesus' messiahship can in no way
be decided on the basis of the title Messiah alone, but the problem of Jesus'
relationship to the title Son of man must also be brought in,[31] just as we need
to pay attention to the fact that our research has shown that no decision at all
can be reached about Jesus' authority claim solely from the promiscuously
and functionally employed titles (Messiah, Son of man, Son of God, etc.), but
that Jesus' historical activity as a whole needs to be kept in view.[32] If we take
all this into account, we are forced to conclude that the kerygma, with its talk
about Jesus as the Messiah who went to his death in pursuit of his mission,
is based on Jesus' actual authority claim, which it, however, comprehends in
title form in a definitive way hardly thinkable apart from the Easter events.
Thereby the proclamation of the kerygma is both historically comprehensible
and independent.

That is totally the case when the kerygma speaks of Jesus' vicarious death.
Here also it is possible to trace historically how the kerygma came to its soteriological assertion, and precisely through such analysis the intrinsic value of
the kerygma emerges clearly.

Of the numerous Synoptic sayings in which Jesus' death is interpreted, none
can with certainty be traced back to Jesus himself, according to the present
state of research. Everywhere, in the passion predictions, the Lord's Supper
tradition, or even in Mark 10:45, the famous ransom saying, the interpretive
faith of the community appears to be involved.[33] Therefore, the question about
these words is exactly the same as the one about the kerygma: with what right
and on what basis is Jesus' death to be designated as an expiatory event? The
answer has to be that the right to arrive at such an understanding comes from
looking back on Jesus' work and from the new Easter encounter with the crucified and risen one.

With regard to Jesus' work we have already made clear that for the sake of
his intention to bring into existence the messianic era of peace Jesus came into
conflict with Jewish and Roman authorities and was condemned to die on the
cross. Whoever sees that cannot easily deny that precisely this threatening
conflict, which was already in the offing early on in Galilee, was seen as such
by Jesus, particularly since not only the fate of John the Baptist, his teacher,
was before his eyes but also, according to Luke 13:31-33, the widely held
Jewish idea of the violent end of the prophets was evidently on his mind.
Despite that Jesus went up to Jerusalem. As he did so we don't know how he
envisioned his death. But one should also not deny that for a possible interpretation of his death a whole series of Old Testament patterns stood at his disposal, on the basis of which his death could have been seen by him both as
part of God's plan and as an expiatory sacrifice for his cause and for his
people. These patterns range from Isaiah 53, to the idea of the martyr-messiah
in Zech. 13:7ff. and the atoning martyrdom of the pious in general, to the concept of the suffering righteous person as God's child whose death had

emblematic significance. Under these circumstances we cannot simply dismiss the idea that at his last meal in Jerusalem Jesus spoke with his followers about his impending fate and declared his willingness to die for his mission and his followers. But it is just this that is not certain historically, and we arrive at an acceptable developmental analysis of the soteriological proclamation of Jesus' death in the kerygma only if we also take the Easter events into account.

For wherever the disciples ran off to on the night of the trial, the Synoptic tradition leaves no doubt that all Jesus' friends, including Peter, finally abandoned him out of disappointment and fear. Under these circumstances the Easter appearances to Peter, the twelve, and other former disciples of Jesus must, among other things, also have had the character of a reencounter and a new encounter with Jesus, indeed a reencounter and a new encounter beyond the abyss of his death on the cross and of the failure of which they themselves were guilty. Put differently, in the Easter appearances the former disciples of Jesus discovered that Jesus, through his death and despite their guilt, took them anew and for good into that eschatological community whose reality they had, together at table with the earthly Jesus, already pondered and experienced. But if the Easter epiphany of Jesus to Peter and the others proved to be the new start and founding of the ultimate community of reconciliation—a fact that is confirmed by the greeting of peace inherent in some appearance stories (Luke 24:36 v.1.; John 20:19, 21) as well as the accounts of the so-called appearance meals that belong here (Luke 24:28ff.; Acts 1:4; 10:41), then it was extremely natural to ponder the significance of Jesus' death on the cross with reference to this new reconciliation reality and to use Old Testament ideas of atonement and substitution to make its kerygmatic significance clear. Talk about Jesus' reconciling death thus proceeds from the Easter experience of reconciliation, and by looking at the scripture and surveying Jesus' work it interprets his death as a work of God that inaugurates reconciliation once and for all.

V

If the origin both of kerygmatic formulas and of narratives about Jesus as the messianic reconciler can be reconstructed in the way we have sketched, and if we bear in mind that without the living Old Testament tradition neither a pre- nor a post-Easter kerygmatic understanding of Jesus would have been possible, then we can make our summation.

The question was and is how and to what extent Jesus' proclamation and fate should be incorporated into a theology of the New Testament. Our finding is this: *Jesus' words and deeds are to be incorporated into a theology of the New Testament as a presentation of his mission as the messianic reconciler, which is what he himself wanted to be and what through his death and resurrection he for faith once and for all became.* Eberhard Jüngel once coined the fine hermeneutical statement: "The remarkable thing about the existence of the earthly Jesus [is] that his life was in fact an actualization of the word about the reign of God."³⁴ We can now give concrete content to this statement by saying: Jesus worked and suffered as the incarnation of God's word about reconciliation, and for that very reason he was already proclaimed as reconciler by the kerygma of the pre-Pauline community. This proclamation has an eschatological value of its own on the basis of the vision faith gained at Easter. But insofar as a biblical theology of the New Testament has the task of showing historically and theologically how the Christian missionaries arrived at their proclamation of Jesus Christ and how this proclamation then developed, the presentation of the mission, work, death, and resurrection of Jesus as the messianic reconciler belongs to the development of such a theology, indeed belongs at its beginning, so that one can recognize and reconstruct the way the kerygma came to be what it is, the gospel of reconciliation.

NOTES

1. H. Conzelmann, *Jesus,* trans. J. R. Lord, ed. J. Reumann (Philadelphia: Fortress Press, 1973), 87–96.
2. H. Conzelmann, *An Outline of the Theology of the New Testament,* trans. J. Bowden (New York: Harper & Row, 1969), xvii.
3. Ibid., xviii.
4. F. Hahn, "Methodologische Überlegungen zur Rückfrage nach Jesus," in *Rückfrage nach Jesus,* ed. K. Kertelge, QD 63 (Freiburg: Herder, 1974), 11–77 [= *Historical Investigation and New Testament Faith* (Philadelphia: Fortress Press, 1983), 35–105].
5. E. Lohse, *Grundriss der neutestamentlichen Theologie* (Stuttgart: Kohlhammer, 1974), 18.
6. H. von Campenhausen has good reason to say, "It is necessary to see Old Testament history as real history that moves forward and leads to a certain inner maturity, critical stage, and dialectic at whose end stands Jesus, the crucified and risen one" ("Tod und Auferstehung Jesu, als 'Historische Fakten,' " in *Moderne Exegese und historische Wissenschaft,* ed. J. M. Hollenbach and H. Staudinger [Trier: Spee-Verlag, 1972], 101 [94–103]). On this problem, in addition to the Old Testament literature listed in my essay, "Das Bekenntnis zur Auferweckung Jesu von den Toten und die Biblische Theologie," *ZTK* 40 (1973): 374ff. (365–403), see now also the fine essay by T. Holtz, "Zur Interpretation des Alten Testaments im Neuen Testament," *TLZ* 99 (1974): 19–32.
7. Lohse, *Grundriss,* 14.
8. Ibid., 15.
9. Leonhard Goppelt, *Theology of the New Testament,* trans. J. E. Alsup, 2 vols. (Grand Rapids: Wm. B. Eerdmans, 1981), 1:281.
10. R. Bultmann, *Theology of the New Testament,* trans. K. Grobel, 2 vols. (New York: Charles Scribner's Sons, 1951–55), 1:3. Among those who insist on this position today are W. Schmithals, *Jesus Christus in der Verkündigung der Kirche* (Neukirchen-Vluyn: Neukirchener Verlag, 1972), 60ff.; 80ff.; and, for different reasons, G. Strecker, "Die historische und theologische Problematik der Jesusfrage," *EvT* 29 (1969): 453–76.
11. In quite diverse theological directions this happens, in my view, in J. Jeremias, *New Testament Theology. The Proclamation of Jesus* (trans. J. Bowden [New York: Charles Scribner's Sons, 1971], 310–11 [and passim]); H. Braun, *Jesus of Nazareth: The Man and His Time* (trans. E. R. Kalin [Philadelphia: Fortress Press, 1979], 10ff. [and passim]), and S. Schulz, "Die neue Frage nach dem historischen Jesus" (in *Neues*

Testament und Geschichte. Festschrift für Oscar Cullmann zum 70. Geburtstag, ed. H. Baltensweiler and B. Reicke [Zürich: Theologischer Verlag, 1972], 33–42).

12. While U. Wilckens, *Die Missionsreden der Apostelgeschichte* (WMANT 5, 2d ed. [Neukirchen-Vluyn: Verlag des Erziehungsverein, 1963], 70 and frequently), spoke of an essentially Lukan composition, Hans Conzelmann, *Die Apostelgeschichte* (HNT, 2d ed. [Tübingen: Mohr, 1972], 10, 71–73), has already stressed the use of traditional material in Peter's sermon, which (also in his opinion) bears a heavily Lukan stamp. Then I myself have called attention to the heavily traditional elements in Acts 10:34ff. in my book *Das paulinische Evangelium,* vol. 1: *Vorgeschichte* (FRLANT 95 [Göttingen: Vandenhoeck & Ruprecht, 1968], 277–79). At the same time, O. H. Steck, referring to F. Hahn, *Christologische Hoheitstitel* (Göttingen: Vandenhoeck & Ruprecht, 1963), 116–17, 385ff. [ET: 1969] spoke about the traditional character of the christological material in the mission sermons and made the interesting conjecture that the format of the Lukan sermons summoning Jews to repentance, a format that in modified form appears in Acts 10:34ff., was not first created by Luke but must be traced back to Jewish proselytizing sermons in Palestine and the Diaspora; cf. Steck's book, *Israel und das gewaltsame Geschick der Propheten,* WMANT 23 (Neukirchen-Vluyn: Neukirchener Verlag, 1967), 267ff. In addition, H. Schürmann (*Das Lukasevangelium,* pt. 1, HTKNT [Freiburg: Herder, 1969], 16, 180) and E. Kränkl (*Jesus der Knecht Gottes* [Regensburg: Pustet, 1972], 78ff) have also referred to the traditional form of our text. Under these circumstances it appears legitimate to me, along with E. Lohse (*The Formation of the New Testament,* trans. M. E. Boring [Nashville: Abingdon Press, 1981], 118–19, and *Grundriss,* 20) to treat our text (again), at least vv. 37–43, as pre-Lukan tradition in outline and fundamental message, taken up and reworked by Luke, of course. From this one can see how clearly Jesus was proclaimed as the Christ (by means of narrative material).

13. On the translation problem in Acts 10:36 and its traditional character see my *Paulinisches Evangelium,* 148, 162, and 279, n. 1.

14. Deuteronomy 21:23 was probably invoked by the Jews in order to interpret Jesus' crucifixion as a curse upon blasphemers and false messiahs. Cf. G. Jeremias, *Der Lehrer der Gerechtigkeit,* SUNT 2 (Göttingen: Vandenhoeck & Ruprecht, 1963), 133–35; my essay "The End of the Law" (chap. 8 in this volume, see esp. p. 139); Lohse, *Grundriss,* 82; and H. W. Kuhn, "Jesus als Gekreuzigter in der frühchristlichen Verkündigung bis zur Mitte des 2. Jahrhunderts," *ZTK* 72 (1975): 33ff. (1–43), which contains valuable new source material. Under these circumstances it is possible and historically appropriate to classify the contrast pattern (which appears not only in Acts 10:39–40, but also in 2:36 and 5:30–31), a pattern that for its context works with the same Deuteronomy passage the Jews used as part of the early Christian reaction to that dangerous Jewish interpretation. I do this, as indicated in the paraphrase above, as follows: I see the contrast words "You crucified him, but God raised him" as an older preliminary stage of that law-critical reply Paul himself developed and then used soteriologically in Gal. 3:13. If pre-Pauline early Christian apologetics spoke only of the fact that with the resurrection God made the crucifixion itself a saving event, Paul's interpretation is both law-critical and soteriological: Jesus endured the accursed death on the cross vicariously, in order to free us from sin and end the law's accursed reign.

15. If any would wish to contest this, they would need to assume first about the tradition and then about Luke that they had not reflected on how Jesus' death and resurrection had become the basis for the forgiveness of sins. In the light of the earliest formulary material such as Rom. 4:25; 1 Cor. 15:3–5; or the words firmly anchored in the Lord's Supper material, "(died) for us," I regard this assumption over against the tradition as unjustified in the same measure as I find in dire need of modification the opinion expressed again and again, most recently by Kränkl (in his work cited in n. 12), 119–20, 209, 213–14, and G. Delling, *Der Kreuzestod Jesu in der urchristlichen*

Verkündigung (Göttingen: Vandenhoeck & Ruprecht, 1972), 83–97 that the proclamation about Christ in Acts is soteriologically deficient. In such a view it is unnoticed or accorded insufficient importance that Luke not only provides an extensive Lord's Supper account (Luke 22:14ff.) but also stresses with particular intensity in Acts the inauguration of salvation through the forgiveness of sins, Acts 2:38; 10:43; 13:37–38; 22:16; 26:18 (cf. Delling, *Der Kreuzestod Jesu*, 88–89). On this issue see also the careful statement of W. G. Kümmel, "Lukas in der Anklage der heutigen Theologie," *ZNW* 63 (1972): 159 (149–65).

16. Hahn, "Methodische Überlegungen," 68.
17. G. Bornkamm, *Jesus of Nazareth*, trans. I. and F. McLuskey, with J. M. Robinson (New York: Harper & Row, 1960), 75–81.
18. Conzelmann, *Jesus*, 51–52.
19. Jeremias, *New Testament Theology*, 109.
20. Ibid., 116.
21. N. Perrin, *Rediscovering the Teaching of Jesus* (New York: Harper & Row, 1967), 102.
22. Lohse, *Grundriss*, 35.
23. Goppelt, *Theology of the New Testament*, 1:132.
24. Lohse, *Grundriss*, 49.
25. M. Hengel, *Was Jesus a Revolutionist?* trans. W. Klassen, Facet Books, Biblical Series 28 (Philadelphia: Fortress Press, 1971), 15, and *Victory over Violence. Jesus and the Revolutionists*, trans. D. E. Green, intro. R. Scroggs (Philadelphia: Fortress Press, 1973), 54–55.
26. Hahn, "Methodische Überlegungen," 41ff.
27. Conzelmann, *Jesus*, 84. Conzelmann speaks here about the original historical element in the passion narrative and evaluates it as follows: "At several places there may still be traces of an eyewitness report (e.g. Mark 14:51; 15:21, 40?). It must be conceded that the length of Jesus' stay in Jerusalem has not been established. According to Mark, everything happened in a week, but this is a redactional scheme. In any case it is . . . certain that Jesus went to Jerusalem in order to place before his people in their very center, at the place of the temple and of the highest authorities, a final decision. Naturally his appearance must have been interpreted by the leadership of the people as an attack on the foundations of religion and the nation. So, just as it is narrated, they seized him with the aid of one of the disciples . . . and handed him over to the Roman procurator, Pontius Pilate, who at that particular time was residing in the city. It is established that Jesus was executed by the Romans (and not by the Jews) since crucifixion is a Roman form of capital punishment and not a Jewish one," 84–85.
28. Cf. on this H. Gese, "Anfang und Ende der Apokalyptik, dargestellt am Sacharjabuch," in *Vom Sinai zum Zion*, BEvT 64 (Munich: Kaiser, 1974), 228ff. (202–30).
29. J. A. Fitzmyer, "The Contribution of Qumran Aramaic to the Study of the New Testament," *NTS* 20 (1973/74): 391–94 (382–407).
30. Hengel, *Was Jesus a Revolutionist?* 15. On what follows, cf. Hengel, *Victory over Violence*, 54–56.
31. I am no more convinced than are Hengel, *Victory Over Violence*, 55–56 (n. 112), and C. Colpe, *TDNT* 8:438, 439–41, or Jeremias, *New Testament Theology*, 257ff., that all Synoptic Son-of-man sayings are later creations of the community, as Lohse now also asserts, *Grundriss*, 45. See my essay mentioned in n. 6, 392ff.; the problem cannot be discussed here in detail, of course.
32. Although they ascribe all the so-called titles in the Synoptic tradition to the theology of the community, neither Bornkamm, *Jesus of Nazareth*, 172, nor E. Käsemann, "The Problem of the Historical Jesus" (in *Essays on New Testament Themes*, trans. W. J. Montague, SBT [London: SCM Press, 1964; Philadelphia: Fortress Press, 1982], 37–38 [15–47], nor Lohse, *Grundriss*, 49, for example, deny that,

as Bornkamm puts it, "Jesus actually awakened Messianic expectations by his coming and by his ministry and that he encountered the faith which believed him to be the promised Saviour" (172). Käsemann even says, "The only category which does justice to his claim (quite independently of whether he used it himself and required it of others) is that in which his disciples themselves placed him—namely, that of the Messiah" (38).

33. The Tübingen dissertation by Werner Grimm, "Weil ich dich lieb habe. Der Einfluss der deuterojesajanischen Prophetie auf die Botschaft Jesu" (doctoral diss., University of Tübingen, 1973), has shown (with consequences that are not at issue here), among other things, that behind Mark 10:45 stands not primarily Isaiah 53 but above all Isa. 43:3ff. (261–316). Thus the well-known ransom word is based on an integrative interpretation of Isa. 43:3ff. and 53:11–12 that, in addition, reflects the Lord's Supper tradition (cf. J. Roloff, "Anfänge der soteriologischen Deutung des Todes Jesu," NTS 19 [1972/73]: 50ff. [38–64]). Thus, from a history-of-traditions perspective it is in my opinion easier to understand this saying from a post-Easter than from a pre-Easter perspective.

34. E. Jüngel, "Jesu Wort und Jesus als Wort Gottes. Ein hermeneutischer Beitrag zum christologischen Problem," in *Unterwegs zur Sache*, BEvT 61 (Munich: Kaiser, 1972), 129 (126–42).

CHAPTER 2

Vicariously Giving
His Life for Many, Mark 10:45
(Matt. 20:28)

Critical New Testament scholarship has a hard time today giving a clear historical answer to the question who Jesus of Nazareth was and how he understood his death. The debate over Mark 10:45 (Matt. 20:28) is symptomatic of this. It is still debated whether the saying, whose wording is identical in the two Gospels (with the exception of the introductory particle, *kai gar* in Mark and *hōsper* in Matthew): "the Son of man also came not to be served but to serve, and to give his life as a ransom for many," is a substantially authentic saying of Jesus or an early post-Easter creation of the Hellenistic Jewish-Christian community. If one believes the majority view among exegetes, it is an interpretive saying coined by the community in reflection on Jesus' death.

I

The best place to learn about the present state of the discussion and the extensive literature on Mark 10:45 is in Rudolf Pesch's brilliant commentary on Mark.[1] While Pesch uses significant arguments to support the historical reliability of the Markan tradition about the Lord's Supper (Mark 14:22–25) and consequently stresses that "by interpreting his death as expiatory" Jesus affirmed "that the saving nature of his mission encompassed also his death,"[2] he considers Mark 10:45 a secondary formulation that probably arose in the Greek-speaking Jewish-Christian community.

In reaching that conclusion Pesch argues as follows:[3] Mark 10:45 is not a combination of an originally independent saying about service ("For the Son of Man also came not to be served but to serve") and a ransom saying originally unconnected with it ("[the Son of man] came to give his life as a ransom for many"). Tradition-historical research makes the independent existence of these two sayings unlikely. Rather, v. 45 is a unified secondary composition intended to conclude the community rule in Mark 10:41–44 (authentic in substance) by reference to Jesus' example. The attachment of v. 45 to vv. 41–44 by means of *kai gar,* which corresponds, for example, to the christological grounding used in Rom. 15:2–3, is pre-Markan, since Mark does not use *kai gar* as a redactional connective particle. As in other sayings of Jesus also formulated by the early church (Matt. 11:19/Luke 7:34; 19:10), there is a looking back on Jesus' completed mission as the Son of man by means of the verb *ēlthen;* thus the title Son of man is part of this subsequent reflection. Although the tradition about and celebration of the Lord's Supper surely played a part in the formulation of v. 45, according to Pesch, the saying about serving is not limited to service at meals but is meant comprehensively and points back to v. 43: the exalted figure of the Son of man does not seek the service to which he's really entitled; his putting his life on the line for others is meant to serve as an example for the community. Verse 45b, *kai dounai tēn psychēn autou lytron anti pollōn,* is an interpretive statement that gives greater specificity to the saying about service in v. 45a. The formulation cannot with any certainty be traced back to a Semitic original, but it "certainly has been influenced by the Lord's Supper tradition and by the christological appropriation in early Hellenistic Judaism of the new meaning given by Jesus to the expiatory concept in Isa. 53:10–12."[4] As in Ecclus. 29:15; 1 Macc. 2:50, and many other passages *dounai tēn psychēn autou* means to surrender one's life; in the concept of the substitutionary and atoning surrender of life the martyr traditions of 2 Macc. 7:37 and, above all, 4 Macc. 6:29 are particularly close to our text. The New Testament *hapax legomenon lytron,* "with [its] notion of equivalence and of substitution, is based on *kōper*" rather than directly on *'āsām* of Isa. 53:10.[5] The phrase *anti pollōn* depends on Isaiah 53 and Mark 14:24. In Luke 22:24–27, which is a partial parallel to Mark 10:41–45 (par. Matt. 20:24–28), Pesch sees "a Lukan transposition of Mark 10:41–45 into the Lord's Supper setting" with clear indication of "Lukan redaction of Mark."[6] 1 Timothy 2:6 is a Hellenized variant of Mark 10:45.

Pesch's observations and analyses are excellent. The only question is whether his conclusion, that this tradition is secondary, is convincing. It appears more likely to me that in Mark 10:45 (Matt. 20:28) we have (in substance) authentic Jesus tradition rather than a tradition derivative either from the theology of the early Christian community or simply from Old Testament–Jewish martyr tradition.[7] This authentic tradition parallels and supports Pesch's historical understanding of Jesus' interpretation of his death as found in the (Markan) Lord's Supper tradition; but the saying did not originate in the Lord's Supper tradition of the early community. The Old Testament supports me in this view of things. It is absolutely indispensable for understanding the mission of the earthly Jesus and makes it possible to explain Mark 10:45 (Matt. 20:28) as a unity not only on the basis of Isa. 53:10–12 but especially of Isa. 43:3–4 and Dan. 7:9–14.

I take my justification for concentrating in what follows solely on Mark 10:45 (Matt. 20:28) from the insight emphasized anew by Pesch that the saying was attached to its present context for the first time by the pre-Markan connective particle *kai gar*[8] and that it thus was probably transmitted independently of Mark 10:41–44.[9]

II

The view, developed especially by Joachim Jeremias,[10] that there is in 1 Tim. 2:5–6 a Hellenized variant of Mark 10:45 (Matt. 20:28), is today a scholarly commonplace. If one, first of all, compares 1 Tim. 2:5–6 with the formulations and traditions of the Pauline epistles, similarities and differences appear. 1 Timothy 2:5–6 is based on acclamations like 1 Cor. 8:6 and Eph. 4:5–6, but, in contrast to them, it is expanded by statements that do not yet occur in Paul. When it says in 1 Timothy, "For there is one God, and there is one mediator between God and men, the man Christ Jesus, who gave himself as a ransom for all . . . ," in a supplementing of Paul's Christology "Mark's Semitic wording [is given] a more pronounced Greek flavour in every word."[11] The incarnationally appropriate term "man" corresponds to "Son of man," an ambiguous term to the ears of Greek hearers; in place of the Semitism *dounai tēn psychēn autou*, 1 Timothy has *ho dous heauton;* the hapax legomenon *lytron* is rendered by the Hellenizing compound *antilytron* (used only once in the NT), and in place of the Semitizing *anti pollōn* the appropriate interpretation *hyper pantōn* appears. 1 Tim. 2:5–6, as well as Mark 10:45 (Matt. 20:28), is concerned with a comprehensive interpretation of Jesus' mission as the mediator of salvation. If one makes a precise comparison of both texts, it also can be seen that 1 Tim. 2:5–6 appropriates more than just Mark 10:45b. Since, as Pesch correctly established, we have no indication of the independent circulation of a ransom saying like "The Son of man came to give his life as a ransom for many,"[12] we must conclude that at least the reference to the "man" Christ Jesus in 1 Tim. 2:5–6 comes from Mark 10:45a. Even the reference to the self-offering mediator between God and humanity could substantially be based on Mark 10:45a/b, but in our context that can remain open. It is sufficient for us to establish that Mark 10:45 (a and) b finds a Hellenized echo in a confessional formula in 1 Tim. 2:5–6, and that it is among the sources on which the Christology of the Pastoral Epistles draws in supplementing the inherited Pauline tradition. Said differently: it follows from 1 Tim. 2:5–6 that Mark 10:45 (Matt. 20:28) counts among the traditions that in addition to Paul became authoritative for deutero-Pauline Christology.

III

What is the source of this tradition, written in semitizing Greek and apparently indispensable for the Christology of 1 Timothy? The critical answer so common today, that it stems from the context of the early Christian theology of the Lord's Supper, stands on a very weak foundation. Neither *lytron*, the word so particularly characteristic of Mark 10:45 (Matt. 20:28), nor the concise formulation *anti pollōn* is typical of the New Testament Lord's Supper texts. These speak of the covenantal blood of Jesus, poured out *hyper pollōn* (also: *peri pollōn*); they avoid the word *lytron* (or *antilytron*). Also missing in the Lord's Supper context are the title Son of man and the saying about Jesus' "serving" (= *diakonein*).[13] But one should expect a christological formulation alleged to have grown out of the early Christian Lord's Supper tradition to reflect clearly the language of this tradition! The Lord's Supper texts and Mark 10:45 (Matt. 20:28) overlap only in a single word, *pollōn*, which in my view points to Isa. 53:10–12. There is really no compelling evidence for deriving Mark 10:45 from the Lord's Supper context; Mark 10:45 (Matt. 20:28) is related to the Lord's Supper tradition only with respect to subject matter.

One could now change course and say that in Mark 10:45 (Matt. 20:28) we are dealing with a formulation of the Hellenistic Jewish-Christian community that is based precisely on Isa. 53:10–12, the typical early Christian proof text. The only trouble with this answer is that it too lacks convincing support. The designation Son of man does not come from Isa. 52:13—53:12; nor does our text's term *diakonein*. The Septuagint, whose use we should presuppose in the Hellenistic Jewish-Christian community, designates the servant of God as *ho pais mou* and has for his service *douleuein*. The word *lytron* is also missing in the Septuagint. Points of contact between Mark 10:45 (Matt. 20:28) and the Septuagint text of Isa. 52:13—53:12 are found only insofar as the Septuagint designates the servant of God in v. 11 as an *eu douleuonta pollois* and speaks in v. 12 of the great inheritance the servant of God will receive because his life has been given up (by God) to death *(paredothē eis thanton hē psychē autou)*, because he has borne the sins of many and been handed over (by God) on account of their sins *(kai autos hamartias pollōn anēnegken kai dia tas hamartias autōn paredothē)*. Thus the similarities between our saying and the Septuagint translation of the Suffering Servant song are restricted, strictly speaking, to the following three words: *(para-)didonai, psychē autou, polloi.* In my opinion these words are sufficient to establish a dependence of Mark 10:45 (Matt. 20:28) on Isaiah 53, but they cannot sustain the thesis of the derivation of the entire saying from the community's interpretation of Isaiah 53.

Consequently one cannot designate Mark 10:45 (Matt. 20:28) as a creation of the Hellenistic Jewish-Christian community since the necessary marks of derivation are missing.

IV

Those who go behind the Greek text of the saying in search of a possible Aramaic (or Hebrew?) original tread on contested ground. Jeremias established the authenticity of Mark 10:45(b) precisely on the assertion "that it relates word for word to Isa. 53:10f., and indeed to the Hebrew text."[14] Jeremias continues:

Accordingly, in Mark 10:45b, *lytron*, which in the Septuagint (twenty times) denotes the ransom money for the firstborn, for slaves to be set free, for ground and land, for life forfeited, has the wider meaning of substitutionary offering, atonement offering, which *'āšām* has in Isa. 53:10.[15] Many exegetes have followed Jeremias in this interpretation of *lytron* as a rendition of *'āšām* Isa. 53:10. The only problem is that *'āšām* is never (!) translated by *lytron*. The primary meaning of *'āšām* is "sin offering," while *lytron* corresponds to the Hebrew word *kōper*. But *kōper* is absent in Isaiah 53! Thus the reference to Isaiah 53 is not convincing even if one has recourse to the Hebrew text.[16]

Should one then abandon recourse to a Semitic original of our saying? I don't think so. For it is striking that Mark 10:45 (Matt. 20:28) is readily capable of retranslation into Hebrew as well as Aramaic. This evident possibility of retranslation is the case for only a few passages in the Synoptic tradition and cannot be a sheer coincidence. In the Hebrew translation of the New Testament by Franz Delitzsch, Mark 10:45 reads: *kî ben-hā 'ādām . . . lô' bā' lĕma'an yĕšāratûhû kî 'im-lĕšārēt wĕlātēt 'et-napšô kōper taḥat rabbîm.* As an Aramaic translation Gustaf Dalman has suggested: *bar nāšā' lā' 'ātâ dĕyištammaš 'ellā dîšammēš wĕyittēn napšēh purqān hulāp saggî' în.*[17] *Kōper* is regularly translated by *purqān* in the Targumim, where *saggî' în* corresponds to the Hebrew *rabbîm.* A look at the Syriac translations of Mark 10:45 (Matt. 20:28) shows that Dalman is also right to use the root *šmš* for the Greek *diakonein.*[18]

From the retranslations it is once again shown that the saying does have points of contact with Isaiah 53 but cannot simply be derived from that passage. The Masoretic text and Delitzsch's translation have a total of two words in common, *napšô* and *rabbîm.* Thus we cannot be dealing with a saying composed by the Palestinian community on the basis of the Hebrew text of Isaiah 53. Rather we have a Son-of-man saying that can without difficulty be retranslated into Aramaic (Hebrew) and that has points of contact with Isaiah 53.

V

Since it is for various reasons denied that the title Son of man in Mark 10:45 (Matt. 20:28) was part of the original form of the text[19] and since Pesch sees the entire formulation "the Son of man . . . has come" as a sign of the text's secondary nature (see above), we need to begin once more, but without losing sight of the Semitic versions of the text.

It is well known that "in the New Testament, apart from the sayings of Jesus and three Old Testament quotations" [of Dan. 7:13 in Rev. 1:13 and 14:4 and Ps. 8:5 in Heb. 2:6—Stuhlmacher], the title Son of man "occurs only in Acts 7:56, on the lips of Stephen. Otherwise, it is completely absent."[20] I agree with Jeremias that the only historical explanation for this situation is that after Easter the community remembered Jesus' self-designation as the messianic Son of man, but, for various reasons not to be discussed here, it refrained almost totally from producing new Son-of-man sayings outside the gospel tradition. All the non-gospel passages Jeremias mentioned above speak of the glory of the Son of man, Jesus Christ. But Mark 10:45 (Matt. 20:28) speaks of the Son of man who refuses worshipful service and becomes the servant himself. The difference between those post-Easter references and the ransom saying is quite significant!

If one compares the saying with Dan 7:9–14 and the Son-of-man tradition dependent on this text in *1 Enoch*, a strange contrast emerges once again. In Daniel and *1 Enoch* the Son of man is made ruler and judge, to whom the service of angels and the adoration of the nations are due. In Mark 10:45 it is precisely this place of honor that the Son of man rejects, and he describes as the goal of his mission to be himself the ransom before God for the many lost (at the judgment).[21] It has been asked again and again where the verb *diakonein* in Mark 10:45 (Matt. 20:28) comes from. It corresponds not to the *LXX* of Isa. 53:11, which uses *douleuein* of the servant of God, but instead to an Aramaic root *šmš*, as the Syriac version confirms. This root occurs in only one place in the Old Testament, namely Dan. 7:10, which speaks of the service myriad angels render God, who had taken his place on the judgment throne. A fully parallel reference to the angels as the servants (= *mĕšārĕtîm*) of Yahweh occurs in Ps. 103:21. In Dan. 9:13–14, the Son of man is given rule over all nations, who are to serve him. In *1 Enoch* 45:3–4, 61:8–9, and 62:2 the Son of man himself sits on God's throne of judgment, the nations fall down before him, and the (avenging) angels are present to serve him in the judgment.[22] The history-of-traditions location of *diakonein* in Mark 10:45 (Matt. 20:28), which Delitzsch and Daiman correctly translated by the roots *šrt* and *šmš*, is the exalted Son-of-man tradition in Daniel 7 and the Ethiopic Enoch apocalypse! The word play "not to be served but to serve" means that the Son of man freely chooses the service of expiatory self-sacrifice over the heavenly place of honor as the worshiped Lord of the judgment.[23] The rendering of both verb forms with *diakonein* doesn't correspond, it is true, to septuagintal usage. But the varied use of the verb by Josephus is evidence enough that the word was current in Hellenistic Judaism, and not only specifically for table service but also for the Jewish life of service to God,[24] for the priest's service of the people (at Passover),[25] for the life to which Samuel was called,[26] and for the discipleship of Elisha.[27] The title Son of man and the verb *diakonein* (= *šrt/šmš*) belong very closely together in Mark 10:45 (Matt. 20:28) and stand in unmistakable contrast to the biblical Jewish Son-of-man tradition. Does this contrast stem from the community? Despite Hartwig Thyen's opinion pointing in this direction,[28] we have no actual historical evidence for this.

Within the Synoptic tradition we are to reckon with a secondary Son-of-man saying (only) if two conditions are met. There must be a clearly older Synoptic parallel that does not have the title Son of man, and the language and overall tendency of the saying in question must point to the theology of the community. These conditions are not met in Mark 10:45 (Matt. 20:28). There is no direct path in either direction between Mark 10:45 and the saying in Luke 22:27, "For which is the greater, one who sits at table, or one who serves? Is it not the one who sits at table? But I am among you as one who serves."[29] The Lukan saying is more firmly tied to its context (Luke 22:24–27) than is our logion, which has only a redactional connection to vv. 41–44. Despite its Semitic flavor,[30] it shows marks of Lukan style;[31] besides, there are analogous sayings in Ecclus. 32:1 and in rabbinic literature.[32] Mark 10:45 (Matt. 20:28), by contrast, is without analogy and is independent of the context of table fellowship and table service presupposed in Luke 22:24–27.

Especially in the light of the retranslations of Mark 10:45a, it is not evident that the formulation *ho hyios tou anthrōpou . . . ēlthen* (in this verse and in Matt. 11:19/Luke 7:34) looks back at the completed mission of Jesus (Pesch). In fact, v. 45 is a programmatic saying. But as Jeremias has shown,[33] *bā' lĕ 'ătā' lĕ* simply has the meaning "has the mission," "intends," "must," or "wants to," so that the sense of v. 45a is, "The Son of man does not want. . . ." Naturally this does not mean to deny that the Greek formulation *ouk ēlthen* could be read and understood in the post-Easter situation in the sense of looking back on Jesus' work. But in the case of Mark 10:45 (and, as I see it, also of Matt. 11:19 par.), it took on this meaning only later.

Certainly Mark 10:45 is closely connected with the sayings about the suffering Son of man.[34] But this is still no argument against the originality of the title Son of man (connected with *diakonein)!* Among the sayings about the suffering Son of man, at least the mysterious saying "the Son of man is delivered into human hands" is original.[35] That could also be true of Mark 10:45 (Matt. 20:28), since here the Synoptic passion predictions given their final form by the community (Mark 8:31ff. par.) are specifically not continued or reproduced.

Since our saying as a whole can be derived neither from the theology of the primitive Christian community nor from the biblical Jewish Son-of-man tradition; since it also does not simply grow out of Isaiah 53 or reproduce the pattern of Jesus' passion predictions, but instead presents an unparalleled and yet wholly Semitic formulation, we can conclude: in all likelihood Mark 10:45 (Matt. 20:28) is an authentic saying of Jesus.[36]

There is also positive evidence for the authenticity of this saying. It was provided by Werner Grimm in his Tübingen dissertation, *Weil ich dich liebe. Die Verkundigung Jesu und Deuterojesaja.*[37] Grimm called attention to the astonishing verbal parallels between Isa. 43:3–4 and Mark 10:45. While there is only a partial connection between our saying and Isaiah 53, the Hebrew text of Isa. 43:3–4 and Mark 10:45 have remarkably significant things in common. And yet Isa. 43:3–4 plays no significant role in early Christian arguments from Scripture; thus the verbal parallels between Isa. 43:3–4 and Mark 10:45 confirm the nonderivative character of the ransom saying. According to the translation in Claus Westermann's commentary,[38] these verses declare:

(3) For I, Yahweh, am your God, the Holy One of Israel, your Saviour, I give (*nātattî*) Egypt as your ransom (*koprĕkā*), Ethiopia and Seba in exchange for you (*taḥtêkā*),

(4) because you are precious in my eyes, and honored, and I love you. And I give people[39] in return for you (*wĕ'ettēn 'ādām taḥtêkā*), and nations for your life (*taḥat napšekā*).

If one compares the Hebrew expressions in parentheses with Mark 10:45, the parallel expressions are easy to recognize. The true verbal equivalent of *lytron,* namely *kōper,* occurs in Isa. 43:3–4; the repeated *taḥat* corresponds exactly to *anti (pollōn),* and the striking saying about the Son of man who will give his life finds an interesting equivalent in *wĕ'ettēn 'ādām:* the Son of man in Mark 10:45 takes the place of the people whom Yahweh will give as a ransom for Israel's life *(taḥtêkā* or *taḥat napšekā).*[40]

The points of contact between Isa. 43:3–4 and Mark 10:45 (Matt. 20:28) are more fundamental than the similarities that are already familiar to us between Isa. 53:10–12 and our saying. To say it another way, Mark 10:45 (Matt. 20:28) stands at the point where these two texts from Deutero-Isaiah intersect; but Isa. 43:3–4 delivers the primary accent. At the same time the ransom saying stands in contrast to the Son-of-man tradition of Dan 7:9–14 and the Ethiopic Enoch apocalypse.

VI

Now that we have brought out the tradition-historical setting of the saying and its nonderivative character, pointing back to Jesus himself, we can proceed to a positive interpretation of the ransom saying.

First we need to clarify with precision the meaning of *lytron.* As we have said, *lytron* corresponds to the Hebrew *kōper.* This word occurs frequently in the Old Testament, for example Exod. 21:30; 30:12; Num. 35:31–32; Ps. 49:8; Prov. 6:35; 13:8. In reference to a relationship with God the word signifies "atoning . . . a sort of ransom, always understood as a substitution for one's existence. It is *pidyōn nepeš,* the redemption of an individual life (Exod. 21:30)."[41] With reference to Isa. 43:3–4 that means that Yahweh, the creator of the world, offers up people and nations out of free love for Israel in order to gather anew his chosen people, scattered among the nations, and to give them the life in communion with God and the freedom that Israel itself can no longer achieve. If one interprets Isa. 43:3–4 on the basis of Isa. 45:14–17, then this passage specifically thinks of the nations, in the light of Yahweh's saving activity, turning from their idols to Yahweh and serving Israel. Thus they must give up their idolatrous existence and become the possession of Israel and its God.[42] The motive and driving force for the surrender of the nations for Israel's sake is, according to Isa. 43:3–4, solely the love that led Yahweh to choose Israel.

Here we also have one of the most beautiful and profound statements of what the Bible means by "election." A tiny, miserable and insignificant band of uprooted men and women are assured that they—precisely they—are the people to whom God has turned in love; they, just as they are, are dear and precious in his sight.[43]

The redemption of Israel is made possible through the ransom offered by God out of love in the form of the life of the nations. Later Jewish interpretation refers Isa. 43:3–4 to the last judgment: Yahweh gives the nations over to the verdict of death in order in just this way to save his beloved people Israel.[44] In another context I suggested understanding Jesus' mission and ministry as messianic reconciliation.[45] This can now be stated more precisely by reference to our saying and the reflections we have just made: with his life Jesus himself takes the place of those nations who were to die for Israel; indeed, he takes their place with a willing obedience that unites him with God's saving will. Jesus gives his life vicariously for Israel. The sacrifice of his life is meant to help gain life with God for all those who have lost and forfeited this life.

The people for whom Jesus sacrifices his life are called the "many" in Mark 10:45 (Matt. 20:28) in dependence on Isa. 53:11–12. Also, the expression "to give his life" resembles not only Isa. 43:3–4 but these verses as well. The vicarious sacrifice of Jesus' life thus also takes on the dimensions of the role assigned to the sin offering *('āšām)* of the Suffering Servant in Isa. 52:13–53:12. According to the oldest interpretation we have, Israel itself is to be seen as the Servant. Already in the two Isaiah scrolls from Qumran, "Israel" is read in Isa. 49:3, which is thus to be translated: "He [Yahweh] said to me, 'You are my servant, Israel,/through whom I will be glorified.' "[46] If one follows this clue, then Isa. 52:13—53:12 describes Israel's substitutionary suffering for the nations (= the many). Jesus also takes on this substitutionary suffering of Israel as God's Servant when he gives his life as a ransom for many. His self-sacrifice offers his life vicariously not only for Israel but also for the nations of the world, that is, for all people far from God. *Anti pollōn* is clearly meant inclusively.

In the Armenian translation of the *Testament of Benjamin* (from the second or first century B.C.E.), an interesting tradition not under suspicion of being Christian interpolation is preserved for us at 3:8. It is Jacob's prophecy about Joseph: "In you the prophecy of heaven will be fulfilled that says, 'The innocent will be defiled for the lawless, and the sinless one will die for the ungodly!' "[47] Here, as in Wisd. of Sol. 2:12–20; 5:1–7,[48] expressions from Isaiah 53 and its principal point are applied to the substitutionary suffering of a righteous individual. In the light of this application, no tradition-historical problem is created by applying to Jesus the expressions of Isaiah (43:3–4 and) 53 that in the original are understood collectively. The possibility of such an application lay readily at hand for Jesus. He himself contributed the interpretation of the messianic Son of man as the Suffering Righteous One and the Suffering Servant.

The Son-of-man tradition that came to Jesus from Dan. 7:9–14 and *1 Enoch*[49] is a complex phenomenon. This tradition is a meeting ground for traditions about the divine judge of the world, about the Messiah as the bearer of the wisdom and righteousness of God, and about the Servant of God.[50] But the Son of man is always an exalted figure appointed to judge the world and not one who suffers. Besides, according to *1 Enoch* 98:10, there is no ransom for sinners at the last judgment (before the Son of man), but only this word of woe,

> know that you are ready for the day of destruction. And do not hope that you will live, you sinners; rather you will go and die, . . . for you know no ransom, for you are ready for the day of the great judgment and for the day of distress and great shame for your spirits.[51]

The warning that there is no possibility of ransom rests on Ps. 49:7–9:

> Truly no man can ransom himself,
>   or give to God the price of his life,
> for the ransom of his life is costly,
>   and can never suffice,
> that he should continue to live on for ever.

This passage as well as Isa. 43:3–4 was interpreted eschatologically in Jewish exegesis.[52] According to Mark 8:36–37 (Matt. 16:26), this eschatological interpretation was known to Jesus. To be sure, the perspectives in these traditions change as he uses them.

When Jesus rejects the service of angels and the worship of the nations that are his due as the messianic Son of man and instead describes his mission as the dedication of his life to serving (culminating in his substitutionary self-sacrifice) the many, he gives a decisive reinterpretation to the image of the Son of man as the world's judge. According to Jesus, the Son of man is primarily the faithful witness to the reconciling and saving will of God! His way is the way of humility and of communion with sinners (Matt. 11:19/Luke 7:34); his call to take up the cross and follow him points precisely to this way, which is the way of love (Mark 8:34–35, par.; Matt. 10:38–39, par.); he sees his resurrection and exaltation as vindication of this way (Mark 14:62); but his glory will consist in being the eternal witness to the reconciling love of God and in judging the world precisely in this way (Luke 12:8–9; Mark 8:38; Matt. 25:31–46). Thus Jesus himself is the embodiment of that creative and sacrificial love of God given classical expression in Isa. 43:3–4. Since Jesus gives his life in an expiatory death for the many, he keeps them from death at the judgment and gives them a new existence before God. By vicariously giving his life for many, Jesus is the sacrifice God himself chooses but that Jesus also takes upon himself and offers in order to save sinners from destruction. It is precisely this willingness to offer himself that forms the inner core of Jesus' messianic mission.

According to the Lord's Supper narratives as Pesch has rightly stressed anew, Jesus persevered in his saving mission all the way to death and understood his death as an atonement for the many, and this is confirmed and underscored by Mark 10:45 (Matt. 20:28). Accordingly, New Testament scholarship doesn't need to be at a loss to answer the important question of how Jesus understood his mission and his death. It can answer that Jesus ministered, suffered, and endured an expiatory death as the messianic reconciler. But the messianic reconciler is the embodiment of the love of God that elects and redeems the lost, as Deutero-Isaiah testifies with special urgency and promise.

NOTES

1. R. Pesch, *Das Markusevangelium*, pt. 1 (Mark 1:1—8:26); pt. 2 (Mark 8:27—16:20), HTKNT (Freiburg: Herder, 1976–77); pt. 2 is hereafter cited as Pesch, *Markus* 2.

2. Pesch, *Markus* 2:362; cf. also R. Pesch, *Wie Jesus das Abendmahl hielt* (Freiburg: Herder, 1977), 69ff.

3. On what follows see Pesch, *Markus* 2:162–67.

4. Pesch, *Markus* 2:163.

5. Pesch, *Markus* 2:164.

6. Pesch, *Markus* 2:163, 165.

7. I am here attempting to sharpen and correct the very preliminary view about Mark 10:45 (Matt. 20:28) that I expressed in the essay "Jesus as Reconciler" (chap. 1 in this volume, p. 10).

8. Cf. Pesch, *Markus* 2:162, and H.-W. Kuhn, *Ältere Sammlungen im Markusevangelium*, SUNT 8 (Göttingen: Vandenhoeck & Ruprecht, 1971), 174–75.

9. "In Mark 10:45 we are dealing with an originally separate logion that became attached to Jesus' instruction of his disciples [= vv. 41–44, Stuhlmacher] through verbal parallels (*diakonos*, v. 43—*diakonēthēnai* and *diakonēsai*, v. 45)" (H. Thyen, *Studien zur Sündenvergebung im Neuen Testament und seinen alttestamentlichen und jüdischen Voraussetzungen*, FRLANT 96 [Göttingen: Vandenhoeck & Ruprecht, 1970], 155 [hereafter cited as Thyen]).

10. "Das Lösegeld für Viele (Mark 10:45)," *Judaica* 3 (1947–48): 249–64, now in Jeremias, *Abba* (Göttingen: Vandenhoeck & Ruprecht, 1966), 216–29 (hereafter cited as "Lösegeld"), summarized and sharpened in J. Jeremias, *New Testament Theology. The Proclamation of Jesus*, trans. J. Bowden (hereafter cited as Jeremias, *New Testament Theology*) (New York: Charles Scribner's Sons; London: SCM Press, 1971), 292–94.

11. Jeremias, *New Testament Theology*, 294.

12. Cf., in addition to Pesch, *Markus* 2:162, Thyen, 156, n. 1.

13. In his essay "Anfänge der soteriologischen Deutung des Todes Jesu (Mark 10:45 und Luke 22:27)" (*NTS* 19 [1972–73]: 38–64 [hereafter cited as Roloff]), J. Roloff develops the thesis "that *first*, the motif of Jesus' serving has its location in a very old layer of the Lord's Supper tradition, and that *second*, within this context it was originally interpreted in the sense of Jesus' sacrifice of his life" (p. 62). Mark 10:45 appears to him as a formulaic abbreviation and dogmatic summary of the Lord's Supper tradition, and he believes that in Mark 10:45 he has the *locus classicus* on the basis of which in the Greek world the stem *diak-*, which primarily signifies waiting tables and personal service, attained the specific ecclesiastical meaning known to us from the New Testament. I do not believe Roloff's double thesis is defensible. As I tried to show above, Mark 10:45 cannot be derived from the Lord's Supper context. If the Lord's Supper context (together with Mark 10:45) had given the decisive impetus for the New Testament reinterpretation of the stem *diak-*, one would expect a significant use of this stem in the Lord's Supper context, the very thing for which all evidence is lacking. However important this text may be for the establishment of the early Christian concept of service, it attains this significance directly from Jesus and not via the indirect route of eucharistic, dogmatic reflection by the early Palestinian community.

14. Jeremias, *New Testament Theology*, 292.

15. Jeremias, *New Testament Theology*, 292–93.

16. That this thesis of Jeremias' is not linguistically demonstrable even by recourse to the Hebrew text of Isaiah 53 was shown already in 1959 by C. K. Barrett, "The Background of Mark 10:45" (in *New Testament Essays. Studies in Memory of T. W. Manson*, ed. A. J. B. Higgins [Manchester: Manchester Univ. Press, 1959], 1–18 [hereafter cited as Barrett]). W. J. Moulder ("The Old Testament Background and the Interpretation of Mark 10:45," *NTS* 24 [1977–78]: 120–27 [hereafter cited as Moulder]), recently attempted to defend Jeremias, but he again arrives only at the (not accidentally) imprecise formulation that Mark 10:45 is an unusual reproduction of Isa. 53:12, as is true also of Phil. 2:6–11, or an adaptation of the entire Suffering Servant song as in the Philippians hymn as well.

17. G. Dalman, *Jesus-Jeshua. Studies in the Gospels*, trans. P. Levertoff (New York: Ktav, 1971), 118.

18. Cf. J. A. Emerton, "Some New Testament Notes: III. The Aramaic Background of Mark 10:45," *JTS* N.S. 11 (1960): 334–35; in the rendering of *diakonein* by *šmš* in the Old Syriac, the Peshitta, and a Palestinian-Syriac gospel lectionary, Emerton sees a confirmation of the fact that the translators had no interest in reproducing the root ^c*bd* from Isaiah 53.

19. For example, by C. Colpe, *TDNT* 8:448; J. Jeremias, "Die älteste Schicht der Menschensohn-Logien," *ZNW* 58 (1967): 166 (159–72), and *New Testament Theology*, 293; K. Kertelge, "Der dienende Menschensohn (Mark 10:45)," in *Jesus und der Menschensohn. Für A. Vögtle*, ed. R. Pesch and R. Schnackenburg, with O. Kaiser (Freiburg: Herder, 1975), 235 (225–39—hereafter cited as Kertelge).

20. Jeremias, *New Testament Theology*, 264–65.

21. Especially Barrett (8ff.) and Thyen (156–57) have called attention to this contrast.

22. J. Theisohn (*Der auserwählte Richter*, SUNT 12 [Göttingen: Vandenhoeck & Ruprecht, 1975], 15ff. [hereafter cited as Theisohn]) shows that the vision of the Son of man in *I Enoch* 46:1–2 depends, down to individual details, on Dan. 7:9–10, 13–14. Thus the connective path we have drawn with reference to "serving" can be traced with tradition-historical precision.

23. Moulder, 122–23, appropriately compares Mark 10:45 with Phil. 2:6ff: "he was in the form of God, [but] did not count equality with God a thing to be grasped, but emptied himself, taking the form of a servant, being born in the likeness of men. And being found in human form he humbled himself and became obedient unto death, even death on a cross."

24. Josephus *Ant.* 18.280.

25. Josephus *Ant.* 10.72.

26. Josephus *Ant.* 5.344: Samuel is consecrated for *diakonia tou theou*.

27. Josephus *Ant.* 8.354: Elisha is Elijah's *mathētēs* and *diakonos*.

28. Thyen, 157: "Could there be . . . in Mark 10:45 a criticism by 'Hellenistic' circles of the messianology of the primitive community? A polemical intention of this kind explains best and most clearly, in any case, the exceptional use of the title Son of man in our saying." Thyen can draw this conclusion because, by appeal to P. Vielhauer, "Gottesreich und Menschensohn in der Verkündigung Jesu" (in *Aufsätze zum Neuen Testament*, TBü 31 [Munich: Kaiser, 1965], 55–91), he asserted previously "that *all* synoptic Son of man sayings are the work of the post-Easter community" (p. 156, emphasis Thyen's).

29. The complications and hypothetical steps to which the derivation of Mark 10:45 from the Lukan saying about service leads are shown, for example, by Roloff, 59, n. 2.

30. Cf. M. Black, *An Aramaic Approach to the Gospels and Acts*, 3d ed. (Oxford: Clarendon Press, 1967), 228–29 and Jeremias, *New Testament Theology*, 292–94.

31. J. Wanke, *Beobachtungen zum Eucharistieverständnis des Lukas auf Grund der*

lukanischen Mahlberichte (Erfurter theologische Schriften 8 [Leipzig: St. Benno Verlag, 1973], 65, n. 222) says Luke 22:27 contains "a series of characteristic Lukan expressions *en mesǭ; ho diakonōn; egō de*," and to establish that he points to H. Schürmann, *Jesu Abschiedsrede, Luke 22:21-38* (NTAbh. 20.5 [Münster: Aschendorff, 1957], 79ff.). It is generally acknowledged that, compared to Mark 10:41-44, Luke 22:24-26 shows Hellenistic redaction; cf., for example, Jeremias, "Lösegeld," 226-27, and Schürmann, *Jesu Abschiedsrede*, 65ff. Schürmann, on p. 92, describes Luke 22:24-26, 27 as a whole as "merely a more remote variant tradition of Mark 10:41-44, 45."

32. Cf. Str-B 2:257 (at Luke 22:27).

33. Jeremias, "Die älteste Schicht der Menschensohn-Logien," 166-67.

34. Cf. Schürmann, *Jesu Abschiedsrede*, 85-86, who expressly warns against declaring Mark 10:45 inauthentic, and Colpe, *TDNT* 8:448, 455; Colpe also regards v. 45b as a substantially genuine saying of Jesus.

35. Jeremias, *New Testament Theology*, 282.

36. For a discussion of the criterion of nonderivability brought into use here, see R. Bultmann, *The History of the Synoptic Tradition* (trans. J. Marsh, rev. ed. [New York: Harper & Row; Oxford: Blackwell, 1972], 270), and E. Käsemann, "The Problem of the Historical Jesus" (in *Essays on New Testament Themes*, trans. W. J. Montague [London: SCM Press, 1964; Philadelphia: Fortress Press, 1982], 37): "In only one case do we have more or less safe ground under our feet; when there are no grounds either for deriving a tradition from Judaism or for ascribing it to primitive Christianity. . . ."

37. W. Grimm, *Arbeiten zum Neuen Testament und Judentum 1* (Bern: Herbert Lang, 1976), 231-77 (hereafter cited as Grimm).

38. C. Westermann, *Isaiah 40-66. A Commentary*, trans. D. M. G. Stalker, OTL (Philadelphia: Westminster, 1969), 114 (hereafter cited as Westermann).

39. Westermann, 114, with *BH*³ proposes changing *'ādām* in v. 4 to *'ădāmôt* ("countries"); in the light of the attestation of *'ettēn hā' ādām* (sic!) in 1QIsaᵃ and *wĕ'ettēna 'ādām* (sic!) in 1QIsaᵇ, I consider this conjecture unnecessary.

40. Grimm, 254, thinks that the striking *hā' ādām* in 1QIsaᵃ envisions a specific person whom Yahweh intends to sacrifice, "since the context excludes the possibility that the interpolated article *h* is intended generically here"; but a comparison of 1QIsaᵃ and 1QIsaᵇ (cf. n. 39 above) suggests that the article is intended generically. This, of course, has no effect on the fact that Jesus could apply the Hebrew *'ādām* or *hā' ādām* to his own mission as (Son of) man.

41. H. Gese, "The Atonement," in *Essays on Biblical Theology*, trans. K. Crim (Minneapolis: Augsburg Pub. House, 1981), 95. The very unfortunate historical discussion over whether a developed concept of atonement is to be presupposed already for Jesus' time or whether it was Hellenistic Judaism in the second half of the first century C.E. that was first impelled to consider the expiatory significance of the suffering of the martyrs and the righteous should, in the light of this essay, be ended as quickly as possible. For the vicarious suffering of the righteous, which effects the forgiveness of sins for others, and for the efficacy of the righteous person's prayer we now have clear pre-Christian evidence in the *Targum of Job* from Cave 11 at Qumran (11QtgJob), col. 38.2-3 (to Job 42:9-10): "and God heard his [Job's] plea and forgave (3) them [Job's friends] their sins for his [Job's] sake." This "for Job's sake" corresponds exactly to *dia Iōb* in the LXX of Job 42:9, to which Martin Hengel has called my attention. It goes beyond the Masoretic text and shows that 2 Macc. 7:37-38 and 4 Macc. 6:26ff.; 16:16-25 have much older roots than is sometimes assumed. On this issue cf. J. Gnilka, "Martyriumsparänese und Sühnetod in synoptischen und jüdischen Traditionen," in *Die Kirche des Anfangs. Für Heinz Schürmann*, ed. R. Schnackenburg, J. Ernst, and

J. Wanke, Erfurter Theologische Studien 38 (Leipzig: St. Benno Verlag, 1978), 223–46.

42. On this interpretation cf. Gese, "The Atonement," 114, n. 13.

43. Westermann, 118.

44. Cf. Grimm, 244–46, for a reference to and quotation of Mek. 21:30; Exodus Rabbah, 11, to 8:19, and Sipre Deut. 333, to 32:43.

45. Cf. "Jesus as Reconciler" (chap. 1 in this volume).

46. The translation follows Westermann, 206. Westermann translates ǎšer-bēkā 'etpā'ar with "you, in whom I will be glorified," while I, following Westermann's interpretation and formulation on 208ff., would rather say, "you, through whom I will be glorified."

47. On the transmission of the text and the translation of the passage see J. Becker, Untersuchungen zur Entstehungsgeschichte der Testamente der zwölf Patriarchen, AGJU 8 (Leiden: Brill, 1970), 51–57, and idem, "Die Testamente der zwölf Patriarchen," in Unterweisung in lehrhafter Form (Gütersloh: Mohn, 1974), 132.

48. On the connection between this "diptych" and Isaiah 53, cf. L. Ruppert, Jesus als der leidende Gerechte? SBS 59 (Stuttgart: KBW Verlag, 1972), 23–24, and G. W. E. Nickelsburg, Jr., Resurrection, Immortality, and Eternal Life in Intertestamental Judaism, HTS 26 (Cambridge: Harvard Univ. Press, 1972), 68–70 (hereafter cited as Nickelsburg).

49. With J. Jeremias, TDNT 5:687, n. 245, and others, I date the Similitudes (chaps. 37–71) of 1 Enoch in the last third of the first century B.C.E.

50. Dan. 7:15ff. can be understood as a transformation of the old concept of the Messiah; see Gese, "The Messiah," in Essays on Biblical Theology, 152ff. In 1 Enoch the Son of man is called "the Righteous One" in 38:2; 53:6; and frequently; "the Chosen One" in 45:3ff.; 49:2; and frequently; "the Anointed One" in 48:10 (61:7). In 1 Enoch 48:4, Isa. 42:6 and 49:6 are applied to him, and in 49:3–4 and 62:2ff., Isa. 11:2–5. On the individual history-of-traditions issues see Theisohn, passim, and Nickelsburg, 68–78.

51. Michael A. Knibb, The Ethiopic Book of Enoch, 2 vols. (Oxford: Clarendon Press, 1978), 2:231–32.

52. Cf. Grimm, 243–44, and Jeremias, "Lösegeld," 222.

CHAPTER **3**

The New Righteousness
in the Proclamation
of Jesus

The formation of New Testament tradition begins in Jesus' time and has in Jesus Christ its crucial point of reference. With respect to so important a biblical theme as "righteousness," we face a peculiar situation. The well-known texts from the Sermon on the Mount that have been so influential in Christian history, about hungering and thirsting for righteousness (Matt. 5:6), about the higher righteousness required of Jesus' followers (Matt. 5:20), as well as about seeking God's reign and righteousness (Matt. 6:33), do not belong to the earliest layer of the tradition. Rather, these are sayings that elucidate Jesus' sermon with the help of the term "righteousness," sayings that are especially characteristic of the Gospel of Matthew. This is true also of Matt. 3:15. Matthew, the "First Gospel" among the Synoptics in terms of actual influence in the church, emphatically locates Jesus' way and word under the heading "righteousness," while in the primary tradition going back to Jesus himself there are only occasional references to "the righteous" (Mark 2:17 par.; Luke 15:7; Matt. 25:37, 46) and to "being justified" (Luke 18:14; Matt. 11:19 par.). Programmatic statements by Jesus about the word righteousness are lacking.

One can conclude from these findings that thoughts and deeds of righteousness were not especially characteristic of Jesus' proclamation and that only with the Christian community that believed in Jesus was new interest in the old biblical theme of righteousness to be found.[1] I would like to warn against such a conclusion. *To me it seems much more likely that Jesus' messianic life of righteousness provided the extent and direction for his community's reflection on this theological concept.*[2] What broke forth in Jesus as a new reality was caught by his post-Easter witnesses in narratives and in the terminologically inflexible language of proclamation. The following historical and also biblical-theological reflections support this view.

JESUS' ENCOUNTER WITH THE
THEME "RIGHTEOUSNESS"

We know that Jesus complied with John the Baptist's preaching of repentance and that he submitted himself to John's baptism of repentance (Mark 1:9–11 par.). John's baptism sealed those who repented from the wrathful judgment of "the Coming One," whom the Baptist proclaimed, and, as Matt. 21:32 says by means of an old biblical expression also used by early Judaism, set them on "the way of righteousness" (cf., for example, Prov. 8:20; 16:31; *1 Enoch* 99:10). "The way of righteousness" is the way of turning from sin and turning to deeds that accord with God's righteous will; as Judaism put it, to deeds that were in accord with God's righteous commands (cf. Prov. 17:23; Ps. Sol. 14:2; *1 Enoch* 94:4–5). Through John the Baptist Jesus consciously followed the call to this "way of righteousness." He was ready to serve God "in holiness and righteousness before God" all the days of his life (Luke 1:74–75). So through the Baptist, Jesus was confronted with the question of a life of righteousness before God, and indeed, when one reads the Baptist's preaching of repentance to people in all walks of life in Luke 3:7–9 par., confronted by it with utmost seriousness. Jesus could not avoid this question, nor did he desire to.

Jürgen Becker[3] and Friedrich Lang[4] have made it likely that the mighty "Coming One" who the Baptist said would follow him, the one who would baptize with the Spirit and with fire, was none other than the Son of man coming "in the clouds of heaven." He is the one spoken of in Dan. 7:13–14; *1 Enoch* 45:3–6; 46:3ff.; 47:2ff.; 49:2ff.; 61:7ff.; 62:2ff.; and 4 Ezra 13:3ff., 25ff. According to this whole tradition the Son of man has the task of inaugurating God's reign over the world. He is set upon God's throne of judgment and, with the help of the angels who serve him, judges the nations of the world. He will destroy God's enemies, hand the unrighteous over to the punishment they deserve, and secure justice and peace for the righteous who experienced suffering and death on earth. He does this because, according to *1 Enoch* 48:4, he is the one entrusted by God with the messianic task of setting things right and serves as the "light of the nations" of whom Isa. 42:6 and 49:6 speak; because in him "dwells the spirit of wisdom, and the spirit which gives understanding, and the spirit of knowledge and of power, and the spirit of those who sleep in righteousness" (*1 Enoch* 49:3;[5] cf. Isa. 11:2ff); because he "has righteousness" and is the one "with whom righteousness dwells" (*1 Enoch* 46:3), righteousness that, according to Isa. 9:6–7; 11:4; and Jer. 23:6, is to be the mark of the Messiah. For "Son of man" and "Messiah" are titles that overlap one another in the Enoch apocalypse (cf. *1 Enoch* 48:10; 52:4).[6] The judgment by the Son of man is the messianic judgment of Isa. 11:3ff.: "the Lord of Spirits (set him[7] [the messianic Son of man]) on the throne of his glory, and the spirit of righteousness was poured out upon him, and the word of his mouth kills all the sinners and all the lawless, and they are destroyed before him" (*1 Enoch* 62:2; cf. also *4 Ezra* 13:9ff., 27ff.). In

John the Baptist's preaching of repentance, then, Jesus was also confronted with the figure of the messianic Son of man who was to judge the world, who was supposed to come imminently in the clouds of heaven and set up God's reign, the just eschatological world order. For Jesus, who heeded John the Baptist's call for repentance, "holiness and righteousness before God" (Luke 1:74–75) and God's universal righteous order, which was to be set up by the Son of man–Messiah at the last judgment, were unavoidable themes. Jesus committed himself to these themes and *with his whole way of life he blazed a trail for a new understanding of the righteousness of God and of righteousness before God.*

THE NEW RIGHTEOUSNESS IN JESUS' MESSIANIC ACTIVITY

From the very beginning of his public ministry Jesus came forward as a proclaimer of the reign of God. According to the accounts in all three Synoptic Gospels (and according to Acts 1:22 and 10:37–38 as well), Jesus began his own proclamation immediately after his baptism in the Jordan by John. More precisely, Jesus came forward as a prophetic evangelist of the reign of God that was now breaking in (Mark 1:14–15). The special tradition on which Luke draws has him read Isa. 61:1–2 in the synagogue in his hometown of Nazareth and add, "Today this scripture has been fulfilled in your hearing" (Luke 4:21). So Jesus set out to proclaim to the "poor" spoken of in that prophetic word the inbreaking of God's reign, to bring sight to the blind, to free the captives, to raise up the downtrodden. He did this by the power and inspiration of the Spirit of God. Since Jesus understood his work of proclamation in the light of Isa. 61:1–2, he also defined God's reign as salvation for the poor and those locked into a life apart from God.

The reign of God had a threefold dimension for Jesus. In the Lord's Prayer he taught his disciples to pray that God's reign would come now (Matt. 6:10/Luke 11:2), that is, that God's will would be carried out fully in heaven and on earth. This endtime reign of God also included the kingdom of God in which the righteous are to sit at table with Abraham, Isaac, and Jacob (Matt. 8:11/Luke 13:29) and triumph over the unrighteous (Luke 16:19–31). Jesus chose twelve disciples to reign over the twelve tribes of Israel in the endtime and to enjoy eschatological table fellowship with him (Luke 22:29–30). He himself looked toward the heavenly banquet (Mark 14:25). God's reign and God's coming kingdom were for Jesus inseparable. Interestingly, Jesus did not stop with these two aspects but added a third: he saw the reign of God already breaking in in his own ministry! Jesus expressed this present aspect in unmistakable terms: "if it is by the finger of God that I cast out demons, then the kingdom of God has come upon you" (Luke 11:20). He gave encouragement to the poor by direct reference to God's reign: "Blessed are you poor, for yours is the kingdom of God" (Luke 6:20; Matt. 5:3). Even children were in his eyes not too small for the reign of God: "Let the children come to me, do not hinder them; for to such belongs the kingdom of God" (Mark 10:14).

Or consider his very shrewd reply to the Pharisees' question about when the reign of God was coming: "The kingdom of God is not coming with signs to be observed; nor will they say, 'Lo, here it is!' or 'There!' for behold, the kingdom of God is in the midst of you!" (Luke 17:20-21). In the final analysis, "in the midst of you" can only mean that in Jesus' words and deeds the reign of God is already breaking in and is in that sense present now.[8]

No Jew at that time could conceive of the reign of God without thinking of God's righteousness, which characterized this reign. The psalms that proclaim God's kingship (97, 98, 99 and others) explicitly extol God's righteousness, which brings justice to the whole world. The messianic judgment by the Son of man that inaugurates the reign of God is according to *1 Enoch* 62:13ff. to inaugurate the time in which the righteous will be glorified and enjoy eternal table fellowship with the Son of man. According to the expectations of the Essene community at Qumran, "the Prince of the congregation," that is, the Davidic Messiah, is to set up the reign of God for Israel by judging the poor with righteousness, that is, by that power that is promised the Messiah in Isa. 11:2ff. (cf. 1QSb 5:20ff.). Finally, in the eleventh petition of the so-called Eighteen Benedictions, a prayer used in the synagogues already in Jesus' time, it says, "Restore our judges as in former times and reign over us, you alone. Blessed are you, Lord, who loves justice." Without the salutary righteousness that establishes justice, there was and is for a Jew no kingdom of God and no reign of God. Historically, therefore, Jesus' proclamation of the reign of God must also be thought of in combination with the idea of righteousness, which was fundamental to God's reign.

Diligent attention to that kind of connection produces a significant yield. In the Old Testament the righteousness of the king reigning in the name of Yahweh, and then later the righteousness of the Messiah, shows itself as he receives those deprived of their rights, especially widows, orphans, aliens, and the poor, and helps them find justice (cf. Psalm 103 with Psalm 72 and Isa. 11:1-5; 16:4-5; Jer. 23:6; and 1QSb 5:20ff.). In a fully analogous way Jesus saw himself called especially to bring into fellowship with God the poor and outcasts living apart from God. We have just spoken of his calling the poor blessed (Luke 6:20/Matt. 5:3). According to Mark 2:17 par. and Luke 15:11-32, Jesus' mission was concerned far more with sinners than with righteous keepers of the law. Jesus says that God rejoices more over one repentant sinner than over ninety-nine righteous people (Luke 15:7). In the parable of the laborers in the vineyard Jesus makes it clear that God is far more interested in being graciously generous than in calculating each person's degree of righteousness. In the well-known parable of the Pharisee and the publican Jesus pronounced God's forgiveness on the publican, who was unrighteous as far as the law was concerned and who confessed that he was guilty before God, while he withheld forgiveness from the Pharisee, who could remind God that he did more than the law required and that his righteousness made him better than other people. Both parables point to a conflict characteristic of Jesus' proclamation. While Jesus' Pharisaic opponents could support their understanding of the law with traditions that surface in Psalm 26 or Ezekiel 18 and Job 31, the sinners to whom Jesus appealed rested their hope on God's righteousness that manifests itself as willingness to forgive sinners (cf., for example, Psalm 143). An understanding of righteousness that focuses primarily on the precise wording of the Jewish law and that expects blessing for the righteous and punishment for the unrighteous is in opposition to the understanding of God's righteousness as compassion that leads to vindication. Jesus was an advocate of the righteousness of God that helped people find life. Thus he broke through the Pharisees' interest in measuring and classifying everybody's performance and followed in his own way the messianic tradition of the Old Testament and of ancient Judaism.

JUSTIFICATION AS THE FORGIVENESS OF SINS

If we tarry a bit longer with Luke 18:9-14, this passage can make it clear to us that in his messianic determination to set things right Jesus is supported by an Old Testament and Jewish tradition that expressly treats God's righteousness as help to find life. This tradition is evident in the individual and collective penitential prayers in Psalm 51; Ezra 9:6-15; Neh. 9:9-37; and Dan. 9:4-18. It also appears in the prayer formulas at the end of the *Manual of Discipline* from Qumran (1QS 10:9—11:22), in liturgical fragments from Qumran Cave 4 (4QDib Ham), in prayers of supplication in 4 Ezra (cf. 8:36), and also, for example, in the penitential "Our Father, our King" ascribed to Rabbi Akiba (died 135 C.E.). In all these prayers of supplication by an individual or the whole community, the suppliants always expressly mention their guilt, which is manifest in the face of Yahweh's gracious deeds and revealed will, their weakness, and their failure, and in all these prayers God's judicial "no" to this guilt is acknowledged. In other words, God is declared to be right, the sinner(s) wrong. But then these texts continue by appealing to God's faithfulness and righteousness, which is able to and does do more than restrain injustice and punish sinners. God is implored to help the threatened life of the sinner, and this very help is praised as the crowning confirmation of God's righteousness. According to our prayer texts God shows himself to be righteous precisely in this, that as the righteous judge he is and continues to be he helps the guilty find new life and forgives their sins. In Ps. 51:1, 14, 15 we read:

(1)   Have mercy on me, O God,
          according to thy steadfast love;
       according to thy abundant mercy
          blot out my transgressions. . . .
(14) Deliver me from bloodguiltiness, O God,
          thou God of my salvation.
       and my tongue will sing aloud of thy deliverance.
(15) O Lord, open thou my lips,
          and my mouth shall show forth thy praise.

4 Ezra 8:36 says, "For in this, O Lord, thy righteousness and goodness will be declared, when thou art merciful to those who have no store of good works." The "Our Father, our King" concludes with the words, "Our Father, Our King, be gracious to us and hear us, for we have no (good) works to show; show us righteousness and faithfulness and save us."

The publican in Luke 18:13 cries out to God in the style of this same tradition of repentance and God "justifies" him, that is, through forgiveness God the gracious judge helps him find a new basis for existence. *Jesus expresses here in story form the principle of the justification of sinners.*[9] According to this parable, however, this justification does not come about by God's simply disregarding his no to sin; instead, through this no he helps the sinner find new life! *For Jesus, God's righteousness is more than a judicial meting out of appropriate punishments and rewards; the righteous God helps the repentant find new life through the forgiveness of sins.*

That we are really on the right track with this interpretation of Jesus' messianic understanding of justice is shown by nothing more clearly than by his eating with tax collectors and sinners (Mark 2:13–17 par.; Luke 19:1–10). This earned Jesus the bad reputation (probably by appeal to Deut. 21:18ff.) of being "a friend of tax collectors and sinners" (Matt. 11:19) and evoked the reproach "This man receives sinners and eats with them" (Luke 15:2). In Palestine in Jesus' time, table fellowship, eating together, was seen as a concrete manifestation of fellowship, peace, and reconciliation. Jesus' eating with sinners becomes in the fullest sense a parabolic action expressing the reign of God.[10] We have already seen that Jesus also looked forward to the eschatological table fellowship with Abraham, Isaac, and Jacob. In *1 Enoch* 62:14, table fellowship with the Son of man is seen as the quintessence of the salvation the righteous await: "And the Lord of Spirits will remain over them, and with that Son of Man they will dwell, and eat, and lie down, and rise up for ever and ever."[11] Since Jesus repeatedly spoke of himself as the Son of man, it is not an overinterpretation if we regard his fellowship meals as an intentional preview of precisely the heavenly table fellowship of the Son of man with his own spoken of in *1 Enoch* 62. But the new accent Jesus gives is quite unmistakable: Jesus' table companions are no longer those who on the basis of their deeds are found righteous at the judgment but rather those who in the light of the judgment appear to be impious and wicked. By speaking forgiveness to this circle of people, sinners cut off from God, by expressly inviting them to the table (Luke 14:21) and admitting them into his company, he personally lived out the parable of the Pharisee and the publican and made himself the advocate of the life-creating righteousness of God that goes beyond merely punishing evil.

THE OBLIGATION TO LEAD A NEW LIFE

The way Jesus lived gave a new dimension to the life of those restored by him to communion with God. They received as a gift a share in a righteousness that sustained their lives in a way they did not deserve, a righteousness to which they could entrust themselves anew. But this also made a total claim on them; Jesus never proclaimed cheap grace. It is once again a parable that serves as a sign of this, the parable of the unmerciful servant in Matt. 18:23–35. Matthew introduces this with a saying that calls for unlimited forgiveness. In direct opposition to the unrestrained revenge of the so-called song of Lamech (Gen. 4:23–24), Jesus advocates unlimited forgiveness (Matt. 18:21f.). In the parable itself Jesus suggests that God's forgiveness, which exceeds every human measure, is the last opportunity for life before the judgment for the person to whom this forgiveness is granted. Whoever does not take up the salvation-creating righteousness of God shown him or her in forgiveness—that is, whoever is not prepared to show forgiveness and thereby open a new possibility of life for someone else—incurs the punishment from which Jesus would like to save sinners. According to Jesus, it is entirely possible to forfeit the grace of God.

In no sense did Jesus simply abolish the holy will of God revealed in the law given on Sinai. Rather, Jesus boldly made visible the original will of God found in and behind this law of Moses (cf. Matt. 19:8) and bound his followers no longer simply to the law but to this true will of God. With his "but I say to you" in the so-called antitheses in the Sermon on the Mount (Matt. 5:21–48), Jesus put himself above the authority of Moses. He epitomized God's ultimate will in the command to love, and meant thereby a love that also applies to the enemies who are persecuting his disciples (Matt. 5:43–48 par.). By such love the disciples conform themselves to the God who gives sun and rain to the just and unjust, that is, who holds to the gracious "commitment" he made to Noah in Gen. 9:12ff. According to Jesus' proclamation, his disciples are to conform their lives entirely to God's righteous behavior, which is and offers more than a guarantee that a deed receives an appropriate reward. *God's righteousness, Jesus declares, is measured by love, and thus for Jesus love is what the law is all about.*

The life-and-death importance Jesus attaches to living this new righteousness can be seen in his parable about the last judgment in Matt. 25:31–46. The parable speaks of the coming judgment by the Son of man/judge of the world and has all the marks of authenticity.[12] Salvation or condemnation is decided for those who will one day stand before the eschatological judge by whether or not they have cared for their fellow human beings in need. According to this parable (Jesus as) the Son of man identifies himself so completely with these very people in need, the hungry and the desperately thirsty, the poor and sick, the prisoners and strangers, that all deeds of love shown or denied them are shown or denied him. The Son of man is most intimately associated with the poor and the weak. As far as the examples of help enumerated in the parable are concerned, every Jew of that period knew that feeding the hungry, attending the sick, clothing the poor, etc., were "works of mercy," that is, works that correspond to the goodness and righteousness of God. Isa. 58:6ff. enumerates the works that are marks of the "fast" really acceptable to God, that is, of true repentance:

to loose the bonds of wickedness,
to undo the thongs of the yoke,
to let the oppressed go free,
and to break every yoke;
(7) . . . to share your bread with the hungry,
and bring the homeless poor into your house;
when you see the naked, to cover him,
and not to hide yourself from your own flesh.

Then in v. 8 a blessing follows. If the people perform the deeds of this "fast" Yahweh really loves,

Then shall your light break forth like the dawn,
and your healing shall spring up speedily;
your righteousness shall go before you,
the glory of the Lord shall be your rear guard.

In *T. Jos.* 1:4–6 God himself is praised for these very acts:

These brothers of mine hated me and the Lord loved me, they desired to kill me and the God of my fathers preserved me, they cast me into a well and the Most High drew me forth. I was sold into slavery and the Lord of all freed me, I was led into captivity and his mighty hand aided me, I was beset by hunger and the same Lord himself nurtured me. I was alone and God comforted me, I was in sickness and the Most High was my visitor, in prison and the Most High (showed favor to me). . . .[13]

The parable in Matthew 25 is obviously formulated on the basis of a tradition that denotes the works that according to Jewish understanding distinguish the righteous and correspond to God's own righteousness. At the same time it made the "new" righteousness Jesus lived and expected of his followers a criterion at the last judgment. Jesus understood the new righteousness he actualized to have eschatological quality and significance.

JOHN THE BAPTIST'S QUESTION

John the Baptist had demanded of penitent Jews at the Jordan genuine righteous deeds and announced the imminent coming of the one who would baptize with fire, that is, the Son of man, the eschatological judge. Jesus repeatedly claimed the authority of the messianic Son of man for his work on earth (cf., for example, Mark 2:10, 28 par.; Matt. 1:19 par.; Luke 12:8 par.). He called the people to repentance just as the Baptist had (cf. Mark 1:15 par.; Luke 13:1–9). But his support for the poor and lawless and his meals with tax collectors and sinners were certainly not signs warning of harsh treatment at the last judgment. Under these circumstances it is easy to understand historically that the Baptist one day sent a message to Jesus asking if he really was the "Coming One" (Matt. 11:2–3 par.). Jesus' answer, characteristic of his veiled manner of self-revelation, is of extreme interest for what we are discussing:

Jesus answered them, "Go and tell John what you hear and see: the blind receive their sight and the lame walk, lepers are cleansed and the deaf hear, and the dead are raised up, and the poor have good news preached to them. And blessed is he who takes no offense at me" (Matt. 11:4–6 par.).[14]

That Jesus' answer is once again dependent on Isa. 61:1–2 is clear from the start. Jesus wanted to be the prophetic evangelist to the poor and saw himself empowered by the Holy Spirit to heal the sick and to restore to communion with God those condemned by the law and despised by Jewish groups who interpreted the law rigidly. The response Jesus sends the Baptist is far more than a general interpretation of his activity with Isa. 61:1–2 (and other texts, especially Isa. 35:5–6) in the background. There is a striking absence in the text of references to Jesus' exorcisms, while the healing of lepers is introduced without regard to the tradition in Isaiah. In Matt. 11:2–6 par. Jesus shows himself to be the advocate of a messianic righteousness that radically contradicted the concept of righteousness and holiness advocated in the most pious groups among his people.

In the Essene texts from Qumran the stipulation is made for the eschatological gathering of Israel that no one afflicted with uncleanness may be admitted to the community:

> No one who is afflicted by any form of human uncleanness is to be admitted to the community, nor is anyone who becomes so afflicted to maintain his position within it. Similarly, no one who is afflicted with a bodily defect, who is stricken in hands or feet, who is lame or blind or deaf or dumb, or has any visible bodily defect, is to be admitted to a place among the "dignitaries" for "holy angels are in the congregation" (1QSa 2:4–9).[15]

According to the Temple Scroll from Qumran no blind or unclean person, no leper, and, indeed, no dead person may be in the holy city in which God dwells. The dead are to be buried outside the city. For lepers and others who are unclean, ghettos are to be established in order to protect the city from pollution (45:11–18; 48:10–17). The Essene community regarded these rigorous purity regulations derived from Num. 5:24ff. as binding for how they were to live. According to the *Manual of Discipline* (1QS 9:6), the Dead Sea community wanted to build, by virtue of their perfect behavior, "a holy of holies, and a house of unity for Israel." By their perfect obedience they wanted to atone for the wickedness of the rest of Israel. The regulations in the Temple Scroll and the *Manual of Discipline for the Future Congregation of Israel* (1QSa) served for the Essenes at Qumran as authoritative prototypes on which to model their present behavior.[16]

The Pharises, who opposed Jesus, had established as the ideal religious life one that in the Jews' day-to-day existence preserved a purity corresponding to the cultic demands placed on the Levites. The Essenes exceeded this Pharisaic ideal in that they demanded of themselves a level of purity in which God's presence could be experienced by humanity and human presence endured by

God without having the impure human consumed by God's holiness. They were thinking of the purity of the high priest in the Holy of Holies (cf. Lev. 16:3ff., 11ff.). The blind and lame, the lepers and deaf, the dead and lawless had no business in God's presence according to the Essene concept of holiness. Even in the Mishnah (*m. Ḥag.* 1:1) it states that deaf-mutes, imbeciles, children, those of doubtful or double sex, women, slaves who have not been freed, the lame, blind, sick, aged and so forth are not subject to the obligation to appear in the temple. Matt: 11:5–6 stands in clear opposition to the Essenes' and Pharisees' concept of holiness and righteousness.

Jesus opposed this concept clearly and repeatedly. The parable of the Pharisee and publican in Luke 18:9–14, which we have already considered, is not the only sign of that. In a manner highly infuriating to those who hold a Pharisaic conception of what is right, Jesus' call for repentance in Luke 13:1ff. sets aside the common view that one's fate is a punishment for particular individual sins.[17] In fact, the well-known word of Jesus in Mark 7:15, "there is nothing outside a man which by going into him can defile him; but the things which come out of a man are what defile him," sounds like a virtual declaration of war against the Pharisaism of his time. But where the Pharisees took offense at Jesus, there the Essenes must have been all the more furious. In any case, Jesus' answer to John the Baptist lists as the primary addressees of God's message of salvation and of Jesus' messianic attention precisely that group of people who according to Essene and Pharisaic notions of holiness and righteousness ought to be isolated in ghettos in order to safeguard the purity of Israel before God and his holy angels.

The list of deeds enumerated in Matt. 11:2–5 par. is especially characteristic of Jesus' ministry. Jesus had actually given sight to the blind (cf. only Mark 8:22–26; 10:46–52). He healed the lame (Mark 2:1–12 par.) and made clean those afflicted with leprosy (Mark 1:40–45 par.; Luke 17:11–19). He healed some people who according to Old Testament and Jewish perspectives had been relegated to the sphere of death (Mark 1:32–34 par.; 3:10ff. par.; 5:1–10 par.), and in God's stead restored to communion with God those who had come to be separated from him (Luke 15:11–32, esp. v. 32). Moreover, the tradition contains accounts of Jesus' power over death that warrant our careful reflection (for example, Mark 5:21–43 par.; Luke 7:11–17).[18] The blessing addressed to the poor (Matt. 5:3/Luke 6:20), which I have already mentioned several times, demonstrates, along with Jesus' behavior, that his proclamation about God's reign applied in special measure to that group considered by people (who assumed they were echoing God's view) to be disreputable have-nots. An authentic tally of Jesus' messianic saving activity lies hidden behind Matt. 11:5–6. That also makes the function of the two verses understandable in the context of the Baptist's question. The "Coming One," whom Jesus embodies, the messianic Son of man as Jesus understands him, is the evangelist to and advocate of the outcasts! This is precisely what this answer gives the Baptist's disciples to understand and ponder. This understanding of his mission put Jesus in conflict not only with the Pharisees' and Essenes' understanding of holiness but also with his "teacher" John's expectation of the one who would baptize with fire, and so he wisely added, "And blessed is he who takes no offense at me!"

JESUS' READINESS TO EFFECT ATONEMENT

Jesus' striking proclamation of messianic righteousness that opens up new life for the "poor" brought him into intense conflict with the understanding of righteousness held by the most pious among his people, a conflict that in the end cost him his life. The Synoptic tradition, which also in this context merits careful historical attention[19] rather than wholesale critical doubt, shows that Jesus consciously faced this conflict and endured it to the end.

We have already seen, by means of the two parables of the unmerciful servant (Matt. 18:23–35) and the last judgment (Matt. 25:31–46), that Jesus viewed his attention to sinners and the commitment to righteousness that shaped this attention in an eschatological light. The so-called parable of the wicked winegrowers (Mark 12:1–9 [10–12] par.) shows in addition that he equated rejecting him with being condemned at the judgment of God.[20] The endtime dimension of Jesus' deeds of righteousness and the claim that he came on an eschatological mission are not easy to deny. But it is equally difficult to deny that Jesus encountered vehement rejection and, in the end, deadly hostility from the leading Jewish groups of his time, the Pharisees, the Essenes, the Sadducees, and the high priesthood. Even the adherents of the ruler of his home territory, Herod Antipas, called the Herodians in Mark 3:6, were hostile toward Jesus. In the face of this animosity from many sides, posing a serious threat that must have been clear to Jesus ever since the death of John the Baptist, Jesus by no means abandoned his messianic way. But from then on he faced the possibility that he would have to die in Jerusalem as had many of Israel's prophets before him (Luke 13:33; cf. Neh. 9:26; 2 Chron. 36:16). For Jesus also spoke of the baptism of death that awaited him (Luke 12:50; Mark 10:38–39) and made enigmatic reference to the Son of man being "delivered up": "The Son of man will be delivered into the hands of men" (Mark 9:31 par.).[21] The passive voice is obviously used here, in keeping with pious Jewish practice, to avoid direct reference to God's name. So what is meant is that God will deliver the Son of man into human hands. The fate of the Son of man, that is to say, Jesus' own fate—death—was determined by God. But according to Jesus' proclamation, God's intention for a sinner was life and not destruction. Under these circumstances we must integrate Mark 9:31 par. with Jesus' understanding of God's will and say: Jesus saw the hour coming in which, in accord with God's will, he would still have to stand up even for those who wanted to get rid of them. Said differently: *Jesus saw himself as sent to persevere in his mission to the end and to die a death that did not exclude even his enemies from God's life-creating righteousness.*

Mark 10:45 par. transmits to us a much-debated saying of Jesus that in my opinion dare not be approached only as a confessional formula of the post-Easter community.[22] The saying reads: "For the Son of man also came not to be served [by angels and people] but to serve, and to give his life as a ransom for many." If we compare this word of Jesus with the familiar Old Testament–Jewish tradition about the messianic Son of man who is to judge the world, we can see a clear contrast. The Son of man/world judge is set upon God's throne according to Dan. 7:13 and the further interpretation of this original tradition in the Enoch apocalypse (see above, pp. 31–32); he executes judgment with messianic authority; the nations worship him, and the angels of God serve him. For the time of his way on earth Jesus rejected this majestic understanding of the sending of the Son of man. Instead of expecting the nations to worship him and angels to serve him, he himself chose the way of service, humility, and suffering. Jesus wanted to be God's messianic Son precisely in his suffering as the ransom "for many." The statement that the Son of man willingly relinquishes the majesty conferred on him by God and sees his mission in serving the "many" by the vicarious surrender of his life is something totally new in the context of Jewish tradition at that time.

The statement implies at least the following: The expression "to give his life as a ransom for someone" might go back to Isa. 43:3–4. That passage speaks of Israel's rescue, purchased by God at the cost of human life:

> I give Egypt as your ransom,
> Ethiopia and Seba in exchange for you.
> (4) Because you are precious in my eyes,
> and honored, and I love you,
> I give men in return for you,
> peoples in exchange for your life.

In order to save Israel's life, Egyptians, Cushites, and Sabeans must be destroyed in the midst of their idolatrous existence (cf. Isa. 45:14ff.). In the Aramaic *Tg. Isa.* 43:3–4 is understood from the perspective of the exodus from Egypt: as God destroyed the Egyptians as they were passing through the Red Sea, in order to save the Israelites, so also entire peoples are sacrificed for Israel as the people are gathered out of the exile. In a liturgical fragment from Qumran based on Prov. 21:18 and related to the subject of this tradition, it says: "and you will sacrifice the evildoer as our ransom" (1Qf 34.3:1, 5). The "you" here is surely God, and "our" refers just as clearly to the Essene community destined for salvation. If we understand Mark 10:45 from this background, then it was Jesus' intention to sacrifice his life in place of the many. The "many" are to be enabled to live before God because the Son of man surrenders his life for them.

According to Isa. 53:10–12 it is the mission of the Suffering Servant to give his life as a sin offering for "many." The sin offering of the Righteous Servant of God shall "make many to be accounted righteous," that is, take away their sin in the sight of God so that they can stand before God and encounter God anew. Not only Isa. 43:3–4 but also Isa. 53:10–12 forms the background for the statement of Jesus we are considering.[23] He gives his life as a sin offering for many, who have forfeited their life before God and have no ransom of their own to use (cf. Mark 8:37 par.). According to the context of Isa. 53:10–12, the "many" are the kingdoms and peoples of the world. For the ones who should actually serve the Son of man and come under his judgment, the Son of man gives himself into death.

Behind this word of Jesus quite clearly stands the atonement-theology concept of ransom and sin offering, that is, the idea that someone who stands before God as a sinner can be spared from destruction through the vicarious sacrifice of the life of another. The concept of atonement Jesus takes up here has a great deal to do with God's righteousness and his judgment. Jesus surrenders himself to God's death sentence in order to spare the "many" from the destruction that awaits them in God's judgment. God's judgment of sinners is expressly acknowledged by Jesus to be legitimate. But God's righteousness is to show itself as a power creating new life for sinners in this way, that the sinner-destroying no (in biblical terms, the wrath of God) strikes the Son of man who takes the place of sinners and not those who are really guilty. Jesus' parables about the judgment and our saying show that Jesus, who understood God's righteousness as salvation for the poor and the lawless, did not envision and live this salvation by giving up God's righteous judgment but by presupposing and confirming it. By the vicarious sacrifice of his life Jesus wanted to affirm God's judgment and at the same time enable God to appear as the one who said no to sin because he wanted to open the way for life. God's righteousness is not exhausted in the execution of judgment. Instead, by virtue of the vicarious surrender of Jesus' life, God's judgment becomes the source of a new righteous life for "many." As Isa. 53:10ff. puts it, Jesus interceded with God for sinners and by virtue of his sacrificial death opened for them the way to new life.

The Son of man, according to biblical Jewish tradition, is the anointed one sent by God. Since Jesus associated himself intimately with the Son of man and pursued his course on earth as the Son of man who came to serve, he understood his mission to be from God and in fulfillment of God's will. This bond of obedience between Jesus and his heavenly Father gives a final, deeper dimension to the fate that awaits him, which according to Mark 9:31 is from the hand of God, and to the understanding of righteousness that lies behind Mark 10:45. This dimension emerges in Isa. 43:3–4 when it says there that God himself will supply the ransom for Israel. If we see that as a starting point for understanding our ransom saying, it attains its true soteriological depth: it is God's own will that the many, instead of receiving the death sentence, attain salvation through the vicarious sacrifice of the life of the Son of man, Jesus, acting in complete obedience to God. Thereby *God's righteousness shows itself to be God's work of salvation, by which God himself brings about atonement for many, achieving this by the "vicarious life-giving" (Existenzstellvertretung–Hartmut Gese) of the Son of man, Jesus, whose life and work are from God.* Mark 10:45 shows us that for Jesus, God's righteousness includes God's role as judge, but that this righteousness is at the same time far more than God's meting out of reward or punishment. *In the proclamation of Jesus, God's righteousness is measured first and foremost by God's love and mercy.* It is in judgment that God's righteousness shows itself to be the power by which God makes things right for the very people who come before him poor and without a leg to stand on. The Lord's Supper texts, Mark 14:22–25 par. and 1 Cor. 11:23–26, show that on the night of his departure Jesus once again explicitly consecrated himself to be a sacrifice "for many" and thereby maintained to his death the view of righteousness we have set forth.[24] Jesus proclaimed and actualized God's righteousness as salvation and love for the poor. By the sacrifice of his life he guaranteed that God is more interested in the life of the poor and sinners than in the death of the wicked.

It is not by chance that these last statements were formulated in connection with Ezek. 18:23, 32. All the essential components of Jesus' understanding of righteousness are Old Testament and Jewish in origin and Jesus' ideas about righteousness can only be appropriately understood by recognizing their roots in the language and experience of the Israelites. Not only is it the case that "righteousness" in the majority of its Old Testament occurrences is a semantically positive word used in reference to relationships, and that both the messianic tradition about righteousness and also the talk in Israel's penitential prayers about God's righteousness as that which makes things right are prefigurings of Jesus' actions and proclamation. But in addition, the cultic and noncultic traditions about atonement, according to which atonement is a salutary institution of God's and the act of atonement is seen as "coming to God by passing through the sentence of death,"[25] were at hand for Jesus. The interpretation of Isaiah 53 with reference to the suffering of a righteous individual is found already in Wisdom of Solomon 2—5 and in an Armenian version of *T. Benj.* 3:8 that presumably has not undergone Christian editing. In that passage the prophecy of Jacob about his son Joseph reads, "In you the prophecy of heaven will be fulfilled that says that the innocent one shall be defiled for the lawless and the sinless one shall die for the ungodly." Perhaps even the messianic interpretation of the Suffering Servant song in the Targum existed in Jesus' time, but this must remain an open question.[26] It is certain, however, that Jesus knew the tradition about the vicarious suffering and intercession of the martyrs of Israel (2 Macc. 7:3–4; 4 Macc. 6:26ff.), about the violent death of the prophets (cf. Neh. 9:26; 2 Chron. 36:16), and about the martyr-messiah in Zech. 12:10. What is new historically is the crystallization of all these individual traditions in the messianic work of righteousness done by the suffering Son of man, Jesus of Nazareth. *Through his willingness to make vicarious atonement Jesus gave a new direction to Old Testament language and experience precisely with respect to the righteousness of God and to the righteousness people have in the sight of God and live out in the world.*

CROSS AND RESURRECTION

Jesus' righteous activity points beyond his individual life. Jesus shared the resurrection faith of wide circles of early Judaism (cf. Mark 12:18–27 par.). With the Baptist's proclamation of the "Coming One" as his starting point,

Jesus connected his work on earth as closely as possible with the impending judgment by the Son of man: "And I tell you, every one who acknowledges me before men, the Son of man also will acknowledge before the angels of God" (Luke 12:8). In the parable of the last judgment, Matt. 25:31–46, he speaks of judgment by the coming Son of man on the basis of the standard Jesus himself lived and demanded, identification with the poor and needy. In his messianic confession before the Sanhedrin, which made his death a certainty, he himself pointed to the coming of the Son of man in the clouds of heaven. Since the roles of Messiah and Son of man already overlap (in Dan. 7:13ff.[27] and) in the Enoch apocalypse, it makes little sense historically to assume for Jesus something different from such overlapping. His answer to the high priest's question, "Are you the Christ, the Son of the Blessed?" is, "I am; and you will see the Son of man seated at the right hand of Power, and coming with the clouds of heaven" (Mark 14:61–62).[28] This answer can only mean that Jesus acknowledged his messianic mission before the Jewish councils. At the same time he anticipated his eschatological exaltation at the right hand of God, and before the Jewish council he had already announced his coming as Son of man to judge the world. On earth Jesus wanted to be the serving messianic Son of man who would suffer vicariously for many; he wanted to be this confident of his acceptance and exaltation by the God who is not God of the dead but of the living (Mark 12:27).

This means that Jesus' concept of righteousness had decidedly eschatological moorings. His righteous activity on earth was the proleptic actualization of the eschatological judgment by the Son of man before and on the throne of God. As far as Jesus' work and claim are concerned, the righteousness he lived was really eschatologically new. But that does not at all mean that this righteousness met no opposition. Quite the contrary. It was Jesus' life of righteousness that first entangled him in the deadly conflict with Jewish authorities that ultimately ended in his death. *The execution of Jesus on the cross was the historical result of the messianic justice he brought.* Despite the fact that he predicted his suffering and exaltation (Mark 9:31 par.; 14:62 par.), the cross also became the great crisis for this messianic justice.

From the Synoptics we know that even before his condemnation by the Jewish council and the Romans, Jesus was forsaken by all his followers. They probably feared that Jesus' whole company of followers would be persecuted and so out of fear they hid. Jesus' Jewish opponents viewed him as a law-despising deceiver and blasphemer (Deut. 13:6, 11; 17:12) who thought he was the messiah, and in their view he had to be blotted out of Israel.[29] No fools politically, they turned him over to Pilate as a potential messianic insurrectionist. After a short trial Pilate had him whipped and, not wanting to take any political chances, crucified. For the Romans crucifixion was a gruesome deterrent. For the Jews in the New Testament era it was more than that. For them the crucifixion of a blasphemer and law-despiser was the implementation of God's curse in accord with the Torah! Deuteronomy 21:22–23 states the following:

And if a man has committed a crime punishable by death and he is put to death, and you hang him on a tree, his body shall not remain all night upon the tree, but you shall bury him the same day, for a hanged man is accursed by God; you shall not defile your land which the Lord your God gives you for an inheritance.

These old stipulations are applied by ancient Judaism to crucifixion. We learn the way they did that principally from the Temple Scroll at Qumran, in which it says in col. 64:6–13:

. . . If (7) a man informs against his people, and delivers his people up to a foreign nation, and does harm to his people, (8) you shall hang him on the tree, and he shall die. On the evidence of two witnesses and on the evidence of three witnesses (9) he shall be put to death, and they shall hang him on the tree. And if a man has committed a crime punishable by death, and has defected into (10) the midst of the nations . . . and has cursed his people the children of Israel, you shall hang him also on the tree, (11) and he shall die. And their body shall not remain upon the tree all night, but you shall bury them . . . the same day, for (12) those hanged on the tree are accursed by God and men; you shall not defile the land which I (13) give you for an inheritance.[30]

The historical background of these regulations is probably the mass crucifixion of Pharisees by the Jewish king Alexander Jannaeus in 88 B.C.E. The Pharisees had invoked the aid of the Seleucid king Demetrius III against Alexander, and after the Syrians withdrew, Alexander took revenge on his rebellious opponents in a most gruesome manner. Jannaeus' action is in a certain sense concealed in the text of the Temple Scroll. Traitors against Israel's religious independence and faith should be hanged on a tree, that is, crucified; they are "accursed by God and [humanity]." If Jesus was regarded by his enemies as a blasphemer and seducer into unbelief who deserved to die, then his crucifixion by the Romans could rightly be interpreted on the basis of Deut. 21:22–23.

When viewed from the perspective of the Temple Scroll, the connection of Deut. 21:23 with Jesus' crucifixion discussed in John 19:31, Gal. 3:13, and Justin *Dialogue with Trypho* 89.2 and 90.1 probably originated in pre-Christian polemic. It presumably goes back to Jesus' Jewish opponents. If this is so, then a quite fundamental antithesis arises with respect to Jesus' crucifixion. While Jesus himself fulfilled his mission as Son of man by the vicarious sacrifice of his life; while he died for sinners, including his enemies, and in the face of death awaited his exaltation to the right hand of God, even his closest followers forsook him out of fear that they themselves would be hunted down, and his Jewish opponents believed that he deservedly met his end under the curse that God in the Torah had hung on those who betray Israel's faith. *Jesus' crucifixion demonstrates that his righteous messianic activity was opposed so thoroughly that precisely with his claim of bringing eschatological righteousness he was believed to be forsaken by God and humanity, branded an enemy of the holy Jewish faith.* Moreover, the Romans put on the cross a superscription meant to warn every Jew: this is the fate of anyone who tries to set himself up as messianic king (Mark 15:26 par.)! The question about the validity and legitimacy of Jesus' messianic work of righteousness could not be put more radically. Before Easter this question received no compelling answer. *Only the exaltation of the crucified one to the right hand of God enabled Jesus to appear as the messianic Son of God vindicated by God who really had walked his way of the new righteousness in God's name (Acts 2:36; Rom. 1:3–4; 1 Tim. 3:16). Not until Easter did Jesus, the crucified one whom God raised, appear as the personification of God's saving righteousness (1 Cor. 1:30).*

NOTES

1. A. Dihle, s. v. "Gerechtigkeit," *RAC* 10:306: "As far as this can be drawn from the Synoptic Gospels as witnesses to earlier community tradition, righteousness did not characterize what was essentially new in Jesus' preaching."

2. For a totally different view, see G. Strecker, "Biblische Theologie?" in *Kirche. Festschrift für Günther Bornkamm zum 75. Geburtstag,* ed. D. Lührmann and G. Strecker (Tübingen: Mohr, 1980), 425–45, esp. 430, n. 25. My thesis, that one may with good reason put Jesus' words and deeds under the heading "the new righteousness," is regarded by Strecker as "a building that rests on a hazardous foundation, when one considers that not a single *dikaiosunē* reference in the New Testament can with any likelihood be traced back to Jesus himself (including, of course, the verb in Luke 18:9, 14)." I do not share Strecker's skepticism about all the Synoptic references to righteousness. For support I only point here to the following works: H. Schürmann, "Die vorösterlichen Anfänge der Logientradition" (in *Traditionsgeschichtliche Untersuchungen zu den synoptischen Evangelien* [Düsseldorf: Patmos, 1968], 39–65); G. Stanton, "Form Criticism Revisited" (in *What About the New Testament? Essays in Honor of C. Evans,* ed. M. D. Hooker and C. Hickling [London: SCM Press, 1975], 13–27); B. Gerhardsson, *The Origins of the Gospel Tradition* (Philadelphia: Fortress Press, 1979); and the Tübingen dissertation by R. Riesner, *Jesus als Lehrer. Eine Untersuchung zum Ursprung der Evangelienüberlieferung,* WUNT 2d ser. 7 (Tübingen: Mohr, 1981).

3. J. Becker, *Johannes der Täufer und Jesus von Nazareth,* BibS(N) 63 (Neukirchen-Vluyn: Neukirchener Verlag, 1972), 34ff.

4. F. Lang, "Erwägungen zur eschatologischen Verkündigung Johannes des Täufers," in *Jesus Christus in Historie und Theologie. Ntl. Festschrift für H. Conzelmann zum 60. Geburtstag,* ed. G. Strecker (Tübingen: Mohr, 1975), 459–73, esp. 470–71.

5. M. A. Knibb, *The Ethiopic Book of Enoch,* 2 vols. (Oxford: Clarendon Press, 1978), 2:135.

6. On this point and with reference to my argument as a whole, see the important essay by M. Hengel, "Jesus als messianischer Lehrer der Weisheit und die Anfänge der Christologie" (in *Sagesse et Religion. Colloque de Strasbourg* [Paris: Presses universitaires de France, 1979], 147–88, esp. 177ff.). Hengel's argument is strengthened and supported by H. Gese, "Die Weisheit der Menschensohn und die Ursprünge der Christologie als konsequente Entfaltung der biblischen Theologie," *SEÅ* 44 (1979): 77–114.

7. (Translator's note: the translation of *1 Enoch* 62:2 here is that of Knibb, *Ethiopic Book of Enoch* [see above, n. 5], 2:150, except that Knibb begins the quote, "the Lord of Spirits sat . . . ," and I have substituted Stuhlmacher's understanding of this part of the text; the identification in square brackets is Stuhlmacher's.)

8. Cf. W. G. Kummel, *Promise and Fulfilment*, trans. D. M. Barton, SBT 23 (London: SCM Press, 1957), 32ff.

9. J. Jeremias, *The Parables of Jesus,* trans. S. H. Hooke, rev. ed. (New York: Charles Scribner's Sons, 1963), 141–42, was correct in stating this. My criticism of Jeremias *(Gerechtigkeit Gottes bei Paulus,* FRLANT 87, 2d ed. [Göttingen: Vandenhoeck & Ruprecht, 1966], 245–46) is in need of revision.

10. O. Hofius, *Jesu Tischgemeinschaft mit den Sündern,* Calwer Hefte 86 (Stuttgart: Calwer Verlag, 1967), esp. 19ff.

11. Knibb, *Ethiopic Book of Enoch,* 2:152.

12. Cf. J. Friedrich, *Gott im Bruder? Eine methodenkritische Untersuchung von Redaktion, Überlieferung und Traditionen im Mt. 25:31–46,* Calwer theologische Monographien 7 (Stuttgart: Calwer Verlag, 1977); on p. 164ff. there is also relevant material about the so-called "works of love" treated in what follows.

13. *The Armenian Version of the Testament of Joseph,* intro., ed., and trans. M. E. Stone, Texts and Translations 6 (Missoula, Mont.: Scholars Press, 1975), 15–17, altered slightly.

14. W. G. Kümmel ("Jesu Antwort an Johannes den Täufer. Ein Beispiel zum Methodenproblem in der Jesusforschung" in *Heilsgeschehen und Geschichte,* 2 vols. [Göttingen: Vandenhoeck & Ruprecht, 1965–78], 2:177–200) has convinced me that the arguments I offered against the authenticity of this text in my book *Das paulinische Evangelium,* vol. 1, *Vorgeschichte* (FRLANT 95 [Göttingen: Vandenhoeck & Ruprecht, 1968], 218ff.), are not convincing.

15. *The Dead Sea Scriptures,* trans. and intro. T. H. Gaster, 3d ed. (Garden City, N.Y.: Doubleday & Co., Anchor Books, 1976), 441.

16. On this complex of material see the essay by H. Lichtenberger, "Atonement and Sacrifice in the Qumran Community," in *Approaches to Ancient Judaism,* ed. W. S. Green, 4 vols., Brown Judaic Studies (Chico. Calif.: Scholars Press, 1978–83), 2:159–71. It was through Lichtenberger that I became aware of the material in the Essene texts related to Matt. 11:5–6.

17. J. Jeremias, *New Testament Theology: The Proclamation of Jesus,* trans. J. Bowden (New York: Charles Scribner's Sons; London: SCM Press, 1971), 183: "In Luke 13:1–5 he expressly attacks the dogma that misfortune is a punishment for the definite sins of particular people. Rather, suffering is a call to repentance, a call which goes out to all." Cf. also John 9:1ff.

18. On this point cf. Kümmel, "Jesu Antwort," 199–200.

19. Kümmel, "Jesu Antwort," 188, asserts quite convincingly that "it appears to be justified from the perspective of historical research to approach the synoptic tradition about Jesus with *critical sympathy"* (emphasis Kümmel's).

20. Along with R. Pesch, *Das Markusevangelium,* pt. 2 (Mark 8:27—16:20), HTKNT [Freiburg: Herder, 1977], 213–24), I am of the opinion that the authenticity of vv. 1b–9 dare not be denied; the community's interpretation does not begin until v. 10, which applies Ps. 118:22–23 to Jesus' resurrection from the dead. I would also like to agree with Pesch when in his book *Das Abendmahl und Jesu Todesverständnis* (QD 80 [Freiburg: Herder, 1978], 105–7), he relates the parable of the wicked winegrowers with Jesus' understanding of his death: "the conflict between the unconditional announcement of salvation that Jesus as God's final messenger brings Israel, and Israel's refusal, which means failure apparently for God's messenger but actually for Israel itself, is resolved by Jesus in that he carries through *his mission as a saving mission unto death* and understands his death as . . . an atoning death for Israel's sake" (p. 107, emphasis Pesch's).

21. For an analysis of the Son-of-man saying in Mark 9:31, which underlies the Synoptic passion predictions, cf. Jeremias, *New Testament Theology,* 281–82.

22. I have sought to establish this, in dialogue with numerous other views, in my

essay "Vicariously Giving His Life for Many; Mark 10:45 (Matt. 20:28)" chap. 2, p. 16 in this volume. As clearly as this saying prepares the way for the atonement Christology of the post-Easter community (and the words about humiliation in Phil. 2:6–11), it cannot be explained simply as a reflection of this Christology. The essential components of the wording are pre-Easter. This is also the view of Martin Hengel, who wants to understand the saying as Jesus' interpretation of what he did at the Last Supper: "Der stellvertretende Sühnetod Jesu," *Internationale katholische Zeitschrift* 9 (1980): 21, 146 (1–25; 135–47) and *The Atonement*, trans. J. Bowden (Philadelphia: Fortress Press, 1981), 73. An evaluation of the saying quite similar to Hengel's is made by T. Holtz in his fine book *Jesus aus Nazareth* (Berlin: Union-Verlag, VOB, 1979), 104. More reserved than Hengel, Holtz, and I is H. Schürmann, "Jesu ureigenes Todesverständnis," in *Begegnung mit dem Wort. Festschrift für H. Zimmerman,* ed. J. Zmijewski and E. Nellessen (Bonn: Hanstein, 1979), 285–86 (273–309). W. G. Kümmel, "Jesusforschung seit 1965: VI Der Prozess und der Kreuzestod Jesu," *TRu* 45 (1980): 333–37 (293–337) accurately states Schürmann's, Hengel's, and my understanding of the tradition, also acknowledging the "precise and well-grounded presentation of the evidence," and yet he regards Mark 10:45 as "a foreign object in Jesus' proclamation" and accordingly doubts "that Mark 10:45 authentically reproduces Jesus' own interpretation of his death." I ask myself whether the tone is still being set for this evaluation of the saying by that "critical sympathy" to which Kümmel himself summoned the interpreters of the Synoptic tradition (see above, n. 19). If Mark 10:45 cannot simply be derived from the Jewish Son-of-man tradition, nor seen as a projection into the past of primitive Christian views about the Lord's Supper (which acquired in the process a Semitic wording), one must in my view agree with the Synoptic tradition that transmits the logion as a saying *of Jesus.* The restraint with which Jesus' death is predicted in his proclamation is also best explained historically: at the center of Jesus' message is the proclamation about the reign of God. The willingness to open for the "many" the way to the reign of God through an atoning death, a willingness that shows itself in the passion predictions, the ransom saying, and the words of institution, emerges only gradually in Jesus' proclamation and is primarily the subject of private instruction of the disciples (cf. Hengel, *The Atonement,* 34–35, 49–50, 71ff.). The saying is therefore neither a "foreign object" nor an (early) formulation by the community. If I am not mistaken, with his alternative interpretation Kümmel wants to guard against the view that, with reference to Isa. 43:3–4 and 53:10ff., Jesus could have understood his own death as a ransom and a sin offering for many (cf. this view already in *Promise and Fulfilment,* 72–73, and then again in *The Theology of the New Testament,* trans. J. Steely [Nashville: Abingdon Press, 1973], 88, 116–17). Not only does Mark 10:45 appear to Kümmel as a formulation by the community but he also regards the saying about the cup in Mark 14:24 as secondary compared to 1 Cor. 11:25 (even though the Markan wording is more difficult than the Pauline). The Markan saying about the cup cannot, therefore (according to Kümmel), be cited as a parallel to Mark 10:45. This argument is also difficult to follow historically. What early Christian author should we suppose subsequently changed a version of the word about the cup (transmitted by Paul) that goes back to Jesus and is easily understandable into the complicated Markan wording? A development from the Markan version through Luke 22:20 to 1 Cor. 11:25 is in my opinion much easier to envision than the movement in the opposite direction postulated by Kümmel. On the whole, I cannot escape the impression that Kümmel's attempt (characteristic of an entire generation) to keep concepts of sacrifice away from Jesus is intended to bar at its starting point the way leading to the medieval theory of satisfaction, because this theory speaks about satisfaction rendered to God through the sacrifice of his Son. This way of thinking is completely unbiblical, and Kümmel is correct to take strong objection to it in his well-known essay, *"PARESIS* und *ENDEIXIS,"* in *Heilsgeschehen und Geschichte, Gesammelte Auf-*

sätze 1933–64, ed. E. Grässer, O. Merk, and A. Fritz (Marburg: Elwert, 1965), 270 (260–270). However, the battle against this theory should not be fought at the expense of the Jesus tradition but with the assistance of better biblical and exegetical argumentation!

23. The way is prepared for the pre-Pauline justification tradition in Rom. 4:25 by Mark 10:45 as well as by the (Markan) words of institution at the Lord's Supper, Mark 14:22, 24, which also point back to Isa. 53:10–12 (and other passages).

24. With J. Jeremias, *Eucharistic Words of Jesus* (London: SCM Press, 1966; Philadelphia: Fortress Press, 1977), and Pesch, *Das Abendmahl und Jesu Todesverständnis,* I regard the Markan words of institution as both the earliest and most difficult version in which these words of Jesus have come to us. This version may well go back to Jesus.

25. H. Gese, "The Atonement," in *Essays on Biblical Theology,* trans. K. Crim (Minneapolis: Augsburg Pub. House, 1981), 114 (93–116). On the Old Testament perspective on atonement see also K. Koch, "Sühne und Sündenvergebung um die Wende von der exilischen zur nachexilischen Zeit," *EvT* 26 (1966): 217–39; Koch, S. V. "Versöhnung," *RGG* (3d ed.) 6:1368–70; and now the comprehensive work by B. Janowski, "Sühne als Heilsgeschehen" (doctoral diss.; University of Tübingen, 1979).

26. It is true that K. Koch, in his study "Messias und Sündenvergebung in Jesaja 53 Targum," *JSJ* 3 (1972): 117–48, assumes "that the targum on the prophets, along with the bulk of its material, goes back to pre-Christian times" (p. 121). But Hengel, in *The Atonement,* 57ff., rightly shows that this can scarcely be said unequivocally on the basis of the sources preserved for us. That Isaiah 53 is interpreted by means of an atonement theology in Aramaic text fragments from Qumran (cf. Hengel, *The Atonement,* 57ff., where he refers to J. Starcky, *RB* 70 [1963]: 492) is, to be sure, significant enough.

27. Gese ("The Messiah," in *Essays on Biblical Theology,* 141–66) shows that we probably already have in the figure of the Son of man in Dan. 7:13 "a transformation of the old messianic concept" (p. 155). Gese also points to this connection in his essay "Die Offenbarung des Gottesreiches und die Erscheinung des Messias," *Zeitwende* 50 (1979): 205–19.

28. In their *Arbeitsbuch zum Neuen Testament* (Tübingen: Mohr, 1975), 368, H. Conzelmann and A. Lindemann consider Mark 14:61–62 to be a tradition consciously drawn up as a "compendium of the Christology of the community," with the intention of helping "to show that all the titles of Jesus—Messiah, Son of God, Son of man—are equivalent." I consider this to be mistaken. Mark 14:61–62 is evaluated with far greater caution and with more historical insight by A. Strobel, *Die Stunde der Wahrheit* (Tübingen: Mohr, 1980), 73–76; "We have here . . . a tradition, peculiar at its core, that expresses, probably in large measure correctly, Jesus' own expectation of exaltation, precisely before the highest court of the Jews at the time of the passover" (p. 75).

29. Very instructive about these issues is Strobel, *Stunde der Wahrheit,* 81ff.

30. *The Temple Scroll,* ed. Yigael Yadin, 3 vols. and supplement (Jerusalem: Israel Exploration Society, 1977–83), 2:288–91.

CHAPTER 4

Jesus' Resurrection
and the View of Righteousness
in the Pre-Pauline
Mission Congregations

Jesus' messianic life of righteousness was radically called into question by his condemnation and execution on the cross. Despite its novelty, it would have remained simply one part of the history of Israel's faith if the Easter events had not led to the reassembling of Jesus' disciples and the establishment of the earliest mission congregation in Jerusalem. The mission congregation in Antioch on the Orontes, founded a short time later by members of the Stephen-circle who were driven out of Jerusalem, was a daughter congregation of the congregation in Jerusalem. Through Barnabas, among others, it always maintained contact with Jerusalem (cf. Acts 11:19ff.). It was from Antioch that the actual gentile mission went forth. This movement received a powerful impetus through Paul, whom Barnabas brought to Antioch a few years after his dramatic call to be Christ's apostle (cf. Acts 11:22–26).[1]

We have to reconstruct for ourselves the ancient texts in which the faith of the pre-Pauline Christian communities is expressed, taking them from the Synoptic Gospels, Acts, and traditional materials quoted in Paul's letters. Since these texts are extremely illuminating with respect to the way the two earliest, and definitely pre-Pauline,[2] Christian congregations thought about righteousness, we can risk taking the approach of an illustrative reconstruction.

THE RAISING OF THE DEAD

We know today that the Israelite expectation of the resurrection grew in an experiential and linguistic development that took hundreds of years.[3] This linguistic development extended far beyond the borders of the Old Testament canon. It included almost all prominent Jewish groups in the New Testament period. The tradition-bound Sadducees constituted the principal exception. It was not only with the Pharisees that they debated the resurrection; the tradition also preserves a debate between the Sadducees and Jesus on this subject (cf. Mark 12:18–27 par.).

For ancient Judaism, belief in the resurrection was the classical expression of confidence in the death-defeating creative power and righteousness of God. In the time during which the New Testament arose this belief found its popular expression in the Eighteen Benedictions, which is a classic summary of Jewish belief. In Jewish synagogues it became and remains "the Tefillah" (*the* prayer par excellence). The second petition of this prayer runs,

> You [God] are strong, humbling the proud, mighty, judging the powerful; you live forever, causing the dead to rise, the wind to blow, the dew to descend; you nourish the living and give life to the dead. May help come for us in an instant. Blessed are you, O Lord, who gives life to the dead.

Israel's whole trust in the one God, who as creator and preserver of the world chose Israel to be his own people, is summed up here in the words "Blessed are you, O Lord, who gives life to the dead." That is, if one takes this benediction, along with the other blessings in this prayer—for example: "You are holy and your name is to be feared; there is no other God but you. Blessed are you, Lord, holy God" or "Forgive us, our Father, for we have sinned against you. Blot out our sin and remove it from your sight, for great is your mercy. Blessed are you, Lord, who forgives much"; and, finally, "May your mercy act upon righteous proselytes, and grant us a good reward with those who do your will. Blessed are you, Lord, the confidence of the righteous"—then one sees at once the context in which God is praised as the one who raises the dead: it is the classical biblical context of his holiness and grace, of his righteousness as creator.

In this context the expectation of the resurrection has a double orientation. God raises the dead so that they can finally receive their due. For the wicked and God's enemies this means that they must answer to the holy God and bear the consequences of their unrighteous deeds. For the righteous, who have experienced persecution on earth, and especially for the Jewish martyrs, being raised means that they will at last receive righteousness from God. They are vindicated before their former tormentors and permitted to enter the eternal glory of God's reign. There is, then, according to Jewish thought a resurrection to salvation and to condemnation, each reckoned on the basis of God's righteousness. Thus it is almost superfluous to stress that "resurrection" always means to be brought to life by God before his throne. In Israelite thought resurrection and being raised are not really to be distinguished; what these words convey is possible only because of God's creative power, which is stronger than death.[4]

THE EARLIEST CHRISTIAN
RESURRECTION FORMULAS

In light of this background and in the face of Jesus' shameful crucifixion, the first brief sentences in which the Easter experience of the first Christian witnesses is expressed appear literally to be earthshaking statements. Let me mention at least two of them which in all probability were already formulated in Jerusalem: "The Lord has risen indeed, and has appeared to Simon" (that is, Peter; Luke 24:34); or, more fully, "Christ died for our sins in accordance with the scriptures, . . . he was buried, . . . he was raised on the third day in accordance with the scriptures, and . . . he appeared to Cephas (that is, Peter), then to the twelve" (1 Cor. 15:3–5). It is immediately clear that these first expressions of faith could only have been formulated within the Old Testament–Jewish linguistic context. "Risen" or "raised," "Christ," "died for our sins," "in accordance with the scriptures" (that is, in accordance with the Bible at that time common to Jews and Christians [which Christians later came to call "the Old Testament"]) are all expressions that have a specific meaning and definite significance in Israelite terminology. Apart from Israelite linguistic history, the Christian confessions quoted above would not have been made.

The three most important assertions made in the resurrection formulas are the following: (1) Jesus of Nazareth has been raised by God; he is Lord and Christ, that is, the Messiah. (2) As the one raised and attested by the power of God, he appeared to Peter and then to the twelve. (3) Jesus died for our sins; the death and resurrection of Jesus happened in accord with the holy will of God found in the Scriptures. Each of these three fundamental assertions is of considerable significance in the context of righteousness.

The first assertion is the most powerful; it is fundamental to Christian faith and to the gospel that is the basis of Christian mission: God raised Jesus of Nazareth from the dead as his Christ. The God of Israel and creator of the world did not abandon in death the messianic Son of man accused by the Jewish council and condemned by Pilate to die on the cross, but summoned him to eternal life before his throne. Instead of ending up on the cross cursed by God and humanity (Deut. 21:22–23), Jesus was raised from the dead by God's power as creator and vindicated before his oppressors. He was and is Lord and Messiah. The "way of righteousness" (Matt. 21:32) which the Son of man followed to his vicarious sacrifice on the cross led him up to God's throne and to God's side. *God exalted Jesus to his right hand; the one who faced controversy on earth and torment and slander on the cross is the truly Righteous One. Henceforth what constitutes righteousness in God's name is to be measured by reference to Jesus, the Lord.*

We have a considerable number of ancient christological texts that illustrate this understanding of Jesus' resurrection. Of ancient Jewish-Christian origin is, first of all, the formula Paul uses right at the beginning of Romans about God's Son, Jesus Christ, "who was descended from David according to the flesh and designated Son of God in power according to the Spirit of holiness by his resurrection from the dead" (Rom. 1:3–4). This formulation, which at first glance might strike one as strange, expresses graphically that Jesus is the Messiah descended from David and that by his resurrection he is the Son of God, appointed to rule. Behind this is presumably Nathan's prophetic word in 2 Sam. 7:12–14, which the Essenes at Qumran had already applied to the coming Messiah (cf. 4QFlor 1:10–11).[5]

In addition to Rom. 1:3–4, reference may be made to Acts 2:30–36, the conclusion of Peter's sermon at Pentecost. Here, besides the prophecy of Nathan, Ps. 16:10 and especially Psalm 110, which is of great importance for the early Christian understanding of the resurrection, are applied to Jesus' resurrection. With the aid of a combination of Ps. 110:1 and Ps. 8:7 typical of Jewish exegesis, Jesus himself had already tried to demonstrate to his opponents that the messianic Son of man is more than a mere son of David (cf. Mark 12:35–37 par.). Jesus' announcement before the Sanhedrin of his exaltation at God's right hand and his return for judgment as the Son of man (Mark 14:62) is supported by Ps. 110:1. Now, with the help of the same psalm reference, the first Christian witnesses make clear what occurred in and with the resurrection of Jesus: God set Jesus on the throne at his right hand and Jesus is to reign as Messiah until God has made all his adversaries a footstool under his feet. The Pentecost sermon ends with the striking words "Let all the house of Israel therefore know assuredly that God has made him both Lord and Christ, this Jesus whom you crucified" (Acts 2:36; cf. also 5:30–31). What Jesus anticipated, his exaltation and installation to his rightful place, has actually occurred! Over against the world that had scorned him, at Easter Jesus was "vindicated in the Spirit" (1 Tim. 3:16).[6] He has been enthroned by God as the "Messiah of righteousness" of whom Jer. 23:5–6, *Tg. Jer.* 23:5–6, and 4QPBless 3 speak as the deliverer of Israel. For those who believe in Christ, God makes Christ their "righteousness and sanctification and redemption" (1 Cor. 1:30). As far as its content is concerned, the expression Paul uses here goes back to the time prior to his call to be an apostle.

From that time on, the first Christians' confession about God and their understanding of what God's righteousness was and what it demanded was grounded in Jesus. If they had formerly prayed in the synagogue, "Blessed are you, O Lord, who gives life to the dead!" the Christians now confessed the God who as the God of Israel and as creator and preserver of the world "raised from the dead Jesus our Lord" (Rom. 4:24; cf. Acts 3:15; 4:10; 4:30; 1 Pet. 1:21, among others). *In these christological confessions Israelite faith and terminology flowed into the initial formulations of the Christian understanding of God and the Messiah. And, conversely, these early Christian confessions we have quoted derive their precise "scriptural" expressive power only from this faith and terminology.*

THE RESURRECTION APPEARANCES

The second statement basic to the Christian confession about the resurrection is added to the first in 1 Cor. 15:3ff., naming the witnesses whom the crucified and risen Jesus provided on earth: "and . . . he appeared to Cephas, then to the twelve" (1 Cor. 15:5). From the perspective of biblical terminology, the verb "appeared" presses us to interpret the appearance of Jesus not only on the basis of the resurrection-appearance narratives in the Gospels but also on the basis of Exod. 3:1–6. Jesus revealed himself as the living Son of God first to Peter, probably in Galilee (cf. Mark 16:7; John 21:1ff.) and then to the twelve, summoned anew to Jerusalem by Peter. In these appearances Jesus was both seen and heard, but as Acts 10:41 expressly remarks, he did not appear openly before everyone but in special encounters that were of faith-evoking significance for those present, as the encounter at the burning bush had been for Moses.

In the context of this discussion, one aspect of these appearances is especially significant. Peter and the twelve had been chosen by Jesus as his companions, as apostles (= messengers) and as future rulers over the twelve tribes of Israel in the endtime (Luke 22:29–30). But one after another they had forsaken Jesus after his final Passover meal with them in Jerusalem. James, the Lord's brother, whom Paul introduced in 1 Cor. 15:7 as another to whom the Lord appeared before he appeared to Paul, had actually rejected Jesus during his earthly ministry. Along with Mary and his brothers he had thought that Jesus was "beside himself" (Mark 3:21).[7] Since all those to whom Jesus appeared were called and received unconditionally by the risen Son of God, they experienced anew and with finality the very acceptance of sinners and rejects into fellowship with God that had been characteristic of Jesus' righteous activity during his earthly ministry.

Since it says in Acts 10:41 that the witnesses who had seen the risen Lord "ate and drank with him after he rose from the dead," we can interpret this scene properly on the basis of Luke 24:30ff. and John 21:12–13: the witnesses to whom the risen Lord appeared saw themselves being received by him anew into that community of reconciliation to which the earthly Jesus' table fellowship with tax collectors and sinners already had sought to give access. In his resurrection appearances to Peter, the twelve, James, and so on, Jesus once again brought into fellowship with himself and his heavenly Father the ones who had forsaken him. With the greeting "Peace be with you!" Jesus conferred on them the peace that flows from reconciliation with him (cf. Luke 24:36; John 20:19) and thereby restored to them that right to live before God that during his earthly ministry they had either rejected completely or forfeited anew on the night of his betrayal. *In the resurrection appearances the Son of man, given his rightful place by God, is seen as reconciler of those who have no rightful claim at all! The experience of Easter and the experience of reconciliation, Easter and the justification of sinners through Jesus Christ, belong together.* The witnesses to the resurrection, enlisted anew into service by Jesus, went up to Jerusalem and established there the first Christian mission congregation. For them Isa. 53:11 had found its fulfillment in Christ: as the servant of God, Jesus had borne the sins of many, enabling them by that very act to stand before God righteous. As those who had been justified, they proclaimed Christ, the risen Messiah, as the personification of the righteousness bestowed on them by God (cf. 1 Cor. 1:30).

THE ATONING DEATH OF THE
SERVANT OF GOD

In this context the third fundamental assertion in the ancient Easter confessions is also easily explained. It runs: Christ died "for our sins" and that happened "in accordance with the scriptures" (1 Cor. 15:3). Three things are combined in this formulation. First and foremost, the fundamental experience we have just discussed finds expression here. The Easter witnesses had experienced that beyond the abyss of their failure and doubt, and beyond his execution on the cross, Jesus met them once more as reconciler. By virtue of this reconciliation experience they now looked back on Jesus' death and finally saw in it an event by which God brought them salvation. They recognized this in the light of the Scriptures[8] and of the passion predictions Jesus had made in their hearing. The Scripture taught (Isa. 52:13—53:12) that the Suffering Servant "shall be exalted and lifted up, and shall be very high (52:13)"; he, the righteous one, will justify many, "because he poured out his soul to death, and was numbered with the transgressors; yet he bore the sin of many, and made intercession for the transgressors" (53:11-12). Jesus had utilized this very tradition about the servant of God, perhaps already in Mark 9:31, but certainly in his word about the Son of man who had come to serve (Mark 10:45), and then once again in the words of institution of the Lord's Supper. He put himself at God's disposal as the ransom spoken of in Isa. 43:3, and once again at his final passover meal in Jerusalem, he surrendered himself to death "for many" (Mark 14:28 par.: 1 Cor. 11:24). Now the Easter witnesses recognized themselves as part of the "many" for whom Jesus died. In the light of Isa. 52:13—53:12 and of Jesus' death, they confessed, "[he] died for our sins in accordance with the scriptures." By this confession Christ's Easter witnesses took over as an explicit statement of the faith they inherited Jesus' own implicit understanding of justification and atonement. But this understanding included a very specific conception of God's righteousness. The disciples inherited this from Jesus as well.

That the first believing community actually did possess the conception of atonement and righteousness we know from Jesus is shown by a traditional christological confessional formula Paul quotes in Rom. 4:25. There are linguistic grounds for assuming that the formula had already been composed in Jerusalem.[9] It reads "[He] was put to death for our trespasses and raised for our justification." It is sure that behind the passive stands the thought that God was at work in the sacrifice of Jesus and in his resurrection.[10] Once again the text is formulated with Isa. 52:13—53:12 as background, and with the aid of Scripture it shows God's saving activity through Jesus: God gave Jesus up to death and raised him from the dead in order to provide in the sin offering of Jesus' life the necessary basis for the justification of those who confess Jesus as their Lord. Our text provides very significant evidence of the fact that "justification" on the basis of Jesus' atoning death was now being spoken of, and explains why this happened already in Jerusalem. This happened in the light of Isaiah 53 and of Jesus' passion prediction in Mark 9:31 par.; 10:45; and 14:24 par. The sin offering of the sinless one, desired by God—the vicarious sacrifice of Jesus' life—made it possible for God the judge to acquit sinners and give them life without any lessening of his no to sin. *God's righteousness provides the basis for new life! As was true already in Jesus' proclamation, God's righteousness is more than mere punitive justice, because in the sacrifice of Jesus' life God himself inaugurated the atonement sinners were unable to provide.* God's righteousness is the power to forgive sins, and Jesus is its guarantor. The *Sitz im Leben* of the formula could have been baptism (F. Hahn).

LIFE TOGETHER IN JERUSALEM

Jesus' new understanding of righteousness had found expression in his messianic life of righteousness. We should probably consider it a reflection of this righteous life, alive in the memory of his former companions, that the primitive congregation in Jerusalem established a community of shared life and faith in which they "had all things in common; and . . . sold their possessions and goods and distributed them to all, as any had need" (Acts 2:44–45; cf. 4:34–35). The report about this spontaneous sharing of goods is not to be judged simply as an idealized construction of Luke the chronicler; reports like the one about Barnabas, a Levite from Cyprus, selling a field (Acts 4:36–37) are too firmly fixed in the tradition for that. Rather it appears to have been an attempt, wholly concentrated on the imminent return of the Son of man, to form a community of faith unencumbered by possessions in which no needy member would have to be in want.[11] Jesus' love command and his various warnings against riches (for example, Mark 10:17–22 par.) molded the thought of those gathered in Jerusalem, as did the remembrance of the Lord's freedom to let his needs be supplied by the well-to-do (cf. Luke 8:1-3).

The real center of the new life together was the "breaking of bread" that took place in private houses amid "rejoicing," that is, singing (Psalm-)prayers of praise (Acts 2:46). In this "breaking of bread" together the table fellowship of Jesus was continued, and the celebration of the Lord's Supper gained its ecclesiastical form in the remembrance of Jesus' farewell meal with the twelve. Jesus' Easter appearance at a meal (Luke 24:30–31, 41–43; Acts 10:41; John 21:12–13) allowed the table fellowship and the basic ideas of the final Passover meal to merge into a new unity: the Christians in Jerusalem celebrated the meal of reconciliation at the table of their crucified and risen "Lord" (cf. 1 Cor. 10:21), for whose rapid return they pleaded with the Aramaic prayer *Maranatha,* "Our Lord, come" (1 Cor. 16:22; Acts 22:20; *Did.* 10:6).[12] *The fellowship of those who believed in Jesus Christ was sustained and reestablished daily through this common celebration of the Lord's Supper.* At this celebration they knew that the risen Jesus was present in the Spirit. Before God and the congregation they remembered the atoning death of Jesus **by** telling about the passion and reciting the account of the Last Supper (Mark 14:22–25); they prayed for his eschatological coming; and as a body they formed the circle of the "many" reconciled to God by Jesus (cf. also 1 Cor. 10:16–17).

Paul shows in Rom. 15:25–26 that the Jerusalem Christians called themselves "the saints." That can only mean that, in accord with an Old Testament model (Lev. 19:2; Deut. 7:6, among others), they understood themselves to be the eschatological people of God sanctified by Jesus' atoning sacrifice. The primitive church's self-designation "church of God," known to us from Gal. 1:13; Acts 8:3; etc., also points to this self-understanding. The history of this tradition begins with the talk about the "assembly of Yahweh" in Deuteronomy 23 and has its exact Semitic equivalent in the Qumran texts, which speak of the "assembly of God" (1QM 4:10). The first congregation in Jerusalem wanted to be God's community of justified saints standing under God's will and bound to him in Jesus.

MISSION AND BAPTISM IN JERUSALEM

The earliest congregation was engaged in missionary activity from the time of the first Feast of Weeks after Jesus' death, that is, since Pentecost, both among the Aramaic-speaking Jews and also the Greek-speaking Jews from the Diaspora who were living once again in Jerusalem. Since even among the twelve (cf. Mark 3:13–19) there were men like Peter and Philip who spoke both Aramaic and Greek (Gal 2:11ff.; John 12:20–21), there was no language barrier to this missionary activity in the synagogues of the Jews from Cyrene, Alexandria, Cilicia, etc. (Acts 2:9). The new converts were baptized and then attached to one of the house churches. Thus there was soon a separation between the predominately Aramaic-speaking believers, the "Hebrews" (Acts 6:1), and those who spoke only or primarily Greek, the "Hellenists" (Acts 6:1). Both groups had their own worship services.[13]

Matt. 28:16–20 and Mark 16:16 show that baptism was understood and administered as a "sacrament of resurrection" instituted by Christ after his resurrection. Jesus had submitted himself to the baptism of repentance administered by John the Baptist, which was to be a seal from the wrath of the judge coming to baptize with the Spirit and fire (Matt. 3:11–12). Jesus derived his claim to eschatological authority from this baptism (Mark 11:27–33 par.). He also appeared to be thinking of it as he spoke of his own impending suffering and death: "I have a baptism to be baptized with; and how I am constrained until it is accomplished!" (Luke 12:50; cf. Mark 10:38–39 par.). By his baptism-death Jesus gave his life as a ransom "for many." Looking back from the perspective of Easter, Jesus' first witnesses saw his whole public way of righteousness as a way that was "already present in his baptism."[14] The disciples of Jesus, called to be witnesses to him and his resurrection, took up from the very beginning the practice of Christian missionary baptism, which was closely related to John's baptism, since they saw themselves endowed with God's Spirit promised in Joel 3:1ff. (cf. Acts 2:24–36). In Jesus, the crucified and risen Son of man and Messiah, the Spirit-baptizer announced by John had appeared, and his witnesses now carried out the baptism of the Spirit for the forgiveness of sins in his name (Acts 2:38). In this context "in the name of Jesus Christ" means to be turned over to Jesus Christ, in whose name the access was now given to full salvation opened up by his life and suffering (Acts 4:12). Ezek. 36:25–27 may well have stood behind this understanding of

Christian Spirit-baptism. If Rom. 4:25 is really an ancient baptismal formula, it gives us a very fine possibility of providing a christological foundation for the forgiveness of sins that takes place at baptism.

THE UNIVERSAL UNDERSTANDING OF BAPTISM
IN THE STEPHEN-CIRCLE

Compared with the "Hebrews," the Hellenists, led by Stephen in Jerusalem and then driven from the city after his martyrdom, sounded decidedly new accents already with respect to baptism. These accents first became evident in Philip's baptism of Samaritans (Acts 8:13) and eunuchs (Acts 8:26–39), as well as his missionary journey all the way to Caesarea (Acts 8:40). Others from Stephen's circle, namely, Diaspora Jews from Cyprus and Cyrene who had been converted to Christ, turned in Antioch to a baptismal mission on Christ's behalf among Greek-speaking Gentiles (Acts 11:19–20). So it was through the Hellenists that the Samaritans, the Jews' archenemies, those whose disabilities excluded them from worship, and even unbelieving Gentiles were summoned to faith in Christ along with faithful (Diaspora) Jews. By baptism the benefit of Jesus' atoning death was applied equally to all these people, and in this way an understanding of justification and reconciliation was operative that looked toward the exalted Christ and went beyond the boundaries of Israel. This missionary practice of the Hellenists is a consequence of Jesus' saving work, grounded in the grace of God, which he carried out not only among tax collectors and sinners but also occasionally among Samaritans and Gentiles (cf. Mark 7:24–30 par.; Matt. 8:5–13 par.; Luke 10:25–37; 17:11–19), and of his death as a ransom "for many," that is, for Israel and the nations. In Matt. 8:11–12 Jesus himself pointed to the time when the nations would make an eschatological pilgrimage to Zion. Through their mission the Hellenists set about getting this pilgrimage under way.

More detail about this foundation for the universal understanding of mission and of baptism is supplied by traditions Paul cites in his letters to Corinth and Rome. They speak of being "washed" (from sin), "sanctified," and "justified" (1 Cor. 6:11), or also of being "called," "justified," and "glorified" (Rom. 8:30).[15] By virtue of their linguistic peculiarity, these expressions, as well as the two christological formulations found in 2 Cor. 5:21 and Rom. 3:25–26, point back to a time before Paul wrote. They might well have come to the apostle from Antioch, that is, from the community that in special measure preserved and developed the heritage of the Stephen-circle. Whether the mission congregation in Antioch originated these baptismal and christological texts or whether they were already in partial use in Jerusalem must remain an open question. The bilingual character of the Jerusalem community makes an early formulation entirely possible. 2 Corinthians 5:21 speaks of God's atoning action through the person of Jesus. Literally translated it reads, "For our sake he [that is, God] made him, who knew no [guilt on account of] sin, to be [an offering for] sin, so that in him we might become the righteousness of God." The second quote is found in Rom. 3:25–26 [the passage quoted below is all in v. 25 in the RSV, but in the Greek it includes part of v. 26—trans.]; once again it speaks of the atonement inaugurated by God in the sacrifice of Jesus. It says: "whom God put forward as an expiation by his blood, to be received by faith. This was to show God's righteousness, because in his divine forbearance he had passed over former sins."

Both of these traditional formulations fit very well into the proclamation of the Stephen-circle and of the Antioch congregation that was launching a mission to the Gentiles. Stephen was stoned by enraged Diaspora Jews after his Jewish opponents made this accusation against him: "we have heard him say that this Jesus of Nazareth will destroy this place [that is, the temple] and will change the customs which Moses delivered to us [that is, the law]" (Acts 6:14). So their accusation was, "Stephen claims that Christ will bring the end of the temple and its worship."[16] This accusation probably was not simply pulled out of the air. In the light of Jesus' words about the destruction of the Herodian temple (Mark 13:1 par.; 14:58 par.), words that were surely not inserted into the Jesus tradition only later; the symbolic act of cleansing the temple (Mark 11:15–17 par.; John 2:14–22), which was a provocation for Jesus' sacrificial death; and his willingness to be the sin offering for Israel and the nations (Mark 10:45 par.; 14:22–25 par.), Stephen's position is quite understandable. Knowing the tradition about Jesus transmitted to him by the twelve and other companions of Jesus, and in the light of Jesus' atoning death for "many" and his Easter exaltation to be Lord and God's Christ, Stephen started with the supreme significance Jesus' atoning death had for all people: with Jesus' substitutionary sacrifice and his resurrection by God it was Stephen's view that all further expiatory sacrifices were obsolete, as was the temple cult in Jerusalem established to carry out these sacrifices.

As evidence for this perspective one can point to the two traditional passages in Paul's letters to which we have just referred. According to 2 Cor. 5:21 God made the righteous and obedient Christ, "who knew no [guilt on account of] sin, to be sin for us," that is, for the sake of the confessing community. The formulation used here in 2 Cor. 5:21 follows the Septuagint wording of Lev. 4:21, 24; 5:12; and 6:18 and has in view the sin offering ritually sacrificed to take away sin. This "sacrifice made on account of sin" can in these passages be referred to in abbreviated language and simply called "sin."[17] It is precisely this abbreviated expression, known from its cultic context, that we have in 2 Cor. 5:21, giving the sentence this meaning: God made Jesus the sinless one to be a sin offering in order to put the confessing congregation in a state of purity and righteousness before God. "The righteousness of God" in 2 Cor. 5:21 designates the new existence of those for whom atonement was made by Jesus' sacrifice. The expression sums up in a phrase the result of the divine act of atonement. This points to the status of holiness possessed by believers, who are acquitted at the judgment, a status conferred and acknowledged by God. As righteousness that proceeds from God's verdict and stands up before his throne of judgment, it is called the righteousness of God. It has its basis in the love and righteousness of God, who in Jesus has destined sinners to life rather than death. 2 Cor. 5:21 celebrates Jesus' surrender to death as a recon-

ciling act inaugurated by God and conferring on the community the righteousness of God. As God's act of reconciliation through Jesus, God's son, it is not
repeatable and nothing more is needed. If this formulation is compared with
the Jewish interpretation of Isaiah 53 in reference to the suffering of the righteous (cited above, p. 43), "the innocent one shall be defiled for the lawless
and the sinless one shall die for the ungodly" (*T. Benj.* 3:8), the roots of
2 Cor. 5:21 in Isaiah 53 become immediately evident.[18] 2 Corinthians 5:21
becomes fully understandable on the basis of Isaiah 53 and the technical cultic
language of Leviticus 4. The Hellenistic-Jewish formulation points to the community in Antioch or the Stephen-circle in Jerusalem.

THE END OF WORSHIP IN THE
JERUSALEM TEMPLE

The second formula that Paul took over from the community around Stephen
and quoted in Rom. 3:25–26 is an expression about Christ's work that is based
on Leviticus 16. In this chapter there is a description of the essential elements
of Israel's most important cultic act, the expiation of the people on the Day
of Atonement. The Day of Atonement was established by God "that atonement
may be made for the people of Israel once in the year because of all their sins"
(Lev. 16:34). The heart of this cultic act of atonement was the entry of the high
priest into the Holy of Holies with the blood of the scapegoat. In the Holy
of Holies, according to Leviticus 16, the Ark of the Covenant was located, with
its lid-structure, the so-called *kappōret*. In our Bibles this word is generally
translated "mercy seat." This refers to the place where God dwells in the
temple, or, as Lev. 16:2 says, "I [that is, God] will appear in the cloud upon
the mercy seat." Lest the high priest be consumed by the presence of the holy
God, he must first bring a sin offering for himself and his household and
through incense hide the *kappōret* from his own view. Only then dare he enter
the Holy of Holies with the blood of the scapegoat and sprinkle the blood
"upon the mercy seat and before the mercy seat" (Lev. 16:15). The significance of the blood for achieving atonement is explained in Lev. 17:11: it
is the bearer of life, and thus belongs to God alone, who gave it to the Israelites
for use "upon the altar to make atonement for [their] souls." Thus the essence
of cultic atonement is the substitutionary sacrifice of a life for the life of
others, which makes possible a new sanctified existence before God. Atonement and new creation belong inseparably together. The ritual for the Day of
Atonement, understood in this way, was carried out in Israel every year until
the destruction of the Herodian temple in 70 C.E. Since the Ark was lost to
Israel in the sixth century B.C.E. and since, according to Jer. 3:16, the Ark was
not to be made again, there was no longer an Ark in the Holy of Holies in
the Herodian temple. Therefore, the cultic act of atonement was carried out
symbolically. The high priest used the incense and sprinkled the blood in an
empty room in the light of God's spiritual presence. This cultic act was per-
formed entirely hidden behind the curtain that separated the Holy of Holies
from the sanctuary. The worshiping congregation learned of the completion

of the act of atonement when the high priest blessed the people publicly after the ritual was over (cf. Ecclus. 50:19–20).

The Day of Atonement had the highest significance for the Israelites. It was celebrated even in the Diaspora, where one could only contemplate the worship in the temple in Jerusalem. The Temple Scroll from Qumran shows that the Day of Atonement was extremely important also for the Essenes, who had separated themselves from the temple in Jerusalem because they believed that the temple had been defiled by the officiating priests, who were in their view ungodly. Every pious Jew in Palestine and in the Diaspora knew what happened on the Day of Atonement in the temple. They knew also what the *kappōret*—or, as the Greek translation of *kappōret* has it, the *hilastērion* (that is, place of atonement)—was, namely, the place of atonement and of the gracious presence of God in the temple on Mt. Zion.

If we look at the formula in Rom. 3:25–26 from this vantage point, we recognize in it the important word we have just mentioned, *hilastērion,* and we flinch involuntarily at the daring expression.[19] Here, with all gravity (and in carefully thought-out, technical priestly terminology) it is said that God publicly installed *Jesus* as the *hilastērion.* Jesus, the crucified and risen Christ, is the place of God's indwelling in Israel and the place where Israel and all God-fearing strangers can find atonement, atonement by virtue of the blood of Jesus poured out on the cross. The hiddenness of the Holy of Holies in the temple has in Rom. 3:25–26 given way to openness on Golgotha and to the light of Easter morning. In Jesus, the obedient Son of man, God has come to humanity and at the same time reconciled this humanity with their God. In Rom. 3:25–26 Jesus is both the God who has come to dwell with humanity and the human being who has vicariously surrendered himself to God for sinners. The atonement effected by Jesus cannot be repeated. It has once and for all been entered into history by God. Wherever this is proclaimed and believed there is no more need for a high priest or a rite of atonement. Therefore, the Jerusalem temple can become (as Jesus said in Mark 11:15–17 par.!) "a house of prayer for all the nations" (Isa. 56:7), and, therefore, instead of the law of Moses "the torah of Christ" (Gal. 6:2) is in effect.[20]

Stephen and his followers had evangelized primarily among those Greek-speaking Jews in Jerusalem who had returned to the holy city in order to be as close as possible to the center of their faith. It must have rendered these orthodox-minded people almost speechless to hear in their synagogues the kind of tones that are struck in Rom. 3:25–26. It is easily understandable that, in an outburst of righteous indignation, they stoned Stephen as a blasphemer, as the law commanded (Lev. 24:14–15). It is just as understandable as the expulsion of the rest of the Stephen-circle from God's city Jerusalem (cf. Acts 8:1ff.).

But with Stephen's martyrdom his faith was not refuted, and the formula we are examining now lived on all the more in the mouth of his Christian friends who were driven from Jerusalem. We must stick with this formula a bit longer. It says that this appointment of Jesus as the *hilastērion,* that is, as the place of God's presence and of atonement, happened "to show God's righteousness." Once again this often-misinterpreted language can be explained on the basis of Israelite tradition. From the penitential prayers of the Qumran community it becomes very clear in what sense God's righteousness was for ancient Judaism at that time the necessary basis for atonement and the forgiveness of sins, namely, as God's grace that effects atonement out of pure mercy. In the *Manual of Discipline* from Qumran (1QS 11:11–15), we read:

> As for me,
>> if I stumble, the mercies of God
>> shall be my eternal salvation.
> If I stagger because of the sin of flesh,
>> my justification shall be
>> by the righteousness of God which endures for ever.
> When my distress is unleashed
>> He will deliver my soul from the Pit
>> and will direct my steps to the way.
> He will draw me near by His grace,
>> and by His mercy will He bring my justification.
> He will judge me in the righteousness of His truth
>> and in the greatness of His goodness
>> He will pardon all my sins.
> Through his righteousness He will cleanse me
>> of the uncleanness of man
>> and of the sins of the children of men,
>> that I may confess to God His righteousness,
>> and His majesty to the Most High.[21]

God's righteousness here is God's grace and mercy, because God atones for the ungodly, receives them anew into his presence, and empowers them to praise God. With this Jewish penitential prayer-language as background, language that was decisive already for Jesus, the language in Rom. 3:25–26 can be understood without difficulty. The installation of Jesus for atonement is a demonstration of God's saving righteousness, because through this installation sinners receive the forgiveness of their sins. God's determination to save sinners is so great that in Jesus Christ he himself lays the ground for their justification and thereby creates for them the possibility and reality of the forgiveness of sins. God's righteousness is praised in Rom. 3:25–26 as righteousness by which God makes things right and establishes order and life. The formula also then continues by saying that the public installation of Jesus as the place of atonement and of God's presence shows God's righteousness, "because in his divine forbearance he had passed over former sins." *God's righteousness provides atonement and thereby effects the remission of sins. It is much more than a retributive power; it is the basis of the new life God opens up in Jesus.*

This profoundly positive understanding of God's righteousness, which agrees completely with Jesus' understanding, is confirmed when we give brief attention to the notion of God's patience.[22] The view that God dealt with Israel graciously and patiently pervades many early Jewish texts. It is firmly rooted in Israelite prayers of repentance, like the prayer in Neh. 9:17:

> But thou art a God ready to forgive, gracious and merciful, slow to anger and abounding in steadfast love, and didst not forsake them [Israel's forebears].

In the so-called Damascus Rule it says of God, "Patience and much forgiveness are with Him to atone for all who turn from transgression" (CD 2:4–5).[23] Finally, in the Wisdom of Solomon God is praised as the "Lord who loves the living." It says of God:

> But thou art merciful to all, for thou canst do all things.
> and thou dost overlook men's sins, that they may repent.
> For thou lovest all things that exist,
> and hast loathing for none of the things
>   which thou hast made,
> for thou wouldst not have made anything
>   if thou hadst hated it.
> How would anything have endured if thou
>   hadst not willed it?
> Or how would anything not called forth
>   by thee have been preserved?
> Thou sparest all things, for they are thine,
>   O Lord who lovest the living (Wisd. of Sol. 11:23–26).

If we turn to Rom. 3:25–26 after looking at these texts, light is shed upon the statement that in (the time of) God's divine forbearance he had passed over former sins. It means that God had stayed his judging wrath until the appearance of Jesus and his installation as the place of atonement in order that sinners could be forgiven and given life. God's patience, meant to offer sinners life and salvation, serves God's life-creating and life-preserving righteousness. There is in our formula no longer any talk of a restriction of the patient and atoning righteousness of God to those in Israel who are truly faithful to the law, as is the case in Jewish texts. The atonement inaugurated by God in Jesus applies to all who confess Jesus as Christ and Lord! The step from a mission only to Jews to a mission among Samaritans and finally even to Gentiles, a step the Stephen-circle dared to take, was well grounded and theologically appropriate when seen from the perspective of this understanding of righteousness. A baptism established with the aid of Rom. 3:25–26 could be universal.[24]

THE LIFE OF RIGHTEOUSNESS IN THE CONGREGATION AT ANTIOCH

Unfortunately, very little has been preserved for us about the life of righteousness among Stephen's followers and the people they baptized. Nevertheless we can identify two things that happened. The first is especially significant. The

baptismal practices of the Hellenists driven from Jerusalem had as a consequence that from that time on Samaritans and the physically disabled, Gentiles
and Jews lived, prayed, and ate together in one Christian congregation. Faith
in Jesus Christ and the bestowal of God's righteousness on them all (2 Cor.
5:21) united Samaritans and Jews, who even up to the period of Jesus' ministry
were separated from one another in hostility (cf. Luke 9:52, 56). But it also
united Gentiles and Jews, who up until then had avoided one another and who
had at times stood in a deep contempt for one another that already in the first
century gave vent to pogroms. *The new faith in Christ and the new righteousness bestowed on the believers worked themselves out in an astonishing actualization of reconciliation between groups that had been religious enemies.* It
appeared as though Paul's famous description of the Christian community,
"For as many of you as were baptized into Christ have put on Christ. There
is neither Jew nor Greek, there is neither slave nor free, there is neither male
nor female; for you are all one in Christ Jesus" (Gal. 3:27–28; 1 Cor. 12:12–
13), was already an operative social reality in Antioch. Righteousness and
reconciliation, indeed reconciliation both with God and with fellow believers,
belonged inseparably together in the new mission congregation.

But the righteousness of faith and communal solidarity also had an effect
on one another! When a famine occurred in Palestine in the forties of the first
century and the primitive church in Jerusalem found itself in a severe eco-
nomic crisis, a collection was made at Antioch for the beleaguered fellow
Christians in Jerusalem (cf. Acts 11:27–30). This collection was in itself an
act of material solidarity with fellow believers which quite clearly lay within
the boundaries of the life of love called for by Jesus himself, of his demand
for the new righteousness. The collection by gentile congregations for the
poor among the "saints" in Jerusalem (Gal. 2:10; Rom. 15:25ff.), which was
decided on a short time later at the Apostolic Council, apparently had this first
collection as a model, and it raised the support of the primitive church in
Jerusalem to a sacred obligation for all gentile Christians. Living Jesus' new
righteousness held Jewish and gentile Christians together despite unmistakable tensions.

Paul was brought to Antioch by Barnabas sometime after his call to be an
apostle of Christ, and together with Barnabas he made his first missionary
journey to Cyprus and Asia Minor (Acts 11:25–26; 13:1–14:28). That the traditions about righteousness that were operative in Antioch were determinative
for Paul can be seen not only in the quotes Paul gives in his letters but also
in Pauline missionary practices. On the first missionary journey Paul and Barnabas, true to the beginnings in Antioch (Acts 11:20–21), baptized Gentiles
into Christ without requiring their circumcision and the consequent adoption
of the whole law of Moses. This baptismal practice caused such offense to a
group of Jewish-Christians in Jerusalem that the legitimacy of such a mission
plan among the Gentiles had to be dealt with at the so-called Apostolic Council in Jerusalem (Acts 15:1–35; Gal. 2:1–10). At this council Paul and Barnabas
successfully represented the missionary interests of the community in
Antioch. The significance of this for us is that we can trace an unbroken line

of tradition from Jesus' life of righteousness to the confession and mission tradition in Jerusalem and Antioch and that we can extend this line to the mission proclamation of Paul. Jesus' new life of righteousness found its valid terminological expression in the theological tradition of the primitive church. This process of formulation reached its high point with Paul.

NOTES

1. For what follows I am indebted to important insights in M. Hengel's *Acts and the History of Earliest Christianity,* trans. J. Bowden (Philadelphia: Fortress Press, 1979) and J. Roloff's commentary on Acts: *Die Apostelgeschichte* (Göttingen: Vandenhoeck & Ruprecht, 1981). With respect to methodology I call attention to T. Holtz. "Überlegungen zur Geschichte des Urchristentums," *TLZ* 100 (1975): 321–32.

2. In "Christologie und neutestamentliche Chronologie" (in *Neues Testament und Geschichte. Oscar Cullmann zum 70. Geburtstag* [Tübingen: Mohr, 1972], 43–67), Martin Hengel has called attention to the fact that it is legitimate to designate as "pre-Pauline" only the first four or five years after Jesus' crucifixion and resurrection.

3. On this, see my essay "Das Bekenntnis zur Auferweckung Jesu von den Toten und die Biblische Theologie," in *Schriftauslegung auf dem Wege zur biblischen Theologie* (Göttingen: Vandenhoeck & Ruprecht, 1975), 128–66, and H. Gese, "Death in the Old Testament," in *Essays on Biblical Theology,* trans. K. Crim (Minneapolis: Augsburg Pub. Co., 1981), 34–59.

4. This is stressed by J. Jeremias, *New Testament Theology. The Proclamation of Jesus,* trans. J. Bowden (New York: Charles Scribner's Sons; London: SCM Press, 1971), 278, n. 1.

5. On the background of Rom. 1:3–4 see esp. U. Wilckens, *Der Brief an die Römer,* EKK 6.1 (Zürich: Benziger Verlag; Neukirchen-Vluyn: Neukirchener Verlag, 1978), 58–61.

6. In the LXX the Hebrew text of Isa. 53:11, "the righteous one, my servant, makes many to be accounted righteous, and bears their iniquities," is applied to the Servant as follows: God will "make righteous a righteous one who wonderfully serves many; and he [the righteous one] will take away their sins." The hymnic statement in 1 Tim. 3:16 could be dependent on this LXX wording; *1 Enoch* 61–63 should also be considered as a background for this hymn.

7. It is not unlikely that there is a connection between the aloofness of Jesus' family, which led to the reaction mentioned in Mark 3:21, the reproach that he was "a glutton and a drunkard" (Matt. 11:19), and the injunction in Deut. 21:18–21. The Deuteronomy passage was still being intensively pondered and interpreted in the Temple Scroll from Qumran (11QTemple 64:1–6) and in the Mishnah (*m. Sanh.* 8:1–5). Seen from the background of this text, both Jesus' disobedience to his family and his table fellowship (cf. particularly *m. Sanh.* 8:2!) appear to be worthy of death. On this issue see N. Perrin, *Rediscovering the Teaching of Jesus* (New York: Harper & Row, 1976), 119ff., and E. Schweizer, *Jesus,* trans. D. Green (Richmond: John Knox Press, 1971), 24.

8. R. Riesner, in his essay "Jüdische Elementarbildung und Evangelienüberlieferung" (in *Gospel Perspectives: Studies of History and Tradition in the Four Gospels,* ed. R. T. France and D. Wenham, 3 vols. [Sheffield: JSOT Press, 1980–83], 1:209–23), and in his dissertation, "Jesus als Lehrer" (diss.; University of Tübingen, 1980), 93–183, called attention to the significance of Jewish education, as conveyed at home, at school, and at the synagogue, for an understanding of the Scriptures, for reading, and for writing. He assumes with good reason not only that Jesus himself bore the imprint of these three institutions but also that "a number of the disciples came

from the religiously aware segment of the Jewish people and consequently they, like Jesus . . . had a good elementary education through their home, synagog, and elementary school." This provides a good explanation for the appeal to "the Scriptures" already present in the earliest stage of the tradition in Jerusalem. Peter and John are called *AGRAMMATOI* and *IDIŌTAI* ("uneducated, common men") in Acts 4:13 only because they lacked the advanced education of the scribes, something Paul had had in addition to this elementary education.

9. On the Semitizing formulation in Rom. 4:25 see Jeremias, *New Testament Theology*, 296-97, and on the traditions behind this text see Wilckens, *Der Brief an die Römer*, 279-80. While Wilckens would like to see in Rom. 4:25 a statement that "Paul himself formulated . . . by adopting traditional motifs," F. Hahn, in "Taufe und Rechtfertigung. Ein Beitrag zur paulinischen Theologie in ihrer Vor- und Nachgeschichte" (in *Rechtfertigung. Festschrift für Ernst Käsemann zum 70. Geburtstag*, ed. J. Friedrich, W. Pöhlmann, and P. Stuhlmacher [Tübingen: Mohr, 1976], 108 [95–124]), considers whether in pre-Pauline times this statement might not have helped to "provide the christological rationale at baptism."

10. W. Popkes, *Christus Traditus* (Zürich: Zwingli Verlag, 1967), 228ff., 263ff.; Jeremias, *New Testament Theology*, 295-96, and Wilckens, *Der Brief an die Römer*, 279-80, point, correctly in my view, to the connections between Mark 9:31 par. and Rom. 4:25.

11. Cf. M. Hengel, *Property and Riches in the Early Church: Aspects of a Social History of Early Christianity*, trans. J. Bowden (Philadelphia: Fortress Press, 1974), 31ff.

12. If Jesus was already addressed as the returning "Lord" in Jerusalem, it is possible that the Pauline designation "the Lord's Supper" (1 Cor. 11:20) can be traced back to pre-Pauline usage.

13. On the discussion that follows see especially M. Hengel's *Between Jesus and Paul: Studies in the Earliest History of Christianity*, trans. J. Bowden (Philadelphia: Fortress Press, 1983), 1–29, and his *Acts and the History of Earliest Christianity*, 69–110.

14. R. Pesch (*Das Abendmahl und Jesu Todesverständnis* QD 80 [Freiburg: Herder, 1978], 115—22), stresses, in my opinion correctly, that primitive Christian missionary baptism remains essentially incomprehensible without reference to Jesus' death as a ransom "for many."

15. For a more detailed analysis of these baptismal texts see Hahn, "Taufe und Rechtfertigung," 104-17. Luz, "Rechtfertigung bei den Paulusschülern," in *Rechtfertigung*, 365-83, deals with the later development of the pre-Pauline and Pauline baptismal traditions.

16. Hengel, *Between Jesus and Paul*, 22. How G. Strecker, *"Befreiung und Rechtfertigung,"* in *Rechtfertigung*, 481, justifies understanding Acts 6:11, 13-14 only as "a secondary Lukan transition into which synoptic material has been incorporated" is not clear to me after Hengel's analysis of the context. A. Strobel, *Die Stunde der Wahrheit* (Tübingen: Mohr, 1980), 22-23; 45, n. 126; 87-88, envisions a legal condemnation of Stephen as a seducer of the people by the Sanhedrin, followed by an unauthorized execution of the death sentence by stoning. In his view the proceedings against Jesus and his execution by the Romans were used by the Sanhedrin as a precedent for the whole process.

17. See my two essays "Recent Exegesis on Rom. 3:24-26 (chap. 6 in this volume, p. 107, n. 40), and "Zum Thema: Biblische Theologie des Neuen Testaments" (in K. Haacker et al., *Biblische Theologie heute*, Biblisch-theologische Studien 1 [Neukirchen-Vluyn: Neukirchener Verlag, 1977], 25-60, esp. 40), as well as Wilckens, *Der Brief an die Römer*, 240.

18. That 2 Cor. 5:18-21 is formulated on the basis of Isaiah 53 has in my view been

pointed out convincingly by O. Hofius, "Erwägungen zur Gestalt und Herkunft des paulinischen Versöhnungsgedankens, *ZTK* 77 (1980): 186–99. Although Hofius regards 2 Cor. 5:21 as a boldly formulated "statement by the apostle" (p. 196), it is my view, as well as that of Wilckens, that we have here a formula that Paul utilizes (see above, n. 17) that Paul naturally does not simply drag in but emphatically affirms! It is only when one assumes the use of traditional material here that the formulaic language of the statement and its place in the context become fully clear.

19. G. Klein wonders in his homily on Rom. 3:21–28 (in *Göttinger Predigtmeditationen* 69 [1980]: 414 [409–19]) about the question "batted back and forth with astonishing passion in many places" exactly how *hilastērion* in v. 25 is to be understood. As long as the centrality of the atonement motif in this text is acknowledged, he regards it as "immaterial whether here the concept of the death of the martyr as a substitutionary atonement is in the background, whether *hilastērion* simply means the 'means of atonement' or whether Jesus is characterized as the place of atonement and of meeting God." Unfortunately in this theologically imprecise way of looking at it, we lose sight of the text's historical daring and its place in the history of traditions. For the pre-Pauline Christology and soteriology of the "Hellenists," it makes a powerful difference whether they had seen Jesus' atoning death merely as the sacrificial death of a (Jewish) martyr or as the end of the ritual of atonement in the Jerusalem temple because Jesus had been established by God as the *kappōret* and Golgotha had taken over the place the Holy of Holies had within the temple! Hebrews 9:5 and Philo *Life of Moses* 2.95, 97 in my opinion speak clearly for the understanding of *hilastērion* as *kappōret*. On the meaning of *kappōret* see now the very fine study by B. Janowski, "Sühne als Heilsgeschehen" (diss.; University of Tübingen, 1979), 198ff.

20. Hengel, *Between Jesus and Paul*, 151, n. 137, conjectures plausibly "that in his remarks about the 'law of Christ' (Gal. 6:2; 1 Cor. 9:21) Paul is taking up an earlier tradition" that was characteristic of the Stephen-circle. The Stephen-circle and the community in Antioch were not simply antinomians, but following Jesus' example they made new value judgments within the law itself.

21. G. Vermes, *The Dead Sea Scrolls in English* (Baltimore: Penguin Books, 1968), 93–94.

22. There is ample material on God's patience and forbearance in D. Zeller, "Sühne und Langmut," *TP* 43 (1968): 59ff. (51–75). I know no compelling reason to follow Strecker, "Befreiung und Rechtfertigung," 502, in asserting that Paul's interpretation of the formula he is quoting begins already with the words *en tē anochē tou theou;* it only begins with *pros tēn endeixin,* as is also asserted, for example, by Hahn, "Taufe und Rechfertigung," 112.

23. Vermes, *Dead Sea Scrolls in English,* 98 (altered).

24. Hahn, "Taufe und Rechtfertigung," 112, argues quite plausibly that the phrase about the forgiveness of sins that had before been overlooked because of God's patience can be explained very well in a baptismal setting. The words *en tǭ autou haimati* in the formula refer to blood as the means of atonement and therefore should not simply be taken as evidence that Rom. 3:25–26 originally belonged in a eucharistic setting (as is proposed, for example, by E. Käsemann, "Zum Verständnis von Röm. 3:24–26," in *Exegetische Versuche und Besinnungen,* 2 vols. [Göttingen: Vandenhoeck & Ruprecht, 1960–64], 1:99–100). Why the reference to the blood of Jesus should be seen as an addition by a pre-Pauline or even post-Pauline transmitter of the tradition, as Strecker, "Befreiung und Rechtfertigung," 502, proposes, is again not clear to me.

CHAPTER 5

The Apostle Paul's
View of
Righteousness

Within the context of the messianic traditions of the Old Testament and of early Judaism, Jesus brought to reality a new righteousness. His legacy was taken up in Jerusalem by the witnesses of his resurrection, especially the Stephen-circle, to be the basis of that mission that programmatically went beyond Israel's borders and sought to win also the Gentiles for Christ the Lord. Paul has a key role in the history of New Testament thinking about righteousness, because he made God's righteousness in Christ the basic content of the missionary gospel. *From the time of the apostle's missionary journeys and letters, the righteousness of God in Christ and the justification of all believers through Christ alone are the inalienable foundations and norms of Christian belief.* Paul made Jesus' work of righteousness the foundation of faith that lives solely on the gospel.

PAUL'S ORIGIN

Paul was a Pharisee from the Diaspora. He grew up in a pious Jewish family in Tarsus, the capital of the province of Cilicia (Acts 22:3). His father was a Roman citizen (Acts 22:28) and a descendant of the Israelite tribe of Benjamin. He named his son Saul after Israel's first king and followed the pious practice of having him circumcised on the eighth day (Phil. 3:5). "Paul" was the Roman name of this young Benjaminite from a well-placed family. According to Acts 22:3 and 26:4 the family moved to Jerusalem sometime after the birth of young Saul.

Paul had a strong religious commitment from his youth. At an early age he joined the Pharisees, a group that took its Judaism seriously and wanted to regulate all of life by the law of Moses. In Jerusalem, at that time the center of true Jewish education, he was trained to be a scribe under Rabbi Gamaliel I (Acts 22:3). As was customary for those with rabbinic training, Paul also learned a trade; out of leather he made tents and other items (Acts 18:3). Today we would call him a leather worker. Some exegetes want to conclude from Gal. 5:11 that before Paul's call to be an apostle he had already been a Jewish missionary in the Diaspora for a time.[1] But in his self-assessment in Gal. 1:13–14 and Phil. 3:6 he only says that he battled "zealously" for the Torah and for the traditions of Torah interpretation handed on by his forebears. He added that he persecuted the church violently, trying to destroy it. Acts 8:1–3 gives something of a picture of Paul's activity as persecutor.

PAUL AS A PERSECUTOR OF CHRISTIANS

If we investigate these events in some detail, interesting findings emerge.[2] We know from Acts 6:9 and from inscriptions that there were in Jerusalem a considerable number of synagogues in which Greek-speaking Jews worshiped. It was in these synagogues that Stephen and his followers arose to dispute with their compatriots, arousing deadly hostility by their criticism of the temple and the law. Paul was a witness to these conflicts. In this way he came to know Christianity already in Jerusalem as a movement that, by appeal to Jesus of Nazareth (who shortly before this had been condemned to a cursed death on the cross and who allegedly arose from the dead and was even exalted to the right hand of God), critically distanced itself both from the sacrificial cult in the temple and the undivided law of Moses. This apostate movement will have appeared just as blasphemous to him as it did to the men who in religious fury stoned Stephen to death. Following this spontaneous religious act of judgment, Paul, with the approval of the highest Jewish court, the Sanhedrin, appears to have proceeded against the Christian sympathizers of Stephen with all the legal means at the disposal of the court and of the individual synagogue congregations. The campaign ended with the expulsion of the Stephen-circle from Jerusalem, that is, actually with the extermination of a significant part of the Jerusalem community. The Aramaic-speaking Jewish Christians in Jerusalem and their friends in Judea at that time learned to fear Paul as an enemy of the faith; but only those in Jerusalem saw him face to face (cf. Gal. 1:22).

When it turned out that Stephen's followers who had been driven from Jerusalem did not allow their mission for Christ to be deterred and indeed gained a firm foothold in significant Jewish Diaspora communities such as the one in Damascus in Nabatea, Paul, armed with letters of recommendation from Jerusalem, set about inciting his fellow-believers to take against those of the Christian sect measures similar to the ones that had been used with success in Jerusalem (Acts 9:1ff.; 22:19). These were the alternatives as he saw them: either the new teaching about the atoning death and resurrection of Jesus, with its critical consequences for the significance of the temple cult and the sole validity of the law of Moses, or the true old fidelity to a faith oriented to the law, especially in its most serious form, the fidelity to the law demanded by the Pharisees.

PAUL'S CALL TO BE AN APOSTLE

The apostle himself and Acts agree in reporting that Paul during his journey to Damascus was bowled over by an appearance of Christ that shook his Pharisaic presuppositions to the core (Gal. 1:15-16; 1 Cor. 9:1; 15:9-10; Acts 9:1-9; 22:6-11; 26:12-18). To the persecutor of Christians appeared the Lord of the persecuted believers, with a glory befitting one who had been exalted to God's right hand and vindicated over against his oppressors as the Son of God! Paul always regarded this appearance of Christ to be equivalent to the Easter appearances to those who had been called to be apostles before him (1 Cor. 9:1-2; 15:9). Like Peter and the other apostles he traced his call as missionary to his encounter with the risen Christ. But with the Easter appearance outside Damascus a theological perception burst forth and a will to mission awoke in Paul that made his apostleship something special. Paul learned outside Damascus that by his zealous advocacy of the law of Moses and its traditional interpretation, of the sacrificial cult in the temple, and of the interpretation of the cross of Christ as a curse that God had deservedly inflicted on Jesus (Deut. 21:22-23), he had actually been fighting against the true will of God in the mission of Jesus, God's Son. He was not in the right; rather the ones whom he had persecuted were, with their faith in Jesus Christ, the Messiah and Lord of the world—the one whom God made humanity's righteousness, sanctification and redemption (1 Cor. 1:30). All who believe in him and become baptized for the forgiveness of sins in the name of Jesus Christ, in which alone salvation is found (Acts 4:12), receive from God that righteousness required at the judgment to enter the eternal reign of God. *Outside Damascus Paul encountered in Christ God's saving will personified; that signified for him, the Pharisee fighting for the Torah, Christ as the "end of the law for everyone who believes" (in Christ and God's work in him, Rom. 10:4).*

With this perception, evoked in Paul by the Risen One, the essential content of his missionary gospel was already given, even before he began with new eyes to study and to accept the story about Jesus and the faith of the Christians, first in Damascus, then also in Jerusalem, and finally in Antioch. With the insight that the crucified and risen Christ was the saving will of God personified, the way of the gospel to the Gentiles was shown even much more fundamentally than with Stephen and his followers. If the true will of God, genuine righteousness, wisdom that fully comprehends God, and the salvation that consists in God's indomitable nearness and love lie hidden in the crucified and risen Son of God (1 Cor. 1:30), then this true will of God and this wisdom point beyond the law from Sinai and call not only Israel but all nations to repent and come to God. Outside Damascus Paul was not moved to abandon Judaism and take up a proclamation of the gospel that was hostile to Jews but rather to move outside the borders of his Pharisaic convictions. Paul came to see that in Christ God had brought the revelation at Sinai to its goal and inaugurated the time announced in the promises in Jer. 31:31ff. and Isa. 2:2-4 (1 Cor. 11:25; 2 Cor. 3:6; Gal. 4:21ff.). From the time of his call to be an apostle, the scribe Paul strove to be a Jew newly enlightened in spirit (Rom.

2:28–29) and obedient to the righteousness of God in Christ, which intends the salvation of the world. The Christian congregations that had been threatened by Paul praised God for the transformation of the persecutor of Christians into an apostle of Christ (Gal. 1:23–24). As long as he lived, however, most of his Jewish coreligionists regarded this change as a fall from faith. With few exceptions they turned a deaf ear to Paul's preaching. Moreover, they now took action against Paul, just as he had previously done against the Stephen-circle and its supporters.

The life of the Diaspora Pharisee won over to faith in Christ was marked with the cross by the gospel about Christ revealed to Paul by his call to be an apostle. Even before he was summoned to Antioch by Barnabas (Acts 11:25–26), Paul was repeatedly beaten in the synagogues for preaching Christ (2 Cor. 11:24).[3] The punishment of flogging with thirty-nine lashes on the breast and the back, in accord with Deut. 25:2–3, was inflicted by the synagogue courts for serious violations of the law; it was life-threatening for those who received this punishment. If we consider on top of this that on his later missionary journeys, according to 2 Cor. 11:25, Paul underwent in addition three beatings with rods at the hands of the Romans (cf. Acts 16:22) and once only barely escaped death by stoning (Acts 14:19–20), then it no longer sounds exaggerated when the apostle writes in Gal. 6:17 that he bears on his body the marks of Jesus.

THE PAULINE GOSPEL ABOUT JUSTIFICATION

From the repeated beatings in the synagogues we can draw the historically reliable conclusion that immediately after his call Paul proclaimed Christ as the sole ground of justification, as the Messiah our righteousness (cf. 1 Cor. 1:30 with Jer. 23:6), and as the end of the law (Rom. 10:4) and lived on the basis of this understanding of his faith. *Thus Paul's proclamation about justification, together with its criticism of the sole validity of the law of Moses, is not only the result of later Pauline reflection about the faith;*[4] *it is the direct consequence of the apostle's encounter outside Damascus with the Son of God, who had been "vindicated in the Spirit" (1 Tim. 3:16).*

If we attempt to grasp Paul's concept of justification, the first resource we have is the apostle's own testimony in Philippians 3, where he writes:

(4) If any other man thinks he has reason for confidence in the flesh, [then] I have more; (5) circumcised on the eighth day, of the people of Israel, of the tribe of Benjamin, a Hebrew born of Hebrews; as to [obedience to] the law a Pharisee, (6) as to zeal a persecutor of the church, as to righteousness [attained] under the law blameless. (7) But whatever gain I had, I counted as loss for the sake of Christ.[8] Indeed I count everything as loss because of the surpassing worth of knowing Christ Jesus my Lord. For his sake I have suffered the loss of all things, and count them as refuse, in order that I may gain Christ (9) and be found [by God] in him, not having a righteousness of my own, based on law, but that which is [won] through faith in Christ, the righteousness from God that depends on faith; (10) that I may know him and the power of his resurrection, and may share his

sufferings, becoming like him in his death, (11) that if possible I may attain the
resurrection from the dead.

This testimony, which Paul himself developed as a pattern for the Christian
attitude he advocated (cf. Phil. 3:15ff.), teaches most beautifully what Paul
understands by "justification."

Justification is the acquittal of an individual who is summoned before the
bar at God's just (last) judgment. In this judgment only those whom God
declares righteous and receives can be acquitted. Paul's own effort as a Pharisee to attain the righteousness demanded at the last judgment, by repentance
and strict fidelity to the law, indeed by a fidelity to the law that proved itself
in his militant "zeal" against the (Christian) despisers of the law, this effort
the apostle regards as a failure. It is a failure in the light of the knowledge
of Christ that had been granted him and not because of any failure on his part
to do what the law demands! Paul expressly emphasizes that in respect to the
Pharisaic norm his righteousness was above reproach. But confronted by the
crucified and risen Christ, he regards this irreproachable self-achieved righteousness as the illusionary high-handedness of pious people who oppose
God's work without any real idea of their true status before God. At the last
judgment no one can rely on self-achieved righteousness based on the law.
Here all that avails is the righteousness given by God for Jesus' sake. That
righteousness is achieved (only) by those who submit in faith to God's atoning
action in Christ and acknowledge Jesus Christ as their Lord and advocate
before God. The righteousness that brings one through the last judgment is
the righteousness God gives by grace because of the intercession of the crucified and risen Christ (cf. Rom. 8:31ff.). The expression used in Phil. 3:9, "the
righteousness from God," agrees exactly with the Hebrew text of Isa. 54:17
and occurs in Aramaic in this place in the *Targum of the Prophets*. In both
cases what is spoken about is the righteousness that God confers on God's servants so that in the judgment they can be victorious over their accusers and
gain salvation. Even in the Isaiah passage this righteousness comes from God
as a gracious gift, and in Paul that is all the more true.

Philippians 3:9 is written with a view to the last judgment, and thus speaks
of the "hope of righteousness," of which Gal. 5:5 also speaks. But Paul can
also speak of "justification" as an event of the past, something the believer
has already received. In doing this the apostle freely adopts the baptismal tradition he inherits (for example, in Rom. 3:24ff.; 4:25; 8:29–30; 1 Cor. 6:11).
But he also formulates the same idea independently and even emphasizes it
by speaking of the reconciliation already conferred on the believer (Rom.
5:1–11). Thus "justification" designates in Paul both the sharing in God's
grace that has already been given by faith and acquittal before God in the last
judgment. The new life is given in baptism, is lived out by those who are
"slaves of righteousness" (Rom. 6:18) and culminates in participation in Jesus'
resurrection glory (Phil. 3:20–21). *If we take Paul at his word, then the justification of which he speaks is a process of becoming new that spans the earthly
life of a believer, a path from faith's beginning to its end.* Life's decisive trans-

formation lies in the faith-awakening encounter with Christ. With this encounter is awakened the believer's righteousness that comes from Christ, whom God made the community's righteousness, sanctification, and redemption (1 Cor. 1:30). The goal of life is having your faith in Christ reckoned as righteousness before God at the last judgment and attaining the resurrection glory into which Jesus has already entered. Between the two poles, the transformation at the beginning and the consummation at the end, lies the believer's life as a life of witness to the crucified and risen Christ who day after day is the believer's Lord and righteousness.

THE APOSTLE'S UNDERSTANDING OF BAPTISM

After his call to be an apostle, Paul himself was baptized in the name of Jesus Christ for the forgiveness of sins (1 Cor. 12:13; Acts 9:17–19). From that time on baptism determined his life; it sealed (2 Cor. 1:21–22) and finalized his membership in the Christian community and his participation in the Spirit of God and of Christ that animated and empowered this community. Irrespective of the unique and unmistakable character of Paul's apostolic commission, he understood baptism as that which confirmed the justification of each individual Christian and as the act of sealing that connected the person to Christ and to Christ's community, by which the baptized receives a share in the Spirit of Christ and in the new life in relationship to God established through Christ.[5] The justification that he himself experienced outside Damascus through God's Christ, the character of which he described in Phil. 3:4–11 and which was sealed for him in his own baptism, is granted to all Christians at their baptism. So as far as justification is concerned, Paul and all baptized Christians are in the same situation: at baptism their lives are changed as was the apostle's; like Paul they are enlisted into discipleship of the crucified and risen Christ (compare Phil. 3:9–11 with Rom. 6:4–11). The following words apply to their life in Christ's community: "For by one Spirit we were all baptized into one body [the body of Christ]—Jews or Greeks, slaves or free" (1 Cor. 12:13). Formulated in individual terms, "if anyone is in Christ, there is a new act of creation; the old order has gone, and a new order has already begun" (2 Cor. 5:17, NEB). Paul adopted the baptismal practice and perspective of the missionary Christianity inspired by the Stephen-circle, with which he came in contact in Damascus and elsewhere. He affirmed the understanding of baptism that he received, but he interpreted it more decisively than it had been from his own transforming experience of justification and thus guarded it against misinterpretations.

THE LORD'S SUPPER AND THE
CONCEPT OF THE CHURCH

Already for those in Jerusalem and Antioch who became Christians before Paul, justification and reconciliation through Jesus' atoning death "for many," a common faith, and a reconciled community belonged inseparably together (cf. Acts 2:42–47). The common celebration of the Lord's Supper was the real center of the community's life. Paul also took over these aspects of the community's life. When he calls the Christian community the "body of Christ" (1 Cor. 12:12–30; Rom. 12:3–8), he means thereby the flock of justified believers brought together into a reconciled community through the vicarious sacrifice of Christ's mortal body (Rom. 7:4; 1 Cor. 11:24–27) in his atoning death for "many." Through baptism believers are incorporated into the "body of Christ." In the celebration of the Lord's Supper, the main features of which, including the account of its institution in 1 Cor. 11:23–25, were probably taken over from Antioch, the community was repeatedly reunited as the "body of Christ" and assured of the life-creating justification and reconcilation that God inaugurated through the atoning death of Jesus. Paul writes in 1 Cor. 10:14–17:

> Therefore, my beloved . . . (15) I speak as to [those who are] sensible . . . ; judge for yourselves what I say. (16) The cup of blessing which we bless, is it not a participation in the blood of Christ? The bread which we break, is it not a participation in the body of Christ? (17) Because there is one bread, we who are many are one body, for we all partake of the one bread.

By virtue of their common celebration of the meal the believers are the body of Christ. But since they partake of "the table of the Lord," they are united for better or for worse with their reconciler, the crucified and risen Christ. Christ will not have his gift treated lightly. For Paul the only alternative to reconciliation is affliction under God's judgment that is already casting its shadow into the present. And God's judgment consists in this, that each person has to bear the consequences of his or her own deeds (1 Cor. 11:27–33).

Under these circumstances it is no longer surprising but rather fully comprehensible historically that Paul incorporated into the language of his own proclamation about reconciliation not only the traditions he received about baptism and the Lord's Supper but also the formulas about justification and reconciliation that came from the mission center Antioch. In 2 Cor. 5:20–21 he summarized what he was to proclaim in this way:

> So we are ambassadors for Christ, God making his appeal through us. We beseech you on behalf of Christ, be reconciled to God. (21) For our sake he made him to be sin who knew no [guilt because of] sin, so that in him we might become the righteousness of God.[6]

In 2 Cor. 5:21 Paul quotes the traditional formulation already familiar to us, with no reduction of its content; in fact, by putting it at the end of his argument, he actually gives it special emphasis. We can see parallels to this treatment in Rom. 3:24ff.; 4:25; or 8:3–4.

THE BATTLE OVER PAUL'S APOSTLESHIP

All his life Paul had to fight for his apostleship and his gospel about justification. As a former persecutor of the community he was burdened with the role of an outsider among the apostles who had been followers of the earthly Jesus. In comparison with them, Paul's missionary preaching appeared quite one-sided and exaggerated. Paul knew Jesus only by hearsay and was thus clearly inferior to Peter. But, above all, in the gospel according to Paul justification and reconciliation through Christ were no longer tied to the presupposition that those who were justified had to be incorporated in the Abrahamic covenant by circumcision (Genesis 17) and obligate themselves to keep the law of Moses. As fundamentally important as this disengagement from the mission of Christ and from the Jewish mission to gain proselytes was for the mission to the Gentiles and as ecclesiastically self-evident as it has become for us today, it was a source of great conflict in the apostle's time.

Paul and Barnabas got those at the Apostolic Council to agree that in the mission to the Gentiles the two of them pursued beginning in Antioch they could categorically dispense with circumcision. For Paul that also meant that the Gentiles were obligated to obey God only in Christ. The "pillars" in the primitive community in Jerusalem, the Lord's brother James and the apostles Peter and John, expressly recognized the work of Barnabas and Paul. They simply directed them both to organize among the gentile Christians a collection for the poor in the congregation in Jerusalem as a sign of the solidarity of Jews and Gentiles in the church (Gal. 2:10). The Jerusalem agreement does not appear to have convinced the hard core among the Jewish Christians in Jerusalem. For Paul's letter to the Galatians shows that they continued to insist on the circumcision of the Gentiles and their incorporation into the Abrahamic covenant and that in the congregations founded by Paul they came in after him to carry on a type of mission that supplemented and countered his. They warned against the gospel from Antioch, especially Paul's gospel, that was allegedly soft on the law, held up to the Galatians the shining example of the real apostles, the original apostles in Jerusalem, and strongly urged them to be circumcised and to submit to the law of Moses.[7] Paul implored the congregations he had founded not to give a hearing to this false "other gospel" (Gal. 1:8–9), not to have second thoughts about the justification through faith in Christ alone that they had received by virtue of his gospel, and not to render this justification null and void through anxious observance of the law. Unfortunately we do not know historically whether the apostle's urgent appeal to the Galatians was successful.

But opposing the radical Jewish Christians in Galatia was not the end of it for Paul. Already in Gal. 2:11–21 a further conflict appears. A short time after the Apostolic Council it appears that James, the Lord's brother, tried to implement in Antioch (and elsewhere) the stipulations listed in what we today call the Apostolic Decree (Acts 15:20–21, 28–29). This demand that uncircumcised gentile Christians abstain from sexual immorality, in the sense of forbidden degrees of marriage (cf. Lev. 18:6ff.), from food offered to idols, from things strangled (that is, from meat that was not ritually slaughtered to remove its blood), and from blood involved an imposition of the minimal commands that according to Leviticus 17 and 18 a God-fearing Gentile living in Israel had to observe. The positive significance of the so-called Apostolic Decree was

that in the mission congregations it made it possible to live together and eat
(the Lord's Supper) together without burdening the Jews who had converted
to Christ with what was expected of them by their former identity as a religion
and a people. According to Gal. 2:11ff., Peter, Barnabas, and a portion of the
Jewish Christians in Antioch affirmed James' addition of this requirement
while Paul saw it as a legalistic accretion and as a falling away by resubmitting
to the law of Moses, and thus sharply rejected it. Out of this come those conflicts that appear in the Corinthian correspondence, in Philippians, and especially in Romans.

In his two letters to Corinth and in Philippians the apostle not only has to
battle against a spiritualizing tendency and an enthusiastic misinterpretation
of his gospel by groups within the congregation, but also has to fight once
again for the legitimacy of his apostleship and his gospel. His opponents in
Philippi and Corinth are probably Hellenistic-Jewish apostles sent by congregations, apostles who find their model in Peter (and in the Lord's brother
James, who supports the mission to the Gentiles with the conditions listed
above).[8] They measure Paul against these models and find his personal appearance in the congregations too lowly. They take offense at his life of suffering
and consider his gospel about the crucified Christ extreme and one-sided.
Paul has to defend the total legitimacy of his cross- and suffering-marked apostleship against these "superlative apostles" (as he ironically styles them—
2 Cor. 11:5; 12:11), and already in 1 Cor. 9:20-21 he has to point out that as
an apostle of Jesus he had not simply become lawless but was a servant of
Christ Jesus, obedient to the true will of God revealed in Christ, the "torah
of Christ" (Gal 6:2).

THE MESSAGE OF ROMANS

In Romans Paul gives a comprehensive survey of his gospel about God's righteousness in Christ. He does this from Corinth, at a time when he is deeply
worried about the future of his mission. He considers his missionary activity
in the eastern Mediterranean finished and wants to press on through Rome to
Spain (Rom. 15:23-24). But before he can undertake this missionary journey
to the West, he has two substantial obstacles to overcome. First, he has to
bring to Jerusalem the offering agreed to at the Apostolic Council and now
completed, but after the battles in Galatia, Philippi, and Corinth he is uncertain how "the saints" in Jerusalem will receive him and his work. Moreover,
he fears—with good reason, as Acts 21:27ff. shows!—personal assaults from
Jews in Jerusalem who had for a long time been hostile toward him (Rom.
15:30ff.). But the visit to Jerusalem is not all that Paul is facing. He must fear
in addition that he will find in Rome closed hearts and closed doors. The con-
tinual controversies in which Paul had been embroiled did not remain
unknown in Rome. Rather, slanderous attacks on the Pauline gospel have
already reached Rome (Rom. 3:8), and people have arisen who create "dis-
sensions" in the congregation and undermine the Christian teaching esteemed
in Rome (Rom. 16:17-18), teaching Paul in his letter affirms again and again.

Paul fears that the criticism brought against him and his gospel could bias the Roman congregation against him and thereby hinder them from actively supporting him in his plans for a mission to the west. He therefore decides to take the very unusual step of giving a comprehensive written report of his gospel to this congregation known to him at that time only from a distance and through friends (named in Romans 16), thereby refuting the objections that had been brought against him. He hoped to be able in this way to secure his future by achieving an understanding with the Romans. Thus, we have to see even in Romans a writing of Paul's that is directed to a very specific historical situation in the congregation. Romans is an exposition of the Pauline gospel motivated by his mission situation, and written to counter the criticism of Paul and his message that had reached all the way to Rome.[9]

THE GOSPEL ABOUT THE
RIGHTEOUSNESS OF GOD

In Rom. 1:16–17 Paul speaks thematically about his relationship to the gospel and its content. He writes:

> For I am not ashamed of the gospel: it is the power of God for salvation to every one who has faith, to the Jew first and also to the Greek. (17) For in it the righteousness of God is revealed through faith for faith; as it is written, "He who through faith is righteous shall live" (Hab. 2:4).

An understanding of these two verses was decisive for the Reformation in the sixteenth century. As Luther, after a long search, discovered that "the righteousness of God" in v. 17 did not mean the righteousness that the inexorable God demands of the believer (at the judgment), but instead the righteousness God confers on the believer by grace, that is, the God-given "righteousness that counts with God," he then saw himself in this Romans text actually standing before the gracious God whom he had long sought and whom he had now found as a God of grace in Christ.[10] The revolutionary consequences of this discovery of Luther's for church history are well known.

If we attempt to discover the original sense of the famous verses, we are struck, first of all, by the statement that Paul is "not ashamed of the gospel." The phrase points to a critical conflict situation in which Paul does not shrink back from standing up for the gospel entrusted to him precisely as it was entrusted to him as an apostle. Even in Rome, despite all the criticism, Paul intends to confess and hold to the gospel about God's righteousness.[11]

In order to comprehend the precise meaning of "the righteousness of God" in Rom. 1:17, an expression the apostle uses repeatedly in his letters, we need to consider vv. 16–17 in relation to the definition of the gospel with which Paul introduces his letter. The opening passage of Romans reads:

> (1) Paul, a servant of Jesus Christ, called to be an apostle, set apart for the gospel of God (2) which he promised beforehand through his prophets in the holy scriptures, (3) the gospel concerning his Son, who was descended from David accord-

ing to the flesh (4) and designated Son of God in power according to the Spirit of holiness by his resurrection from the dead, Jesus Christ our Lord, (5) through whom we have received grace and apostleship to bring about the obedience of faith for the sake of [= in the service of] his name among all the nations (Rom. 1:1–15).

The revelation of the righteousness of God through faith for faith and the essential content of the gospel according to Rom. 1:3–4, that is, the mission of Jesus as the messianic son of David for Israel and his lordship over all the nations of the world as the resurrected Son of God, are for Paul in Romans 1 two inseparable parallel aspects of his gospel. It seems natural to consider these two aspects together on the basis of 1 Cor. 1:30, where Christ is designated as the one "whom God made our [the believers'] wisdom, our righteousness and sanctification and redemption." The righteousness of God revealed in the gospel, of which Rom. 1:16–17 speaks, would then be the righteousness revealed in the mission of Jesus Christ and put into operation by God, from which every individual believer lives, and which is directed to the faith of every individual as its true addressee. The righteousness of God would then be the embodiment of the saving action of God in Christ, which creates new life for believers as they face the judgment.

Whether or not we are on the right track with this interpretation of the righteousness of God in Rom. 1:16–17 (an interpretation that agrees with Luther's but goes beyond his equating of the righteousness of God with the righteousness that comes by faith) must be established by a look at further occurrences of the term in Romans and at the Christian and Old Testament–Jewish history of the term that stands behind the formulation. In 2 Cor. 5:21, Paul had described by "the righteousness of God" the quality of the new life conferred on the believer by virtue of Jesus' atoning sacrifice, that is, the result of God's saving action. Paul did that in agreement with the Jewish-Christian tradition taken up by him there. In another tradition that was already at hand for Paul, one found in Rom. 3:25–26, the same formulation describes the righteous activity by which God effects for sinners forgiveness of sins and new life by virtue of Jesus' atoning death. Thus the Christian tradition about righteousness that blazed the trail for Paul already used our expression to designate both God's own righteous action and the result of this action. In this complex (or, as K. H. Fahlgren has said, "synthetic"[12]) broadness of meaning, the concept handed on to Paul is structured in a way typical of the Old Testament.

Paul preserved this "synthetic" range in Romans quite consciously. One can easily see this in Rom. 3:5; 3:21–26; and 10:3. In Rom. 1:18—3:20 Paul is interested first of all in showing the guilt of Gentiles and Jews before God, the righteous judge. What Paul has found is this: Jews and Greeks are equally guilty in God's sight (3:9–20). In this wider context God's righteousness in 3:5 clearly means God's very own righteousness as judge, on the basis of which he confronts human wickedness with judicial wrath. According to vv. 3–4, however, this righteousness of God is closely associated with God's faithfulness and truthfulness, and this righteousness is vindicated when one tries to put God on trial (Ps. 51:6). So what is in view in Rom. 3:5 is God's own righteousness as judge of the world, the righteousness that sits in judgment on wickedness and sin. The parallelism of God's righteousness, faithfulness, and truthfulness shown in vv. 3–4 again points back to the Old Testament (cf., for example, Ps. 98:2–3, 9). This parallelism shows that even when the focus is on judgment the expression "the righteousness of God" has retained for the apostle a semantically positive meaning.[13]

After Paul has shown in Rom. 1:18—3:20 the universal guilt of Jews and Gentiles and indicated that the law of Moses does not free anyone from this guilt, he speaks in 3:21–26 of the salvation of believers "now" inaugurated through God in Christ without help from the law. The genitive phrase we are investigating, "righteousness of God," occurs four times in the six verses. We already know that in 3:25–26 the apostle makes use of a traditional formula. The passage reads:

> But now the righteousness of God has been manifested apart from law, although the law and the prophets bear witness to it, (22) the righteousness of God [which is attained] through faith in Jesus Christ [and intended] for all who believe. For there is no distinction; (23) since all have sinned and fall short of the glory of God, (24) they are justified by his grace as a gift, through the redemption which is in Christ Jesus, (25) whom God put forward as an expiation by his blood, to be received by faith. This was to show God's righteousness, because in his divine forbearance he had passed over former sins; (26) it was to [show] at the present time that he [God] himself is righteous and that he justifies [the one who lives by] faith in Jesus.

In his highly complex but carefully formulated passage Paul utilizes the tradition about atonement he received from Antioch (which, as we saw above, pp. 58–63, rests essentially on Jesus' own concept of atonement) and makes it the basis of his presentation on justification and redemption. The same process is visible in Rom. 4:25. In this verse he makes a traditional formula he received the centerpiece for the discussion on faith and justification in chapter 4. The Semitizing formulation originating in Jerusalem reworks Jesus' own understanding of atonement in that it interprets death and resurrection on the basis of Isaiah 53. The death of Jesus is the punishment "for our trespasses," Jesus' resurrection the ratification of his sacrificial death by God in the form of the exaltation of the Servant of God who suffered vicariously. Because sins have been expiated and Jesus' sacrificial way has been affirmed by God, "our" (that is, the believing community's) justification can grow out of Jesus' death and resurrection. It is bestowed on everyone who believes in the God who raised Jesus from the dead.

In both Rom. 3:21–26 and Rom. 4:23–25 a genuine continuity becomes visible with respect to the gospel. Jesus' own willingness to be sacrificed, the pre-Pauline mission community's confession of Jesus, their reconciler, and the mission message of Paul are connected in an essentially inseparable proclamatory process. With the perspective on justification he presents in Romans, Paul really is the "ambassador of Jesus" (Adolf Schlatter).

"The righteousness of God" appears in Rom. 3:21–26 with a twofold significance. While in Rom. 3:5 God's righteousness as judge was discussed,
Paul is now concerned about the question of where Jews and Gentiles are to
gain the righteousness that at the judgment is a matter of life or death, since
the works of the law cannot produce this righteousness (3:20). His answer is:
the righteousness that alone avails before God, that is, the righteousness
attained by faith in Christ Jesus and inaugurated by God, has been manifested
by God without help from the law, yet entirely in accord with the testimony
of the Law (that is, the five books of Moses) and the prophets—"the law and
the prophets" here encompassing the Old Testament. In vv. 21–22 Paul uses
"the righteousness of God" as it is used in the tradition found in 2 Cor. 5:21,
that is, as a designation for the blessings of salvation made accessible by God
in Christ and appropriated by faith. The formulations in vv. 21–22 rest closely
on the programmatic sentences in 1:16–17, and they thereby enable us to see
a specifically Pauline concern. It is critically important to the apostle (and
corresponds to his personal call experience) that God's righteousness is
attained solely "through *faith* in Jesus Christ" and that *all* may have a share
in these blessings, and thereby in the new existence of those who are righteous
before God, without needing the support of the law and of their own works.
For Paul the righteousness of God is essentially a righteousness that comes
by faith.[14]

But the way of salvation opened by the righteousness that comes by faith is
for Paul also the only way that is still open for sinners. Whether Jews or Gentiles, they all stand under sin and thereby under an inescapable indictment at
God's righteous judgment. They lack God's glory, which according to Jewish
understanding is that righteousness Adam and Eve originally possessed in
paradise, by which they were creatures who met God without shame and were
preserved by God (cf. the *Apocalypse of Moses* 20—21). But it is God's will
that they once again attain this original glorious righteousness they now lack
and that they attain it through the redemption that God brought about by grace
in Christ. God publicly put Jesus forward as a place of atonement (that is, as
the *kappōret* of Leviticus 16),[15] in order through the sacrifice of the life (symbolized by the blood) of Jesus, God's Son, to achieve for sinners atonement
and forgiveness of sins. Paul expressly adds "to be received by faith" to the
tradition, thus stressing anew that Jesus as the place of reconciliation and of
the presence of God is accessible only by faith. By the tradition he quotes he
then stresses further that this entire saving work is a demonstration of the
righteousness of God. God, the righteous judge, shows his righteousness by
helping sinners through Christ to attain life at the judgment. So in v. 25 it is
once again God's own peculiar righteousness that is discussed, God's righteousness that is more and intends more than merely the carrying out of
punishment; it wants to offer and create new life. In v. 26 Paul once again
expressly repeats that this is to show God's own life-creating righteousness at
the present time, which is contrasted with the past, which was under sin, by
the mission of Jesus (cf. Rom. 1:3–4) and the proclamation of the gospel. This
demonstration is intended to let God be seen as the righteous one whose right-

eousness achieves its goal as God brings about the gracious justification of everyone who lives by faith in Jesus. So in Rom. 3:21–26 "the righteousness of God" means God's own righteousness, which obtains life for the lost (vv. 25–26), and at the same time the righteousness by faith which is made manifest to sinners on the basis of this saving work of God in Christ (vv. 21–22). This righteousness by faith is identical with the glory of God's righteous creatures, glory they lack as sinners (v. 23). *According to our verses "justification" clearly has the dimension of new creation.*

In Rom. 9:30—10:4, within the framework of his long discussion of Israel's present and future in view of the gospel about Christ, Paul contrasts the unexpected attainment of salvation by the Gentiles with the to him painful distance separating from salvation the Israel that up to that time remained closed to the gospel about Christ. The Gentiles, who did not pursue righteousness as the law-observant Jews had, attained righteousness by their faith; but Israel took offense at Christ, went the way of the law apart from faith, and did not attain the righteousness that was the law's goal. Paul knows Israel's zeal for God, but he also knows (from his own experience) that this zeal is a blind zeal (10:3–4): "For, being ignorant of the righteousness that comes from God, and seeking to establish their own, they did not submit to God's righteousness. (4) For Christ is the end of the law, that everyone who has faith may be justified." God's righteousness again has here the comprehensive significance that we observed already in 1:16–17. Up to that time Israel, in ignorance (because they were without faith), missed out on God's saving work in Christ and did not submit to the righteousness by grace manifested by God in Christ, because they clung to the law as the way to saving righteousness. But this way has been superseded by God in Christ. Christ is the end of the law for everyone who believes because in Christ God has already inaugurated and opened to believers that righteousness that the law-observant still think they can and must attain through their own efforts on the basis of the law.

The use of "the righteousness of God" in Romans, in 2 Cor. 5:21, and in Phil. 3:21 cannot be reduced to the formula that it everywhere concerns only the righteousness of faith that is accepted by God, nor again that God's own righteousness in Christ is always in view; both aspects belong indissolubly together. And they cannot be separated by saying that in Christian traditions about righteousness received by Paul God's own righteousness was particularly emphasized while Paul was rather concerned with the individual's righteousness by faith. Paul never criticizes the tradition he receives; rather he expressly acknowledges it. From his own knowledge of Christ, to be sure, he stresses emphatically, and with a previously unknown thoroughness, that the Mosaic law does not lead to the righteousness of God in Christ and that the righteousness brought about by God in the sacrificial atoning death of his Son is equally open to Gentiles and Jews insofar as they believe in Jesus Christ as their reconciler and Lord. So we must take the expression "the righteousness of God" in the "synthetic" comprehensiveness in which Paul, no differently from the Christians in Jerusalem and Antioch, used it, and we must ponder from passage to passage where the apostle's accent lies. *In the one*

*term "the righteousness of God," if one looks at it properly, is comprehended
Paul's understanding of Christ and therewith his whole gospel.*[16]

THE HISTORY OF THE TERM
"RIGHTEOUSNESS OF GOD"

On the use of this term, so important to Paul, and on its history, the following
is to be added. (1) The complex possibilities for the use of the term show up
elsewhere in the New Testament. In Matt. 6:33 the concept is expressly
inserted by Matthew to interpret the Q material he received; it signifies God's
establishment of the saving order that constitutes the reign of God. In James
1:20, in an ethical-wisdom context, "the righteousness of God" means the
deed that finds favor with God (cf. Ecclus. 1:22). 2 Peter 1:1 speaks of the
righteousness of our God and Savior, Jesus Christ, on the basis of which the
post-Easter community has obtained a faith equal in value to the apostle's confession of faith. (2) Thus a look at the Pauline and non-Pauline passages in
the New Testament already shows that with the phrase "the righteousness of
God" we are dealing with a frequently recurring, almost fixed term that pos-
sesses a "synthetically" comprehensive meaning not to be epitomized by us
in a single concept. But "the righteousness of God" always has justice and
judgment in view, and in that context it signifies God's active work and/or
human existence and behavior in accord with that work. (3) The history of
the concept points behind the New Testament into early Judaism and the Old
Testament. K. Koch and H. H. Schmid have shown[17] what great importance
and meaning talk about righteousness has in Israel's worship and in its expectations of judgment and salvation. This Old Testament use of the term was
alive for Paul and the Christian congregations of his time because in worship
they read the Law, Psalms, and Prophets as "Holy Scriptures" and interpreted
them in the light of the revelation in Christ. For them the series of righteous
acts God showed Israel in the course of its history, the so-called *sidqôt* of
Yahweh (Deut. 33:21), Judg. 5:11; 1 Sam. 12:7; Mic. 6:5; Ps. 103:6; Dan. 9:16,
finds its culmination in the mission and resurrection of Jesus (cf. Acts 2:11).
In the Qumran texts we find not only praise for these demonstrations of God's
righteousness (cf., for example 1QS 10:23; 11QPs[a] Plea 19:4–11) but, closely
related to it, a use of the Semitic equivalent of "the righteousness of God,"
namely *sidqat 'el* (1QS 10:25; 11:12, 14, 15; 1QM 4:6), that is an astonishing
parallel to the pre-Pauline and Pauline usage. The most important parallel passage, 1QS 11:11–15, we have already quoted above (p. 62). God, the creator
and righteous judge of the world, helps penitent sinners find new life and forgives their sin, while God clobbers the enemies of the community and
unrepentant sinners with death. Jesus and the pre-Pauline and Pauline texts
about righteousness build on this understanding of the righteousness of God,
which in the New Testament period was present not only in the Essene texts
but also in the Old Testament–Jewish tradition of penitential prayer and in
apocalyptic expectations of judgment (cf., for example *1 Enoch* 61–62; *4 Ezra*

7:26—8:61). Since the understanding of righteousness in the community's texts is oriented totally toward Jesus' mission and atoning death, the righteousness of God appears in them primarily in the light of salvation: God does not want to be simply the judge of unrighteousness but in Jesus Christ the creator and Lord of the world who brings his creatures to life, justifies and saves them.

THE QUESTIONS AT ISSUE IN ROME

According to Rom. 1:16–17, the entire Pauline gospel is summed up in one biblically based concept, "the righteousness of God." Paul hopes his message will be received with understanding by the congregation in Rome. He can also expect this, since he is in agreement with the congregation at Rome, which lived within the Jewish-Christian faith tradition from which it had its origin, in agreement both on their understanding of doctrine (Rom. 6:17; 16:17) and with respect to the Old Testament, which was to be read with Christ as its key and its content (Rom. 7:1; 15:3–4). The traditional formulas that Paul approvingly cites in Rom. 1:3–4; 3:25–26; 4:25, etc., show that the apostle is by no means merely beating the air with this expectation.[18] The Roman congregation was at home in the Old Testament Scriptures from the synagogue and from Christian worship. They were instructed in the traditions of their faith by Jewish-Christian missionaries (Rom. 16:7) before they received Romans. So Paul had good reason to expect common theological ground from which to address the issues.

Apart from the Pauline understanding of the righteousness of God, the following questions in particular appear to be points of controversy in Romans: What was Paul's view of the law, of Christian obedience, and of the last judgment? What was Israel's future according to his gospel? How should one respond to the emperor's oppressive taxation demands, and how can Jewish and gentile Christians live together in the congregation? If we pursue a few of these "test questions" somewhat further, we can complete our picture of Paul's thinking on righteousness.

JUSTIFICATION AND OBEDIENCE

Paul knows that through his Jewish-Christian opponents accusations against him had gotten to Rome to the effect that he overthrows the law (Rom. 3:31) and that with his proclamation about justification he espouses the view "[Let us] do evil that good may come" (Rom. 3:8), or even "[Let us] continue in sin that grace may abound" (6:1), or, finally, "[Let us] sin because we are not under law but under grace" (6:15). Historically one can well imagine that such accusations already stood behind the charge swirling about him in Galatians that with his proclamation he seeks to curry favor with his hearers and that his gospel is tailored for human approval (Gal. 1:10–11). Jewish-Christian accusations of that kind and knowledge of the controversies, mirrored in the letters to Corinth and in Philippians, about the legitimacy of Paul's apostleship and his understanding of law and justification appear to have reached Rome and to have engendered there considerable prejudice against the apostle. Paul reacts to this "slander" (Rom. 3:8) with full clarity: even in Rome he is not ashamed of his gospel (1:16–17) and declares his slanderers to be people whose condemnation by God is fitting (3:8). And he constructs his letter in such a way that he invalidates the reproaches hurled against him and reaches agreement with those to whom he addresses the letter.

The central thesis, that God in Jesus Christ is a God who "justifies the ungodly" (Rom. 4:5), which sounds highly questionable to the ears of those trained in Judaism, but which for Paul himself was indispensable, in no way signifies that God simply dispenses justification on the unbelieving "ungodly" without further ado and that they can keep on indulging in their ungodliness! That central thesis has to sound offensive to everyone who hears the stipulation of Exod. 23:7 that a righteous Israelite dare never "acquit the wicked" and who reads in Prov. 17:15, "He who justifies the wicked and he who condemns the righteous are both alike an abomination to the Lord." According to the statement in Rom. 4:5, God's justifying activity unambiguously contradicts the command of the law, so Paul, with his bold formulation, triggers the question, where under such circumstances is there any longer a distinction between righteousness and wickedness, God's holiness and human sin? Paul's answer is really remarkable. He states that God's gracious justice, established in Christ, takes graced sinners into service from the moment of their baptism, into the service of righteousness (Rom. 6:18–23). According to Paul justification leads directly to sanctification. Those who have met in Christ their reconciler have also found in him the crucified and risen Christ of God, their Lord (Rom. 7:4), and, for better or worse, they remain under obligation to this Lord till judgment day (14:7ff.). Christ the reconciler pleads before God's throne for those who are his, so that all the days of their lives and even at the last judgment they can console themselves with the justification they have through him. Nothing can separate them from the love of God in Christ, their Lord (8:31–39). And yet the apostle does not allow a false security about salvation and indifference to demonstrating faith by actions to develop, since he shows that justified believers continue to be threatened daily by a life apart from the Spirit of Christ and that they must fight against falling away from the protecting presence of Christ and falling victim to death at the judgment (8:8–11).

In Paul's letters the call for a faith that lives righteously never stops with the basics, with abstractions. Two examples must suffice to show this in our particular context. The admonition of 1 Cor. 6:1–11 became highly significant for the development of an autonomous canon law.[19] Justification and living righteously in the congregation are here connected quite directly by Paul. The apostle considers it to be very inappropriate that it comes to legal and property battles at all among the Corinthians justified and sanctified by faith and baptism (6:11). He would consider it much more appropriate if Christians would neither defraud nor wrong one another at law and in that context reminds them (probably in the light of Matt. 5:39) that Christians are to endure wrong without defending themselves (6:7–8). But if legal controversies really become unavoidable, then they should at least be settled before a competent Christian and not tried before unbelievers (6:1–6). Paul considers it to be intolerable when unbelievers excluded from God's lordship and reign sit in judgment over the affairs of congregation members dedicated to Christ in baptism, "washed" from their sins, and designated to be eschatological judges of the world. Therefore he demands that the Corinthians give up this deplorable practice at once!

The second example leads us from Corinth back to Rome. As was already the case in Corinth, so also in Rome there was controversy over whether Christians could drink wine dedicated to pagan gods and partake of food offered to idols (food that, in addition, had not been prepared according to the regulations for slaughter in Deut. 12:20–25). In Romans 14 Paul discusses in detail this question, which is highly relevant for the common meals of the congregation in Rome, composed of Jewish and gentile Christians. Although Paul himself shares the view of those who hold the enjoyment of this wine and meat to be permissible, he considers it to be totally wrong when the so-called strong in faith make a show of their freedom and by their practices cause a crisis of conscience for other Christians whose faith is more scrupulous and weak. In this situation he demands of the "strong" that they give up all food that causes difficulty to others. What the Apostolic Decree tries to solve with the aid of minimal legal demands is handled by Paul as a question of mutual responsibility among Christians, without recourse to the so-called Noachite commandments. Rather, Paul's rationale is, "For the kingdom of God is not food and drink but righteousness and peace and joy in the Holy Spirit" (14:17). *The love shown to the members of the congregation in Jesus' sacrificial death and the manner of their life together should be in clear agreement with one another!*

THE PROBLEM OF THE LAW

Behind the question put to Paul in Rome about justification and obedience emerges at once a second, more fundamental question. If God by his own justifying action in Christ has turned aside from sinners the curse of the law, and if Christ is "the end of the law . . . [for] every one who has faith" (10:4), what is then, in Christ, the status of the law and of God's holy will proclaimed in the law? Whoever lived through the battle in Galatia and stood on the side of Paul's critics could also have spread in Rome the view that Paul "overthrow[s] the law by this faith" (Rom. 3:31) and asserts that "the law is sin" (7:7). Such accusations must have taken hold against the apostle all the more as from Corinth the view probably also reached Rome, then capital of the world, that Paul had become a person who lived apart from the law (1 Cor. 9:21) and that his stance should presumably be distinguished from Peter's. The apostle felt himself challenged to the extreme by such attacks, and he called upon his whole training as a Scripture scholar in order to give the Romans more accurate information. He did this without departing from his fundamental thesis, that God has inaugurated justification in Christ apart from the law and that God's promise to justify those who believe preceded circumcision and the revelation at Sinai (Rom. 4:9ff.; 5:20; cf. Gal. 3:6–18).

Paul's argument has two stages. In stage one he rejects outright the view that he abolishes the law through faith and counters that he actually upholds the law, that is the law of faith (Rom. 3:27–31)! He offers the evidence for that in Romans 4. According to the account in the Torah, Abraham's faith is reckoned to him by God as righteousness (Gen. 15:6); this action of justifying Abraham by faith is prior in time to the covenant of circumcision attested in Genesis 17. Thereby the Torah gives testimony to the priority of justification by faith over the covenant of circumcision and the giving of the law at Sinai. Thus Paul is honoring the voice of the Torah and not overthrowing it. When he speaks of Abraham as the father of those who believe, the Torah is with and not against him.

But how is it with the giving of the law at Sinai, that is, the law of Moses? Paul addresses the law of Moses in a second stage of his argument. Two things are true of the Torah. Historically the law of Moses only came onto the scene when sin and its consequence death, beginning with Adam, had been holding sway for a long time. Thus the law addressed sinners, and it increased their sin in that from that time on it exposed them legally as transgressors against the revealed will of God. At the same time it goaded them on in the illusory hope that through their own efforts they could achieve righteousness before God (5:20). How futile this hope is Paul makes clear in Rom. 7:7ff., after he has expressly appealed to the Roman congregation's knowledge of the law in 7:1. So the apostle is aware that he is expecting his addressees to do some biblical reflection, but he is counting on being understood by the congregation in Rome, trained in Jewish Christianity. The person he uses as an example in Rom. 7:7ff., a person in whom every biblically trained reader can discover his or her own "I," is Adam, specifically Adam in paradise under the protective command of God (cf. Genesis 3). This one command of God is for Paul (as for Jewish exegesis of his time) the prototype of the whole law. Instead of remaining under this command's protection, Adam let himself be led into disobeying the command and became a victim of sin. Now the command or law of God can no longer help him; rather it denounces him as a guilty lawbreaker, which he continues to be even if he later obeys the law again and thereby wants to attain life (once more). This is the picture: the law cannot help him reenter paradise, not even if with all his might he strives to fulfill the law. Despite the law the "glory of God" (Rom. 3:23) remains lost for Adam (and for every other person who is "Adam"). Only God can help the person, and in Christ that is what God has done! As Paul shows in Rom. 8:3, God sent the requisite offering for sin[20] in the form of his own sinless Son, Jesus Christ. God has surpassed Abraham in Genesis 22 in that God actually sacrificed his own Son, in order to reopen for sinners the locked gates of paradise by virtue of Jesus' atoning death and to lead those who are justified through Christ back to his original will. Those for whom God has provided atonement and justification in Christ are for Paul, according to Rom. 8:4–5, the true fulfillers of the just demands of the law. They are this as people who have been led back to the gates of paradise by Christ and who have heard the life-preserving will of God from the mouth of their Lord, crucified and raised for them. By virtue of his atoning death and his resurrection Jesus restored the command of God, or the law, to its original paradisiacal function. Or, to put it another way: *the law of Sinai, which increases and condemns sin, has by virtue of Jesus' atoning death become the torah of Christ, which proclaims God's demand as the command of love, thereby agreeing with the life-preserving will of God in paradise.*

Paul could certainly not have spoken of this transformation of the law of Moses into the law of Christ (Gal. 6:2; 1 Cor. 9:21) by virtue of Jesus' atoning death if he himself had not encountered Christ outside Damascus as the "end of the law." Into this fundamental experience were then incorporated information about the "law of Christ" from Christians in Damascus inspired by the Stephen-circle and Peter's reports about Jesus' own critical handling of the Torah from Sinai (cf. Gal. 1:18; 2:7–8). The traditions assembled by Matthew in the Sermon on the Mount under the theme of the new righteousness show even now that Jesus incorporated the Torah of Sinai into the messianic torah he proclaimed and that he taught and demanded as its center the command to love your enemy.

The discussion in the last paragraph is of significance for an understanding of Paul because the apostle in Romans once more takes up the law, raised to a new validity in Christ, namely in Romans 12 and 13. The giving of the ceremonial law, which was an indispensable part of the law for him as a Pharisee and for every Jew really true to the law (cf. Rom. 9:4!), is not discussed here any more than it is in Rom. 7:7—8:11 or in the proclamation of Jesus. Rather, in 12:14, with a clear allusion to Matt. 5:44, the discussion is about loving your enemy, and, as in Mark 12:28–34 par., loving your neighbor appears as the essential summary of all God's commands (Rom. 13:8–10). The agreement that exists between Paul and Jesus, not only in regard to the understanding of atonement, but also in the critical evaluation of the Mosaic law and its epitome in the command of love, is surely no mere coincidence. The Pauline view of the law, controversial all the way to Rome, can be traced in stages through Peter and the Stephen-circle all the way back to Jesus himself. *Paul is "the ambassador of Jesus" (A. Schlatter), even with respect to the proclamation of the will of God for those who believe.* In the light of his encounter with the exalted Christ outside Damascus he thought through his own Pharisaic understanding of the law and that of the Christian mission congregations that supported him and in this way constructed his proclamation about the new obedience of those set free by justification from sin and separation from God. For Paul justification does not lead to antinomianism; instead, it leads to obedience to the will of God, to which Jesus brought validity again in his messianic mission.[21]

THE FATE OF ISRAEL

There remains the final question, an agonizing one for Paul and all Jewish Christians of his time, of Israel's fate before God. Right up to the time of the composition of Romans, the majority of faithful Jews remained closed to the gospel. The appearance of Paul as an apostle of Jesus Christ was for them an unparalleled provocation. From the beginning they attacked the preaching of this apostate with every legal measure the synagogues possessed (2 Cor. 11:24–25), plotted attacks on the apostle's life (Acts 20:3), arrested Paul in the temple in Jerusalem during his collection visit (Acts 21:27ff.), and even took an oath to kill Paul when he was already in Roman custody (Acts 23:12ff.). Paul was well aware of this hostility (Rom. 15:31). Therefore, it cannot have surprised him that also in Rome the question was raised about the implications of his gospel for Israel and for the advantages of the Jews as God's chosen people. The first ones in Rome with a basis for such questions were the former proselytes, who were in an especially precarious place over against the synagogues, and those Jews by birth who had been converted. So Paul's discussion in Rom. 3:1–9 and 9–11 is directed in the first instance to them. In these sections of the letter his argument is very direct. He identifies himself with his addressees and asks, for example, "What then? Are we Jews any better off? . . ." (3:9), or says, "Brethren, my heart's desire and prayer to God for them [that is, the unbelieving Jews] is that they may be saved!" (10:1).

To the question wherein, in the light of the gospel, the advantage of the Jews remains and what the benefit of circumcision is, Paul answers in Romans 3: "To begin with, the Jews are entrusted with the oracles of God" (3:2), and that is true even if, like the Gentiles, they stand under sin and therefore appear as sinners in God's just judgment (3:9). God has assumed a special obligation toward Israel. In Romans 9—11 Paul takes up this thought once more and discusses it thoroughly. God's promise to rescue his people stands firm and cannot fail (9:6). For the sake of Israel Paul, like Moses, would gladly let himself be accursed and cut off (9:3; cf. with Exod. 32:32). But since God has not granted him this wish, the apostle can work for Israel's salvation only by bringing his mission to the Gentiles to its appointed conclusion as quickly as possible, through this work making his still-unbelieving fellow Jews "jealous" (of the Gentiles who have already attained salvation), and in this way helping to inaugurate the time in which God will fulfill the promise of salvation given to his people (11:13–14, 25). Indeed, God will fulfill it by the event of the return of his son Jesus Christ in the form of the Redeemer-Messiah coming from Zion, as Israel had been promised (11:26; cf. with Isa. 59:20–21). The hour of salvation for all Israel will strike, according to Paul, on the day of the return of the crucified and risen Christ. At the day of judgment he will bring salvation to Israel in that he appears as the personification of the righteousness of God promised to Israel. God destined Israel not for destruction but for salvation, and this salvation will consist in the justification of God's people through the Redeemer-Messiah, Jesus Christ. God consigned all, that is, Gentiles and Jews, to unbelief in order in Christ to have mercy on all (11:32). *The goal of history and of God's promise is, according to Paul, the righteousness of God in Christ for Gentiles and for Jews.*

SUMMARY

The gospel about the righteousness of God in Christ has a universal dimension, according to Paul's presentation in Romans. It embraces history from Adam until the return of the Messiah Jesus Christ from Zion. It is the gospel about the mission of Jesus to save every believer by the grace of God, who destined his chosen people, together with the Gentiles, not for destruction but for life in communion with God.

Unfortunately we do not know how the congregation in Rome received Paul's letter. And Paul did not reach Rome as a free man but only as a defendant and a Roman prisoner (Acts 28:11–31). Strikingly, Luke is silent about Paul's reception by the Christians in Rome.[22] But in *1 Clement*, written to the Corinthians about 96 c.e. by Clement of Rome, Paul is called a martyr for the faith who "taught the whole world righteousness" (5:7). So Paul's gospel did not die away in Rome completely unheard and with it his view of righteousness, which still binds the apostle, for all his unmistakable independence, with the Christians before and beside him and above all with Jesus himself.

NOTES

1. This is the view of E. Barnikol, *Die vor- und frühchristliche Zeit des Paulus* (Kiel: Mühlau, 1929), 18ff., and G. Bornkamm, *Paul*, trans. D. M. G. Stalker (New York: Harper & Row, 1971), 10–12. This view is contested, correctly in my opinion, for example by F. Mussner, *Der Galaterbrief*, 2d ed. (Freiburg: Herder, 1974), 358–59, and H.-D. Betz, *Galatians*, Hermeneia (Philadelphia: Fortress Press, 1979), 268–69.

2. On what follows, compare the study by M. Hengel, *Acts and the History of Earliest Christianity* (Philadelphia: Fortress Press, 1979), 81ff.

3. L. Goppelt, *Apostolic and Post-Apostolic Times*, trans. R. Guelich (London: A. & C. Black, 1970), 74, points out that the whippings mentioned in 2 Cor. 11:24 "must have taken place before the beginning of his work in Antioch, because after this time he no longer appeared before the courts of the synagogues." C. K. Barrett, *The Second Epistle to the Corinthians* (New York: Harper & Row, 1973), 296, agrees with Goppelt and proposes that Paul was punished by the Jews for his association with the Gentiles in violation of the purity laws and his table fellowship with them.

4. This is the view especially of G. Strecker, "Befreiung und Rechtfertigung. Zur Stellung der Rechtfertigungslehre in der Theologie des Paulus," in *Rechtfertigung. Festschrift für E. Käsemann zum 70. Geburtstag*, ed. J. Friedrich, W. Pöhlmann, and P. Stuhlmacher (Tübingen: Mohr, 1976), 479–508, and, in my opinion less convincingly, H. Hübner, *Das Gesetz bei Paulus*, 2d ed. (Göttingen: Vandenhoeck & Ruprecht, 1980).

5. In his essay "Das Verständnis der Taufe nach Römer 6" (in *Bewahren und Erneuern. Festschrift zum 80. Geburtstag von Kirchenpräsident a.D. Professor D. Theodor Schaller,* published by the Protestant Landeskirchenrat d. Pfalz [1980], 143 [135–53]), F. Hahn correctly stresses that on the basis of Rom. 6:5 we can understand baptism in Paul "in the sense of an effective sign and act": the person baptized is incorpo-

rated into the death of Jesus and set into a grace-empowered life "that still awaits the completion of the existence-with-Christ that begins in baptism" (144).

6. On 2 Cor. 5:18-21 see especially the essay of O. Hofius, "Erwägungen zur Gestalt und Herkunft des paulinischen Versöhnungsgedankens," *ZTK* 77 (1980): 186-99. On the traditional character of v. 21, see above, pp. 59-60.

7. On this understanding of the conflict in Jerusalem, see my book *Das paulinische Evangelium*, vol. 1: *Vorgeschichte* (Göttingen: Vandenhoeck & Ruprecht, 1968), 63-108.

8. F. Lang, my emeritus colleague in Tübingen, has helped me in my search for an answer to the complicated question about the opponents who deprecated Paul in Philippi and Corinth. See, in addition, G. Friedrich, *Der Brief an die Philipper*, 14th ed., NTD (Göttingen: Vandenhoeck & Ruprecht, 1976), 131-34. On Paul's missionary situation see my essay "Weg, Stil und Konsequenzen urchristlicher Mission," *Theologische Beiträge* 12 (1981): 107-35.

9. At my instigation, M. Kettunen has sought to substantiate anew this historically illuminating view of Romans as a letter directed to a live issue in the congregation in his dissertation, "Der Abfassungszweck des Römerbriefs," Annales academicae scientarum Fennicae, Ser. Dissertationes Humanarum Litterarum 18 (Helsinki, 1979).

10. On this issue see E. Jüngel, "Gottes umstrittene Gerechtigkeit," in *Unterwegs zur Sache*, BEvT 61 (Münich: Kaiser, 1972), 67ff. (60-79).

11. Cf. W. Schmithals, *Der Römerbrief als historisches Problem* (Gütersloh: Gerd Mohn, 1975), 91-93. While Schmithals envisions only the "inevitable conflict with the synagogue in Rome" and the "public consequences of this conflict" (92), in my opinion Paul also has in view the dispute with Christians who were stirring things up in Rome against him and his gospel.

12. K. H. Fahlgren, *şĕdāqā nahestehende und entgegengesetzte Begriffe im Alten Testament* (Uppsala, 1932), especially 52ff.; reprinted in *Um das Prinzip der Vergeltung in Religion und Recht des alten Testaments*, ed. K. Koch (Darmstadt: Wissenschaftliche Buchgesellschaft, 1972), 126ff. (87-129).

13. In *THAT* 2:514 (507-30), s. v. *şdq*, Klaus Koch offers the appropriate explanation for what we have found. According to his analysis, the following is true of the juridical use of "righteousness" in the Old Testament: "In juridical usage . . . the 'righteousness' of the judge never stands in the foreground (as would be the case in German usage), but instead the restoration of the *şĕdāqā* of the plaintiff or the accused through acquittal and restoration of their undiminished . . . existence, of which the condemnation of the 'unrighteous,' that is, the wicked opponent, is a part. In the background there appears to be a concept of justice according to which every litigation grows out of a disturbance of a relationship which needs to be set right" (514).

14. That the righteousness of God is promised to those who have faith and that it is received and experienced by faith is new over against the pre-Pauline tradition about righteousness. Here we are in fact looking at a particular Pauline emphasis. But with respect to this emphasis it should not be overlooked that Paul also worked out his Christology entirely from the point of view of the actualization of the righteousness of God. It is true that traditions such as those in Phil. 2:6-11; 1 Cor. 1:30; Rom. 3:25-26; and 4:25 are handed on to Paul, but for him the sending of Jesus into the world, his atoning death "for us," his resurrection, his work as the Risen One, his messianic Parousia from Zion (Rom. 11:26ff.), his intercession for believers at the last judgment (Rom. 9:31ff.), and his conquest of death (1 Cor. 15:25ff.) are united in such a way that in this entire christological event the righteousness of God succeeds in bringing salvation (see my essay "On Pauline Christology," chap. 10 in this volume). It is therefore a one-sided view of the apostle's concept of righteousness to point only at the experience of righteousness through faith without at the same time speaking of the

history-spanning actualization of the righteousness of God through the mission, death, resurrection and return of Christ.

15. I am presupposing here once again the analysis of Rom. 3:24ff. which I offered in the Festschrift for W. G. Kümmel (reprinted as chap. 6 in this volume).

16. With these assertions I am attempting to take a new position in the debate about the meaning and history of "the righteousness of God" in Paul. A lively continuing debate has followed upon E. Käsemann's brilliant essay " 'The Righteousness of God' in Paul," in *New Testament Questions of Today,* trans. W. J. Montague (Philadelphia: Fortress Press, 1969), 168–82. In my dissertation *Gerechtigkeit Gottes bei Paulus,* 2d ed. (Göttingen: Vandenhoeck & Ruprecht, 1966), I tried to support and extend Käsemann's position in greater detail. But judged from today's perspective, my work had three fundamental weaknesses. First, it treated the concept of the righteousness of God too rigidly as a fixed *terminus technicus* that always and only meant God's own righteousness. Second, there was in the book insufficient discussion of the significance of the atoning death of Jesus as that which made justification possible. For that reason no genuine continuity was apparent between Jesus, the mission congregations in Jerusalem and Antioch, and Paul. Third, when I wrote my study it was not yet clear to me that one must not make a strict tradition-historical separation between the Old Testament and early Christian apocalyptic texts. Therefore, the continuity in the history of transmission from the Old Testament to the early Jewish and the earliest Christian texts is not treated fully enough. H. Graf Reventlow, *Rechtfertigung im Horizont des Alten Testaments* (Munich: Kaiser, 1971), 113, has proven to be correct in his formulation that one, "starting with Old Testament thought about 'righteousness,' [should give] the Pauline concept of 'the righteousness of God' a comprehensive meaning. Then the alternatives that have arisen in the discussion about this formula—whether 'of God' is to be understood as a subjective or an objective genitive, whether the phrase is to be understood soteriologically or eschatologically, as theology or anthropology— quickly show themselves to be too narrow." Those who have criticized Käsemann and my dissertation have hardly taken any notice of my attempts at a further clarification of the complex verbal structure and overall meaning of "the righteousness of God" in my three essays "The End of the Law" (chap. 8 in this volume); "On Recent Exegesis of Romans 3:24–26" (chap. 6 in this volume); and "Zum Thema: Biblische Theologie des Neuen Testaments," in Biblisch-theologische Studien 1 (Neukirchen: Neukirchener Verlag, 1977), 43ff. (25–60). Prominent among these critics are R. Bultmann, *"DIKAIOSYNE THEOU"* in *Exegetica. Aufsätze zur Erforschung des Neuen Testaments,* ed. E. Dinkler (Tübingen: Mohr, 1967), 470–75; H. Conzelmann, "Die Rechtfertigungslehre bei Paulus," in *Theologie als Schriftauslegung. Aufsätze zum Neuen Testament* (Munich: Kaiser, 1974), 191–206; G. Klein, "Gottesgerechtigkeit als Thema der neuesten Paulus-Forschung," in *Rekonstruktion und Interpretation. Gesammelte Aufsätze zum Neuen Testament,* BEvT 50 (Munich: Kaiser, 1969), 225–36; idem, "Predigtmeditationen über Röm. 3:21–28," *Göttinger Predigtmeditationen* 69 (1980): 412ff. (409–19); and E. Lohse, "Die Gerechtigkeit Gottes in der paulinischen Theologie," in *Die Einheit des Neuen Testaments. Exegetische Studien zur Theologie des Neuen Testaments* (Göttingen: Vandenhoeck & Ruprecht, 1973), 209–27. In any case, I regard it as a one-sidedness on a par with that of my own former thesis that they all assume the righteousness of God in Paul primarily means the righteousness obtained by faith and see therein what is characteristic of Paul's view of righteousness compared with the pre-Pauline tradition. Their assessment has its basis not only in exegesis but also in the decidedly Lutheran stamp of all the authors I have named. E. Käsemann has once again laid out his view of the matter in his *Commentary on Romans,* trans. G. W. Bromiley (Grand Rapids: Wm. B. Eerdmans, 1980), 23ff. Then recently U. Wilckens, *Der Brief an die Römer,* EKK VI, 1 (Neukirchen-Vluyn: Neukirchener Verlag,

1978), in two excursuses on "Gerechtigkeit Gottes" (202–33) and "Zum Verständnis der Sühne-Vorstellung" (233–43), and K. Kertelge. s. v. "DIKAIOSYNE," *EWNT* 1:790ff. (784–96), have discussed the issues of interpretation that are decisive today so instructively that I am in extensive agreement with them and can point to their expositions. How the German discussion about the meaning of the righteousness of God in Paul is viewed in America is shown by Manfried T. Brauch in the (unsatisfactory) "Appendix: Perspectives of 'God's righteousness' in recent German discussion," in E. P. Sanders, *Paul and Palestinian Judaism* (Philadelphia: Fortress Press, 1977), 523–42.

17. K. Koch, s. v. *ṣdq, THAT* 2:507–30; H. H. Schmid, *Gerechtigkeit als Weltordnung,* BHT 40 (Tübingen: Mohr, 1968); idem, "Rechtfertigung als Schöpfungsgeschehen," in *Rechtfertigung. Festschrift für E. Käsemann,* 403–14. The objections that Koch, "sdq," 516, and J. Halbe, " 'Altorientalisches Weltordnungsdenken' und alttestamentliche Theologie," *ZTK* 76 (1979): 381–418, raise against Schmid's systematizing discussion of righteousness as a world system appear to me worthy of attention. To be sure, it is significant that in the *Book of Mysteries* from Qumran (1Q27) the eschatological righteousness dawning upon the world is expressly called the "norm" or "order" of the world (*tîqqûn tēbēl*). In my view, one must ask Schmid for a more precise differentiation between wisdom and righteousness.

18. K. Berger, in "Neues Material zur 'Gerechtigkeit Gottes' " (*ZNW 68* [1977]: 266–75) and in *Exegese des Neuen Testaments* (Heidelberg: Quelle and Meyer, 1977), 162 and often, believes that the Roman congregation could only understand the phrase "the righteousness of God" as it was commonly understood in its Hellenistic-Jewish environment, that is, forensically, as God's demanding and standard-setting judicial holiness. As interesting as Berger's collection of material is in many ways, his thesis appears to me quite improbable. The Roman congregation was made up of a number of converted Jews like Aquila and Prisca (Rom. 16:3, 7) and several so-called God-fearers, who were, it's true, regarded by the Jews as uncircumcised Gentiles, but who from the synagogue were well acquainted with the Old Testament Scriptures. Cf. Schmithals, *Römerbrief,* 63–91. In addition, K. Beyschlag, *Clemens Romanus und der Frühkatholizismus* (Tübingen: Mohr, 1966), has called attention to the fact that according to *1 Clement* there must have been active in the Roman congregation from early on a Jewish-Christian community tradition that did not derive from Paul, but to which, rather, he tried to conform where possible in his letter to Rome. If Schmithals and Beyschlag are correct, and if the references to Jewish-Christian tradition in Romans given by O. Michel throughout his commentary *Der Brief an die Römer,* 14th ed. (Göttingen: Vandenhoeck & Ruprecht, 1978), are not entirely mistaken, then the Old Testament and Jewish-Christian tradition provide the primary context from which to reconstruct how the righteousness of God was understood in Rome. Berger's noteworthy late examples from the Armenian Philo, the *Testament of Abraham,* a grave inscription from the third century C.E., etc., have in my view only secondary significance compared with the background this tradition provides. On this problem see also Kettunen, *Abfassungszweck,* 73–81.

19. On 1 Cor. 6:1–11 see especially the two important works by E. Dinkler, "Zum Problem der Ethik bei Paulus, Rechtsnahme und Rechtsverzicht (1 Kor. 6:1–11)," in *Signum Crucis, Aufsätze zum NT und zur Christlichen Archäologie* (Tübingen: Mohr, 1967), 204–40, and L. Vischer, *Die Auslegungsgeschichte von 1 Kor. 6:1–11. Rechtsverzicht und Schlichtung* (Tübingen: Mohr, 1955).

20. Wilckens, *Der Brief an die Römer,* 239, n. 754, correctly stresses that Rom. 8:3 is not to be translated "God sent his own son in the likeness of sinful flesh and for sin . . . ," but "God sent his own son in the likeness of sinful flesh, indeed as an offering for sin." Paul is following here the language about sacrifice in the LXX at Lev. 4:3, 14, 28, 35, etc., as he does in 2 Cor. 5:21.

21. I have attempted to provide information about the contexts in which Paul's understanding of the law is to be viewed in my essay "The Law as a Topic of Biblical Theology" (chap. 7 in this volume). There is definitely a historical continuity from the Old Testament to Jesus' understanding of the law and from this to Paul.

22. J. Roloff, "Die Paulus-Darstellung des Lukas," *EvT* 39 (1979): 523–24 (510–31), calls attention to Luke's strange silence about Paul's arrival in Rome and, on the basis of *1 Clem.* 5.2 and Phil. 1:15ff, speculates that "intrigues fed by group rivalries" in Rome "were partially responsible for the bad turn the case against Paul finally took."

CHAPTER 6

Recent Exegesis on Romans 3:24–26

I

Exegesis on Rom. 3:24–26 appears today more than ever to end inconclusively. It has not been clarified decisively whether and to what extent Paul is citing traditional material in these verses, what this tradition means for him and for his theology of justification, and in what manner the text connects justification and the death of Jesus. It is sufficient to illustrate this unclarity with a few examples from recent literature.

Ernst Käsemann, in his commentary on Romans, has supported the analysis and interpretation of the passage he presented in 1950/51 in *Die Zeitschrift für die Neutestamentliche Wissenschaft:*[1] The "abrupt change in sentence structure"[2] from v. 23 into v. 24 signals "the fragment of a hymn" as does the terminology in the following verses which is uncommon for Paul or totally foreign to him, a fragment cited by the apostle and (critically) interpreted with the aid of his own interpolations. The fragment encompasses vv. 24–26a with the exception of the following six words: probably *dōrean tē autou chariti* in v. 24 and certainly *dia pisteōs* in v. 25. Verse 26b, *pros tēn endeixen* etc., is to be understood as the apostle's continuation and commentary. The fragment belongs to early Jewish-Christian tradition about the Lord's Supper. It speaks of the atonement, forgiveness, and justification wrought in the death of Jesus by God himself for the community as the covenant people of God, and it is taken up by Paul for the sake of this fundamental declaration, which the apostle, of course, expands to apply to all believers.

Käsemann has not let himself be dissuaded from this interpretation, which rests on Rudolf Bultmann's trailblazing analysis of the traditions in the passage,[3] despite repeated criticism. He is not dissuaded by the stylistic argument of Eduard Lohse,[4] which was made more precise by Klaus Wengst,[5] that the choice of words in v. 24, except for the one expression *apolytrōsis*, is to be ascribed totally to the apostle himself and that with the relative pronoun connecting v. 25 to v. 24 we have a decidedly better and clearer starting point for a quotation, so that we are to reckon with pre-Pauline tradition only in vv. 25–26a. Nor is he dissuaded by Gottfried Fitzer's attempt to strike vv. 25c–26a, that is, the entire phrase from *eis endeixen* to *en tę anochę tou theou*, as a "minimally appropriate gloss on the Pauline text."[6] Fitzer seeks to remove this text and Paul in general, far from thoughts about sacrifice and to understand *hilastērion* in the light of the understanding of *kappōret* (Exod. 25:22; Lev. 16:2; Num. 7:89, etc.) as used in the Septuagint and in Philo. For Fitzer *hilasterion* is not an "expiatory sacrifice or means of atonement" but the "place of God's presence, of God's grace, at which, through the manipulations of the priests, that is, through the cultic rites of sanctification, the grace of God is actualized."[7]

Nor has Käsemann been talked out of his exegesis by Leonhard Goppelt[8] and Stanislas Lyonnet,[9] who both take *hilastērion* to be equivalent to *kappōret* in Leviticus 16, Goppelt wishing to understand it with less specificity than Fitzer as "mercy seat," Lyonnet, with greater specificity than Fitzer, as the place of the presence of God, of revelation and atonement. Finally, the attempt to understand the text as a whole as genuinely Pauline, for example, by Otto Kuss[10] or Herman Ridderbos,[11] Käsemann correctly regards as a relapse into the difficulties out of which his differentiation between pre-Pauline expressions and Pauline interpretive additions was precisely meant to lead.

These perplexities become clearly apparent when Ridderbos interprets Rom. 3:24ff. to mean that

> God has shown the [judging and condemning] power of his righteousness in Christ, by giving him for others as a means of propitiation in death. The idea is then joined to this [by Paul] that God till this moment had not meted out the punishment on the sins of men that was due them, but passed over them in his forbearance, i.e. in his withholding of the judgment. Now, "in the present time," God has abandoned this attitude of waiting, however, and shown his [judging] righteousness, in the death of Jesus.[12]

This interpretation not only pushes aside the attempt at all tradition analysis and the whole recent discussion about the Semitic background of the phrase "the righteousness of God," but also what Werner George Kümmel showed about our text long ago, that *paresis* is not to be translated here by "passing over" or the like but by "remission," and *endeixis* by "demonstration" and not by "proof."[13]

Actually, this brief review has yielded discouraging evidence that exegesis has gone around in circles on this passage in recent years and is once again bogged down in old difficulties, and one is inclined to speak of insoluble problems or even of intradisciplinary roadblocks that prevent exegesis from reaching any clear knowledge about the text. But as admittedly difficult as it is to interpret our verses and as little as one can absolve present New Testament interpreters from setting up their own scholarly roadblocks, it would be just as unfortunate if we were to give up on a solution of the problems of this very text. Indeed, what is at issue in Rom. 3:24–26 is not only the christological foundation of the Pauline gospel about justification but also the relationship of the apostle to the christological tradition he received and with that also the question of the place of Paul in the history of early Christian proclamation.

II

If we wish to make progress, it seems advisable to discuss the interpretation of Rom. 3:24–26 that at present is most influential, that of Eduard Lohse.[14] Lohse's literary-critical analysis and overall interpretation is not only confirmed and defended by his student Herbert Koch,[15] but also drawn upon directly or in substance by Hans Conzelmann,[16] for example, just as extensively as by Wolfgang Schrage,[17] Klaus Wengst,[18] Gerhard Delling,[19] Günter Klein,[20] Eduard Schweizer,[21] Ulrich Wilckens,[22] and Georg Eichholz.[23] An even greater number of exegetes follow its religiohistorical thesis (because it is established in detail by a proven expert on ancient Judaism) that *hilastērion* in our text is not to be equated with *kappōret* but, on the basis of 4 Macc. 17:21–22, more generally with expiatory sacrifice. The opponents of this thesis, who wish to affirm the equation of *hilastērion* and *kappōret*, have to my knowledge failed up to now to study Lohse's arguments directly and also to criticize them when that appears necessary. It is just this that is to be attempted in what follows, because not all arguments that Lohse offers are equally convincing, and the impression grows that the interpretation of Rom. 3:24ff. as a whole remains so controversial because its fundamental literary, historical, and theological problems have not really been discussed thoroughly.

First of all, with respect to the literary-critical differentiation of tradition and Pauline redaction, Lohse's thesis that the quoted traditional phrase begins only in v. 25 and is prepared for in v. 24 only by means of the traditional term *apolytrōsis* (= redemption, forgiveness of sins; cf. Eph. 1:7; Col. 1:14) is clearer and more adequately supported than all alternative theses. A break between v. 23 and v. 24 is not really demonstrable; except for the word just mentioned, the phrase is wholly Pauline in formulation. However, in vv. 25, 26a, apart from the Paulinizing addition *dia pisteōs*, un-Pauline expressions abound. Moreover, v. 26b (*pros tēn endeixen* etc.), written by Paul as a parallel to v. 25, is more readily understandable as a continuation and an elaboration of the tradition by the apostle himself. So we have to reckon here with Paul's quoting of a tradition which, like Phil. 2:6ff.; 1 Tim. 3:16; 1 Pet. 2:23; but also Rom. 4:25, begins with a relative pronoun.

If one goes on to ask the intent of this tradition, virtually everything depends on understanding the word *hilastērion* (written without an article). Tradition historical and history-of-religions considerations suggest a double possibility for understanding the word. *Hilastērion* in the Septuagint and in the Hellenistic Judaism represented by Philo of Alexandria became a technical term for *kappōret*[24] and seldom appears in extrabiblical Greek in the sense of an initiatory offering or expiatory offering, which often consists of a stele dedicated to the divinity.[25] In addition to this a few references document a use of the adjective *hilastērios* in the Septuagint,[26] in Josephus,[27] and in so-called profane Greek.[28]

Since the context and Rom. 3:25–26a point to Jewish-Christian tradition—only in that context is it meaningful to speak of atonement through the blood of Jesus, of Jesus' appointment as the means of atonement, of remission of sins as a demonstration of the righteousness of God, etc.—Lohse is rightly at pains to explain the use of *hilastērion* against the background of the biblical use of the adjective and noun. But the conclusion is that *hilastērion* cannot be an equivalent for *kappōret* but that one must presuppose an (independent) concept formation in which *hilastērion* has the sense of *hilastērion thyma*, that is, expiatory sacrifice. As evidence Lohse points to 4 Macc. 17:21–22, and he conjectures that *hilastērion thyma* could also have stood earlier in the phrase quoted in Rom. 3:25–26a and that Paul then replaced *thyma* with his addition *dia pisteōs*. The idea is apparently this, that from an original adjectival use in the pre-Pauline Jewish-Christian formula a substantive *hilastērion* = expiatory sacrifice, was formed only by the Pauline redaction.

Now this is not really a simple argument, and it is made more difficult by the fact that up to now we have evidence for *hilastērion* = expiatory sacrifice (rather than expiatory inscription or expiatory stele) neither in the Septuagint nor elsewhere. Only once, in a fragmentary Egyptian papyrus from the second century c.e., is there talk of *hilastērious thysias*, that is, of making an expiatory sacrifice.[29] Thus what Lohse proposes as a solution is a hypothetical concept formation on the analogy of the scarce materials in profane Greek. Whether such a new word formation is probable on Jewish-Christian soil, when there existed there from the Septuagint and from Hellenistic Judaism an established technical use of *hilastērion* = *kappōret*, one may and must ask, in any case. For Lohse comes to his hypothesis only because a typological equation of Christ with the *kappōret* = *hilastērion* appears rather improbable to him.

Now Lohse does fully acknowledge that such a typological equation could make good sense to Jewish-Christians. He thinks that the picture drawn in the text of the installation of Jesus as the *kappōret* and of the expiation through his blood "would be understandable for Jewish-Christians and would compare the atonement attained in Christ antitypically with the atonement that was possible under the old covenant."[30] Despite the theology about the Ark and atonement cultivated in Judaism into the rabbinic period, this equation nevertheless appears to him unlikely in respect to our text: first of all, because a comparison of Christ = *kappōret* is not supported by the context and also because Paul in quoting a tradition would have had "to show his readers through some indication that he was thinking of the cultic object from the old covenant";[31] second, because in the Septuagint, aside from the interpretive explanation in Exod. 25:16 (17), where *kappōret* is reproduced by *hilastērion epithema*, it is always given with the article, *to hilastērion* (as also in Heb. 9:5); and so also in Rom. 3:25–26 "a further identification of the term must have been given, such as *hilastērion epithema* or *to hilastērion*";[32] because, third, the Ark stood hidden in the Holy of Holies, while the text specifically emphasizes that Jesus was publicly installed as the *hilastērion*. But a contrast between Jesus as the new *kappōret* and the old hidden one can, according to Lohse, "be made likely neither from the context nor by reference to 2 Cor. 3:6ff.; and finally, in the fourth place, because in a comparison of Christ with the *kappōret* this very comparison would "go awry in that precisely the blood of Christ would have to be poured out on the *kappōret* which he would himself be. If the *kappōret* were to be thought of at all, one would much rather have expected that the cross rather than Christ himself would have been so designated."[34] Taken together these four points show that "the view according to which *kappōret* is to be understood with *hilastērion* is not to be maintained."[35]

With respect to Lohse's first argument, a careful distinction is to be made between the intention and linguistic possibilities of the pre-Pauline tradition and the appropriation of the material in its context in Romans. If the traditional phrase originates from Jerusalem or from the Hellenistic Jewish–Christian congregation in Antioch established by the Stephen-circle, an antitypical contrast between the former place of revelation and of atonement in the temple, which was hidden and merely envisioned, and the one which now has been publicly established by God himself in the person of Jesus—such a contrast is in that context not only meaningful but indeed very likely, because the Stephen-circle was driven out of Jerusalem because of its criticism of the temple and the law (cf. Acts 6:13). In this circle our traditional material could actually have been used with the intention of supporting this criticism of the temple, in such a way that the highest cultic ritual, carried out once a year in the temple by the high priest on the people's behalf on the Day of Atonement (Leviticus 16), would be completed and once and for all surpassed through Christ's sacrificial death, so that a cultic atonement is from this time on no longer required. In this way the Christology of Hebrews, which extensively develops this thesis, would already be prepared for in Jerusalem or Antioch by the Stephen-circle. Thus the charge of possible unclarity cannot be applied to the Jewish-Christian tradition itself.[36] Nor can it be applied with reference to the congregation in Rome, for it later, in 1 Peter, *1 Clement*, and the *Shepherd of Hermas*, shows itself to be so heavily under the influence of Jewish Christianity in its theological tradition and manner of thinking that already in the middle of the first century an understanding of Jewish-Christian tradition is to be assumed for it. This is especially the case since this tradition appears to take up a technical term of atonement theology known outside the Septuagint and, in addition, since all the motifs and statements that come together in Rom. 3:24–26—new creation and the forgiveness of sins, the possibility of forgiveness through atonement by means of blood, the institution of such reconciliation as a demonstration of the salvation-bringing righteousness of God, etc.—were localized for Jews and Jewish Christians especially in that theology of the atonement that had its Old Testament center in Leviticus 16.[37]

Lohse's second objection can hardly be sustained either. Since the article is not normally used in New Testament formulas, in definitions, and with predicate nouns (cf., for example, Rom. 1:16–17; 3:20; 4:25; 8:3–4; 2 Cor. 5:21; Col. 1:15, 20b, etc.), the absence of the article before *hilastērion* in Rom. 3:25 is no longer surprising, for the word stands here as the predicate.[38] Paul or even the Christian transmitters before him would have had to put the article in the text only if he or they would have had to reckon with an inadequate understanding of the formula by their congregations. However, for this traditional text itself, coming from Jerusalem or Antioch, this suspicion does not arise, and it is also difficult to substantiate it for the Jewish-Christian-oriented congregation in Rome, especially since this congregation not only espoused a Jewish-Christian theology (see above) but also very likely gave a hearing to the Jewish-Christian agitation directed against Paul (Rom. 3:8; 4:31; 6:1, 15; etc.).

We have already touched on Lohse's third argument above. At this point we still need to ask, first of all, if there are parallels for the antitypical element clearly embedded in the text which sees in the atonement conferred by God through the death of Jesus the superseding and ending of the Old Testament temple worship. There are such parallels in the Markan passion tradition that extends back to Jerusalem (cf. Mark 15:38) and then, with the desired compass and clarity, in Hebrews (cf. especially Hebrews 9, 10, and 13:10ff.). So Rom. 3:25–26a stands in a line of tradition that was formulated independently of Paul and that extended from Jerusalem to the Jewish Christianity of the post-Pauline period.[39]

But as far as Paul himself is concerned, it appears noteworthy to me that in a way analogous to that in Hebrews he affirms the "once for all" character of the death of Jesus (cf. Rom. 6:10 with Heb. 9:12; 10:10); speaks of the death of Jesus as an expiatory sacrifice no less clearly than that epistle does (simply compare Rom. 8:3–4 and 2 Cor. 5:21[40]); asserts as does Heb. 9:24 the heavenly intercession of the Risen One for his community (cf. Rom. 8:34); and, finally, contrasts with the desired clarity old and new, the time of the old and of the new covenant, the righteousness of the law and the righteousness of God, and that precisely in a cultic context. If Lohse does not want to see 2 Corinthians 3 as evidence for that, one must point to the Pauline Lord's Supper formula, which emphasizes the inauguration of the new covenant through Jesus' atoning death, 1 Cor. 11:23ff. Then Rom. 5:1, 2, 9–10 is also to be recalled, where in a clear appropriation of cultic concepts there is reference to justification by virtue of blood, that is, by virtue of the atonement effected by Jesus' death; the eschatological benefit of justification is described as gaining "access" to God; and an explicit identification is made between justification and reconciliation. One cannot, therefore, say that the cultic-typological antithesis of Rom. 3:25–26 would be totally uncommon in Romans. And that would be especially the case in the context of an argument in which, as in Rom. 3:20 and 3:21ff., the old reality of the law and of the wrath of God is contrasted with the new reality (attested in the Old Testament!) of the righteousness of God and of faith.

Finally, Lohse's fourth and last argument will not really hold either. Inasmuch as he says that the installation of Jesus as the *kappōret* involves the inconsistent concept that Jesus as the place of atonement would be sprinkled with his own blood, Lohse is in my view in danger of an underinterpretation of the theology of the Ark that was already highly developed in the priestly tradition in the Old Testament. According to Exod. 25:17–22, the *kappōret* is a lid-structure found atop the Ark; it is also the place of meeting with Yahweh and of his self-disclosure. In Lev. 16:13ff., where the actual atonement rite of the Day of Atonement, the sprinkling of the Holy of Holies with blood by the high priest, is described, the description is formulated with evident care: first the high priest is to cover the *kappōret* with rising incense, lest he die if he sees God face to face (cf. Isa. 6:5). When he has done this he is then to sprinkle once with his finger some of the blood "on the front of the mercy seat" and then seven times "before the mercy seat."[41] We are dealing here with a merely symbolic rite that is to be sharply differentiated from the pagan taurabolium. The merely suggestive nature of the ceremony is underscored by the fact that in the Holy of Holies there was no longer an actual Ark, to say nothing of a physical *kappōret*. Rather, the high priest carried out the atonement rite, according to Lev. 16:14, at the place where Yahweh was believed to be present, although he could not be seen. Only in this way can one then also understand the stipulations in the tractate *Yoma*, that the high priest should stand in the Holy of Holies filled with smoke at the place where he has burned incense and sprinkled the blood "once upwards and seven times downwards," but, as is the case with someone wielding a whip, "not as though he had intended to sprinkle upwards or downwards."[42] Thus the Old Testament–Jewish ritual itself already fundamentally moves beyond anything that can be visualized concretely. This is all the more the case if this rite is now held up as the interpretive model for Jesus' death and resurrection and the saving work God carried out through them. The text of Rom. 3:25–26a only says that God publicly made Jesus the place of meeting with God, of his revelation, and of the reconciliation that has been brought about by virtue of the atonement effected in Jesus' sacrifice of his life, in his blood. So God himself has in the death and resurrection of Jesus made himself known as the one who meets humanity and makes atonement, and this event, the revelation of reconciliation, is beyond human imagining as much as the thesis of Hebrews that Christ is at the same time the high priest and the sacrifice.[43]

So Lohse's four arguments against an identification of Jesus Christ with the *kappōret* are not at all satisfying. Even less satisfying is the interpretation he proposes, the linguistic difficulty of which we have already discussed. Since in Lohse's view Jesus cannot be regarded in Rom. 3:25–26a as the *kappōret*, and since he regards as, among other things, too vague the proposal of Hans Lietzmann,[44] Werner Georg Kümmel,[45] C. H. Dodd,[46] Paul Althaus,[47] Ernest

Käsemann,[48] and others that *hilastērion* is to be interpreted as "the means of atonement," he refers to 4 Macc. 17:21–22: the Jewish martyrs become

> as it were, a ransom for the sins of our nation.
> (22) And through the blood of those devout ones and their death as an expiation, divine Providence preserved Israel that previously had been afflicted.[49]

Lohse interprets the Maccabees text and at the same time connects it with Rom. 3:25–26:

> The martyrs in the Maccabean period died for the sins of the nation. But their death brought atonement, which became effective by virtue of their shed blood. God accepted their death and because of it rescued Israel. As we had already seen, Hellenistic Judaism understood the death of the martyrs as a sacrifice and expressed the atoning power of their death by the use of sacrificial language. It follows from this that it seems most natural to assume also for Rom. 3:25 the picture of sacrifice and to supplement *hilastērion* with the word *thyma*. It is not impossible that this word could actually have stood in the Jewish-Christian phrase that Paul adopted. For the words *dia pisteōs* interpolated by Paul could have displaced that word. But, in any case, the words that follow, *en tǭ autou haimati*, also support understanding *hilastērion* as an expiatory sacrifice.[50]

Is this view probable? That is doubtful, and not only on linguistic grounds. First of all, the text of 4 Macc. 17:21–22 is not certain precisely in reference to the word of interest to us, *hilastērion*. While Alexandrinus speaks of the atoning death of the martyrs, *tou hilastēriou thanatou autōn*, Sinaiticus reads *tou hilastēriou tou thanatou autōn*, meaning that the death of the martyrs was a *hilastērion*. It is the usual scholarly practice to follow the reading of Alexandrinus, printed by H. B. Swete in his text,[51] without, of course, a real textcritical discussion of such a decision.[52] Lohse also follows this reading.[53] Nevertheless, if one considers the decided Hellenistic ring of the text, which seeks to make understandable to a Greek-thinking circle of hearers the idea of the vicarious, penitential suffering of the martyrs, an idea it received from 2 Macc. 7:30–38,[54] and since the 4 Maccabees text seeks to do this with tentative Greek circumlocutions—v. 21 speaks quite unbiblically of "having as it were become a ransom" [*hōsper antipsychon*] for the sins of the nation[55]—the reading of Sinaiticus, followed by Rahlfs in his text and R. B. Townshend in his translation,[56] appears worthy of full consideration. It interprets the death of the martyrs as a *hilastērion*, that is, as an expiatory offering to divine providence, which corresponds to the language of Greek inscriptions. That this reading would be altered by Christian users of 4 Maccabees into the version in Alexandrinus, which in the light of Rom. 3:25–26a and the technical biblical language of *hilastērion* = *kappōret* is less offensive, is at least as probable as the common assumption of a secondary origin of the article in Sinaiticus by dittography.

Nevertheless, whether we follow the one text or the other, it remains to be observed that in either case there is no reference at all to an expiatory *sacrifice* of the martyrs.[57] What is said is only that the suffering of the martyrs should serve as a ransom and atonement for the nation. Sacrifice, atonement, and substitution are, it's true, very close to one another in the Old Testament and in Jewish thought, but all texts do not emphasize each aspect in the same way, as 2 Macc. 7:30–38 and 4 Macc. 17:21–22 show. If one wants to parallel 4 Macc. 17:21–22 with Rom. 3:25–26, then from this perspective the common understanding of *hilastērion* as a means of atonement, which Lohse rejects, is much more likely than his own interpretation.

But there are still two further considerations that speak against Lohse's view. In the LXX *protithesthai* is not a technical term for offering a sacrifice. But in a cultic context *protithesthai* is used for setting out publicly the so-called shewbread (cf. Exod. 29:23; 40:23; Lev. 24:8; 2 Macc. 1:8, 15). *Proetheto* in connection with a sacrificial concept would thus be an unexpected term, while the expression makes good sense insofar as what is intended by it is the public putting forth of Jesus as the place of atonement and of meeting with God. The expression *en tǭ autou haimati* also points in the same direction. According to Lev. 17:11–12, blood is the means Yahweh gave (!) the Israelites with which cultic atonement may be brought about. Naturally this blood is acquired through the slaughter of a sacrificial animal, but the phenomenon of the sacrifice does not for that reason need to be emphasized in every passage in which blood is spoken of. In Rom. 3:25–26 the element of Jesus' sacrifice remains unemphasized, and what is emphasized is that God himself, in his salvation-bringing righteousness, has effected atonement in the surrender of the life of Jesus. In Rom. 8:3 and 2 Cor. 5:21, on the other hand, the emphasis is put on the fact of sacrifice, while the idea of atonement is the accompanying motif. The accent that the text in Rom. 3:25 puts on atonement through blood becomes easily understandable if with *hilastērion* the *kappōret* as the place of atonement is in view. If, on the other hand, one speaks of the expiatory sacrifice of Jesus, *en tǭ autou haimati* functions as an interpolation into the text, with the grammatical connection of which the exegetes have great difficulty, as is known. But one must see that these problems once again arise only out of imprecise exegesis.

Finally, it remains to be asked where the primary point of comparison might have lain for the first Christians who had originally formulated our tradition. It was their kerygmatic task to express effectively and appropriately the reconciliation-effecting saving work of God in the death and resurrection of Jesus, saving work that overshadowed everything that came before. The question is, which interpretive resource was more appropriate for them in this situation, the suffering of the Jewish martyrs that is presented in 2 Maccabees 7 as a penitential act and only in 4 Maccabees 6 and 17 as vicarious punitive and expiatory suffering, or the ritual and events of the Day of Atonement? If one considers the immense significance of this day in Jerusalem itself until the destruction of the temple in 70 C.E. and then the great celebrations of this day in the synagogues of the Diaspora, recourse to Leviticus 16 was in my opinion much more likely for those early Christian interpreters than to thoughts of the martyrs, with whose help precisely the singularity of the atoning action of God in Christ was much more difficult to express than with the aid of an antitypal reference to the celebration of the Day of Atonement.

If we return the tradition in Rom. 3:25-26a to its original proclamatory situation and allow it its own unmodified message, then it proclaims the inauguration of Jesus as reconciler who surpasses Leviticus 16. Old Testament-Jewish theological concepts then appear as essential assertions of the text which are now used christologically;[58] the statements in the passage are in harmony with one another, and, besides, Hebrews 9 confirms to a tee the Jewish-Christian message the tradition intends to convey (cf. esp. 5:11ff., 15).

III

As surely as it is to be granted Lohse that "through form- and tradition-historical analysis of this passage all that can be achieved is a very high degree of probability,"[59] just as clearly it appears to me that the tradition in Rom. 3:25-26 can be interpreted more adequately from the context supplied by Leviticus 16 than by Hellenistic-Jewish martyr theology or, indeed, by Greek references from inscriptions and papyri. This conclusion, which was a surprise to me,[60] has consequences for the question of what the tradition originally meant and how Paul himself then utilized and interpreted it. As far as both questions are concerned, I am happy that I can again agree with Lohse. Whether one locates the tradition already in Jerusalem itself or, as he prefers, only in Antioch, it appears to be connected originally with the idea of the (eschatological) people of God: in fidelity to his covenantal promise, that is, to his righteousness, God has reconstituted the eschatological covenant people by putting forth Jesus as the reconciler, thereby surpassing and abolishing the ritual in Jerusalem that effects atonement for the nation by hidden actions in the Holy of Holies. By virtue of the atonement that in Jesus God himself arranged and guaranteed for the people, their sins of the past are forgiven, so that out of this atonement a holy, new people of God emerges.

In this fundamental assertion the tradition points to the Pauline-Lukan Lord's Supper formula, which also gives instructions for the celebration of the establishment of the new covenant by virtue of the expiatory death of Jesus and unites the new eschatological people of God into the body of Christ. If one sees this connection, then the interpretation Paul gives the tradition has to be seen not merely as a critique, to say nothing of a qualitative correction,[61] but, with Lohse, as a consistent continuation and elaboration.[62] If the superseding of the Old Testament-Jewish saving event is emphasized already in the tradition, the apostle consistently advances this line when by the interpolation of *dia pisteōs* in the tradition itself and then by its incorporation into its context in 3:21-24, 26bff., he emphasizes two things: one gains participation in Christ as reconciler "by faith" (alone), and faith is the way of salvation opened and given for everyone, that is, not only the Jews but also the Gentiles, that is, for every person (vv. 22, 26b). The people of God as the community of the new covenant is thus constituted from all nations and no longer only from members of Israel. This first and primary accent of the Pauline use of

the tradition stands beside the second, that righteousness as the saving **activity**
of God is now open to everyone who in faith acknowledges Christ as reconciler, since God justifies precisely the person who so believes. The righteousness of God as the universal saving activity of God which procures the
justification of everyone who believes, this is the second accent Paul makes
in our context.[63]

If one asks, finally, how Paul himself conceives justification by faith in
Christ, our text lets us see that what makes justification possible also for the
apostle is precisely the atonement wrought by God in the offering of Jesus'
life, a thesis that is confirmed and strengthened by reference to Rom. 4:25;
5:1–11; 8:1ff., 31ff.; 1 Cor. 1:30; 2 Cor. 5:21, etc. By faith this atoning work
of salvation, embodied in the person of the Risen Crucified One, is acknowledged to have happened "for us," and therewith Christ is also acknowledged
as Lord over life and death, believers experience God's acquittal, freeing them
of their sins, and gain Christ as Lord and advocate. This total event, called
"justification" (*dikaiōsis*) already before Paul according to Rom. 4:25, is
experienced as the new creation of the sinner, that is, as guarantee of that freedom, righteousness, and glorious existence that Adam possessed in paradise
but lost as a sinner (cf. *Life of Adam* 20–21), which since then has been lost
to sinners caught up in Adam's fate (Rom. 3:23; 5:12ff.); it can be bestowed
and conferred on them anew only through the favor of God the righteous creator who has turned to those who believe in Christ. So the justified one is *kainē
ktisis* (2 Cor. 5:16). Since precisely this idea of new creation through atonement and forgiveness in the Old Testament[64] and in Judaism[65] was connected
especially with the celebration of the Day of Atonement and what it effected,
our deliberations have of themselves come full circle.

We can therefore return to the question asked at the beginning and answer:
it is very likely that in Rom. 3:25–26a the apostle takes up pre-Pauline soteriological tradition. In form and content this tradition may well go back to the
Stephen-circle. By typological recourse to Leviticus 16 and with an eye toward
the atonement made in the temple in Jerusalem each year on the Day of Atonement, the installation of Jesus as the reconciler is proclaimed in the formula,
an installation in which God shows his fidelity to his promises and his covenant by forgiving all former sins. The cultic celebration of the Day of Atonement is abolished and superseded by virtue of this act of God, because the
atonement granted definitively by God in Christ once and for all renders
superfluous further cultic atonement ritual. The apostle adopts this tradition
approvingly and with it lays the christological foundation for his theology
about justification. Justification through Christ is established also for Paul
precisely in the atonement that God opened in the surrender of Jesus' life and
acknowledged as completed and effective in the resurrection of the Crucified
One (cf. also Rom. 4:25). So Paul does not speak critically of the soteriological foundation of justification in Jesus' atoning death but in continuity and
agreement with the confessional formula he received, which goes back to
Jerusalem. This point of continuity is both underscored and confirmed by

1 Cor. 15:3ff. or by the Pauline Lord's Supper tradition. What the apostle emphasizes beyond the tradition in Rom. 3:25–26 is the will of God to give to believers from all over the world, and only to them, access to the atonement opened up in Christ and to confer it on them. Justification for Paul shows itself to be the reconciliation and new creation of all people who experience for themselves and acknowledge (cf. Rom. 10:9) the atonement completed in the death of Jesus and eschatologically ratified in his resurrection. That Paul also resolved christologically the difficulty possibly still inherent in the old tradition, whereby the atonement effected by God in Christ applied only to the sins of the past, resolving it in that for him Christ as the Risen One remains to the end of the world the justifier and reconciler of all who believe, is now to be mentioned by reference to Rom. 8:31ff., though it cannot receive treatment here. Yet this reference is important, for without it, it would remain incomprehensible how for Paul justification no longer signifies only a soteriological aspect of his gospel but the whole of it.

NOTES

1. E. Käsemann, "Zum Verständnis von Römer 3:24–26," *ZNW* 43 (1950/51): 150–54, reprinted in *Exegetische Versuche und Besinnungen*, vol. 1, 5th ed. (Göttingen: Vandenhoeck & Ruprecht, 1967), 96–100.

2. This and the following references are to E. Käsemann, *Commentary on Romans*, trans. and ed. G. W. Bromiley (Grand Rapids: Wm. B. Eerdmans, 1980), 95ff.

3. R. Bultmann, *Theology of the New Testament*, trans. K. Grobel, 2 vols. (New York: Charles Scribner's Sons, 1951–55), 1:46–47.

4. *Märtyrer und Gottesknecht*, FRLANT 64, 2d ed. (Göttingen: Vandenhoeck & Ruprecht, 1963), 149, n. 4.

5. K. Wengst, *Christologische Formeln und Lieder des Urchristentums*, SNT 7 (Gütersloh: Gerd Mohn, 1972) 87, points out (correctly) that the continuation of the phrase in v. 23 with a participle in v. 24 is nothing unusual for Paul. According to BDF he actually "loves" to continue with a coordinating participle (or several) after a finite verb (no. 468.1; cf. 2 Cor. 5:12; 7:5; 10:14–15).

6. G. Fitzer, "Der Ort der Versöhnung nach Paulus," *TZ* 22 (1966): 161–83 (here, 165).

7. Ibid., 171.

8. L. Goppelt, "Versöhnung durch Christus," in *Christologie und Ethik. Aufsätze zum Neuen Testament* (Göttingen: Vandenhoeck & Ruprecht, 1968), 147–64 (here, 155).

9. S. Lyonnet and L. Sabourin, *Sin, Redemption, and Sacrifice. A Biblical and Patristic Study*, AnBib 48 (Rome: Biblical Institute, 1970), 162.

10. O. Kuss, *Der Römerbrief. Erste Lieferung*, 2d ed. (Regensburg: Pustet, 1963), 159ff. The view is maintained by Kuss in *Paulus. Die Rolle des Apostels in der theologischen Entwicklung der Urkirche* (Regensburg: Pustet, 1971), 167.

11. H. N. Ridderbos, *Paul: An Outline of his Theology*, trans. J. R. de Witt (Grand Rapids: Wm. B. Eerdmans, 1975), 166ff.

12. Ibid., 167 [de Witt's English translation of Ridderbos' Dutch has been altered slightly to agree with the German translation Stuhlmacher is using, which at points crucial to Stuhlmacher's argument (see n. 63 below) seems truer to the Dutch original—trans.]

13. W. G. Kümmel, "paresis und endeixis. Ein Beitrag zum Verständnis der paulinischen Rechtfertigungslehre," in *Heilsgeschehen und Geschichte*, 2 vols. (Marburg: Elwert, 1965–78), 1:260–70, esp. 267–68.

14. Cf. Lohse, *Märtyrer und Gottesknecht*, 149ff., and Lohse's essay, "Die Gerechtigkeit Gottes in der paulinischen Theologie," in *Die Einheit des Neuen Testaments. Exegetische Studien zur Theologie des Neuen Testaments* (Göttingen: Vandenhoeck & Ruprecht, 1973), 209–27, esp. 220ff.

15. H. Koch, "Römer 3:21–31 in der Paulusinterpretation der letzten 150 Jahre" (doctoral diss.; University of Göttingen, 1971).

16. H. Conzelmann, "Die Rechtfertigungslehre des Paulus: Theologie oder Anthropologie?" in *Theologie als Schriftauslegung. Aufsätze zum NT*, BEvT 65 (Munich: Kaiser, 1974), 191–206; here, 198–99.

17. W. Schrage, "Das Verständnis des Todes Jesu im Neuen Testament," in *Das Kreuz Jesu Christi als Grund des Heils*, ed. F. Viering, 3d ed. (Gütersloh: Gerd Mohn, 1969), 49–89 (here, 78) and Schrage's further essay, "Römer 3:21–26 und die Bedeutung des Todes Jesu Christi bei Paulus," in *Das Kreuz Jesu*, ed. P. Reiger, Forum Heft 12 (Göttingen: Vandenhoeck & Ruprecht, 1969), 65–88, esp. 77ff.

18. Wengst, *Christologische Formeln*, 87ff.

19. G. Delling, *Der Kreuzestod Jesu in der urchristlichen Verkundigung* (Göttingen: Vandenhoeck & Ruprecht, 1972), 12–13. Delling, however, regards only v. 25a (with the exception of *dia pisteōs*) as a pre-Pauline quotation.

20. G. Klein, "Gottes Gerechtigkeit als Thema der neuesten Paulus-Forschung," in *Rekonstruktion und Interpretation. Ges. Aufsätze zum NT*, BEvT 50 (Munich: Kaiser, 1969), 225–36 (here, 230–31).

21. E. Schweizer, "Die 'Mystik' des Sterbens und Auferstehens mit Christus bei Paulus," in *Beiträge zur Theologie des Neuen Testaments. Neutestamentliche Aufsätze, 1955–70* (Zürich: Zwingli-Verlag, 1970), 183–203 (here, 200).

22. U. Wilckens, *Das Neue Testament. Übersetzt und kommentiert von Ulrich Wilckens* (Zürich: Theologischen Verlag, 1971), 508ff.

23. G. Eichholz, *Die Theologie des Paulus im Umriss* (Neukirchen: Neukirchener Verlag, 1972), 190ff. On this book and its interpretation of Röm. 3:24ff. see my article "Theologische Probleme gegenwärtiger Paulusinterpretation," *TLZ* 98 (1973): 721–32, esp. 726ff.

24. Cf. F. Büchsel, *TDNT* 3:319–20. Lyonnet, *Sin, Redemption, and Sacrifice*, 159ff.

25. Cf. A. Deissmann, *"HILASTĒRIOS* und *HILASTĒRION*—eine lexikalische Studie," *ZNW* 4 (1903): 193–212; Büchsel, *TDNT* 3:320; and Lyonnet, *Sin, Redemption, and Sacrifice*, 155ff.

26. Cf. the translation of *kappōret* in Exod. 25:16 (17) with *hilastērion epithema*, 4 Macc. 17:22 (on which see below).

27. *Ant.* 16.182: Herod the Great, because he had desecrated David's tomb, built at the entrance to the tomb a *hilastērion mnēma*, that is, a marble expiatory stele.

28. Cf. Büchsel, *TDNT*, 3:319, and Lyonnet, *Sin, Redemption, and Sacrifice*, 156.

29. Papyrus 337 in B. P. Grenfell, A. S. Hunt, and D. G. Hogarth, *Fayum Towns and their Papyri* (London: Offices of the Egyptian Exploration Fund, 1900), 313.

30. Lohse, *Märtyrer und Gottesknecht*, 151.

31. Ibid.

32. Ibid.

33. Ibid.

34. Ibid., 152.

35. Ibid.

36. So also Eichholz, *Die Theologie des Paulus im Umriss*, 193.

37. The significance for postexilic Israel of the Day of Atonement and the atonement brought about on it can hardly be overestimated. It becomes clear from the principal texts: Leviticus 16; 23:26–32; Num. 29:7–11, as well as from Ecclus. 45:16; 50:5ff., and the Mishnah tractate *Yoma*. Possibly the penitential prayers in the *Manual of Discipline* from Qumran and the praise of the righteousness of God which atoned for and created anew the one who prayed (1QS 11:12ff.) are also to be connected with the tradition and theology of the Day of Atonement, which was also observed by the Essenes. Cf. 1QpHab 11:6ff. and M. Weise, *Kultzeiten und kultischer Bundesschluss in der "Ordenregel" vom Toten Meer*, SPB 3 (Leiden: Brill, 1961), 75–82 and, in addition, H. Bardtke, "Literaturbericht über Qumran. 7. Teil: Die Sektenrolle 1QS," *TRu* 38 (1973/74): 257–91 (here, 282–83). Cf. on this subject also n. 57 below.

38. This conclusion, noted by BDF, nos. 252.2 and 258.2, also escaped W. D. Davies in his analysis of Rom. 3:24ff.; for him the absence of the article is essentially the decisive argument against a direct equation of Christ and the *kappōret (Paul and Rabbinic Judaism,* 4th ed. [Philadelphia: Fortress Press, 1980], 239–40).

39. Hebrews 13:22–24 shows that this Jewish Christianity sees itself to be fully connected to Paul and his disciples.

40. In Rom. 8:3 *peri hamartias,* in accord with the common usage of the LXX, signifies the sacrifice for sin, the Hebrew *hattāt* (cf., for example, Lev. 4:3, 14; 5:6, etc.). Since the same sin offering in the same context can also be designated simply *hamartia* (Lev. 4:21, 24; 5:12; 6:18; etc.), 2 Cor. 5:21 might also be understood, parallel to Rom. 8:3, as saying God made the sinless Jesus a sin offering for us so that we might be justified through him. On both translations in the LXX see Suzanne Daniel, *Recherches sur le vocabulaire du culte dans la "Septante,"* Études et Commentaires 61 (Paris: Klincksieck, 1966), 301ff.

41. Leviticus 16:14. I am following here the understanding of the text found in M. Noth, *Leviticus. A Commentary,* rev. ed., OTL (Philadelphia: Westminster Press, 1977), 123.

42. *M. Yoma* 5:3a, H. Danby, *The Mishnah* (Oxford: Oxford Univ. Press, 1933), 168.

43. So already Eichholz, *Die Theologie des Paulus im Umriss,* 193.

44. H. Leitzmann, *An die Römer,* HNT 8, 5th ed. (Tübingen: Mohr, 1971), 48–50.

45. Kümmel, "Paresis und endeixis," 264.

46. C. H. Dodd, *The Epistle of Paul to the Romans,* Moffatt New Testament Commentaries, 14th ed. (London: Hodder & Stoughton, 1960), 54–55.

47. P. Althaus, *Der Brief an die Römer,* NTD 6, 11th ed. (Göttingen, Vandenhoeck & Ruprecht, 1970), 33–34. Beside this understanding Althaus puts as a second the equation of Jesus with the *kappōret.*

48. Käsemann, "Zum Verständnis von Römer 3:24–26," 99, and *Commentary on Romans,* 97.

49. The Greek text reads: (21) *hōsper antipsychon gegonotas tēs tou ethnous hamartias* (22) *kai dia tou haimatos tōn eusebōn ekeinōn kai tou hilastēriou thanatou autōn, hē theia pronoia ton Israēl prokakōthenta diesōsen.*

50. Lohse, *Märtyrer und Gottesknecht,* 152.

51. H. B. Swete, *The Old Testament in Greek according to the Septuagint,* vol. 3 (Cambridge: Univ. Press, 1912), ad loc (see above, n. 49).

52. A. Deissmann [whose translation, printed in E. F. Kautzsch, *Die Apocryphen und Pseudepigraphen des Alten Testaments,* 2 vols. (Hildesheim: Ohms, 1962), 2:174, is used by Lohse—trans.] gives no justification whatever for his reading. Büchsel, *TDNT* 3:319, n. 7, merely says, "The reading *dia tou hilastēriou tou thanatou autōn* is not to be preferred." Lyonnet, *Sin, Redemption, and Sacrifice,* also follows Alexandrinus without any explanation.

53. Lohse, *Märtyrer und Gottesknecht,* 71, n. 2; here as well it is said about the reading of Sinaiticus, with only a reference to Deissmann and Büchsel (see above, n. 52), that it is "probably to be regarded as secondary."

54. Cf. Lyonnet, 156f.: "it cannot be denied that the vocabulary of that apocryphal book reveals generally quite a Greek coloring and particularly in the quoted passage. Not only must the allusion to 'divine Providence' (similarly in 9:24 and 13:19; in the LXX only [157] in Wis 14:3) be noted, but also the typically Greek word antipsuchon, used, for example, by Lucianus and Dio Chrysostomus instead of the equally typical biblical word antilutron, which is unknown in profane literature. It does help, indeed, to compare the very Jewish narrative of 2 Maccabees 7 (especially verses 37f.) with the same narrative in 4 Macc 6:27f. and 17:20–22. It appears at once that the author of the Fourth Book of Maccabees evolved Jewish notions, evoked in the Second Book of Maccabees by means of a Greek terminology which carried meanings familiar to Greek readers." On the character of 4 Maccabees as a strongly Hellenizing diatribe, cf. L. Rost, *Einleitung in die alttestamentlichen Apokryphen und Pseudepigraphen einschliesslich der grossen Qumran-Handschriften* (Heidelberg: Quelle and Meyer, 1971), 80–82.

55. The same concept emerges in the parallel passage 6:28–29. There the martyr Eleazer prays in the midst of his torture: "Be merciful to your people, and let our punishment suffice for them. (29) Make my blood their purification, and take my life in exchange for theirs" *[hileōs genou tō ethnei sou arkestheis tē hēmeterą autōn dikę. (29) katharsion autōn poiēson to emon haima kai antipsychon autōn labe tēn emēn psychēn].* 4 Maccabees thus combines with martyrdom the concept of vicarious suffering as punishment and penance, a thought entirely foreign to Rom. 3:25–26, into which it can be inserted only by an inappropriate interpretation.

56. In R. H. Charles, *The Apocrypha and Pseudepigrapha of the Old Testament in English,* 2 vols. (Oxford: Clarendon Press, 1964), 2:683; Townshend translates vv. 21–22: "they having as it were become a ransom for our nation's sin; and through the blood of these righteous men and the propiation of their death, the divine Providence delivered Israel that before was evil entreated."

57. So also Wengst, *Christologische Formeln,* 89, n. 10. It is read differently, for example, by J. Jeremias, *Abba* (Göttingen: Vandenhoeck & Ruprecht, 1966), 221 and 327, n. 8. As a correction of his earlier attempt to understand Rom. 3:25 on the basis of Isa. 53:10 (cf. the original version in *TWNT* 5:704, n. 399, with the reworking in *Abba,* 200), he points to the reading of Sinaiticus in 4 Macc. 17:21–22 and wants to understand *hilastērion* there and in Rom. 3:25 as an expiatory sacrifice.

58. Besides the material already presented, it is to be pointed out that in Old Testament and Jewish thought, atonement is seen as offered and given by Yahweh, as in Rom. 3:25–26a; Lev. 17:11; Deut. 21:8; Ps. 65:3; 78:38; 79:9; Jer. 18:23; Ezek. 16:63; 2 Chron. 30:18; Dan. 9:24; *m. Yoma* 3:8d; 4:2e; 6:2b; that the righteousness of God is understood as action that confers salvation and forgiveness: Ps. 65:2–6; Isa. 46:12–13, compared with 43:25 and 44:21–22 as well as 45:8; Dan. 9:16–18; 1QS 11:14; *4 Ezra* 8:36 (here, to be sure, it is already a view that is criticized; cf. W. Harnisch, *Verhängnis und Verheissung der Geschichte,* FRLANT 97 [Göttingen: Vandenhoeck & Ruprecht, 1969], 237–38); and that, finally, in an atonement-and-forgiveness context there can also be reference to the forbearance of God: Exod. 34:6–7; Neh. 9:16–17; 1QH 17:17–18; CD 2:4–5, and D. Zeller, "Sühne und Langmut. Zur Traditionsgeschichte von Röm. 3:24–26," *TP* 43 (1968): 51–75 (here, 64ff.).

59. Lohse, "Gerechtigkeit Gottes," 221.

60. I have for a long time tried to understand Rom. 3:24ff. in dependence on Käsemann and Lohse (cf. *Gerechtigkeit Gottes bei Paulus,* vol. 1, FRLANT 87, 2d ed. [Göttingen: Vandenhoeck & Ruprecht, 1966], 86–87), but I now see in this interpretation difficulties too great to allow me to follow it any longer. In the face of quite sparse

and at times very unsatisfactory Old Testament literature on the topic of atonement and reconciliation, I am greatly indebted to my colleague Hartmut Gese that in a joint seminar on this topic he brought me to a new understanding of the atonement texts in the Old Testament, which are too much neglected by us Protestants, and I can only urgently hope that in the foreseeable future he publishes what he presented there.

61. Thus Klein, "Gottes Gerechtigkeit," 230, n. 12.

62. Lohse, "Gerechtigkeit Gottes," 222: "In full agreement Paul takes up this confession, but he gives it an interpretation that lets what it says come forth with incomparably greater emphasis." Similarly Eichholz, *Theologie des Paulus,* 189–90.

63. Cf. Lohse, "Gerechtigkeit Gottes," 222. I also accept the criticism he offers there of the one-sidedness of my dissertation, but allow myself to call attention to the fact that in this criticism Lohse has not paid any attention to my attempt to sharpen and correct my own view, published long before he wrote his article, in "The End of the Law" (chap. 8 in this volume; see esp. p. 149, n. 28 and p. 151, n. 39). Of greater theological importance than such understandable roadblocks in collegial conversation is, of course, the fact, also stressed by Lohse, that neither the tradition nor Paul himself sees the righteousness of God as a punitive power demanding expiation. This latter idea, stressed for the tradition by Bultmann, *Theology of the New Testament,* 1:46, and H. Thyen, *Studien zur Sündenvergebung,* FRLANT 96 (Göttingen: Vandenhoeck & Ruprecht, 1970), 165, and actually extended to Paul himself by Ridderbos, *Paul,* has nothing to do with our text but grows out of late patristic and orthodox dogmatics.

64. The high priest, who on the Day of Atonement made atonement first for himself and then, once reconciled, for the people, comes forth from the Holy of Holies, according to Ecclus. 50:5, as *doxastheis,* that is, as a transformed new creation, and is pictured in vv. 5ff. almost with messianic attributes.

65. By virtue of the atonement on the Day of Atonement the Israelites are regarded in rabbinic tradition as new creations (cf. Str-B 2:422), and even glorious statements about the expiation and new creation of the pious in 1QS 11:13ff. and 1QH 3:19ff. appear to belong in Leviticus 16's wider sphere of influence (see above, n. 37). The material presented by J. Jeremias, *Infant Baptism in the First Four Centuries,* trans. D. Cairns (Philadelphia: Westminster Press, 1960), 32ff., also shows, of course, how the idea of new creation could be separated from its original cultic context and connected with the tradition about repentance and conversion in general.

CHAPTER 7

The Law as
a Topic
of Biblical Theology[1]

Hans Hübner has recently called attention to the fact that the topic "law," highly controverted to this moment in Old Testament, New Testament, and systematic theology, is a fundamental topic of biblical theology.[2] Hübner leaves open the question of how the Old and New Testaments are to be related to one another in the context of biblical theology, also excludes early Judaism from his deliberations, and confines himself to the question: "Which aspect of the Old Testament law or which understanding, perhaps also which misunderstanding of this law, is the object of theological reflection at each point in the course of New Testament tradition?"[3] We can get beyond the difficulties that arise with a perspective encompassing so long a period of time if we follow Gerhard Ebeling's suggestion, well established in the history of theology, that a biblical theology in which an account should be given of the understanding of the biblical witness as a whole demands in "the contemporary theological situation . . . the intensive co-operation of Old and New Testament scholars."[4] Where the chance for such cooperative work exists, the prevailing points of controversy about the law are by no means resolved, but this cooperation guards against the shortening of perspectives that threatens to occur from an approach proceeding only from the Old or only from the New Testament. Since a narrowing of perspective and the formalization of the items under investigation are fundamental problems particularly in the secondary New Testament literature on the topic of the law, the cooperation appropriately demanded by Ebeling can be a special help to New Testament scholars when they strive to give an accurate presentation on the problem of the law.

With respect to the following theses and elucidations, I owe Hartmut Gese special thanks. In 1976 at a meeting of the Biblical Theology Task Force of the Wissenschaftliche Gesellschaft für Theologie at Bethel, Gese read a paper on the topic "law" from an Old Testament perspective.[5] He advocated a con-

---

For Walther Zimmerli on his Seventieth Birthday

cept there that in a highly independent way ties together and advances the two discussions of the understanding of the law in the Old Testament that are in my opinion especially valuable for New Testament scholars, the presentations of Gerhard von Rad[6] and Walther Zimmerli.[7] Gese thereby extricates New Testament exegetes from the danger of having to choose between von Rad and Zimmerli. The choice is: Shall one, following von Rad's masterful interpretation oriented to the Decalogue and Deuteronomy, see in the law at any given time the whole of Yahweh's will revealed to Israel; pursue with him a succession of reinterpretations of the law through Israel's history; but finally, take in the bargain the need to speak of a radical reinterpretation occurring in the New Testament texts? This reinterpretation "goes farther back than Judaism and links up with the practice of the prophets," which means, however, that "the Old Testament Law as such often cannot keep up with its new Christian interpretation, and that it does not seem of itself to yield the interpretation given it by Christian understanding."[8] Or shall one side with Zimmerli's essentially more theologically precise presentation? That would mean seeing in the law a "command" accompanying and guarding the covenant Yahweh made with his people, which "has the power to push the person or the whole people of Israel outside the covenant."[9] A survey of the history of interpretation of the phenomenon of the law in the Old Testament that follows Zimmerli would lay heavier stress on the atonement tradition in P and on the announcement of the eschatological torah and the new covenant found in Jer. 31:33–34 and Isa. 2:1ff. and would then see the fulfilment of that announcement in the appearance of Jesus.[10] If one agrees with Gese, it is the task of the New Testament theologian, before making any theological judgments or choices, first to take into account the complex whole in the formation of the Old Testament tradition, and only in the light of this whole to ask where and how the basic interpretive decisions were made by Jesus and Paul and in the Gospel of John. I accept this challenge, and in that regard I share Gese's opinion that in a discussion of the primary issues of biblical theology it makes no sense historically to put only the so-called Masoretic canon of the "Old Testament" in relationship to the New Testament Scriptures. At the time of the origin of the New Testament Scriptures the Old Testament was completely open, and comprised in addition to the writings contained in the present Masoretic canon also the great wisdom traditions and the collections of apocalyptic traditions.[11]

In what follows I have an overarching concern with the fundamental question, important for biblical theology, whether and how far the principal New Testament statements about the law can be regarded as biblical in the light of the whole Old Testament tradition. In order to keep my presentation clear and within the desired brevity, I summarize it in a set of theses, which I elaborate one by one.

1. Biblically the question of the law is the question of the way of life *(Lebensordnung)* revealed and set down by God for Israel and the nations of the world.

With this thesis I attempt to do justice to a threefold task. We must discover, first of all, the basic intention of the tremendously complex terminology about the law in the Old and New Testaments as well as in Judaism in the biblical era. This terminology extends from the individual "precept" in priestly and wisdom material to the cosmic universal law in Sirach 24; from the ten "words" of the Decalogue through Psalm 119 to the examples of so-called early Jewish "torah ontology" assembled by Martin Hengel;[12] but it also includes a direct or a transferred use of *nomos* by Paul, in James, and in the Apostolic Fathers. The expression "way of life" does justice most adequately to this widely diverse way of speaking and at the same time guards against the formalization and abstraction that is usual in respect to the law (in the New Testament).

The expression "way of life" attempts, second, to do justice to the fact that in the Old Testament as well as in New Testament and Jewish texts we are always dealing with a manifestation that encompasses God's entire will for humanity's whole existence, which can be followed but also violated, fulfilled but also despised. Accordingly, "signs of the blessed life" *(Lebenswohlordnung)* and "warning signs along life's way" *(Lebensanordnung)*—the terms are Eberhard Jüngel's—curse and blessing, are included in the way of life in the law.

It is true of this complex way of life, third, that it is understood as something revealed equally in Old and New Testament texts: in it God reveals his will to the whole people, to the congregation, and to the individual within them and thereby makes accessible to those addressed a way of life that these addressees could not come to on their own but that they rather are to see as something disclosed to and demanded of them. I am certainly aware that with the suggested definition decisions are made, and yet I don't see that these decisions could be avoided in the light of the biblical and Jewish texts we have.

2. In the Old Testament we can see not only diverse lines of tradition with respect to the understanding of the law but also a historical sequence of stages of increasing experience with the law.

With the help of tradition-historical analysis we can today point to lines of tradition with respect to the understanding of the law in the Old (and in the New) Testament, which point, for example, from the Decalogue to Deuteronomy and from there to Psalms 1, 19, and 119 and to the wisdom perspective on the law that comes into view in Sirach 24 as well as in Baruch 3 and 4; or from Ezekiel to P and back to Sirach 24. (There is an analogous situation in the New Testament, where clear lines of tradition go from Jesus to the Stephen-circle and from there to Paul, or from law-observant Jewish Christianity in Palestine to James and the Gospel of Matthew as well as to the famous formulation in *Barn.* 2:6, according to which the "way of life" provided for Christians no longer consists in the cultic laws about sacrifice but in the *kainos nomos tou kyriou Iēsou Christou, aneu zygou anankēs ōn* ["new law of our Lord Jesus Christ, which is free of the yoke of necessity"]). As von Rad already saw with his reference to the qualitative difference between the law perspective of the Decalogue, of preexilic judgment prophecy, of Deuteronomy, and then of the P tradition, the substance of these lines of tradition is understood only when exegesis also illuminates the historical and religious experiences that accompany and evoke the various stages in the interpretation of the law. This demand on biblical exegesis, advocated equally today by Gese, Hans Heinrich Schmid[13] (and for the New Testament above all by Ulrich Luck[14]), and rejected, in my opinion too hastily, by Hans-Joachim Kraus,[15] can only be fulfilled methodologically when the individual texts are not detached from the historical situation in which they arose but are understood in the context of this situation as an expression of a particular experience of the world and encounter with God. If one interprets in this fundamental way, this correlative way that goes beyond mere text-bound or context-oriented exegesis, one moves with Gese beyond von Rad and Zimmerli to the stages of experience with the law named in the following thesis.

3. This series of stages begins with Israel's experience of being chosen by Yahweh at Sinai to a way of life that is today exemplary, a way of life comprehended in the Decalogue; on the basis of prophetic preaching about judgment this very way of life is understood in Deuteronomy as a way of life of the believing community of Israel; then in the P tradition, building on Ezekiel, there is an understanding of the law as an ordering of Israel's encounter with Yahweh's holiness; finally, the Deuteronomic and the priestly understandings of the law form the basis of the discovery that emerges in the postexilic period, that in its Torah Israel participates in the creative wisdom of God and thereby in the order of creation for the whole cosmos.

If one recognizes these stages, not only does the tremendous complexity of the Old Testament understanding of the law become clear but also it becomes comprehensible how Israel, in the grasp of the revelation of Yahweh's will that would not let this people go, evolved to a form of belief by which it not only coped with the severest historical catastrophes, the loss of political independence and expulsion from their religious home, but also masterfully overcame the problems that were posed for Israel in the Hellenistic era. If we turn our attention from the Decalogue to the comprehensive sapiential understanding of the law in Sirach 24, we see that the all-encompassing view of life lived under Yahweh that already characterized the Decalogue was by no means lost in the postexilic period but instead was expanded universally. The conception of the ordering of the world that emerges in Job 28, Baruch 3—4, and Sirach 24 not only enables the Jew to rest in Yahweh's will in every place in the (ancient) world and in every particular life situation, but also explicitly incorporates even the nonhuman creation into Yahweh's ordering will. The identification of torah and wisdom in the postexilic period has under these circumstances a definite world-opening, life-affirming meaning and should no longer be misunderstood today as an abandonment of the original faith in Yahweh. Anthropologically, the sapiential widening of the understanding of the torah is supported by the view that humanity, as God's creation and by virtue of the forgiveness (constantly renewed cultically) of their guilt, is fully able to remain in the way of life disclosed to and demanded of them by Yahweh (cf. Ecclus. 15:11–20; 21:11). We should, of course, immediately note that this very understanding was by no means unopposed in the Old Testament itself.

4. The revolutionary expansions of the way the law was experienced were accompanied in general by a growing awareness of the failure of the nation, the community of faith, and the individual in their existence before Yahweh. This very awareness corresponds to the insight into the human need for renewal and into the provisionality of the law of Moses from Sinai, an insight that emerged repeatedly from Jeremiah and Ezekiel on.

In the judgment preaching of the classical prophets of judgment it already becomes clear that no sphere of life may be kept from Yahweh, and that where this nevertheless happens, guilt arises and a broken existence is revealed. This broken existence before Yahweh is experienced, as Isaiah 6 already shows, all the more intensely the more clearly people see themselves standing before the majesty and holiness of God. This very experience of sin (embracing the whole people, the faithful community, and the individual Israelite within them) leads in Jeremiah and the prophet-priest Ezekiel to a radical anthropological and theological insight about the law. In order to be able really to fulfill the will of Yahweh and encounter God, Israel and the individual pious person need a new creation. But even the Torah revealed at Sinai, Israel's way of life, according to (Jeremiah and) Ezekiel bears marks of historical provisionality and of a deficiency that makes it once again in need of change. Instead of simply leading to life, the Torah from Sinai by virtue of its very words leads to involvement with guilt from which only a new creation can deliver. Israel and the individual pious person will be able truly to encounter Yahweh only when this people and every individual believer are changed and created anew by the Spirit of God, and even the Torah is revealed anew. The most distinctive evidence for this thoroughly daring conception is, on the one hand, Jer. 31:31ff. and, on the other hand, Ezek. 36:22–28; 37 as well as the critical survey of the history of revelation in Ezekiel 20 (cf. especially vv. 25–26[16]).

5. The Torah from Sinai, according to Isaiah, Micah, Jeremiah, and Ezekiel, is moving toward an eschatological transformaion and new revelation. This new revelation applies first to Israel, but according to Micah and the Isaiah tradition it also includes the gentile world. Insofar as the new revelation goes forth from Zion, one can speak of an eschatological "Zion torah" that corresponds eschatologically to the Torah from Sinai.

The texts to be cited in connection with this thesis, Isa. 2:2–4; Mic. 4:1–4; Isa. 25:7–9; Jer. 31:31ff.; Ezekiel 20; 36:22–28; 40—48, etc. naturally come, first of all, from diverse periods and situations. But they combine into a comprehensive concept all the more clearly the more one reads them as common elements of tradition in the one prophetic canon. Jeremiah 31:31–34 speaks most clearly about the transformation and new eschatological revelation of the Sinai Torah to a people of God renewed to spontaneous obedience. The context of this chapter links this new revelation with the announcement of the reestablishment of Jerusalem (cf. Jer. 31:38ff.). Isa. 2:2–4 and Mic. 4:1–4 speak of eschatological instruction for all nations going forth from Zion. According to the apocalyptic expectation of Isa. 25:6ff., one day the nations shall assemble on Zion for the eschatological *todah* meal [*toda-Mahl*; the *todah* is a thank offering, which has its cultic setting in a celebrative meal (cf. Gese, *Essays on Biblical Theology,* 82, 128–39)—trans.] possessing full knowledge of God and freed from the sentence of death. With this, Isa. 2:2–4 (and Mic. 4:1–4) have reached their goal. Ezekiel 20 in vv. 25–26 indicates the ghastly provisionality of the Sinai Torah, but also looks for a time of the new knowledge of Yahweh and of the new obedience of Israel to the true will of Yahweh. This looking once again concentrates on Zion (cf. Ezek. 20:40ff.). Ezekiel 36 continues this theme and designates Israel's renewal to genuine obedience to the revealed will of God as a work of the Holy Spirit. The constitutional model contained in Ezekiel 40—48 goes beyond the Sinai Torah, in some respects markedly so, and definitively makes Jerusalem and the new temple the place of Yahweh's presence on earth. If one considers the convergences in what all these texts are saying, it is possible to speak with Gese of the expectation of an eschatological "Zion torah" that corresponds eschatologically to the Torah from Sinai. This eschatological torah is not simply identical with the Sinai Torah. It goes forth not from Sinai but from Zion, the eschatological dwelling of God. Because of the gift of the Spirit and the destruction of death this torah is to be of itself clear and livable. In its midst stands the *todah,* the thank offering after rescue from the peril of death. The torah that goes forth from Zion no longer applies to Israel alone, nor separates them, the people of God, from the Gentiles, but is directed to all nations. Since in this way the First Commandment comes to be observed perfectly and universally, the Zion torah brings to eschatological completion what was expressed in the Sinai Torah only in historical provisionality.

6. In the todah piety of many psalms, the Zion torah is already experienced as Yahweh's present claim on humanity.

We know from Judaism and the New Testament, especially with regard to the eschatological treasures of salvation, the mode of experience and expression according to which God's eschatological Spirit, the reign of God, the grace and joy of the eschaton, etc., are experienced as breaking in already at this time and as shaping the present, and yet are to attain their full reality only in the future. This anticipatory structure of language and experience is also characteristic of the Old Testament. It is essential not only for an understanding of the prophetic proclamation of the word but also, as Gese has shown in his essay on Psalm 50, for the encounter with the Zion torah. The suppliant in Psalm 50 knows that in the *todah,* that is, in the total self-surrender to Yahweh in the context of the thank offering, one can break through the barriers of ritually prescribed obedience and already in the present participate in that will of Yahweh whose revelation from Zion shall one day fill and shape the whole world. The content of this will of Yahweh can be discerned by a new interpretation of the Decalogue.

7. **The understanding of the Torah from Sinai as a comprehensive, eternal order of creation and the dialectic of a provisional Sinai Torah and an eschatological Zion torah are not reconciled systematically in the course of the development of Old Testament tradition.**

The understanding of the law in the priestly writings—an understanding that orients the life of faith on earth to the heavenly archetype of what has been revealed and grounds it in the miracle of the atonement established by Yahweh (on the Day of Atonement)—can no more be identified with the Deuteronomic understanding than the expectation (and present experience) of the Zion torah can simply be identified with the wide stream of tradition that flows from the Decalogue to Deuteronomy and from there over Psalm 119 to Sirach 24 and Baruch 3 and 4. In Sirach 24 and Baruch 3 and 4 participation in the eternal and true order of creation is already awaited from the Sinai Torah. According to the traditions that speak of the Zion torah, such participation is possible only when the Sinai revelation is completed from Zion. Under these circumstances we must say that the Old Testament understanding of the law remains in contention into the late stages of the tradition.

8. **Early Judaism does not solve the systematic problem of the dialectic between the Sinai Torah and the eschatological Zion torah. Although the eschatological texts are handed on and the Qumran community even knows an eschatological expansion of the Sinai Torah, the primary intention of early Jewish theology of the law lies in the endeavor to portray the Torah of Moses as the ground of all being and of the entire life of faith before Yahweh.**

Concerned since the Maccabean period with the religious identity of Israel and of Jewish faith in God, early Judaism in Palestine and in the Diaspora joins the mainstream of the sapiential interpretation of the law that culminates in Sirach 24 and in Baruch 3 and 4. All existence, all thought, and the whole life of faith are assigned to the Torah of Moses as the eternally valid life-creating revelation of God. In the *Book of Jubilees* (second century B.C.E.) this happens in such a way that a distinction is made between the first torah (2:24; 6:22), which regulated the world already in its primal condition in paradise, and the Torah first revealed to Moses on Sinai. The "first torah" contains the order of creation that culminates in the establishment of the Sabbath. It is incorporated into the law entrusted to Moses on Sinai, in which all periods of time until the day of the new creation are traced out. On that day God will erect his sanctuary on Zion and appear to the whole world as the holy one. In *Jubilees* 1 the promise of Ezek. 36:22–28 is applied to the renewal of the righteous to full obedience to the torah and to a true knowledge of God which is associated with the day of new creation.

This also happens in the *Manual of Discipline* from Qumran (cf. 1QS 4:19ff.). The Essenes from Qumran expand the Torah and the Prophets through their own inspired scriptures.[17] Indeed, in their Temple Scroll they possess (according to information from Yigael Yadin) "the sealed book of the law that was in the ark" (CD 5:2–3), that is, a supplementary revelation to the Torah from Sinai, spoken by Yahweh himself. But there is no reference among them to a new eschatological torah.

The early Pharisaism that Paul then confronts with the crucified and risen Christ does not stand far from the way of thinking we have sketched out. As is already true of *Jubilees,* this Pharisaism stresses the primal creation of the torah and speaks in *Psalms of Solomon* 17 and 18 of the fact that the Messiah will restore Israel to true fear of God (which, in fact, means leading her to obedience to the eternally valid torah) and cleanse Jerusalem of all uncleanness. But there is no talk of a change of the torah itself.

The rabbis in the post–New Testament period carry the line of this one-sided evaluation of the Sinai Torah further. For the time of eschatological fulfillment they await "not a *new* torah . . . , but the perfect and final understanding of the existing one."[18]

Esteem for the Sinai Torah as the eternal revelation of God is also characteristic of Diaspora Judaism. Philo's allegorizations of the Torah are intended to integrate the entire intellectual cosmos of antiquity with the Torah and not to assimilate the Torah to this cosmos. In *Migr.* 89—93 he expressly resists attempts to sublimate or even to nullify the Torah with the aid of symbolic interpretations.

With this early Jewish interpretive direction, which naturally always had to carry along with it that anthropological compromise already discussed above (cf. esp. *m. 'Abot* 2:1d; 3:1,15), the biblical statements about the Zion torah cannot, of course, be thought to be taken care of. Rather, there is articulated in them an expectation of a new, spiritual-eschatological way of life for all people that is only partially brought in, in part actually suppressed, by the early Jewish exegetes.

9. The understanding of the law in the Old Testament (which was not yet canonically delimited in the first century C.E.) and in early Judaism—an understanding that was open and in dispute—forms the linguistic and experiential base from which all New Testament theology of the law begins.

If we move from the Old Testament, which at the turn of the eras and in the first century C.E. was not yet delimited in a fixed canon, and from the early Jewish traditions to the New Testament, first of all a very elementary historical fact is to be noted. Jesus and the leading New Testament witnesses were born Jews and for them the Old Testament (that is, the Torah, fixed since the fifth century B.C.E., the canon of Prophets, since the third century B.C.E., likewise clearly defined, and the not yet firmly fixed collection of "writings") was Holy Scripture. Under these circumstances one may assume that the Old Testament theology of the law, in itself open, together with the early Jewish exegetical traditions we have just sketched briefly, provide the linguistic and experiential base from which discussion of the law in the New Testament proceeds. This linguistic and experiential base is decisive in a twofold sense. First, in the language and interpretive tradition of Israel the New Testament witnesses inherited a particular kind of world view and a particular pattern of experience with which they articulated their faith. Second, this very world view, inherited from the Old Testament, also appeared to them to be religiously definitive because it was disclosed by the sacred Scripture, and the Old Testament remained the revelatory record also for Christians. Under these circumstances Old and New Testament are not separable from one another, neither tradition-historically nor theologically, although the proper interpretation of the Old Testament has been in dispute between Jews and Christians since the time of Jesus. This interpretation is expressed both by recourse to certain individual passages and with reference to the biblical language pattern as a whole.

10. Jesus' understanding of the law can be read most clearly from the tradition of the double command to love God and your neighbor, from the so-called antitheses in the Sermon on the Mount, from the saying about clean and unclean (Mark 7:15 par.), and from his claim to have authority over the Sabbath.

If, at the threshold of the New Testament, we first ask about Jesus' handling of the law, we must, given the way New Testament research operates today, seek those traditions in which this handling is mirrored authentically. The selectivity which that requires dare not obscure the fact that Jesus' handling of the law was embedded in the testimony his whole life gave. Every individual saying of Jesus about the law must therefore be interpreted against the whole of his activity for the reign of God in the spirit of sonship. Only if we interpret in this comprehensive way do we have in view the reality that Jesus saw in the torah. The tradition about the double command to love God and your neighbor (Mark 12:28–34; Matt. 22:34–40; Luke 10:25–28) is authentic[19] and characteristic of Jesus in that the double command here is no longer only (as in the *Testaments of the Twelve Patriarchs* and in Philo)[20] an illustrative summary of the will of God that is accessible only in the torah as a whole; with Jesus the will of God is exclusively concentrated in this double command. On the basis of this double command the Mosaic Torah can be evaluated critically by Jesus and, where that appears necessary to him, he can go behind it to seek God's original intention. The antitheses in the Sermon on the Mount make this process clear. It is true that the famous saying about clean and unclean in Mark 7:15; Matt. 15:11 actually pulls the Pharisaic ideal of levitical purity in the everyday life of the Jews off it hinges. But in that regard the saying is biblical and also establishes the authentic original will of God as Jesus understood it, as Jesus here carries out a process completely analogous to that in Psalm 50. Jesus goes behind the Pharisaic purity regulations for the sake of getting people to submit completely to the will of God (cf. Mark 7:13). This repeated reaching back on Jesus' part to the genuine original will of God (cf. Mark 10:2–12 par.) does not really become clear without Jesus' claim to be "Lord of the Sabbath" (Mark 2:28; Matt. 12:8; Luke 6:5). The background for this claim is the esteem for the Sabbath, in evidence starting with the P tradition and once again expressly affirmed in

Jubilees, as that special sanctified day on which Israel is already able on earth to participate in the holy condition the world knew at the beginning and shall know in the future. From the background of this way of thinking Jesus' claim of lordship over the Sabbath reveals no mere antinomianism. Rather it means that with Jesus' ostentatious healings on the sabbath, with his word of forgiveness, and in the freedom he grants his disciples on the Sabbath, that holy order of existence is inauguarated on earth that hitherto had been regarded as a mark of the eternal world of God. Jesus claimed, in other words, the authority to bring by his words and deeds eschatological salvation to the world estranged from God (on this see also the aprocryphon in the D text of Luke 6:5). With this claim then is also unearthed the comprehensive spiritual reality in which Jesus' individual statements about the torah have their place.

11. The critique, deepening, and focusing of the law that appear together in Jesus become most readily understandable if Jesus appeared with the claim that as the Son of man/Messiah inaugurating the eschatological reign of God he was also the messianic fulfiller of the torah. In and with Jesus the eschatological reality of the Zion torah is made manifest.

In our context I would like to indicate briefly and in a thetical way that Jesus himself, the testimony about his ministry and his death in Jerusalem, and the development of the Jesus tradition are historically understandable to me only if Jesus actually came making a messianic claim and if he put forward that claim under the sign of the title that in like measure related him to God and humanity—the title Son of man. The combination of the Son of man and Messiah traditions was transmitted to Jesus indirectly by the Enoch tradition and directly by the proclamation of the Baptist.[21] But even if some cannot bring themselves to this historical perspective and want to remain with the fragmentary thesis of Ernst Käsemann,[22] Günther Bornkamm,[23] and Eduard Lohse,[24] according to which Jesus, although claiming no messianic title for himself, nevertheless came forward with unique messianic authority, Jesus' handling of the law must be related to this very authority claim. We can do this biblically very well if we recall the Old Testament expectation of the Zion torah. On the basis of this expectation one can understand Jesus' criticism of the law of Moses and the establishment of the genuine original will of God by the power of the Spirit that followed on its heels as a unified process. Jesus establishes the eschatological will of God which characterizes the reign of God and involves all those for whom the reign of God is inaugurated through him. Jesus' table fellowship can without difficulty be related to this process of setting up the eschatological will of God. As *1 Enoch* 62:14–15 shows, this table fellowship anticipates on earth the heavenly table and reconciliation fellowship in which the Son of man will one day stand with those who are righteous before God. Jesus' table fellowship finds its earthly seal as Jesus, at the last Passover meal with his followers, declares his willingness, translated into an actuality on the next day, to go to death to attain unending communion with God for the poor and guilt-laden entrusted to him by God. The Synoptic Lord's Supper texts and the Pauline tradition on the Lord's Supper in 1 Cor.

11:23ff. see in this substitutionary surrender of Jesus' life the eschatological fulfilment of Exod. 24:8 and Jer. 31:31ff. Thus one can say that in and with Jesus the eschatological way of life of the reign of God, the "Zion torah," is revealed. At the same time it becomes clear why Judaism at that time could under no circumstances accept, but rather perceived as blasphemous, Jesus' claim to be the fulfiller of the torah (cf. the saying in Matt. 5:17, redactionally reworked, it's true, by Matthew, but in my opinion to be traced to Jesus himself, and the so-called transfiguration story that refers to the completion of the Law and the Prophets in Jesus' person and word).

12. The content of the new way of life inaugurated and demanded by Jesus is characterized by the righteousness of God, which helps those apart from God to find in Jesus' person life in communion with God and thus puts them in the freedom of love.

If one asks wherein the eschatological way of life inaugurated and demanded by Jesus has its thematic center, one can only answer with two biblical words, in righteousness and love. The category of righteousness suggests itself biblically as soon as one attempts to relate to one another Jesus' help for the weak and disfranchised, his concern for children and the sick, the Beatitudes, which stand under the sign of Isa. 61:1ff., and his proclamation of the reign of God in the parables, all viewed in the light of the messianic claim made for his mission. A look at the great messianic traditions in the Old Testament, above all Isa. 9:1–6 and 11:1–9, then makes the word "righteousness" unavoidable (as a messianic way of acting that brings the world separated from God under God's order of salvation). The word "love" is brought to mind by the double command, by the sixth antithesis (Matt. 5:43–48; Luke 6:27–28, 32–36) and by Jesus' great parables about love (esp. Luke 15:11–32 and 10:27–37). In his person Jesus was the embodiment of the righteousness and love of God and for that very reason he demanded of his disciples the practice of love and of the new righteousness.

13. By his testimony to and emblematic actualization of the new way of life in righteousness Jesus risked conflict with all influential Jewish groups of his time. At the climax of this conflict he was put under the curse of the Mosaic law and crucified.

The facts with which this thesis deals are in plain view. Jesus' claim that as proclaimer of the reign of God he was also the messianic fulfiller of the torah led him into a fundamental conflict with the Pharisaism of his time. His refusal to share the Zealots' understanding of the First Commandment and to let himself be made the religious spearhead of the war of liberation against Rome earned him the Zealots' animosity. The Sadducees became Jesus' enemies as he began to shake not only the authority of the Mosaic Torah but also the cultic regulations of the temple. Under the accusation, cleverly chosen in the light of Jesus' ministry, that he was a messianic pretender, Jesus after his arrest was handed over by the Sanhedrin to Pilate, by whom he was crucified after a short trial. The execution of Jesus on the cross fully gave Jesus' ene-

mies the possibility of putting him, the blasphemer and betrayer of the tradition of the faith of Israel, under the curse of the Torah as it is stated in Deut.
21:22–23. The Temple Scroll from Qumran (col. 64:6–13) today shows clearly
that pre-Christian Judaism already applied Deut. 21:22–23 to the execution of
Jewish lawbreakers and interpreted the death of such apostates from the faith
as a curse by God and humanity. The interpretation of Jesus' death in the light
of Deut. 21:22–23, which can be seen in John 19:31ff.; Acts 5:30; 10:39;
13:19; and Gal. 3:13 might well not be, therefore, only of Christian origin. It
appears rather to be a Jewish polemical thesis which the Christians up to Paul
found hard to refute.

**14. Early Christians understood Jesus' resurrection as a vindication of the
crucified one by God. It was experienced by those who forsook Jesus on the
night of his betrayal, who doubted him or even fought against him, as a read-
mission or new admission, proceeding from the Risen One, into the community of reconciliation.**

If one goes from the death of Jesus under the curse pronounced by the
Mosaic Torah to the New Testament texts that speak of Jesus' resurrection and
his appearance to the Easter witnesses, these texts reveal at least two fundamental experiences. Christologically it is said, according to Acts 2:36, that
God made the very Jesus whom his enemies crucified Lord and Christ. The
Christ hymns of Phil. 2:6–11 and 1 Tim. 3:16 describe the resurrection of
Jesus as his enthronement and as "vindication," that is, Jesus' installation into
his heavenly prerogatives as Son. When Paul sees the crucified one as "Lord"
and "Son of God" (1 Cor. 9:1; Gal. 1:15–16) the cursed one from the cross
appears instead as the Son attested by God and invested with the Old Testament name of God, "Lord" = *kyrios*.

The appearance stories show even more. Here not only is Jesus seen as the
one whom God eschatologically vindicated after his shameful death on the
cross, but the experience is also stated (in narrative form) that this Jesus
reestablished with the witnesses of his appearance that community of reconciliation that is symbolized for Israel in eating together. The resurrection witnesses know themselves to be taken anew through Jesus, the Risen One, into
the state of shalom with God which they themselves violated by betrayal or
even by fighting against the Christian faith.

**15. While the interpretation of the death and resurrection of Jesus as an aton-
ing and reconciling event was common property for early Christians on the
basis of these experiences, varied consequences were drawn from the death
and resurrection of Jesus in respect to the law.**

The Easter experiences we have outlined, which in my view are the foundation of and catalyst for the early Christian theology of mission and, before
that, the foundation of all faith in Jesus as "Lord" and "Messiah," are articulated soteriologically in an exemplary fashion in language about Jesus' atoning
death. This language runs from the Jerusalem beginnings through the entire
New Testament tradition, and in the early Christian celebration of the Lord's

Supper it is in symbolic reality both experienced and proclaimed. Despite all the differences between the Synoptics, Paul, and the Gospel of John, one can speak of a common early Christian tradition also with respect to the Lord's Supper. It is, on the other hand, different with the question of what consequences Jesus' death and resurrection have for the Christian life under and with the Mosaic Torah. That this question will indeed be answered differently becomes clear the moment one considers the controversial outcome of the Old Testament theology of the law and, in addition, Jesus' own dialectical way of dealing with the Mosaic Torah, with which he associated himself in the double command but which he also criticized and went behind. Under these tradition-historical circumstances one could press toward both a synthesis, reflected on christologically, of faith in Christ and obedience to the Mosaic Torah, and a dialectic on the law, also reflected on christologically, worked out completely from an Easter perspective in discipleship to Jesus, without abrogating the Old Testament as Holy Scripture. In the one case, beginning with Christ one followed the understanding of the law climaxing in Sirach 24 and Baruch 3 and 4 and applied Jesus' claim to be the fulfiller of the torah only to a christological modification of the Sinai Torah. In the other case, one adhered more strongly to the traditions pointing to the Zion torah and saw oneself supported in this position by Jesus' criticism of the Pharisees and the temple as well as the Easter events. In the New Testament from early on we find both kinds of Christian theology of the law present and in conflict with one another.

16. Significant groups of early Christians attempt a synthesis of the Mosaic Torah and faith in Christ; its touchstone is the command of love, understood radically and universally on the basis of Jesus' behavior. Today this synthesis is most clearly recognizable in the Gospel of Matthew and in James.

In the history of early Christianity efforts at such a synthesis can be seen from the earliest period. The predominantly Aramaic-speaking part of the primitive Jerusalem community that remained in association with Israel went this way. At the Apostolic Council this way is defended, militantly by the "false brethren" (Gal. 2:4) hostile to Antioch's law-free mission to the Gentiles, conciliatorily by James and the Jerusalem "pillars" (Gal. 2:9). As the polemics in Paul's letters and in Acts 21:15ff. show, both groups accompany and criticize Paul's missionary way to its end. In the Gospel of Matthew and in James the effort at a synthesis finds its historically most potent canonical manifestation to this day. In both documents the way of a gentile mission without circumcision is in my opinion expressly affirmed, and by appeal to Jesus a Christian way of life is taught that is obedient to the will of God as it is revealed in the Mosaic Torah and interpreted by Jesus through an eschatological focus on the radical command of love.

According to Matthew, Jesus fulfills the Mosaic Torah in his work and sacrificial way and also instructs those who are his, following his example, to fulfill this very Torah in such a way that the righteousness of Christians is better than the formal righteousness of the Pharisees and scribes. The rigoristic tradition of Matt. 5:18–19 (in which historically one may suspect not the voice of Jesus but probably that of an early Christian legalism like that the "false brethren" advocated), which was not originally in conformity with the intention of the Gospel of Matthew, was incorporated by the evangelist into his own agenda as he wrote Matt. 5:17-20, probably because he had to defend his gospel on two fronts, against the charge of antinomianism, directed against him and other early Christian communities from the side of the synagogue, and also against a Christian abrogation of the law that could arise above all in the wake of Pauline theology.[25]

The Mosaic Torah fulfilled by Jesus and reinterpreted by him in the sense of a radical love for the neighbor is called in James (in accord with Old Testament and Jewish wisdom theology) the "royal law" or the "law of freedom" (James 2:8, 12).[26] With these expressions James, from a Christian perspective, links up with the extolling of the Mosaic Torah as we find it artfully elaborated, for example, in Psalm 119.

This synthesizing form of the Christian understanding of the law which takes off from the Gospel of Matthew and the letter of James has become extremely influential in the church's history. *Barnabas* 2:6 stands clearly in this line.

17. Other groups in early Christianity understand the relationship between the Mosaic Torah and faith in Christ in an essentially more dialectical way. With Jesus' substitutionary giving of his life they regard the institution of cultic atonement in the temple as fulfilled and superseded. In Jesus' mission, death, and resurrection the time of the new covenant's "obligation" and of the eschatological torah has begun. The time has also come in which even the non-Israelites may be assembled under the rule of Jesus as "Lord." This line of thought can be seen most clearly today in the traditions of the Stephen-circle and in the Epistle to the Hebrews.

The possibility of the dialectical perspective on the law sketched above is realized first in the Stephen-circle, with explicit appeal to Jesus' criticism of law and temple (cf. Acts 6:13-14). The mission of the Stephen-circle to Samaria and even to a eunuch, described in Acts 8, appears to be inspired by Isa. 56:1ff.[27] After the martyrdom of Stephen it finds its actual center in Antioch on the Orontes and gains world prominence finally through Paul. If, as I believe, Rom 3:25-26[28] and 1 Cor. 11:23ff. are characteristic of the thinking of this Hellenistic-Jewish missionary Christianity, one can immediately see why here faith in the atonement once for all established by God in Jesus' death abolishes the temple cult; why the community by virtue of the atonement sees itself transferred into the time and reality of the *kainē diathēkē;* and why thereby also its new eschatological view of the torah breaks forth. Martin Hengel recently conjectured that Paul took over from the Stephen-circle the much-puzzled-over term "the torah of Christ" (Gal. 6:2; 1 Cor. 9:21).[29] However that may be, Hebrews, with its interpretation of the sacrifice of Christ on the basis of Leviticus 16 and its emphasis on the covenant "obligation" of Jer. 31:31ff., established for Christians by this sacrifice, stands most clearly in the line of the Stephen-circle. Therefore, one has to read Hebrews as a document of that missionary Christianity that, emanating from Antioch, supported Paul and sympathized with him without having a proclamation identical to his.

18. Paul stands in the tradition-historical line of the Stephen-circle. Nevertheless he owes his dialectical theology of the law directly to his call to be an apostle. In connection with this call Christ appears to him as the "end of the law" (Rom. 10:4).

According to Acts 11:25–26 Paul is brought to Antioch by Barnabas. A few years later Paul, together with Barnabas, (successfully) defended at the Apostolic Council in Jerusalem the principal concerns of the mission theology espoused in Antioch. So Paul stands directly in the mission tradition pointing from Jerusalem to Antioch and represented by the Stephen-circle, which Paul, as an enemy of Christians, encountered already in Jerusalem. But as clear as these historical connections are, one dare not make Paul simply a consistent advocate of the mission-theological tradition he received in Antioch. In his own reports of his call the apostle insisted emphatically that he received his law-critical gospel directly from God and his risen Son; thus he was an apostle of equal right and equal authority with the Jerusalem apostles and the others called before he was. If one takes these statements in Galatians 1, 1 Corinthians 15, 2 Corinthians 4 and 5, Philippians 3, and Rom. 1:1ff. seriously, and does not omit from historical consideration that, according to 2 Cor. 11:22–33, beginning in Damascus Paul was subjected to persecutions by Jews and gentile authorities, one can in my opinion not sustain the view, frequently advocated again today, that Paul's theological criticism of the law is only a late consequence of his preaching about Christ.[30] Since Paul sees outside Damascus the Jesus accursed by the torah on the cross as the "Son" and "Lord" exalted to the right hand of God, he experiences at the same time and in concert with this Christophany that God's gracious will with Jesus, his Son, outreaches the curse of the law. Or, expressed with Rom. 10:4, Paul sees and recognizes in Jesus, the risen Son of God, the "end of the law" for faith.[31] Precisely because he experiences this, Paul knows himself to be called as apostle to the Gentiles. And because he proclaimed this from the beginning, he was persecuted by the synagogue forthwith in precisely the same way in which he as an enemy of Christians had previously persecuted Jewish Christians in Jerusalem and as far as Damascus who had fallen away from the Mosaic Torah to Christ. Even if we find the actual literary explication of Paul's theology of the law only in the two Corinthian letters, Philippians, Galatians, and Romans, that is, in missionary documents from the height of the Pauline mission between 52 and 57 C.E., the Pauline gospel about Christ was from the beginning a gospel about justification that was critical of the law for the sake of Jesus Christ and not the proclamation—only gradually developing into a law-critical message about justification—of a confession of Christ with which "Jewish theology . . . could see the accompanying danger of a falling away from Judaism,"[32] without anyone being able to indicate precisely why in that case the Jews inflicted against the proclaimer of this confession the lashes typically used for blasphemy against the law and why the Romans in addition inflicted the flogging used to punish open insurrection.

19. The Pauline theology of the law will be properly understood only if one can combine undiminished the following four lines of assertion: (a) By virtue of the death and resurrection of Jesus, the Christian community already lives in the time and actualization of the "obligation" of the new covenant from Jer. 31:31ff. (b) The time of freedom from the Mosaic law has begun for the community in and with Christ. (c) The community has to confirm its new freedom in the power of the Holy Spirit under the "torah of Christ" (Gal. 6:2). (d) The "torah of Christ" has its center in the love command and in the fundamental demands of the Decalogue; in this torah of Christ the spiritual intention of the Torah from Sinai reaches its goal.

The Pauline interpretation of the law is "the most intricate doctrinal issue" in the theology of the apostle[33] not only because Paul's terminology about the law is highly nuanced but also because the development of his teaching about the law is diversely accented. It is developed by the apostle on constantly changing fronts. In the Corinthian correspondence Paul turns to oppose an early Christian enthusiasm on one side and a Jewish-Christian anti-Pauline agitation (inspired by Jerusalem?) on the other. In Galatians he needs to resist Christian Judaists. In Philippians he must withstand a group similar to the one in 2 Corinthians. Finally, in Romans Paul is concerned with undercutting the Jewish-Christian polemic that was building against him in Rome, a polemic emanating from Corinth and Philippi, perhaps also Galatia. He attempts to warn the community against the agitators and to win them for a gospel the apostle considers in full agreement with the Christian teaching into which the Romans were baptized.

Since all these letters arose within a short time of one another, one should in my opinion measure neither Galatians by the yardstick of Romans nor on the other hand Romans by the yardstick of Galatians, nor should one try to regard all Pauline utterances on the law merely as preliminary stages of the theology of the law that the apostle really brought to a systematic completion only in Romans.[34] It is considerably more appealing historically first to show the main features that predominate in each of the letters mentioned and afterward to combine them in such a way that a unity emerges that can be thought of biblically and reconstructed logically as flowing from the apostolic commission given to the Pharisee-turned-Christian Paul.

Four main features appear thereby. (1) According to the Pauline Lord's Supper tradition, and according to 2 Cor. 3; 5:17—6:2; and Gal. 4:21ff., the community reconciled with God by the death and resurrection of Jesus already lives (under persecutions!) in the time and in the service of the new covenant's "obligation." Unconverted Israel lives only in anticipation of this time (Rom. 11:25ff.). (2) As Paul emphasizes in Galatians, in Philippians 3, in Rom. 6:15ff., and in Rom. 9:30—10:4, the time of freedom from the Mosaic law has already begun for the Christian community. Also, according to 1 Cor. 9:19-23 Paul no longer stands simply under the Mosaic Torah. (3) The freedom from the Mosaic law is, however, to be confirmed by the congregation, under the power of the Holy Spirit conferred in Christ, in the service of righteousness (Rom. 6:18ff.; cf. Philippians 3) that is, in the doing of God's commands (1 Cor. 7:19). Therefore, Paul can also say in 1 Cor. 9:21 and Gal. 6:2 that he himself and Christians stand in obedience to the "torah of Christ" (an expression, as mentioned above, that he possibly borrowed from the Antiochene theology of mission that went back to the Stephen-circle).[35] (4) This "torah of Christ," as 1 Cor. 9:21 clearly shows, is not identical with the Mosaic Torah, but in it, according to 1 Cor. 7:19; Gal. 5:14; Rom. 8:3–4; 13:8–10, the intention of the Torah from Sinai reaches its goal and (just as in the proclamation of Jesus!) the love command, deepened to include love for enemies, together with the fundamental demands of the Decalogue are required as valid expressions of God's will. Thus, according to Paul, Christians are not despisers but doers of the revealed will of God newly established in Christ. How can these four lines of expression as Paul understood them be combined biblically?

20. A historically and biblically comprehensible combination of these four series of statements emerges above all when one understands the "torah of Christ" as the eschatological equivalent of the Mosaic Torah in obedience to which and under whose curse Jesus died on the cross. The "torah of Christ" is the Zion torah that Jesus inaugurated when he underwent his expiatory death in fulfillment of the Sinai Torah and in this way freed it from the oppressive curse upon it and sinners since the Fall.

Since Paul in Galatians as well as in Romans repeatedly reflects on the weakness of the law of Moses as an institution, it does not appear to me adequate to seek the unity of the four lines only in an existential dialectic, as if the Pauline theology of the law were an interpretive device that only becomes understandable from the anthropology of the apostle.[36] If one observes the precisely weighed words of the "missionary canon" (G. Eichholz) of Paul in 1 Cor. 9:19–23 and bears in mind also Jesus' proclamation of the "Zion torah," together with the Old Testament tradition that is its foundation, one actually can, in my opinion, combine the four lines undiminished. The torah of Christ under which Paul stands and under which he puts Christians is the Zion torah inaugurated by Christ through his obedient death. It is not simply identical with the reality of the Mosaic Torah to which Israel in Paul's time holds firm while rejecting the gospel, but it brings the Mosaic Torah's spiritual intention to its goal in that it is its eschatological fulfillment. Since Jesus died the accursed expiatory death on the cross, the Mosaic Torah is, according to Paul, fulfilled and also freed from the power of sin that had ruled over the Torah as well as over humanity since Genesis 3. Through Jesus' expiatory death, therefore, not only is humanity freed for its true creaturely existence in communion with God in Christ but the torah is also eschatologically transformed and put in force as a way of life the community is to fulfill and as an open space for the community's renewed creaturely existence before God. As the way of life of the new covenant's "obligation" from Jer. 31:31ff., the eschatologically transformed Mosaic Torah is the eschatological torah of Zion that now applies to all nations and that, by virtue of the gift of the Holy Spirit, which for Paul is Christ's presence on earth, enables a spontaneous acting in love.

21. Accordingly Paul not only teaches the Christian community a new ethical use of the Mosaic law but also calls it to obedience to the new and finally restored will of God which eschatologically corresponds to and fulfills the Torah from Sinai. According to Paul the community no longer stands under the law of Moses but already in the "law of the Spirit of life [opened] in Christ Jesus" (Rom. 8:2). The creative wisdom of God is revealed to the community no longer in the law of Moses but in Christ alone.

Under the presuppositions we have outlined it is in my view an oversimplification and not really illuminating for an exact understanding of the Pauline view of justification to maintain that Paul speaks in his letters always only about one Mosaic Torah, and that, while distinguishing between the status of the sinner under the law and that of the believer in freedom over against the law, he endeavors in his parenesis to require Christians to fulfill the law of Moses.[37] This interpretation could accord with the post-Pauline reflection in the Pastoral Epistles (cf. 1 Tim. 1:8–9), already somewhat oversimple in comparison to Paul himself, but I cannot regard it as genuinely Pauline. It would make the Pauline position and the way of suffering Paul traveled from the Apostolic Council on incomprehensible from a historical perspective. When Paul in Rom. 8:2 speaks of the "law of the Spirit of life [opened] in Christ Jesus"; when he says he by no means overthrows the law but establishes it as *nomos pisteōs* (Rom. 3:27–31); when he in Romans 7 and 8 shows with consummate skill that the holy, righteous, and good law, which (according to the Jewish tradition taken over by Paul) already applied to Adam in paradise and which with the Fall came under the power of sin, has been freed by the sacrificial death of Jesus from the clutches of sin and from the weakness to which the flesh's manipulation subjected it, so that the righteous demand of this transformed law now (finally) finds its fulfillment in the Spirit-directed life of Christians, then he does not simply teach the perfect keeping of the Mosaic Torah by Christians but rather says that the torah through Christ is really freed for the first time for the life-sustaining function accorded it in paradise. With the advent of sin and the curse of Genesis 3 this function was lost. Even the law revealed to Moses on Sinai could no longer perform it. But through Christ's victory over sin it is finally (re-)attained. Paul merely hints at these relationships in Rom. 5:12ff. and 7:7ff.[38]

Of greater concern to him than reflecting on the lost primal state of humanity, the world, and the torah was the new situation inaugurated by Christ for those who believe, in which that will of God is finally realized which was, to be sure, already revealed to Israel in the Sinai Torah but not really obeyed. Paul can say quite boldly in Rom. 9:31 that Israel in its effort to pursue the torah of righteousness did not attain this torah. It is revealed and present only in Christ. While the Gentiles practice idolatry and the Jews keep trying to catch sight of God's creative wisdom in the law of Moses and by virtue of the Mosaic Torah, that wisdom by which the world is sustained (1 Cor. 1:30; 2:6ff.; 8:6) has already appeared to Christians in Christ Jesus. In Christ, then, that eschatological way of life of which Jer. 31:31ff. speaks has already been revealed for faith, though its worldwide revelation and implementation is, according to Paul, still in the future.

22. Paul's dialectical theology of the law has an independent parallel in the Johannine tradition about Jesus' "new commandment" (John 13:34).

One could hesitate a moment and wonder whether the situation with Paul is really as presented if the Fourth Gospel, tradition-historically entirely independent of Paul, did not reveal that it stands in precisely the same place as Paul's letters in terms of its reflection and proclamation about the issue. According to John 1:17 the Torah was given through Moses, but the grace and truth of God appeared only through Jesus Christ, indeed through Jesus Christ who as the Son of God is also God's creative Word and thus the wisdom of God in person. Moses is related to and subordinated to the Christ-Logos by John. In John 5:39-47 Jesus challenges the Jews who ask him about his authority and legitimacy to search Moses and the Scriptures of the Old Testament because these bear witness to Jesus in his authority as the one sent by God. But in 13:34 this very Jesus, of whose messianic mission Moses and the prophets write (John 1:41, 45), gives his disciples the love command as an (eschatological) new command and as a way of life for the struggle they have to endure in the world with the help of the Paraclete after his departure.[39] Here, in essence, the very same statement is made about the *entolē* given to Christians as in Paul, when he speaks of the "torah of Christ" that is binding on Christians, including himself. Only in John the appeal to the Jesus tradition is much clearer than in Paul; the likelihood that Paul's interpretation of the law is rooted in the Jesus tradition can be shown only indirectly (especially from Romans 12 and 13).

23. The differences between the synthesizing theology of the law in Matthew and James on the one hand and the dialectical understanding of the law by Paul and the Johannine tradition on the other cannot be completely resolved, because they are each connected with a different conception of faith and justification (at the last judgment).

In a comparison of the two principal lines of New Testament understanding of the law we are now considering it must be observed that all the tradition-bearers under discussion relate their messages to Jesus, his mission, and his saving work, culminating in his death and resurrection, but that the situations to which Paul, John, James, and Matthew direct their messages differ greatly. But even if one takes this into account, no unified summary of the New Testament—christological understandings of the law is possible. That this is not possible is shown not only by the situation of humanity before God in Matthew (cf. 5:48; 19:21), James (1:13ff.), Paul (cf. especially Rom. 1:18—3:20; 7:7—8:11), and John (cf. 3:16–21; 6:44ff.), who reflect on this human situation with

varying degrees of critical intensity, but also, at one with this, by the difference in their statements about justification and the last judgment. It is true that
Paul, John, Matthew, and James all proceed from the assumption that only
the person who does God's will will be justified at the last judgment, but they
use this common base to make extremely different statements about the role
of faith and works at the judgment.

James, in this respect wholly within a Jewish wisdom perspective, clearly
stresses that only faith and works give the Christian any hope of being vindicated at the last judgment, and the Gospel of Matthew, with its ideas about
the church and the powerful parables about the last judgment, points in the
same direction, despite the central statement (taken from Mark 10:45) about
Jesus' death as ransom in Matt. 20:28 and the Lord's Supper tradition in
26:26ff., which is sharpened into an express reference to the forgiveness of
sins. But Paul expressly states that the promise that the crucified and risen
Christ will intercede for believers in the last judgment and that they will
finally be vindicated applies even if they with their actions fail in the sight of
God (cf. Rom. 8:31ff.; 1 Cor. 3:11–15). The apostle adds that even for Israel,
hardened and locked in unbelief, the hour of final vindication through Christ,
the redeemer going forth from Zion, will come, and God's uncanceled promise of salvation for his own people will come true (Rom. 11:25–32). Since
especially 1 John stresses the enduring validity of the *hilasmos* effected by the
expiatory sacrifice of Jesus' life and the miracle that God in Christ forgives
sin even when the human heart sees no possibility of that (1 John 1:6ff.; 2:1ff.;
3:19–20; 4:9–10, etc.), the Johannine school is again in essential agreement
with Paul without being dependent on him. Thus, despite various points of
contact and their common appeal to Jesus, the two principal lines of New
Testament understanding of the law continue to have different accents also in
their soteriological conclusions.

24. Since Paul and the Johannine tradition, with their dialectical-
eschatological understanding of the law, are more closely connected to Jesus
than are Matthew and James, Matthew and James should not be seen as
equivalent to but as correctives of the Pauline-Johannine understanding of the
law.

Today we can see that historically the dialectical theology of the law in Paul
and the Fourth Gospel and its accompanying Christology agree in a substantially greater measure with Jesus' new proclamation and imposition of the will
of God and his mission as reconciler[40] than does the attempt at a synthesis
of obedience to the law and faith in Christ as it was practiced after Easter by
a part of Jewish Christianity, an attempt at synthesis that originally impeded
the mission to the Gentiles, and, despite decisive correctives, continued to be
characteristic of James and Matthew. Under these circumstances there can be
no question of giving equal theological value to Paul, the Johannine school,
Matthew, and James. Nevertheless, James and the Gospel According to Matthew continue to be an indispensable historical and theological corrective to
the Pauline-Johannine understanding of faith. The history of early Christianity

(and the ancient church) shows that the Pauline congregations and the Christian circles that were under the influence of the Fourth Gospel were susceptible to enthusiasm, lovelessness, and gnosticizing tendencies to a higher degree than the (Jewish) Christianity behind James and Matthew. Precisely the Pauline and Johannine understanding of Christianity needed a corrective pointing it back to Jesus and a constantly renewed self-definition. Both were already carried out in the New Testament by James and the First Gospel. Since it can be shown historically that Matthew and James found early Christian Paulinism (and Johannine esotericism?) a challenge, the four complexes of tradition coordinate to one another historically. But their place in the canon makes the church depend on them all the more in order really to find an understanding—tied to Jesus—of faith and of the way in which faith might live before God today.

25. The topic "law" is an unresolved fundamental problem for a biblical theology that connects the Old and New Testaments. This fundamental problem does not separate the two Testaments from one another but aids in a more precise understanding of their indissoluble connection.

According to our reflections as a whole, "law" (as a way of life) is not a topic over which a biblical theology would have to fall apart. With far greater right one could say that a theology of the law remains of necessity fragmentary insofar as it does not approach this topic in the Bible as a whole. The question about the law is posed for the New Testament by the Old Testament with all clarity, and with this question the question of humanity and its way of life before God is also asked. The bearers of the New Testament tradition decisively address the question of the law without arriving at an uncontroverted common answer. The controversial nature of the Old Testament understanding of the law thus carries over into the New Testament. Nevertheless, in the New Testament a new, fully decisive point of reference becomes visible in the person and work of Jesus and in his resurrection from the dead. The New Testament is of one mind on the necessity, since the appearance of Jesus Christ, of testing all biblical discussion about the law on Jesus Christ as the wisdom of God in person, appointed for us by God. The discussion is from a New Testament perspective also biblically legitimate only to the degree in which it really deals with this wisdom and the way of life in conformity to it.

NOTES

1. The following set of theses grew out of my seminar in winter semester 1976/77. And it was also tremendously instructive for me to be able to discuss the theses, first of all on February 24, 1977, with the Editorial Board of *Die Zeitschrift für Theologie und Kirche*, and then, on March 29, 1977, in Zürich with the editors and authors of the *Evangelisch-katholischer Kommentar zum Neuen Testament* and the *Biblischer Kommentar*. Since it has been my conviction and experience that exegetical theology in particular grows from common critical discussion of the texts and their truth (and is considerably impoverished when individual exegetes respond to one another only in writing with their in part highly subjective "But I say unto you . . . ."), I have rethought

and reworked my set of theses after each discussion. Therefore I am indebted to all those who have helped me to modify and sharpen my statements.

2. H. Hübner, "Das Gesetz als elementares Thema einer Biblischen Theologie?" *KD* 22 (1976): 250–76.

3. Ibid., 253.

4. G. Ebeling, "The Meaning of 'Biblical Theology,' " in *Word and Faith*, trans. J. Leitch (Philadelphia: Fortress Press, 1963), 96.

5. The paper contained the basic ideas that Gese has now spelled out in greater detail in his new book, *Essays on Biblical Theology*, trans. K. Crim (Minneapolis: Augsburg Pub. House, 1981), in the two essays on "The Biblical View of Scripture" (pp. 9–33; see esp. 25ff.) and "The Law" (pp. 60–92). Gese graciously offered his paper for further discussion in my seminar on the law in Paul and Jesus (see above, n. 1). The insight into the stages through which the interpretation of the revealed torah passed, which is my starting point in what follows, I owe to him. Besides the two studies just mentioned I point to his presentation of the phenomenon of the torah in the following essays: "Erwägungen zur Einheit der Biblischen Theologie" and "Der Dekalog als Ganzheit betrachtet," both in *Vom Sinai zum Zion BEvT* 64 (Munich: Kaiser, 1974), 11–30 and 63–80, as well as "Psalm 50 und das alttestamentliche Gesetzesverständnis," in *Rechtfertigung. Festschrift für E. Käsemann zum 70. Geburtstag,* ed. J. Friedrich, W. Pöhlmann, and P. Stuhlmacher (Tübingen: Mohr; Göttingen: Vandenhoeck & Ruprecht, 1976), 57–77. H. Seebass takes up Gese's tradition-history perspective in his article "Zur Ermöglichung biblischer Theologie," *EvT* 37 (1977): 591–600, see esp. 599.

6. G. von Rad, *Old Testament Theology,* trans. D. M. G. Stalker, 2 vols. (Edinburgh: Oliver and Boyd, 1962–65), 1:187–279; 2:388–409.

7. W. Zimmerli, "Das Gesetz im Alten Testament," in *Gottes Offenbarung. Gesammelte Aufsätze,* TBü 19 (Munich: Kaiser, 1963), 249–76; *Das Gesetz und die Propheten* (Göttingen: Vandenhoeck & Ruprecht, 1963), esp. 68–93; *Old Testament Theology in Outline,* trans. D. Green (Atlanta: John Knox Press, 1978), 109–40.

8. Von Rad, *Old Testament Theology,* 2:407.

9. Zimmerli, *Das Gesetz und die Propheten,* 78 (and frequently).

10. Zimmerli, "Das Gesetz im Alten Testament," 272–76.

11. Cf. Gese, "Erwägungen zur Einheit der Biblischen Theologie," 12–18, and "The Biblical View of Scripture," 9–14.

12. M. Hengel, *Judaism and Hellenism*, trans. J. Bowden (Philadelphia: Fortress Press, 1974), 169–75.

13. Cf. especially Schmid's essay "Altorientalische Welt in der alttestamentlichen Theologie," in *Altorientalische Welt in der alttestamentlichen Theologie* (Zürich: Theologischer Verlag, 1974), 145–64.

14. U. Luck, *Welterfahrung und Glaube als Grundproblem biblischer Theologie* (Munich: Kaiser, 1976).

15. H.-J. Kraus, "Theologie als Traditionsbildung?" *EvT* 36 (1976): 498–507.

16. See on this passage Gese's new essay, "Ezekiel 20:25f. und die Erstgeburtsopfer," in *Beiträge zur Altestamentlichen Theologie. Festschrift für W. Zimmerli zum 70. Geburtstag,* ed. H. Donner, R. Hanhart, und R. Smend (Göttingen: Vandenhoeck & Ruprecht, 1977), 110–51.

17. For this formulation as well as for the knowledge of the view of Y. Yadin mentioned below I am indebted to M. Hengel's kindness.

18. P. Schäfer, "Die Torah der messianischen Zeit," *ZNW* 65 (1974): 34 (27–42).

19. On the earliest stage of the double-command tradition see R. H. Fuller, "Das Doppelgebot der Liebe," in *Jesus Christus in Historie und Theologie. Neutestamentliche Festschrift für H. Conzelmann zum 60. Geburtstag,* ed. G. Strecker (Tübingen:

Mohr, 1975), 317–29. Since the double command emerges in Judaism only in the context of a series of commands and in combination with the demand to keep the whole law, I regard the exclusive status of the double command in the Jesus tradition as authentic, while Fuller believes that Jesus is following Jewish wisdom tradition, without, of course, being able to offer examples of an exclusive regard for the double command in such tradition.

20. On the place of the double command in the Testaments and on the relationship between the fear of God and philanthropy in Philo see the very excellent presentation by A. Nissen, *Gott und der Nächste im antiken Judentum. Untersuchungen zum Doppelgebot der Liebe*, WUNT 15 (Tübingen: Mohr, 1974), 230–44; 498–502. Nissen shows that neither the Testaments nor Philo come in question as a source of the double command in Jesus.

21. On the proclamation of the Baptist, see F. Lang, "Erwägungen zur eschatologischen Verkündigung Johannes des Täufers," in *Jesus Christus in Historie und Theologie*, 459–73.

22. E. Käsemann, "The Problem of the Historical Jesus," in *Essays on New Testament Themes*, trans. W. J. Montague, SBT (London: SCM Press, 1964; Philadelphia: Fortress Press, 1982), 37–45.

23. G. Bornkamm, *Jesus of Nazareth*, trans. I. and F. McLuskey with J. M. Robinson (London: Harper & Row, 1963), 227ff.

24. E. Lohse, *Grundriss der neutestamentlichen Theologie* (Stuttgart: Kohlhammer, 1974), 43–50.

25. The opposition to a "crass Hellenistic Christianity" in Matt. 5:17–20, emphasized above all by G. Bornkamm, "Wandlungen im alt- und neutestamentlichen Gesetzesverständnis," in *Gesammelte Aufsätze*, 4 vols.; vol. 4, pt. 2 (Munich: Kaiser, 1971), 73–80 (73–119), is, according to a suggestion by Hengel, to be supplemented through evidence of a synagogue polemic against those "heretics" who attacked the authority of the Torah (cf. Str-B 4:2, 1033–34, 1052ff.).

26. Cf. U. Luck, "Der Jakobusbrief und die Theologie des Paulus," *TGl* 61 (1971): 161–79.

27. There is an interesting connection between Mark 11:17 par. (with a quotation of Isa. 56:7), the accusation against Stephen in Acts 6:13–14, and the mission of Philip, which, with its turning to the Samaritans and the Ethiopian eunuch, appears to implement Isa. 56:3ff.

28. See my essay "Recent Exegesis on Rom. 3:24–26," (chap. 6 in this volume).

29. M. Hengel, *Between Jesus and Paul. Studies in the Earliest History of Christianity*, trans. J. Bowden (Philadelphia: Fortress Press, 1983), 151.

30. Although they accent individual details diversely, this is the view common to Hübner, "Das Gesetz," 264–72; G. Strecker, "Befreiung und Rechtfertigung," in *Rechtfertigung*, 479–508; and U. Wilckens, "Christologie und Anthropologie im Zusammenhang der paulinischen Rechtfertigungslehre," *ZNW* 67 (1976): 64–82.

31. See on this, in greater detail, my essays "The End of the Law" and "Eighteen Theses on Paul's Theology of the Cross" (chaps. 8 and 9 in this volume, esp. pp. 156–58). I hold to the formulation "end of the law" despite the essay of P. von der Osten-Sacken, "Das paulinische Verstandnis des Gesetzes im Spannungsfeld von Eschatologie und Geschichte," *EvT* 37 (1977): 549–87, esp. 568; that this is the case is a consequence of the theses that follow, since Paul's understanding of the law must be spoken of with more precision than has been customary up to now.

32. Strecker, "Befreiung und Rechtfertigung," 484.

33. H. J. Schoeps, *Paul*, trans. H. Knight (Philadelphia: Westminster Press, 1961), 168.

34. Thus Hübner, "Das Gesetz," 264ff.

35. Of interest for the relationship between Paul and the Stephen-circle is not only

this connection but also the fact that in Gal. 2:18 the apostle uses "the terminology of the temple logion . . . *(katalyein, oikodomein;* cf. Mark 13:2; 14:58; 15:29; Matt. 26:61; 27:40a; Acts 6:14; John 2:19), which was also brought into direct relationship with the law by Stephen in Acts 6:14, F. Hahn, "Das Gesetzesverständnis im Römer- und Galaterbrief," *ZNW* 67 (1976): 53, n. 76 (29–63).

36. Cf. H. Conzelmann, *An Outline of the Theology of the New Testament,* trans. J. Bowden (New York: Harper & Row, 1969), 228.

37. Against U. Wilckens in his frequently reprinted essay "Was heisst bei Paulus: 'Aus Werken des Gesetzes wird kein Mensch gerecht'?" EKKNT, *Vorarbeiten* 1 (Neu-kirchen: Neukirchener Verlag, 1969), 51–77, esp. 76; now in *Rechtfertigung als Freiheit. Paulusstudien* (Neukirchen-Vluyn: Neukirchener Verlag, 1974), 77–109, esp. 109; also against Wilckens is Hahn, "Das Gesetzverständnis," 61, n. 95.

38. In the light of the talk about Adam's transgression of the commandment in Rom. 5:14 and the *nomos* or the *entolē hē eis zōēn* already given Adam in Rom. 7:7, 10, I regard as too strong Hahn's statement that Paul "never [reflects] on a 'primal state' in which the law was fulfilled without sin" (Hahn, "Das Gesetzverstandnis," 62). On the Israelite tradition guiding Paul in both passages, see, for example, in addition to Genesis 2 and 3, the *Apocalyps of Moses* 13–28 or *4 Ezra* 7:11ff., and O. Betz, s.v. "Adam," *Theologische Realenzyklopödie* 1:417–18 (414–24). As little as it is seen to be a con-tradiction in *4 Ezra* to speak of the commandments already given to Adam and the gift of the law to the fathers first on Sinai (compare 4 Ezra 7:11 with 9:29ff.), just as little is it for Paul, the former Pharisee, a contradiction to speak of the gift of the *nomos* already to Adam and the revelation of the *nomos* only a long time after Adam's trans-gression (or even only 430 years after the promise of righteousness by faith given Abraham, cf. Gal. 3:17).

39. On the redaction-historical problem and on how far the "new" command to love one another (John 13:34) is to extend, see R. Schnackenburg, *The Gospel According to St. John,* trans. D. Smith and G. A. Kon, pt. 3, HTKNT (New York: Crossroad, 1982), 53–55; Hf. Thyen, " '. . . denn wir lieben die Bruder' (1 Joh. 3:14)," in *Recht-fertigung,* 527–42; and S. Pancaro, *The Law in the Fourth Gospel* (Lieden: Brill, 1945), 443ff.

40. See my essay "Jesus as Reconciler" (chap. 1 in this volume).

CHAPTER 8

"The End of the Law." On the Origin and Beginnings of Pauline Theology[1]

Protestant theology is presently confronted with the urgent task of reflecting anew on its essence. It needs to do this in view of a changed world and conscious of the responsibility it bears to its tradition and its church. In such reflection it dare not choose to disregard its heritage for the sake of pressing contemporary problems nor should it, out of concern for this heritage, stop with the confessions and language of its past. Rather, a theology of the gospel can rediscover its identity only if, in both freedom and obedience, it works out its true heritage in the present, with an eye to the future.

If we ask what the heritage of Protestant theology is, the answer may be: the gospel is Protestant theology's heritage as well as the compelling basis of its present responsibility. But this answer is still too provisional. No one can, and no one should, claim an agreement between the gospel and theology. Above all, however, the controversy on how the gospel is to be defined extends today into the congregations themselves. But if the gospel is in dispute, then Protestant theology can achieve a determination of its essence—to which it is called anew—only as it asks anew about the gospel and, while it pursues this question, is at the same time concerned to gain a clear perception of its real tasks in the present.

In this situation all theological disciplines are equally summoned to seek the truth and, in my opinion, that still means to seek it primarily in the form of a theologically reflected interpretation of Scripture.[2] It would therefore definitely be an error to assume that within Protestant theology the two exegetical sister disciplines of Old and New Testament hold a monopoly on Scripture interpretation. Rather all theological disciplines have a role in a responsible interpretation of Scripture. Precisely in the present theological situation, it is both important and valuable for New Testament scholars to know that they need to bring the exegetical findings of their search for the gospel into a discussion involving all theological disciplines. The mutuality of these disciplines does not excuse New Testament scholars, of course, from theological accountability for the whole, but for many phases of the work it permits them to concentrate on particular aspects of the scholarly task and, in any case, requires of them modesty. That is because looking at the whole of theology makes them aware of how much exegetical statements that are primarily historically oriented are in need of expansion and correction with respect to the whole theological enterprise and to hermeneutics. Once this is established, then exegetes will, of course, also be able to offer freely what they have to contribute from their own special subject matter, the New Testament, to theology's reflection on its task.

I

As little as the New Testament can be reduced to the Pauline tradition, just as surely the figure and proclamation of the apostle Paul come to the foreground as soon as the question of the gospel arises, and with it the question of determining the essence of Protestant theology. When it comes to the gospel and to defining the task of a theology appropriate to the gospel, then an investigation of Paul takes preeminence because the apostle first elevated the word "gospel" to be essentially the quintessence of Christian revelation and proclamation and thereby first also set himself the task of theological reflection on the proclamation of this gospel.[3] Theological reflection in this context has the task of giving specificity to the content of the apostolic proclamation and guarding it from manifold misunderstandings. Whatever may have been the direction of the tradition-historical lines between the Pauline proclamation and the evangelists, who began to write only after Paul, through his theological struggle for the gospel Paul in fact prepared the way for the composition of the Gospels. He thereby also presented criteria for an understanding of the work and fate of Jesus appropriate to the gospel which to the present could be surpassed neither theologically nor historically; rather, apart from these criteria there was always a clear misunderstanding of Jesus' many-sided work.

Paul summarized his whole struggle for a theological understanding of Jesus' person in the pregnant thesis in his first letter to the Corinthian congregation: "For I decided to know nothing among you except Jesus Christ and him crucified" (2:2). It is convenient that this statement is not just one thesis among others expressing Paul's Christology but also defines the content of the Pauline gospel itself and thus designates the center of Pauline thinking. The center of the apostle's proclamation is determined by Christology and, even more precisely, by the death and resurrection of Jesus and thus by the cross. What is interesting about the Pauline proclamation, however, is the fact that his theological reflection is not merely done, as it were, casually or as an afterthought. Rather, it is precisely his encounter with Christ that forces the apostle to use every means at his disposal to think through his proclamation of Christ. Paul became the leading theologian of the first primitive Christian generation because God in Christ compelled him to do theology.

II

The statements I have just made are not uncontroversial, and I therefore need to justify them with supporting argumentation. To be sure, the vast majority of exegetes today admit that the apostle's theological thinking was an existential task for him. But the question of where the center of Paul's theology lies is in dispute. If it was still objectively and tradition-historically certain beyond a doubt for Adolf Schlatter that Paul was to be understood only as the ambassador and witness of Christ, that is, on the basis of his Christology,[4] Rudolf Bultmann drew a new picture of Paul's theology and proclamation from a perspective on early Christian tradition history altered by the history-of-religions school. The center of Pauline thought in Bultmann's view is no longer Christology as such but the person confronted by the message about Christ, the kerygma, in his or her stance before God.[5] This view of Pauline theology, with certain modification, has gone into the portrayals of Paul by Günter Bornkamm[6] and Hans Conzelmann[7] and controls the discussion today.

In fact one must grant Bultmann that Schlatter's view of early Christian tradition-history is in need of correction. One will further have to acknowledge that an unmistakable peculiarity of Paul's lies in his sketch of a theological anthropology that stands alone in the New Testament.[8] Finally, we are able to stress with Bultmann that Pauline theology does not deal with the world and humanity as they are in themselves, but constantly sees the world and humanity in their relation to God. Every assertion about God is simultaneously an assertion about humanity, and vice versa. For this reason and in this sense Paul's theology is, at the same time, anthropology. But since God's relation to the world and humanity is not regarded by Paul as a cosmic process oscillating in eternally even rhythm, but is regarded as constituted by God's acting in history and by humanity's reaction to God's doing, therefore every assertion about God speaks of what he does with humanity and what he demands of it. And, the other way around, every assertion about humanity speaks of God's deed and demand—or about humanity as qualified by the divine deed and demand and by its attitude toward them. The Christology of Paul likewise is governed by this point of view. In it, Paul does not speculatively discuss the metaphysical essence of Christ, or his relation to God, or his "natures," but speaks of him as the one through whom God is working for the salvation of the world and humanity. Thus, every assertion about Christ is also an assertion about humanity and vice versa; and Paul's Christology is simultaneously soteriology.[9] If one did not want to admit this and also praise the systematic level of Bultmann's presentation of Paul, one would in my view miss the "act of seeing" that Schlatter regards as one of the qualities needed by an exegete.

To be sure, such an acknowledgment of Bultmann's views does not mean that we could omit objections to his basic plan. As far as I can see, it is not historically appropriate for Bultmann to treat the question of the Jewish law in Paul only in the context of anthropology and here only as a logical ultimate description of the situation of the person in perplexity over against God. Nor does one in my view do justice to Paul's proclamation when, paralleling the interpretation of the law, christological questions are taken up only as anthropological reflections in the mirror of faith and not given a dominant position in the foreground. But, finally, the hermeneutical and structural questions of theology we meet today have become too urgent for us to content ourselves any longer with the model of existential interpretation that holds sway in Bultmann as the sole pattern for a theological interpretation of Scripture.[10]

Now these objections are, taken as a whole, not new. The historically oriented presentation of Paul by Martin Dibelius and Werner Georg Kümmel already puts the accent opposite Bultmann's.[11] Ernst Käsemann's interpretations of Paul grow out of an evaluation of the problem of the law and of Christology in the apostle that is new compared to Bultmann's.[12] The "Prolegomena zu einer Theologie des Paulus im Umriss" set forth by George Eichholz also recommend a presentation of Paul that proceeds from Christology,[13] and they thereby continue the line of interpretation that Karl Barth took already in 1940/41.[14]

Under these circumstances it is high time to risk formulating a presentation on Paul that takes up the objections raised against Bultmann, but that in doing so thankfully appropriates Bultmann's references to the soteriological foundation of the Pauline proclamation and at the same time seeks to think through the open question about the gospel that today awaits a new answer.

III

If we want to pursue the question of the origins and, consequently, of the structure of Pauline theology, we must in my opinion resolve to take up once again the question of the call of Paul, a question Bultmann pushed ever further into the background in the course of his work on Paul.[15] It has been long established that Paul's call was foundational for his own theology.[16] The psychologizing misuse one could occasionally make of the reserved accounts of Paul's call-vision in no way destroys the theological value that Paul himself ascribed to his call and that an exegesis involved in reconstructing Paul's theology has to consider.[17] The question, much discussed in the past, about the character of Paul's call-epiphany is actually of lesser importance if Schlatter's statement still holds: "The historian has to understand events as they were experienced by the participants,"[18] and if, as is the case with Paul, the participant expressed himself with desirable clarity about the essential significance of what happened to him. Desirably clear, first of all, is the fact that in 1 Cor. 15:8ff., for the sake of the Christ-epiphany granted him, Paul included himself in the list of early Christian resurrection witnesses, as the last and, for the Corinthians themselves, most important.[19] And then, of desirable clarity is especially the apostle's polemically specific utterance in Gal. 1:11–17:

> (11) For I would have you know, brethren, that the gospel which was preached by me is not man's gospel. (12) For I did not receive it from man, nor was I taught it, but it came through a revelation of Jesus Christ. (13) For you have heard of

my former life in Judaism, how I persecuted the church of God violently and tried
to destroy it; (14) and I advanced in Judaism beyond many of my own age among
my people, so extremely zealous was I for the traditions of my fathers. (15) But
when he who had set me apart before I was born, and had called me through his
grace, (16) was pleased to reveal his son to me, in order that I might preach him
among the Gentiles, I did not confer with flesh and blood, (17) nor did I go up
to Jerusalem to those who were apostles before me, but I went away into Arabia;
and again I returned to Damascus.

Thus far the Pauline account.[20]

If one combines this account with the brief reference in 1 Cor. 9:1 ("Have
I not seen Jesus our Lord?") and the well-known confession by the apostle in
Phil. 3:4–11, that since his call he no longer hoped to be justified by God on
the basis of the law but only for Jesus Christ's sake, the following biographical
picture emerges of the career and proclamation of Paul:

The Jew born in Tarsus, named Saul for the first king from his tribe, Benjamin, and having the Hellenistic surname Paul, had his theological education
as a scribe in Jerusalem with Gamaliel the Elder (cf. Acts 22:3).[21] He attached
himself at the same time to the scrupulously law-observant party of the
Pharisees (Phil 3:5; Gal. 1:14) and consequently saw his life's true fulfillment
in service of the Jewish law. His militant zeal for the law caused him to proceed against those Christians who, by appeal to Jesus and with faith in the
risen Christ, began to ignore the law and thereby to cast doubt on its primal
place as revelation.[22] Undertaken with the agreement and approval of the
Sanhedrin, his persecution of those Jewish Christians who had deserted the
law for the new faith begins, according to Acts, already in Jerusalem (Acts
7:58; 8:3) but is attested for us with certainty by Paul himself only for the time
when he expanded his persecution to the Hellenistic Jewish Christians in
Damascus. In the vicinity of Damascus an epiphany of Christ is experienced
by the man who until that time was entirely caught up in the law. That is, he
beheld the crucified Jesus of Nazareth in the glory of the living Son of God
and Lord. Through this experience Paul was designated to enter immediately
into the mission work of the Hellenistic Jewish–Christian congregation he had
just persecuted. From the zealot for the law came the apostle consumed in the
service of the law-free gospel about Christ to the point of martyrdom in Rome.

This very brief summary already shows that the Jewish law as interpreted
by the Pharisees and the gospel about Christ were the two forces that shaped
the life of Paul. If Paul designates himself in his pre-Christian period as a
fanatic zealot for the law (Gal. 1:14; Phil. 3:5–6), he regards himself according to 1 Cor. 9:16 as an apostle handed over to the gospel about Christ as to
a fateful force which drove him on.[23] A glance at the Pauline missionary journeys and the descriptions of his sufferings in 2 Corinthians shows that with
such a remark Paul by no means exaggerated.[24] So we have established that
the two theological forces clearly determinative for Paul's existence were law
and gospel. Of course, we can go beyond such a succinct determination.

IV

That is to say, if we may in Pauline exegesis proceed from the assumption of the tension between law and gospel, without thereby subjecting ourselves from the start to the accusation of a confessionally narrowed point of view,[25] then in glancing at the Pauline letters it strikes us immediately that the gospel for Paul is primarily a christologically determined phenomenon. According to the beginning of Romans, the gospel accords with the prophetic promise in the Old Testament, and it concerns the Son of God, who as the bearer of the promise has his human origin as a descendant of David, but who, since the resurrection of the dead made its proleptic appearance in him, has been installed by God into his office as Son of God and ruler of the world (Rom. 1:2ff.).[26] This christological definition of the gospel is, as especially G. Bornkamm has shown,[27] the key to understanding the famous parallel definition of the gospel in Rom. 1:16–17, according to which the gospel is the power of God for salvation for everyone who believes because in it the righteousness of God is revealed from faith to faith. The righteousness of God means the very faithfulness and grace of God that reveals itself in sending Jesus evokes faith and imparts itself to faith.[28] Finally, if we think about 2 Cor. 4:6, a verse that probably deals with Paul's call,[29] and if we read there once again that for Paul and his hearers the gospel is about the enlightening knowledge of the glory of God in the face of Jesus Christ, then we may also take the apostle at his word in Galatians 1 and accept the equating of the gospel and the revelation of Christ that he established already there. The epiphany granted Paul of the Crucified One as the Son of God in the glory of the Risen One is, then, the gospel itself he received and was to hand on.

Why is the revelation of Christ gospel? Because in this epiphany Christ appears as the end of the law, that is, as the bringer of salvation on the last day. It is proclaimed in the gospel that in Christ and his glory God has already permitted the salvation of the last day to begin. That the fullness of salvation that God prepared for the world is already present as promise in Christ is the fundamental idea of Paul's (anticipatorily conceived) Christology, and it is also a definition of the content of the gospel about Christ and the very substance of the Damascus-epiphany.[30] But that now needs to be spelled out more fully.

How much Paul knew about the message of Jesus before Damascus is today just as controversial as the question of possible interconnections between the Jesus tradition in the Gospels and Paul's apostolic proclamation. But even if we today can no longer reach Schlatter's confident conclusion that Paul knew "the message of Jesus as well as we do,"[31] we can assume that Christian preaching about the Crucified Risen One as the "Lord" and the liberator from the law's all-embracing revelatory claim was prior to Damascus a scandal for Paul, the Jewish persecutor of Christians (cf. 1 Cor. 1:23–24; Gal. 5:11). Indeed, in Deut. 21:23, the Torah itself shows the crucifixion of Jesus, that enemy of the law, to be a curse imposed by God (Gal. 3:13)![32] If Paul prior to his call already knew at least this much about Jesus, that he was crucified by the Romans not as a martyr for the Jewish cause and the law but as one condemned by the Jewish court, and if the Torah identifies such a crucifixion as a curse imposed by God, the alternatives were clear for him (as a persecutor of a community that forsook the law in the name of the risen "Lord"): either God's honor in the law or God's dishonor in faith in the crucified Christ! The knowledge already attained from the apostle's biography, that the pre-Christian Paul was entirely consumed by zeal for the law, strengthens us in this view and permits us to hold to the stated alternatives.[33]

If this view of things is tenable, there is an important corollary. If Paul's pre-Christian zeal and his battle against the law-critical adherents of Christ were understood as honoring God on the basis of the law, then his call showed him that God wants to be honored precisely in Christ. For a Pharisee, as well as for first-century popular Jewish piety in general, belief in the God who raises the dead (at the last day) was a basic article of faith.[34] Thus the resurrection of the dead was for Paul already in his pre-Christian period the quintessence of God's life-creating eschatological activity. If Paul outside Damascus experienced an epiphany of the Crucified One as the living Son of God in glory,[35] or as the "Lord" (raised from the dead), then this meant several things: it meant first and foremost that God, in his eschatological creative power, has already now acted on behalf of the Crucified One, acted in an eschatological and once-and-for-all valid identification of himself with Christ. By the resurrection God has already actualized on the Crucified One the salvation of the last day, and therefore Christ can for Paul be regarded as the "action of the Father" pure and simple, as Conzelmann aptly expresses it.[36] But more than that. The epiphany as resurrected Son of God of precisely the Crucified One cursed by the law must have been the infallible sign that God himself thwarted and annulled the Torah's verdict of death. Put differently: God revealed to Paul the Crucified Risen One as the end of the law. The statement formulated by Paul in Rom. 10:4, "Christ is the end of the law, that everyone who has faith may be justified," is probably in its context theologically a statement with great argumentative force, but even before that it is the quintessence of that which God outside Damascus impressed on Paul, the zealot for the law, in the form of the Crucified Risen One.[37]

Through the Damascus-epiphany Paul came to know Jesus Christ as the end of the law, and the justification of the ungodly without works of the law solely by faith happened to the apostle himself at the same time as and of a piece with this coming to know Christ. The choice of the expression "justification of the ungodly" is in this context not too strong to suit Paul's understanding. For in his fanatical zeal for the law Paul had opposed God's own decision, manifested in the resurrection of the Crucified One, to effect reconciliation apart from the Torah. Despite such opposition, however, Paul is chosen by God to become a servant and preacher of Christ.[38] It is therefore entirely justified when Paul stresses in Gal. 1:15 and 1 Cor. 15:10 that it is only by the grace of God that he is the apostle that he is, and it is once again consistent with this and correct when in Phil. 3:4–11 he describes his call as the event by which he came to know Christ and was justified.[39] Precisely the passage just mentioned impresses upon us that the real gain of justification—if one may use this provocative expression—consists in "the surpassing worth of knowing Christ Jesus my Lord" (Phil 3:8).[40] Justification is, thus, a christological matter through and through, able to be comprehended only on the basis of Christology. If as a consequence of this we can now also proceed from the knowledge that the gospel about Christ revealed to Paul outside Damascus is in itself—and not only in a theological deduction drawn subsequently by Paul—a gospel about the justification of the ungodly through Christ,[41] then this very knowledge compels us to dwell on Paul's Christology as the theme of his life.

If in this Christology the action of God pure and simple is visible as an action on behalf of humanity which ends the law's claim to offer salvation, then one can also understand why Paul does Christology expressly as a Christology of the cross and wants to speak of the lordship of Christ primarily as the lordship of the Crucified One. First of all, there is no doubt, rather it is explicitly to be emphasized, that only the raising of Jesus by God got Paul's thinking started. The proclamation of Paul is legitimated at all only by virtue of the fact that he is a messenger of the Risen One and a witness for God who raised Jesus from the dead (cf. 1 Cor. 15:15).[42] But the Pauline knowledge of Jesus Christ gets its characteristic particularity, its soteriological importance, its pregnant revelatory significance only in the renewed reflection on the cross forced on Paul by the resurrection. The Torah let the cross and, in the cross, the work of Jesus appear to be standing under God's curse. Now, on the contrary, in the light of the resurrection the cross appears as the despoiler that takes away the law's power. Since God himself showed Paul the end of the law in the cross and resurrection of Jesus, the apostle confronted by the Risen One also directed his intellectual energy entirely to the cross. For him and all people the world turned upside down precisely at the cross. If Paul, as we heard already at the beginning of this essay, in Corinth wants to concentrate all his knowledge of revelation solely on Jesus the Crucified (see 1 Cor. 2:2); if Paul, as he says shortly before that (1 Cor. 1:18), wants to understand and proclaim the gospel only as a word about the cross, then this is again theologically argued and theologically reflected language, but before that it is a proclamation that God himself gave Paul and impressed upon him.

If we draw some preliminary conclusions on the basis of what has been presented so far, we get the following result: when Paul speaks of the "gospel," he means the message about the crucified and resurrected Jesus. The Risen One is proclaimed by Paul as the crucified, as the end of the law. Preaching about the Crucified Risen One or preaching about Christ as the end of the law is preaching about the justification of the ungodly. These central statements of his theology, developed by Paul by using all the critical intellectual resources at his disposal, unfold what Paul himself experienced in his Christophany. Because his call was an encounter with the Crucified Risen One in the name and authority of God, Paul in his theology reflects on the work of God, his theology is at the same time proclamation and his proclamation theology, and both unfold the mission of Christ aimed at saving the world. To summarize: Paul unfolds the gospel about Jesus Christ and knows himself to be sent to confront the need of the world in the name of God on the basis of this gospel. But the world that Paul has to confront with the gospel is the world under the law and the human being in its midst.

V

The brief sketch of Paul's life we tried to give and the reflection we did at the end about the christological starting point of Paul's thought both yielded an astonishingly similar result. In both instances we came upon law and gospel as the two forces controlling Paul's life and work. Structurally law and gospel stand in a dialectical tension in Paul. The law constitutes the world of the pre-Christian Paul, the world into which the gospel about Jesus Christ broke unexpectedly as a provision by God that overrides the law. As our reflections showed, the curse of the law and the cross are the framework that helps to give with precision the content of the gospel as saving power. And yet this sequential arrangement of a law preceding the gospel is no longer the point of view that really shaped Paul's thought and proclamation. If we proceed from Paul's thought itself, here it is the gospel that first brings freedom and a possibility of reconsidering the law and its world critically.[43] One can see this from the thought progression in Romans 1. Paul introduces himself here first and foremost as a witness for the gospel and introduces the gospel as the evidence of God's saving power. Not until Paul has laid this foundation (Rom. 1:1–17) does he dare to address the world of Gentiles and Jews, on the basis of the law, about their common fallen state at the judgment, a fallen state from which only God through Christ is able to save (Rom. 1:18—3:20 and 3:21ff.). The revelation of the gospel is thus the condition that makes Pauline theology possible, a theology that revolves around the christological confrontation of gospel and law and for the sake of the gospel ponders the law's power and impotence.

Now, as Hans Joachim Schoeps states, quite correctly in my view, "The Pauline understanding of the law [is] the most intricate doctrinal issue in his theology."[44] It is already a sign of this that, as we just saw, a simple alternative of law and gospel is no longer adequate to capture where Paul stands.[45] Paul interprets precisely the law, if I see things correctly, on the basis of God's action in Christ, and that in a multilayered argument that I can only outline now: With Christ the law, fallen into the clutches of sin and thereby falsely made the basis of the world's claim to be pious or impious in God's sight, reaches its end, the law that is merely a caricature of the good, revealed will of God. Christ himself, however, is subject to the good will of God in the law, and in his own "law of Christ"—given such a provocative name by Paul (Gal. 6:2; cf. 1 Cor. 9:21)—he makes the good will of God visible and valid as the love command. So Christ is the end of the law and yet at the same time the obedient Son who esteems and fulfills the will of God. Thus, as the Crucified

One, he becomes the Lord who rules definitively over the world in God's name. His law of love is no longer the law from Sinai, gone awry under the power of sin, but the law's positive equivalent![46]

To be sure, the lordship of Christ is proclaimed and announced by Paul only in a world in which, as Ulrich Luz puts it so well, "the law is by no means at its end!"[47] The end of the law is proclaimed in the midst of the continuing lordship of the law! Paul himself experiences this most painfully in the fact that the Jews in his time are largely closed to the gospel, and the gentile world, despite Christ, sticks to its own wisdom. So Paul knows himself to be sent to a world and to people who, still subject to the law, are nevertheless already acquitted and are justified in the gospel. So Paul has to serve people who are simultaneously addressed by both the law and the gospel. To proclaim to such people Christ as crucified and as Lord is the goal of his theology. Precisely this apostolic and, if one will, pastoral obligation, shown him in advance in the sacrificial way of Christ, leads Paul quite logically to the topic of anthropology. The apostle's anthropological analyses treat no abstract problems,[48] but they attempt to further the gospel's comprehensibility and urgency in the light of the claim God in Christ makes upon the world and the body of each individual person. Since the battle of Christ for the world will be decided today and here in each individual person (cf. Rom. 8:2–11), Paul devotes himself to the topic of anthropology and the attainment of true humanity with a seriousness sketched out in the New Testament only by Jesus. But this evaluation of humanity for whose sake God sent his Son into the world (cf. Gal. 4:4ff.) should not make us forget the worldwide dimensions in which the theme of anthropology appears in Paul. Anthropology is not the main idea but the "depth dimension" of Pauline thinking,[49] whose essential subject and origin is God's action in Jesus Christ as the Crucified Risen One, or, as Paul also says, Christ as the end of the law.

I conclude my historical section with the question whether it is not time, and just as correct historically as important theologically, to present Pauline theology in the categories coined by Paul himself, the law and the gospel of Christ.[50] Such a presentation could remain thankfully indebted to Bultmann's findings and would perhaps also be in a position to formulate in an impressive way the claim Paul makes for all time with his theology. For it would compel us to rethink today and here, anew and critically, the question of ecclesiastical-theological interpretation of the law and proclamation of the gospel; the question of the so-called rules for life, of the autonomy of the world, and of the freedom of faith.

VI

We had begun with the task before which Protestant theology stands today, that as it inquires about the gospel it must once more remember its identity and ponder its mission. What the theologian occupied with Paul can bring to this total theological task is the indication that the theology of the gospel began as Christology, a Christology of reconciliation in the midst of a still unreconciled world standing under the law. The core of this theology is the word, and this word is the action of God in the world. Protestant theology in my view would not be ill advised if it would remember this, its own starting point, and make clear that the gospel is not today, any more than it once was, an empty formula but the eminently practical word of life and hope, the message about and the encounter with the crucified and risen Christ, who as the Coming One gives us hope and presses us into service.

NOTES

1. Delivered as an inaugural lecture in Erlangen on May 8, 1969, and given at the invitation of the Protestant theological faculty in Bern on June 17, 1969. In preparation for printing the text was reworked slightly and the footnotes were enlarged.

2. Inspired by H. Rückert, G. Ebeling suggested in his habilitation lecture in 1946 defining church history theologically as "the history of the exposition of Scripture" (the lecture is printed in *The Word of God and Tradition*, trans. S. H. Hooke [Philadelphia: Fortress Press, 1968], 11–31). Perhaps exegetes are able to emphasize that for their interpretive task they are still painfully awaiting the implementation of this program. The difficulties, clearly in evidence today, created by a theological exegesis that emancipates itself from the tradition, believing it can relate the text and the present to one another directly, could perhaps have been lessened if exegesis had at the right time been forced by church history to reflect on the tradition that made exegesis possible and with that also on the historical relativity of all exegetical judgments. However that may be, today in any case church history has a key role when it comes to considering the hermeneutical and, with that also, the essential problem of a theological interpretation of Scripture.

3. On the problem and relevance of the Pauline gospel, see now, in addition to my habilitation thesis (*Das paulinische Evangelium*, vol. 1: *Vorgeschichte*, FRLANT 95 [Göttingen: Vandenhoeck & Ruprecht, 1968]), especially E. Grässer's instructive study, "Das eine Evangelium," *ZTK* 66 (1969): 306–44.

4. Cf. A. Schlatter's lecture, "Jesus und Paulus," delivered in 1906, now printed as *Kleinere Schriften*, ed. Theo. Schlatter, vol. 2, 3d ed. (Stuttgart: Calwer Verlag, 1961); the section on Paul in Schlatter's *Theologie der Apostel*, 3d ed. (Stuttgart: Calwer Verlag, 1977), 239–432, esp. 243ff. and 389ff; as well as his article on Paul in the *Calwer Bibellexikon*, 4th ed. (1924): 558b–563b, reprinted in *Das Paulusbild in der neueren deutschen Forschung*, ed. K. H. Rengstorf, Wege der Forschung 24 (Darmstadt: Wissenschaftliche Buchgesellschaft, 1964), 200–213, to which the references are given in what follows.

5. Cf. R. Bultmann's article "Paulus" in *RGG* (2nd ed.) 4:1019–45, and the presentation on the theology of Paul in the *Theology of the New Testament*, trans. K. Grobel, 2 vols. (New York: Charles Scribner's Sons, 1951–55), 1:185–352.

6. Cf. G. Bornkamm's article "Paulus" in *RGG* (3d ed.) 5:166–90, and especially his book *Paul*, trans. D. M. Stalker (New York: Harper & Row, 1971); see my discussion of this in *EvK* 2 (1969): 735. It is to be pointed out that Bornkamm stresses the indissoluble connection between Christology and justification much more strongly than Bultmann himself (see *Paul*, 56, 115–17).

7. Cf. H. Conzelmann, *Outline of the Theology of the New Testament*, trans. J. Bowden (New York: Harper & Row, 1969), 155–286.

8. E. Käsemann has again made that clear in his essay "On Paul's Anthropology"

in *Perspectives on Paul,* trans. M. Kohl (Philadelphia: Fortress Press, 1971), 1–31, esp. 1: "In the whole of the New Testament it is only Paul who expounds what we should call a thoroughly thought-out doctrine of man, although, oddly enough, it already became superficial in the hands of his disciples or was even abandoned by them altogether."

9. *Theology of the New Testament,* 1:191. In agreement with these very statements are Käsemann, *Perspectives on Paul* (1) and Bornkamm, *Paul* (119).

10. I would like to point out explicitly that I am not interested in eliminating existential interpretation. As long as the category of the individual continues to be an enduring theological category (cf. on this Käsemann, *Perspectives on Paul,* 2ff.; Bornkamm, *Paul,* 125–26)—and it continues to be this as long as we have to speak about salvation, judgment, and human responsibility—then existential interpretation is unavoidable. Of course, it is very important what picture of human existence provides the starting point for such interpretation and from what theological perspective it is carried out. It is especially important today, in my view, that we carry out the interpretation conscious of tradition rather than oblivious to it, that Christology and anthropology are not viewed as freely interchangeable, that we learn to interpret the eschatological category of the individual within the social structures in which the person actually lives (and in which, according to Paul, he or she always belongs), and, finally, that we do not identify a christologically constructed eschatology simply with eschatological futurity and thereby cover up the eschatological problem.

11. Cf. M. Dibelius and W. G. Kümmel, *Paul,* trans. F. Clarke (Philadelphia: Westminster Press, 1953), 46ff., 102ff., and now W. G. Kümmel, *The Theology of the New Testament According to Its Major Witnesses: Jesus—Paul—John,* trans. J. Steely (Nashville: Abingdon Press, 1973), 151ff.

12. This comes out with special clarity in Käsemann's programmatic study on "The Righteousness of God in Paul," in *New Testament Questions of Today,* trans. W. J. Montague (Philadelphia: Fortress Press, 1969), 168–92, and in his essay on "Justification and Salvation History in the Epistle to the Romans," in *Perspectives on Paul,* 60–78, esp. 73 and 76, n. 27.

13. Published in G. Eichholz, *Tradition und Interpretation. Studien zum NT und zur Hermeneutik,* TB 29 (Munich: Kaiser, 1965), 161–89, cf. esp. 169, 182, 187–88.

14. K. Barth, *A Shorter Commentary on Romans,* trans. D. H. van Daalen (London: SCM Press, 1959). In addition, I call attention to E. Schweizer, *Jesus,* trans. D. E. Green (Richmond: John Knox Press, 1971), 97ff., and to the fine book about the problem of a christological understanding of Paul's theology by Schweizer's pupil U. Luz, *Das Geschichtsverständnis des Paulus,* BEvT 49 (Munich: Kaiser, 1968).

15. In his article "Paulus" in *RGG* (2d ed.) Bultmann still went extensively into the problem of the "conversion" of the apostle and stressed that the conversion, presented psychologically as a vision of Christ, was for Paul "the decision to surrender his whole former self-understanding, which was called into question by the Christian message, and to understand his existence in a new way" (4:1022); more precisely (4:1023): "Whether Paul wanted to see in a historical fact, which is what the person and fate of Jesus were, the breaking in of the time of salvation, of the new creation, inaugurated by God, and whether he wanted to acknowledge in the cross of Christ the judgment on his former self-understanding as a pious Jew, whether he wanted with that to understand himself in a new way and render the verdict over his former life 'sin or death'— these are what he was asked by the Christian proclamation, and in his conversion he answered, Yes." At the same time, of course, there is already present in this article a warning against the "error" of wanting to derive Pauline theology from the apostle's "conversion experience," since "the question about the content of [Paul's] conversion is a question about his theology itself" (4:1027). Although precisely this last reference in actuality shows that historically the "conversion" event was determinitive for the

Pauline proclamation, the possibility of a psychological derivation of the apostle's theology flashed such strong warning signals before Bultmann's eyes that he became more
and more reluctant to make statements about the Damascus experience. In the survey
of recent research on Paul *(TRu* N.F. 6 [1934]:229–46), he once again takes up the various possibilities for understanding the Pauline conversion, but in his *Theology of the
New Testament,* 1:187–88, he makes only brief reference to the conversion of the apostle
and stresses the (historically undemonstrable as stated) point that Paul was "*won to the
Christian faith by the kerygma of the Hellenistic church*" [emphasis in the original] and
(the historically accurate) point that the conversion of the apostle "was not a conversion of repentance. . . . Rather, it was obedient submission to the judgment of God,
made known in the cross of Christ, upon all human accomplishment and boasting. It
is as such that his conversion is reflected in his theology." The word "conversion" that
Bultmann uses throughout his work is, of course, almost unavoidably misleading. U.
Wilckens, by contrast, in his lecture "Die Bekehrung des Paulus als religionsgeschicht-
liches Problem," *ZTK* 56 (1959): 273–93, correctly points out in the light of the revelation terminology of 1 Cor. 15:8 and Gal. 1:12, 15: "That Paul describes his experience
emphatically in this way as a vision of the risen one has its basis, first of all, in the
fact that he understands the event not so much as his own personal conversion to the
Christian faith but primarily as *a call to be an apostle.* That is, Paul himself does not
speak biographically about his 'Damascus experience' but theologically of his call to
be apostle to the Gentiles in the experience of the revelation of Jesus Christ to him"
(274–75; emphasis Wilckens'). Accordingly, we should speak not of Paul's conversion
but of his *call.*

16. I mention only Schlatter's article "Paulus," 203ff.; W. von Loewenich, *Paul, His
Life and Work,* trans. G. E. Harris (Edinburgh: Oliver and Boyd, 1960), 38ff.;
Dibelius-Kümmel, *Paul,* 46ff.; H. G. Wood, "The Conversion of St. Paul: Its Nature,
Antecedents and Consequences," *NTS* 1 (1954/55): 276–82, esp. 281–82; Wilckens,
"Bekehrung des Paulus," 274; J. Blank, *Paulus und Jesus,* SANT 18 (Munich: Kösel-
Verlag, 1968), 184ff.; P. Seidensticker, *Paulus, der verfolgte Apostel Jesu Christi,* SBS
8 (Stuttgart: Verlag Katholisches Bibelwerk, 1965), 17–18.

17. I find Bornkamm's statements on the topic contradictory. In his book *Paul,* he
emphasizes, "On the subject of his conversion and call to be an apostle Paul speaks
surprisingly seldom. When he does so, it is, however, in important remarks and always
in the context of the exposition of his gospel. This suggests that we should not follow
the common practice of making Paul's own personal experiences and, specifically,
Christ's appearances to him, central, partly on the basis of the vision on the way to
Damascus repeatedly described at length in Acts and partly under the influence of
pietistic tradition and modern psychology. We do best to keep our feet firmly on the
ground, take our lead from what Paul himself says, and not let ourselves be sidetracked
from what for him was the heart of the matter" (p. 39). As Luz, *Geschichtsverständnis*
(see above, n. 14), 387–88, stresses, Paul comes to speak about his "mission call" to
legitimate his apostleship: 1 Cor. 9:1; 15:8ff.; Gal. 1:15–16; cf. Rom. 1:5; 1 Cor. 1:1;
2 Cor. 1:1; Gal. 1:1, 12, and naturally Phil. 3:4ff. The references are surprisingly fre-
quent! Moreover, I don't understand how Bornkamm's statement and his reserve about
treating Paul's call in the light of Christ's appearance to him relate to his own statement
that Christology and justification in Paul are not only inseparable from one another
but are actually the center of the Pauline gospel *(Paul,* 116–17; 248–49), and that "all
controversy apart" self-designations such as " 'apostle called by the will of God,' 'servant of Jesus Christ,' and so on [are] of the utmost importance for Paul" *(Paul,* 164).
Precisely if we, with Bornkamm, do not want to separate the theology of the apostle,
his proclamation, and Paul's history from one another but rather understand and interpret them as a unity (cf. *Paul,* xxvi–xxviii and frequently), it is through his call that
we discover that the Pauline gospel originally was also tied to Paul's individuality as

an apostle, however little it stands or falls with the fate of this individuality. Without agreeing with Wilckens' understanding of the law (cf. my *Paulinisches Evangelium*, 75, n. 4), I therefore consider it correct when he, in "Bekehrung des Paulus," 274, writes, "For as infrequently [?], sparingly, and reticently as Paul speaks of his experience, just as closely connected are these infrequent [?] statements with his whole interpretation of the gospel of Christ—just as basically also the understanding of these statements will contribute to an understanding of the Pauline proclamation as a whole."

18. Article on Paul in the *Calwer Bibellexicon* 204; also good on Paul's call are these words in H. J. Schoeps, *Paul*, trans. H. Knight (Philadelphia: Westminster Press, 1961), 55: "If we wish to understand what happened at this point in the life of the apostle, and what were its consequences, then we must accept fully the real objectivity of the encounter as it is testified in the letters and in Acts." Cf. also Blank, *Paulus und Jesus*, 184–85.

19. If we consider the key eschatological role Paul assigns to his apostleship (illuminating on this is Bornkamm, *Paul*, 49ff.), we will be able to hold to this interpretation of 1 Cor. 15:8 with, for example, Dibelius-Kümmel, *Paul*, 50, or H. Conzelmann, *1 Corinthians*, Hermeneia, trans. J. W. Leitch (Philadelphia: Fortress Press, 1975), 259, against Luz, who would like to translate *eschaton de pantōn* merely with "lastly," its theological significance unstressed, *Geschichtsverständnis*, 388–89. Actually one could say that in the apostle's view "Easter" is present for the Corinthians especially in his proclamation and person; but we cannot go into that further at this time.

20. On this text, see, in addition to my outline in *Paulinisches Evangelium*, 69ff., especially Blank, *Paulus und Jesus*, 208–30, and Grässer, "Das eine Evangelium." I agree to a large extent with Grässer's study and point especially to his fine definition (p. 321): the Pauline gospel "is not a system of statements and doctrines *about* God; rather, it is an event by which God, in a very specific way and with a very specific intention, lets himself be known as the one who calls. His call has power. For with this call *he himself*, God, comes onto the scene, ruling and in control" (emphases Grässer's). In view of the fact that this statement is almost identical with my view of the apostle's gospel, I question the basis for Grässer's reservation about my picture (for example, 342, n. 142), and I further question, in view of my references to the new time opened by the gospel, to the christological content of the gospel and of the definition of the righteousness of God as the reconciling will of God in the work and rule of Christ (*Das paulinische Evangelium*, 68, 79, note, 81ff., 289; also my "Erwägungen zum Problem von Gegenwart und Zukunft in der paulinischen Eschatologie," *ZTK* 64 [1967]: 423–50, and the meditation "Siehe, ich mache alles neu," *LR* 18 [1968]: 3–18), whether he can really say that in my book, "unmindful of all criticism" I bring up "the apocalyptic understanding of Paul for discussion once again with reference to another central theological issue" (in his review in the *Deutsches Pfarrerblatt* 69 [1969]: 672). For my part I still don't understand how Grässer can speak with emphasis about the gospel as a power of God, about God as the calling one, and about God's unlimited power that raises the dead and in that connection only incidentally point out that Paul hereby "stands in Old Testament linguistic tradition" (*Das eine Evangelium*, 324, n. 64, and 325). That Paul not only actually utilized but consciously held on to the Old Testament for theological reasons is certainly also known to Grässer! On this premise, what is the hermeneutical significance of Paul's clearly reflected attachment to Old Testament–Jewish tradition in language and thought, specifically for the proclamation of the gospel about Christ? Moreover, when Grässer grants Käsemann (and me) the possibility of including the history of Jesus of Nazareth as part of the proclamation of the gospel (*Das eine Evangelium*, 331–32), doesn't the search for Old Testament–Jewish components in such a kerygmatic historical account then acquire once more a high theological significance? To these questions, not unimportant for proclamation

today, I do not yet see Grässer giving any answer. Beyond that I wish to take this opportunity to point out once again that it is not my concern, and in my view theologically cannot be my concern, to sketch the Pauline proclamation about Christ into religion-historical, apocalyptic-Jewish structures that were already at hand, picturing it thereby as simply a modification thereof. Rather, on the contrary, what interests me is showing the possibilities for interpretation and expression that Paul gained for the proclamation of his gospel by (consciously) attaching himself to Old Testament–Jewish ways of thinking and speaking.

21. Cf. Schlatter's article on Paul, 201; Dibelius-Kümmel, *Paul,* 33; Bornkamm, *Paul,* 11. Bornkamm's critical question whether Paul's study with Gamaliel might not be the product of Lukan tendencies is in my opinion to be answered in the negative by reference to the new observations about Pauline hermeneutics by J. Jeremias, "Paulus als Hillelit," in *Neotestamentica et Semitica. Studies in Honour of M. Black,* ed. E. E. Ellis and M. Wilcox (Edinburgh: T. & T. Clark, 1969), 88–94.

22. On this see, for example, Kümmel, *Theology of the New Testament,* 150–51; Conzelmann, *Outline,* 164; Blank, *Paulus und Jesus,* 238–48; Bornkamm, *Paul,* 42ff; H. Kasting, *Die Anfänge der urchristlichen Mission,* BEvT 55 (Munich: Kaiser, 1969), 53ff.

23. Cf., besides Käsemann's well-known essay, "A Pauline Version of the 'Amor Fati,'" in *New Testament Questions of Today,* 217–35, Blank, *Paulus und Jesus,* 206–7, and Grässer, "Das eine Evangelium," 318, 321.

24. Cf. the very illuminating presentation of Paul's missionary activity and sense of mission in Bornkamm, *Paul,* 49ff., and E. Güttgemanns, *Der leidende Apostle und sein Herr,* FRLANT 90 (Göttingen: Vandenhoeck & Ruprecht, 1966), esp. 142ff., 154ff.

25. For a recent alternative perspective see R. Bring, *Christus und das Gesetz* (Leiden: Brill, 1969), chap. 2, "Die Gerechtigkeit Gottes und das alttestamentliche Gesetz" (pp. 35–72).

26. In my sketch of "Theologische Probleme des Romerbriefpräskripts," *EvT* 27 (1967): 374–90, I suggested not only explaining the use of the pre-Pauline christological tradition in Rom. 1:3–4 apologetically or ecumenically from a tradition-historical perspective but attempting to interpret the use of such tradition on the basis of the Pauline proclamation of the gospel. Luz, *Geschichtsverständnis,* 111–12, has pointed out in response that "*evangelion* without the article, the connection of prediction and prophets, as well as the expression 'holy scriptures' [are] . . . unpauline," indeed that "primarily [Paul wants] neither to make a statement about the gospel nor to make one about a christology structured by reference to the promise but [to use] both to characterize his apostleship," an apostleship, it's true, "that stands in the service of the proclamation of the gospel and agrees with the saving will of God already proclaimed through the prophetic word." I regard this exegesis as a step backward in comparison with my—admittedly and consciously strongly systematizing—theses. The following are my reasons, which can only be hinted at here: gospel and apostleship are for Paul inseparable and impossible to remove from one another. In addition, G. Klein, in his essay "Der Abfassungszweck des Römerbriefes" (in *Rekonstruktion und Interpretation. Gesammelte Aufsätze zum Neuen Testament,* BEvT 50 [Munich: Kaiser, 1969], 129–44 [an essay that I evaluate in substantially more positive terms than does W. Schmithals, in *EvK* 2 (1969): 609]), has now pointed out, among other things, that in Romans, in contrast to the epistolary prescripts in his other letters, Paul treats the topic of the gospel already in the opening section ("Abfassungszweik," 142). Therefore, precisely if one wants to give an exegetically nuanced interpretation, it is necessary in our passage especially to attend to the phenomenon of the gospel and to regard the reference to apostleship as a convention (which, to be sure, is not for that reason insignificant). The correspondence between the prophetic office and apostleship is a characteristic not

only of the epistolary prescript in Romans but also of the Pauline call-narrative in Gal. 1:15. Finally, the use of substantives without the article is not uncommon in Pauline epistolary prescripts (cf., for example, v. 5, "freely formulated by Paul" according to Luz [*Geschichtsverständnis*, 111–12], with 1 Cor. 15:10). All that still remains is to call attention in passing to the fact that—as Luz himself has brought out very well (cf. *Geschichtsverständnis*, 288, n. 96, and 354–55)—Paul adapts traditions responsibly, as an apostle, so that it is not legitimate without further ado to use the identification of traditions in Paul to declare that traditional thought patterns are theologically less significant than genuine Pauline ones. Since Luz has not avoided this danger fully, I stick to my old suggestion, point once again to the parallel in 1 Cor. 15:8–9, and welcome the agreement of E. Schweizer, *Jesus*, 70, n. 11.

27. G. Bornkamm, s. v. "Paulus," *RGG* (3d ed.) 5:177, and *Paul*, 116–17, 248–49.

28. About the interpretation of this still-controversial expression I wish only to say the following in our context: a righteousness of God other than one that is realized and imparted christologically is not at issue for Paul, but this righteousness of God remains a proof of salvation inseparable from God's work of imparting himself to the world and the sinner in forgiveness and new creation. Käsemann espoused this interpretation of the concept from the beginning, and he has even supported it once again (cf. his two essays mentioned in n. 12, "Righteousness of God in Paul" and "Justification and Salvation History") and, for example, Luz, *Geschichtsverständnis*, 169, n. 128, and U. Wilckens, "Warum sagt Paulus: 'Aus Werken des Gesetzes wird niemand gerecht'?" EKKNT, *Vorarbeiten*, Heft 1 (Neukirchen: Neukirchener Verlag, 1969), 69, n. 51, have correctly seen that this is what I wanted to say. By saying this I would by no means be rejecting criticism of my dissertation as one-sided. To be sure, the tradition-historical solution of the problem, which Bultmann already had in mind and which has been defended anew by Conzelmann, *Outline*, 214–20, and "Die Rechtfertigungslehre des Paulus: Theologie oder Anthropologie?" (*EvT* 28 [1968]: 389–404), and Klein, "Gottes Gerechtigkeit als Thema der neuesten Paulusforschung" (in *Rekonstruktion und Interpretation*, 225–36)—according to which the concept of the righteousness of God designating God's own behavior belongs particularly to the pre-Pauline Christian tradition and the soteriological concept of the righteousness of God, meaning the righteousness of faith, belongs especially to Paul—appears to be an inadmissible simplification of the problem. The double aspect, of a behavior that characterizes God and of the gift of God, is demonstrable already in the pre-Pauline Christian tradition (just compare Rom. 3:24–25, on the one hand, and 2 Cor. 5:21, also a traditional formulation, on the other) and is expressly affirmed by Paul himself, as Rom. 3:26 unambiguously shows. The objection, raised almost stereotypically by Bornkamm (*Paul*, 147) and his pupils F. Hahn (orally) and E. Brandenburger (*Fleisch und Geist*, WMANT 29 [Neukirchen-Vluyn: Neukirchener Verlag, 1968], 222ff.), that when the righteousness of God is understood in the sense of a self-manifesting power of God "surprisingly little is said . . . of the coordination of God's righteousness and faith" (Bornkamm, *Paul*, 147), has already been answered by Käsemann ("Justification and Salvation History," 78). I also do not find the objection compelling, since faith for Paul is not an anthropological principle but the obedience which always depends on the word of the gospel as a recognition of God in Christ (cf. the fine treatment of this in Eichholz, "Prolegomena," 169). I have stressed the indissoluble connection of the righteousness of God and the word of proclamation offered only to faith from the beginning of my work. So the problems are still undecided and are by no means soluble solely with the help of the context analysis brought into the field recently by Klein and Conzelmann in an all too one-sided attack on concept-historical arguments.

29. With H. Windisch, *Der zweite Korintherbrief*, MeyerK 6, 9th ed. (Göttingen: Vandenhoeck & Ruprecht, 1924) 140; Bultmann, s. v. "Paulus" *RGG* (2d ed.) 4:1021–22; Dibelius-Kümmel, *Paul*, 60; Bornkamm, *Paul*, 23; and Seidensticker, *Paulus*, 17,

93, and among others, I refer 2 Cor. 4:6 to Paul's call. The stylized way of speaking noted by Windisch is not strange but is to be interpreted on the basis of Phil. 3:7.

30. Therewith I am stating more precisely what I mean in my habilitation treatise and in my reflections on Pauline eschatology mentioned in n. 20 above by the salvation-prolepsis of the gospel, and at the same time addressing the question put to me by Luz (*Geschichtsverständnis*, 398–99). As I stressed already in n. 20, it is not my view that "the apocalyptic outline of history in its unbroken totality and especially its end [would be] necessary to an understanding of revelation history and Christology," but rather I believe that the Christ event both establishes and triggers historical-theological reflection and eschatological expectation on Paul's part. I already said this in *ZTK* 64 (1967): 445, n. 48, when I there, referring to a formulation of Bornkamm's, subsumed Pauline eschatology under the thesis "Since God has already done everything, you may expect everything from God." Kümmel, for example, has also correctly understood my view in this christological sense ("Die exegetische Erforschung des Neuen Testaments in diesem Jahrhundert," in *Bilanz der Theologie im 20. Jahrhundert*, ed. H. Vorgrimler and R. van der Gucht, 4 vols. [Freiburg: Herder, 1969–70], 2:337 [279–377]). The category of prolepsis or anticipation arrived at in my book on the Pauline gospel by means of tradition analysis and structural analysis of the phenomenon gospel is, thus, filled out christologically by Paul and arrived at by him, as stated more precisely above, not speculatively but on the basis of his call-experience. Of course, this very category also enabled him to think about eschatology christologically, that is, as the completion of the lordship of Christ leading to the glorification of God. Consequently, in the midst of the old world Paul can already live in the sweep of christologically based hope and freedom that are more than all individual futurity, that establish clear goals for his ethical exhortation, and, as expressly affirmed by Luz, that move toward the eschatological glorification of God. Since neither Conzelmann (*Outline*, 206), nor Bornkamm (*Paul*, 197ff.), neither Grässer, (*Das eine Evangelium*, 308, n. 8; 326) nor Luz (*Geschichtsverständnis*, cf. 399–400) gets along without this kind of anticipatory understanding of Pauline Christology, I don't understand why "with the methodological starting point chosen by Stuhlmacher a severe distortion must be feared," for which the "frequently met expression 'prolepsis' for the Pauline understanding of salvation . . . is the vivid [warning flag]" (thus Schmithals in his notice [which strongly distorts my theses, to be sure] about my habilitation treatise in the Theologische Literaturbeilage to the *Reformierte Kirchenzeitung*, 15/16 [August 1, 1969]: 1).

31. Schlatter, "Jesus und Paulus," 24 (cf. 88ff.) and his article "Paulus," 201.

32. That the application of Deut. 21:23 to the crucifixion of Jesus in Gal. 3:13 may be traced to Jewish polemic and ascribed to Paul already in his struggle against the Christians has been shown, following a conjecture of P. Feine's (*Das gesetzesfreie Evangelium des Paulus* [Leipzig: Hinrichs, 1899], 18), by G. Jeremias by reference to the exegesis of Deut. 21:23 in 4QpNah 1:7–8 (*Der Lehrer der Gerechtigkeit*, SUNT 2 [Göttingen: Vandenhoeck & Ruprecht, 1963], 133–35. On this, see also J. Jeremias, *Der Opfertod Jesu Christi*, Calwer Hefte 62 (Stuttgart: Calwer Verlag, 1963), 14; Schoeps, *Paul*, 86–87; Blank, *Paulus und Jesus*, 245, 247–48; Kümmel, *Theology of the New Testament*, 150. On the rabbinic interpretation of Deut. 21:23, cf. not only Str-B 3:544; 1:1012–13, 1034, but also *Tgs. Yerusalmi* 1 and 2 to Num. 25:4 (on this see M. Hengel, *The Charismatic Leader and His Followers*, trans. J. Greig [New York: Crossroad, 1981], 58, n. 77), where crucifixion by Jews is still presupposed and regarded as the carrying out of the *rwgz' dyy* = wrath of God.

33. Since Paul persecutes a Hellenistic-Jewish congregation that in the name of the risen Lord dares to abrogate the law, and since Gal. 3:13, on the basis of the death on the cross, presents a direct polemical connection between the law and (a contested) Christology, it is unnecessary for our interpretation to go into the difficulty that arises

for Wilckens ("Bekehrung des Paulus," 281) that just as in Jewish Christianity faith in the Messiah and the abrogation of the law don't need to be connected, so also for the Pharisee Paul the doctrine of the law and messianology "had little direct . . . connection."

34. Just see the second benediction of the Eighteen Benedictions (W. Staerk, Altjüdische liturgische Gebete, KIT 58, 2d ed. [Berlin: de Gruyter, 1930], 11, 15).

35. The verb Paul uses in 1 Cor. 15:8, ōphthē, characterizes the appearance of Christ as an epiphany by the power of God. Cf. on this the fine overview by J. Kremer, *Das älteste Zeugnis von der Auferstehung Christi*, 2d ed., SBS 17 (Stuttgart: Verlag Katholisches Bibelwerk, 1967), 54ff.

36. Conzelmann, *Outline*, 202.

37. Like Käsemann, *New Testament Questions of Today*, 184, Wilckens ("Bekehrung des Paulus," 277, and "Warum sagt Paulus," 70ff.) also emphasizes the correspondence of the biographical report in Phil. 3:4ff. to the fundamental statement in Rom. 10:4. Cf. further Bornkamm, *Paul*, 16–17, and Blank, "Warum sagt Paulus, 'Aus Werken des Gesetzes wird niemand gerecht'?" EKKNT, *Vorarbeiten*, Heft 1, 79–95, esp. 91.

38. Even more forcefully than Wilckens, "Warum sagt Paulus," 66, Käsemann, in his essay "The Faith of Abraham in Romans 4" (in *Perspectives on Paul*, 79–101), has stressed that Abraham is used by Paul as "the prototype of the justification of the ungodly" (p. 89) and that the formulation that God justifies the ungodly (Rom. 4:5) is "the indispensible key to Paul's doctrine of justification" (p. 84). Käsemann's analysis appears to me incontrovertible. I also agree with his explanations (arrived at in debate with Klein and Wilckens) of the Pauline understanding of salvation history (for Käsemann, a salvation history that finds its continuity in God alone is indeed indispensable for Paul [pp. 86ff.]). But in this context it should be pointed out, without relativizing Käsemann's explanations, that Paul came to a knowledge of the God who justifies the ungodly only through his own call and justification.

39. Somewhat differently from J. Gnilka (*Der Philipperbrief*, HTKNT [Freiburg: Herder, 1968], 194–95), I believe that the terminology about justification in Phil. 3:9–10 doesn't find its way onto Paul's pen only by chance, as a brief parenthetical remark, but that it is formulated with the conscious intention of classifying things precisely. However, as before, I resist making Phil. 3:9 the key to understanding the expression "the righteousness of God" in Paul, as Bornkamm again suggests (*Paul*, 136–37). It is true that we should not make an abrupt separation between Phil. 3:9 and Rom. 10:3, as C. Müller does in his book *Gottes Gerechtigkeit und Gottes Volk* (FRLANT 86 [Göttingen: Vandenhoeck & Ruprecht, 1964], 74), where he states, "The apostle means something entirely different in Phil. 3:9 from Rom. 10:3." Rather, it appears to me to be historically necessary to connect Rom. 10:3 and Phil. 3:9 and to speak of a righteousness of God that discloses itself as justifying, with Phil. 3:9 having in view primarily the gift-character of such disclosure to the individual. More clearly than I demonstrated in my dissertation (*Gerechtigkeit Gottes bei Paulus*, FRLANT 87, 2d ed. [Göttingen: Vandenhoeck & Ruprecht, 1966], 100–101), attention is to be given to the fact that the well-known expression used by Paul in Phil. 3:9, *hē ek theou dikaiosunē*, corresponds to Jewish thinking (thinking that becomes apparent already in Isa. 54:17). Judaism sees in God's Spirit, in his word, and in his patterns of behavior, wrath or righteousness, for example, operative realities, which, since they proceed from God, are effective, as it says, both "from him and before him" (= *m' t* or *mn qdm*). Two examples may clarify that. The Masoretic text of Isa. 61:1 reads, "The Spirit of the Lord is upon me, because Yahweh has anointed me" (*rwḥ 'dny yhwh 'ly y'n msḥ yhwh 'ty*). The targum reads, "The prophet says: 'the Spirit of prophecy from before the Lord is upon me" (*rwḥ nbw'h mn qdm yhwh 'lhym 'ly*). Or, in Isa. 63:1b, a self-designation of Yahweh's reads, "It is I, announcing vindication, mighty to save" (*rb lhysy'*). The

targum has "He said, 'Behold, I reveal myself as I announced vindication, mighty before me is the power to save' " (*sgy qdmy ḥyl lmprq*). The *dikaiosunē ek theou* in Phil. 3:9 is, then, the righteousness that proceeds from God and is effective before him as a gift that is not separable from God himself (in Hebrew perhaps *ṣdqt 'l mn qdm 'lhym* or the like). If one sees these correlations, then the connection between Phil. 3:9 and Rom. 10:3 is clear. But then one will not want to speak of the gift-character of the righteousness of God as the only feature that predominates for Paul but one must see in the righteousness of God in Paul a self-imparting saving power and operative reality revealed to faith. In the operation of this righteousness of God, God and humanity are indissolubly connected as giver and receiver (on this issue cf. also n. 28).

40. On this text see the fine comments in Blank, *Paulus und Jesus*, 231. In reference to Bultmann's thesis (*Theology of the New Testament*, 1:188) that the meaning of Paul's conversion was that "he surrendered his previous understanding of himself; i.e. he surrendered what had till then been the norm and meaning of his life, he sacrificed what had hitherto been his pride and joy (Phil. 3:4–7)," Blank writes, "As correct as the idea of a 'new self-understanding' is, it is nevertheless clear precisely from Phil. 3:4–11 that the apostle's 'self-understanding' is *based on his knowledge of Christ;* it is a christologically and in this context also an eschatologically based self-understanding, eschatologically with reference to the still awaited end, the parousia, but also, as one must say for Philippians, to the end of the apostle's own life. Finally, it should be clear that even according to Phil. 3:4–11 his self-understanding is not based on the 'kerygma,' but on the experience of the reality of the risen one, who himself first made the Yes to the cross possible (cf. the order of vv. 10f.). With these qualifications, offered by the text itself, the idea of the 'gaining of a new self-understanding' has its relative justification" (emphasis Blank's).

41. Agreeing here, for example, with Grässer, *Das eine Evangelium*, 316–17, 338. Grässer also correctly emphasized (316, n. 37) that Paul's teaching on justification should not be pictured as arising only in the battle against Judaizers, in Galatia, for instance. If justification is an explication of Christology, then the polemical enemy against which the justifying God is turned from the start is the sinner pure and simple (cf. Käsemann, "Justification and Salvation History," 70ff.).

42. Cf. Käsemann, "The Saving Significance of the Death of Jesus in Paul" (1967), in *Perspectives on Paul*, 32–59 (54): "just as, historically speaking, the crucifixion precedes the Easter appearances, so for the faith of the primitive church all knowledge of Jesus (in the sense of certainty of salvation) was only possible after Easter. This applies to the one who was incarnate and crucified as well as to the one who was pre-existent and exalted. Nor must we confine this observation to the experience of the primitive church. *It is a basic truth and applies at all periods. If this were not so, a theology of the Word would be quite unjustifiable.* For, according to the testimony of the whole of the New Testament, it is the one who is risen who acts through the Word of proclamation, even when the theme of that proclamation is the 'historical' Jesus" (emphasis mine).

43. Bornkamm has brought this out very nicely (*Paul*, 120–21): "To say what is perfectly correct historically, that the meaning of Christ's coming was deductible from the Law, was, in his view, not enough. Put in such general terms, the statement was true for all the first Christian converts from Judaism. For Paul, however—and for him alone—it also held true when put the other way around: only in the light of Christ could one deduce the status of the law. The law was the basis of, and the limitation put upon, the unredeemed existence of all men, both Jew and Gentile." Cf. also W. Schrage, "Römer 3:21–26 und die Bedeutung des Todes Jesu Christi bei Paulus," in *Das Kreuz Jesu. Theologische Überlegungen*, ed. P. Rieger, Forum Heft 12 (Göttingen: Vandenhoeck & Ruprecht, 1969), 65–88, esp. 70.

44. H. J. Schoeps, *Paul*, 168.

45. That applies also to the catchy phrase coined first by Schlatter (for example, in the article "Paulus," 212 and now adopted primarily by Wilckens ("Bekehrung des Paulus," 285, and "Warum sagt Paulus," 70), that "Christ has replaced the law." With this thesis Paul's whole understanding of the law is up for grabs. It appears to me to be fundamental for this point of view that Moses and Christ are always opposites. Consequently it dare not be said that for Paul Christ has replaced the law, but it must be acknowledged that the matter is much more complex.

46. A. van Dülmen, *Die Theologie des Gesetzes bei Paulus*, SBM 5 (Stuttgart: Katholisches Bibelwerk, 1968), has passionately urged that we have to view the question of the law in Paul from the perspective of Christology but that we have to regard the law itself "as a unified, self-contained entity whose nature does not allow further differentiation" (p. 133, and often). I grant van Dülmen that the solution of the problem of the law solely on the basis of an anthropological dialectic, advocated especially by Bultmann ("Christ the End of the Law," in *Essays Philosophical and Theological*, trans. J. C. G. Greig [London: SCM Press, 1955], 36–66, and *Theology of the New Testament*, 1:259–69), is not adequate alone, as correct as it remains in its context. The thought and discussion on the level of anthropology does, it's true, allow Bultmann and all who follow him to answer in the negative the question pointedly asked already by Schlatter, and now by van Dülmen and Wilckens, whether Paul's teaching on justification doesn't have the goal of making out of sinners who cannot fulfill the law righteous people who can fulfill it. So understood, the Pauline teaching on justification would actually offer only a christological modification of the impressive self-critical piety of the law advocated in the Qumran texts, for example. But this possibility exists only as long as one doesn't go into the concept of the law itself and its inner dialectic in Paul. That is, it appears to me that the exegetes mentioned above have overlooked the basic fact that the apostle, with a boldness that actually breaks out of the Jewish circle of tradition and perspective, discusses the weakness of the law as an institution (examples of this are found in Gal. 3:21 and Rom. 8:3; good on this are O. Kuss, "Nomos bei Paulus," *MTZ* 17 [1966]: 173–227, esp. 218–19, and Blank, "Warum sagt Paulus," EKKNT, *Vorarbeiten*, Heft 1, 89, 94–95)! But since Paul just as unmistakably holds to the will of God in the law (just see Rom. 1:18—3:20 and 7:7ff.) and interprets the "law of Christ" (Gal. 6:2; cf. 1 Cor. 9:21), provocatively so-named by him (hardly by his opponents, as K. Wegenast [*Das Verständnis der Tradition bei Paulus und in den Deuteropaulinen*, WMANT 8 (Neukirchen-Vluyn: Neukirchener Verlag, 1962)], 38, n. 4, and D. Lührmann [*Das Offenbarungsverständnis bei Paulus und in paulinischen Gemeinden*, WMANT 16 (Neukirchen-Vluyn; Neukirchener Verlag, 1965)], 68, hypothesize), as the love command, in analogy to the law of Moses, one must decide to regain the anthropological dialectic of old and new, sinner and righteous also in the discussion about the law itself, the law of Moses and the law of Christ standing over against one another as old and new. They find their continuity only in this, that even in its weakness the law of Moses has to serve the grace of God, and Christ carries out and life-creatively represents this primal will, God's will to love. Since Paul gives Christ, as the preexistent Son of God, precedence over Adam and his guilt, as well as over the giving of the law at Sinai, he can actually think that Christ represents the original will of God as love which, to be sure, expresses itself in the law of Moses, but is not effective to create and preserve life. What in this presentation is "perforce problematic," Luz, who makes such an accusation (*Geschichtsverständnis*, 398, n. 4), must first show, and it would be best if he did this in a treatment of the phenomenon of the law of Christ, left unaddressed in his book.

47. Luz, *Geschichtsverständnis*, 157.

48. I can only agree with Bornkamm *(Paul)*, 129–30, when he stresses that none of the anthropological terms is considered philosophically by Paul. "Just as he never embarks upon abstract discussion of the being of God or the term 'God' or makes crea-

tion an 'article of doctrine,' so, too, he makes no theoretical pronouncements about man."

49. Developed with intensive systematic interest by Käsemann in his study "On Paul's Anthropology," the expression is present already in *RGG*, 3d ed., 2:1275; similar in content is K. H. Schelkle, *Theology of the New Testament*, trans. W. Jurgens, 4 vols. (Collegeville, Minn.: Liturgical Press, 1971–78), 1:111–41, esp. 125ff.

50. In this context several things appear important to me which I can only hint at now: First, it appears to me fundamental to take up the insight offered by G. Bornkamm in his well-known papers "The Revelation of God's Wrath (Romans 1—3)" (in *Early Christian Experience*, trans. P. Hammer [London: SCM Press, 1969], 47–70) and "Gesetz und Natur" (in *Gesammelte Aufsätze*, 4 vols., vol. 2: *Studien zu Antike und Urchristentum*, BEvT 28 [Munich: Kaiser, 1959], 93–118); carried forward by his pupils H. Koester, "NOMOS PHYSEŌS. The Concept of Natural Law in Greek Thought" (in *Religions in Antiquity. Essays in Memory of E. R. Goodenough*, ed. J. Neusner, Sup. to Numen 14 [Leiden: Brill, 1968], 521–41), and E. Brandenburger, *Fleisch und Geist* (here esp. 106ff., 232–33); and independently developed in greater detail by H. Fr. Weiss, *Untersuchungen zur Kosmologie des hellenistischen und palästinischen Judentums* (TU 97 [Berlin: Akademie-Verlag, 1966], here esp. 277ff., 283ff.), and M. Hengel, *Judaism and Hellenism* (trans. J. Bowden, 2 vols. [Philadelphia: Fortress Press, 1974], here esp. 1:171ff., 174–75)—the insight that the torah was a cosmic principle equally for Hellenistic and Palestinian Judaism, so that Hengel dares to speak graphically of an "ontological understanding of the torah" that finds its climax in anthropology (on this see Hengel, *Charismatic Leader*, 31). On the basis of this background it appears requisite to consider the Pauline statements about the law and about wisdom together and to ask if Paul did not also battle against the law as a power holding together the world as a whole and shaping humanity. If the gospel about Christ was supposed to put an end to the polemical claim of such a cosmically significant law, then it would have to be a match for this law. I have sought to show the outlines of this understanding of the gospel in my book *Das paulinische Evangelium:* the gospel, understood as a word of the creator and as a powerful promise, is for Paul actually an entity by whose aid the lordship of the Crucified Risen One can be proclaimed in a way that puts an end to the law and helps God's will to burst forth. When G. Klein (*EvK* 2 [1969]: 736–37) disputes the tradition-historical analyses in my book in all details, he needs to offer better ones, from which I would gladly profit. As far as his doubt about Paul's salvation-history thinking, which also shapes his concept of the gospel, is concerned, I am unable to go along with it, not even when Klein suspects the acknowledgment of *Ioudaiǭ te prōton kai Hellēni* in Rom. 1:16 of being law-oriented thinking. In clear contrast to Klein, Paul did not feel that his insight into God acting on the basis of a saving history to which he continued to be bound was law but an experience of God's faithfulness, which is constitutive for his gospel. On this topic cf. Eichholz, "Prolegomena," 178–79, and also the vigorous criticism that Käsemann (*Perspectives of Paul*, 86ff.) practices on Klein's analysis of Romans 4, which coincides with Kümmel's ("Exegetische Erforschung," 337–38) concern about Klein's formulation. If one sees the connections that have been drawn, then it seems to me the attempt at least needs to be made to construct a picture of the Pauline proclamation about Christ under these historical presuppositions of law and gospel. For this task, recourse to ancient thought forms can certainly not be avoided, and that leads to the final task confronting us. That is to test and to investigate without overhasty hermeneutical criticism whether the Pauline plan doesn't provide the impetus for theological reflection which allows the theology of the word of God to free itself from the rearguard actions it is presently waging and its apologetic isolation and to make it anew what in my view, according to the New Testament, it undoubtedly is: the vital core of all theology.

CHAPTER 9

Eighteen Theses
on Paul's Theology
of the Cross*

Eberhard Jüngel and Jürgen Moltmann are concerned at present with redefining the identity of Protestant theology on the basis of a theology of the cross understood from a trinitarian perspective. New Testament exegesis can only rejoice over this endeavor, because it is thereby challenged to make its own contribution and to ask the question whether it is permissible to locate the center of the New Testament message of salvation in the proclamation of the cross of Jesus Christ. As far as this very question is concerned, the exegetes are indebted to Ernst Käsemann, above all others, that in the past twelve years he has defended with incomparable provocative vigor the thesis *crux sola nostra theologia* (our only theology is the cross), thereby preparing the way for the present theological efforts on behalf of a theology of the cross. But the exegetes also owe Ernst Käsemann a critical answer to his noteworthy attempt to define the saving significance of the cross, in clear association with his teacher Rudolf Bultmann, by emphasizing its dependence on the First Commandment: Christ dies for us as the one who remains obedient to God unto death on the cross; as this sole obedient one he is raised by God and enthroned as Lord of the world; the community participates in the power of the death and resurrection of Jesus, which binds them to God once and for all, by following the Crucified obediently as their Lord, that is, by entering into Jesus' fulfillment of the First Commandment, letting no one be Lord save God in Christ alone, and for that taking up their cross; such followers are able to console themselves in God as their gracious Father in Christ and in the coming resurrection of the dead. If this is the central thought of what Käsemann, viewing Paul and Jesus together, calls the theology of the cross, we now need to ask whether this definition actually coincides with Pauline and Synoptic statements about the cross and, accordingly, whether it can be called a valid summary of the New Testament message about the cross and of the Reformation's *theologia crucis*.

If one is concerned, first of all, about taking stock of Pauline ideas on the

155

topic, a series of conclusions can be drawn that can be summarized in the following theses and elaborations.

1. The proclamation of the cross involves the whole of Pauline theology, focused on critical issues relating to the law and wisdom.

It is unmistakable that the apostle shapes the central assertions of his proclamation about the cross in controversy with the Corinthian enthusiasts, intent on Christian wisdom and pneumatic power (cf. 1 Cor. 1:13, 17; 1:18ff., 23ff., 30; 2:2, 8; 2 Cor. 4:7ff.; 12:7ff.; 13:4), and with the Christian nomism threatening in Galatia (cf. Gal. 2:19–20; 3:1ff., 13; 5:11; 5:22ff.; 6:12, 14, 17). This line of attack does not, of course, mean that with the proclamation of the cross we have a topic that forced itself on the apostle only in a polemical context or that was exhausted in the battle with the Corinthians and Galatians! The passages just cited from Paul's letters are flanked by pointed statements like Phil. 2:8; 3:18; or the language in Rom. 6:6 that defines baptism as being crucified with Christ, and they find their liturgical and discursive echo in Col. 1:20 and Eph. 2:16. If one gives full attention to a concordance of what the proclamation contains in the passages listed, one quickly recognizes that in his theology of the cross Paul discusses nothing less than his justification theology as a whole, together with the question about the legitimacy of his apostleship. Accordingly, the second thesis must read:

2. The crucified Christ appeared to Paul outside Damascus as the Son of God raised from the dead, that is, as the "end of the law," and hence he was viewed by the apostle as the saving revelation of God par excellence; it is this very revelation about which the "word of the cross" in Paul's gospel is speaking.

When Paul consciously calls the gospel about Christ that was entrusted to him the "word of the cross" in 1 Cor. 1:17, 18ff., he thereby summarizes a threefold set of circumstances: by virtue of his epiphany of Christ outside Damascus he has a fully valid call as apostle to the Gentiles and as far as his office is concerned, he is in no respect inferior to the apostles called before him; in his call-epiphany Jesus of Nazareth, who had been condemned to die on the cross under a curse for blaspheming God and violating the law, appeared to him as the glorified Son of God vindicated by God, that is, Christ came as the one in whose death and resurrection the Mosaic law reached the end of its power to condemn sinners (cf. Rom. 10:4); on the basis of his encounter with the risen Christ, the cross of Jesus proved to be for Paul the particular place at which the Mosaic law and Jewish wisdom identified with the law were unmasked as powers that mislead sinners into self-assertion before God and deprived of this power to lead astray and bring death.—If one asks more precisely how Paul understands the death of Jesus and what he means when he speaks of Christ crucified "for us," we must answer:

3. Paul sees in the crucified Christ primarily the Son of God who freed us by the vicarious sacrifice of his life from the curse of the law and reconciled us

to God, who by virtue of his resurrection was installed as Lord of the world and advocate of the community.

As inclined as one may be under Bultmann's influence to view things differently, just as strongly must we insist on this statement of the matter. In Paul talk about the atoning death of Jesus is no traditional relic but the condition that makes his theology of justification and of the cross possible! This becomes clear in this context from 1 Cor. 1:13, 23–24, 30; 2:2, as well as from Gal. 2:19–20; 3:1, 13.

The decisive christological phrases in 1 Corinthians 1 and 2, "crucified for us," "the power of God and the wisdom of God," "righteousness and sanctification and redemption," can be explained in Paul's own writings in no other way than on the basis of Rom. 3:25–26; 4:25; 5:8ff.; 7:4; 8:3–4, 31ff.; 1 Cor. 8:11; 11:23ff.; 15:3–5, 17; 2 Cor. 5:18–21, etc.; and Col. 1:14, 20; 2:14; Eph. 1:7; 2:16ff., offer the deutero-Pauline commentary thereon. Paul adopts on a broader basis Old Testament and Jewish ideas about atonement and sin offering, which Christians before him had already applied to Jesus' death on the cross. In following this tradition he in no way distinguishes between ideas of atonement and substitution as do his modern interpreters, who undervalue historically and theologically the atonement traditions in the Old Testament; rather, he recognizes that it is the vicarious sacrifice of Jesus' life on the cross that makes it possible for believers to be acquitted of their sins by God in the act of justification, to be received anew, and to be entrusted to the Crucified Risen One as their Lord. The idea of a reconciliation established by the death and resurrection of Christ is in fact so important to the apostle and so inseparable for him from the lordship of the Risen One that he—as is later the case for Heb. 7:25; 9:24; and 1 John 2:1–2—can speak of the intercession of the Christ enthroned (as reconciler!) at God's right hand, which also assures those persecuted and oppressed on earth of justification on judgment day (Rom. 8:34).

This is confirmed by Gal. 1:4; 2:19–20; 3:1, 13. Here not only does it become clear that the message about the crucified Christ is the proclamation of that Lord who out of love, that is, in total unity of will with his father, gave himself into death for us and whose sacrifice of his life was the price that "ransomed" us from the curse the law imposed on sinners, but one can also see how Paul establishes his thesis about Christ as the "end of the law" specifically on Jesus' death on the cross. The excerpts from the Temple Scroll from Qumran (Col. 64:6–13) published by Yigael Yadin show today most clearly that pre-Christian Judaism already applied the instruction from Deut. 21:(22,) 23, cited by Paul in Gal. 3:13, to the execution of lawbreakers on the cross and understood the death of these people as a curse by God and humanity. That the Jews also interpreted Jesus' crucifixion in this way is attested not only by the well-known passages in Justin's *Dialog with Trypho* 89.2 and 90.1, but already by John 19:31ff., together with the ancient apologetic "contrast pattern" in Acts 5:30; 10:39; and 13:29. When the apostle in Gal. 3:13 comes to speak about Deut. 21:23, he thus enters into the early Christian discussion about the understanding of Jesus' death on the cross, but in such a way that he turns the Jewish verdict, that Jesus deservedly died the accursed death as a blasphemer of God and a lawbreaker, critically against the law of Moses: in the death and resurrection of Jesus it is not Jesus who fails but the law (which unjustly cursed the blameless Son of God) in its power to cut people off from a relationship with God. The crucified and risen Christ is therefore "the end of the law, that every one who has faith may be justified" (Rom. 10:4). If Paul had rejected the idea of atonement in the form of the vicarious surrender of Jesus' life, he would have been able to establish only inadequately precisely his all-decisive christological thesis about Christ as the end of the law. Therefore, what made it possible for the apostle to explain the exclusive saving significance of Jesus' death kerygmatically, and, in his time, also apologetically and polemically, hangs on the idea of atonement. Incidentally, that is precisely the same for the Reformation, as Luther's hymn "Dear Christians, One and All, Rejoice" and his Smalcald Articles from 1537 (cf. pt. 2.1) demonstrate quite conclusively.—If one has seen and acknowledged this, one can then go into the other components of the Pauline theology of the cross and say:

4. The crucified Christ, as the community's reconciler and Lord, is also its model and its hope, because he is proclaimed to the community by Paul as the righteous Son of God who in archetypal obedience suffered, and was raised from the dead as the first of those who have fallen asleep.

The obedience of Jesus Christ is spoken of in the well-known Christ-hymn in Phil. 2:6–11 as well as in Rom. 5:17–19 and 8:3–4, for example. How strong Paul's interest in the obedience of Jesus is, precisely in the context of his proclamation about the cross, can be seen in Phil. 2:8. When the apostle speaks of Jesus Christ's obedience, three lines of thought are connected with it: precisely in his self-renunciation and in his obedience Jesus is the blameless and Righteous One, who suffers and dies for God's sake (Phil. 2:7ff.; Rom. 8:3–4; 15:2–3), the Christ who obediently dies is raised by God as "the first fruits of those who have fallen asleep" (1 Cor. 15:20); in both his obedience and his status as first fruits of the resurrected, Christ is the model, Lord, and hope of the community, which is called to the obedience of faith and love and enabled on its way of obedience to remember his way of suffering and take consolation in his resurrection (cf. Rom. 14:15; 15:2–3; Phil. 1:29–30; 2:3ff., 12ff.; 3:20–21, etc.). While the atonement tradition that Paul takes up christologically helps him to explicate *sola gratia* with christological clarity, it is the pattern, deeply rooted in the Old Testament and widely branched, of the suffering and vindicated Righteous One, applied to Christ, (and tied to the concept of preexistence; cf. thesis 11), which enables the apostle to interpret the way of the Crucified and Risen One archetypally. As the Synoptic passion tradition or the statements in Acts about the suffering and death of Jesus as the Righteous One (cf. Acts 3:14; 7:52) show, Paul was in all probability also able for this second strand of his theology of the cross to draw on Christian patterns of interpretation, a finding that is confirmed by talk about the "surrender" of Jesus to suffering and death that occurs in Paul as well as in early Synoptic texts (cf. Rom. 4:25, 8:32 with Mark 9:31; 10:33; 14:41 par.). If one observes that already in the Old Testament and in Judaism traditions about atonement must be distinguished from (not divorced from) traditions that speak of the Suffering Righteous One and that also in the New Testament both strands of tradition continue to be distinguished (not divorced), one recognizes the reason that in his theology of the cross Paul combines both lines of interpretation: the atonement tradition speaks of Jesus' inimitable death and the unique act of God, in the form of the resurrection of Jesus "for us" (for example, Rom. 4:25), "ratifying" the vicarious surrender of Jesus' life as a valid occurrence of atonement; the statements about Christ as the Suffering and vindicated Son of God enable us to see Christ and the community united as those who have to follow God's righteous will and who, as doers of this will on earth, experience suffering.—Now, within the second strand of tradition it is characteristic of Paul that in very special measure he identifies himself as an apostle with the suffering Christ, so that one can say:

5. Paul himself, the apostle of the crucified and risen Christ, becomes the proclamation of the cross for his congregations, in that in his life of suffering these congregations encounter him as the primary living commentary on his theology of the cross.

This fact is shown with all clarity by passages in the Corinthian correspondence (cf. 1 Cor. 2:1ff.; 4:6–13; 2 Cor. 4:7–15; 6:1–10; 11:21–33; 12:7ff; 13:3–4), in Philippians (chap. 3), and in Galatians (cf. 4:12ff.; 5:11–12, and 6:17). The following is therefore added only by way of elaboration. As close as Paul himself comes also to the suffering Christ (for example in 2 Cor. 4:10ff.; 13:4), just as little does he speak in his genuine letters of an atoning power in his apostolic suffering (cf. 1 Cor. 1:13). Only his school (under the influence of Paul's martyrdom?) sees itself justified in speaking in this way (cf. Col. 1:24; Eph. 3:1, 18).—The sufferings that Paul enumerates, in 2 Cor. 11:23ff., for example, are primarily sufferings that arose for him out of his service of apostolic witness, but 2 Cor. 12:7ff. or Gal. 4:13ff. does not allow us to restrict Paul's sufferings to his apostolic-missionary trials; they definitely include physical weakness and sickness.—In general it is striking, however, to how strong a degree Paul interprets his apostolic life under the cross by traditions that can be assigned to the whole Old Testament–Jewish tradition of the Suffering Righteous One. This is true of his apostleship as a whole (compare Gal. 1:15 with Jer. 1:4–5 and 1QH 9:29; 1 Cor. 9:16 with Jer. 20:9) as well as of the particular paralleling of Christ and apostle in 2 Cor. 4:10ff. and 13:4, and the so-called catalogues of trials (cf. to 2 Cor. 4:7ff. especially *T. Jos.* 1:4–7; the citation of Ps. 118:17–18 in 2 Cor. 6:9ff.; the references to Jer. 9:22–23 in 1 Cor. 1:31 [2 Cor. 10:17] with the catalogue in 1 Cor. 4:6–13, etc.).—This is true, in fact, of the concept of *mimēsis*, by aid of which Paul designates himself as a follower of the Crucified One in order at the same time to summon the community to follow him (cf. 1 Cor. 4:16; 11:1; Phil. 3:17), for it is not accidental that in Judaism this concept of *mimēsis* is found, among other places, precisely in the exemplary martyr tradition in 4 Macc. 9:23; 13:9. If one sees this, a further thesis becomes possible and at the same time a differentiation becomes necessary. The thesis is:

6. The suffering apostle, obediently following his task as proclaimer, can understand himself as a model for the community, because he is following on earth Christ, his crucified reconciler and Lord, as the Suffering justified One.

If there can be no doubt, in the light of the references just given, about Paul's summons to follow him, we now need to ask in what sense Paul takes over the Old Testament–Jewish interpretive pattern of the Suffering Righteous One. For precisely in its classic, pre-Christian form (for example in Wisd. of Sol. 2:12–20 and 5:1–7 or *1 Enoch* 103:9–15), as well as consistently later among the rabbis, this pattern describes the fate of the righteous person as an exemplary pious follower of the law who suffers on earth for their fidelity to the law and, purified by their suffering, enters the reign of God and the glory of the resurrection. If the apostle, at best, was in a position to view Jesus' fate in this sense, he had to modify the pattern from the perspective of his theology of justification the moment he adopted it for his own person and as an interpretation of the Christian life in general. He did this in this way, that he— as Philippians 3 classically shows—spoke of himself as the exemplary justified One, who was made to suffer because of his testimony to justification *sola fide,* opened to him and all believers in the cross of Christ, but who held, nevertheless, to this testimony as God's eschatological will to love.—From here the theology of the cross then widens to focus also on the community as a whole.

7. The Christian community and the individual within it experience the redeeming and molding power of the cross of Christ especially in the situation of personal suffering experienced for faith, that is, as the suffering justified ones, who, called to faith by the apostle, follow the crucified and risen Christ as their reconciler and Lord.

In addition to 1 Thess. 1:6–7; 2:14, and Phil. 1:27–30, especially Rom. 5:3ff. and 8:4–39 can serve to illustrate this thesis. In this regard three things are to receive primary emphasis: the sufferings the community undergoes arise as a result of its exemplary Christian life of testimony as well as of the world's apocalyptic fate in which the community is still enmeshed on earth. In its life of discipleship the community is to fulfill the eschatological will of God, revealed in Christ, in the form of the spiritual law of Christ, that is, love (cf. Rom. 8:24 and Gal. 6:2). Finally, the community, in its situation of suffering for Christ's sake, explicitly emphasized by Paul with the help of Ps. 44:23, is able to take comfort in the Crucified and Risen One as the embodiment of the love of God and as the guarantor of its final vindication (Rom. 8:31–39). The crucified Christ is as Lord of the community also its reconciler. Reconciliation, a discipleship of suffering, and hope in the future resurrection of the dead belong indissolubly together in Paul.—We now need to call attention to this matter in greater detail:

8. Just as baptism participates in Christ's life of obedience and suffering as a sign of accomplished atonement and in the hope of resurrection, so also the Lord's Supper enables the baptized to have a share in the communion with God opened up by Jesus' atoning death and places them into discipleship to the crucified and risen Christ until the Parousia.

This thesis connects Paul's statements about baptism and discipleship in Rom. 6:1–23 with his understanding of the Lord's Supper in 1 Cor. 11:23ff. Moreover, it is characteristic of the apostle that according to 1 Cor. 11:26 precisely also the Eucharist, as a sacramental proclamation of Jesus' atoning death, is put in the context of discipleship and hope. So Paul's theology of the Lord's Supper no more allows for a treatment of the soteriological element in Paul's Christology independent of the parenetic element than does Paul's interpretation of baptism, with its principle of being crucified with Christ (Rom. 6:6).—A look at the concept of the "body of Christ," so characteristic of Paul, confirms this inseparability of soteriology and parenesis.

9. The community of the baptized, reconciled to God by the sacrifice of Jesus' life and sharing in his life of obedience and suffering, is called by Paul the "body of Christ."

Precisely when one, after the failure of the attempt to explain the concept of the "body of Christ" on the basis of (pre-Christian) Gnosticism, returns to that which can really be seen in the Pauline texts, one comes to the conclusion summarized in this thesis: according to 1 Cor. 10:16–17 and Rom. 7:4, the congregation is united to be the community of the body of Christ by the power of the sacrifice of Jesus' life, power that gathers and reconciles to God; as a community constituted in this way, it forms the *sōma Christou,* attesting to the lordship of Jesus Christ in the world, subject to the detailed admonition of the apostle found in 1 Cor. 12:4ff. and Rom. 12:3ff. So Paul calls the congregation the body of Christ because it arises from the sacrifice of the life and the body of Jesus Christ, advances the earthly work of the Risen One in the world, and in this work of testimony takes delight in the help of the Spirit and in its own future resurrection.—If one pursues this idea a moment longer, the following thesis arises:

10. The worship of the congregation standing in discipleship under the cross consists, according to Paul, in the worship of God and his Son, in the dedication of their bodies to testimony to Christ on earth, and in the liberating practice of love which bears the burdens of the weak, thus offering Christ to all people; precisely this worship leads the congregation into suffering, but also in this suffering it is enabled to experience the help of the Risen One.

Nowhere in the Pauline epistles can this be seen in a more concentrated way than in Romans 12—15. In this regard only the following deserves special emphasis: the summons to present one's body as a living sacrifice in Rom. 12:1–2 would be misunderstood and totally irreconcilable with Rom. 8:14–15; 26ff.; 1 Cor. 11:20 ff.; 14:26ff.; etc., if one wanted to hear in it the summons to "worship in the work-a-day-world" (E. Käsemann) in such an exclusive way that beyond it the worship of God in prayer, praise, and consolation would be neglected or even abrogated.—It is extremely impressive and worthy of reflection how intensively Paul, precisely in Rom. 12:14ff.; 13:8ff.; 14:15ff.; 15:1ff., 7ff., points to love and to testifying to reconciliation as the essential ingredients of the congregation's life. This is in harmony with 1 Corinthians 13; Gal. 5:14–15; 6:1–2; or Phil. 2:1–11, and underscores to how high a degree, according to Paul, the congregation is to testify that what Jesus is concerned about is love. How this testimony to reconciliation and faith, ventured as a sacrifice of body and life, places the congregation under suffering is shown by 1 Thess. 1:6; 2:14ff.; Phil. 1:29–30 or Rom. 8:35ff.; and in this suffering, according to Rom. 8:4ff., 15, 26, 34, it is the Spirit, with the congregation as the power and presence of the Risen One, that sustains it on its way and leads it through suffering to the love of God.

If reconciliation, discipleship under the cross, and hope belong indissolubly together in this way for the congregation, and if Christ is their reconciler only as their Lord, but as their Lord also the real abiding guarantee of their justification and reconciliation, then in a further thesis we need to point to the whole christological and creation-theology dimension of Paul's theology of the cross, a dimension neglected again and again:

11. It is precisely the crucified and risen Christ whom Paul proclaims as the one through whom God creates and by whom all God's work is brought to completion; thereby Paul's theology of the cross has a universal scope and covers the history that spans from the first day to the day of eschatological redemption.

Tradition-historically Paul's talk about Christ as the *eikōn* of God (2 Cor. 4:4–5), about the Crucified and Risen One as the mediator of creation and redemption (1 Cor. 8:6), or also about Christ as the one whom God made for us the power and wisdom of God (1 Cor. 1:24, 30; 2:6ff.) stands in a specific tradition context that is also constitutive for the deutero-Pauline testimonies to a theology of the cross (Col. 1:20; 2:13–15; Eph. 2:16). The tradition context in question is the joining of priestly and wisdom traditions in the later layers of the Old Testament. By virtue of the joining of these two strands of tradition, the cultic act of atonement, particularly on the Day of Atonement, could be interpreted as God's work of creation and satisfaction carried out through the wisdom of God, as an act through which the fallen world is refashioned and connected once more with its creator. Examples of this kind of tradition occur in Ecclesiasticus 24 and 50, in the temple symbolism of Ps. 46:5–6, and Ezekiel 47; in texts like 3 Macc. 2:1–20; *Testament of Levi* 3 and 18, or even in the saying ascribed to Simeon the Just (3d century B.C.E.) in *m. ʾAbot* 1:2 that the world rests on three things, on the Torah, on worship, and on deeds of love. If then in a Christian context one interprets the cross and resurrection of Jesus as an eschatological atonement event, and if one puts this event into the context of the traditions we have mentioned, then it is possible, indeed necessary, to understand the Crucified and Risen One as the embodiment of the wisdom of God that binds heaven and earth together once more, as the mediator of the new creation God wanted from the beginning, as the heavenly high priest, and as the glorious image of the invisible God. This very thing happens already in Paul in the texts we have mentioned and in Rom. 8:34, and that not in isolation from his proclamation of the cross but, as the material from 1 Cor. 1:21ff., 30–31; 2:2, 6ff.; and Rom. 8:3–4, 31ff. shows, at its center. Accordingly, if one grants the Pauline proclamation about the cross its own genuine voice, one must speak emphatically about the creation dimension of this theology. A natural theology based on a theology of the law and of wisdom is in 1 Cor. 1:18–25 not only made by Paul the antithesis of a theology of the cross but also superseded by Christology and creation theology! To be sure, what is involved here is an act of creation out of death and the destruction of human *kauchēsis*, whereby we again stand on the battleground on which Paul formulated the pertinent arguments of his theology of the cross:

12. When Paul, as in Corinth or Galatia, consciously and exclusively proclaims Christ crucified, he opposes an understanding of Christ and of faith that through pretended strength or presumptuous anxiety threatens to overshadow the unique atonement aspect of the cross of Christ and its aspect of prototypical suffering. Those holding such an understanding need to be shown and therefore attention needs to be called to the fact that God in Christ saves only those who were crushed before him as lawbreakers and who also as believers on earth remain weak and tempted until judgment day.

Since the references pertinent to these observations were already given above in connection with the first thesis, we only need to mention here that "pretended strength" appears to have been the temptation of the pneumatics in Corinth, and "presumptuous anxiety" the false path of nomism urged on the Galatians. Interestingly, on both occasions Paul opposed early erroneous forms of Christian theology, erroneous forms, to be sure, behind which there emerged for him also the false path of Jewish law and wisdom theology he himself took as a Pharisee and a persecutor of the community. In his theology of the cross Paul battled for the existential dimension of experience and faith in his theology of justification, presented for example in Romans 4, according to which God, who calls into existence the things that do not exist, who gives life to the dead, and who raised for our justification the Jesus who was put to death for our trespasses (Rom. 4:17, 25), is a God who creates the ungodly *(ton asebē)* anew out of nothing in that he justifies them by grace alone. Believers, according to Paul, do justice to this creative justifying activity of God in and through Christ only if they continue to recognize their nothingness before God, thus making their boast about the salvation granted them in Christ and their new existence in reconciliation only in their weakness and in their discipleship under the suffering of Christ, who as the Risen One continues to be the Son of God suffering out of love and in love. According to 2 Cor. 12:7–10, Paul himself is the first witness and guarantor of such a life of faith.

But then isn't the Pauline theology of the cross in the New Testament only a plan for the individual? This question, asked and answered in the affirmative (derogatorily) again and again, still needs to be discussed briefly before we can arrive at a theological conclusion. This will be done best by testing whether Paul in his theology of the cross departs from the Synoptic Jesus tradition or if he is close to and continues it. The present state of research, in which Paul at times is located at an extreme remove from Jesus and the Synoptics, makes it necessary to move ahead by first making a tradition-historical observation.

13. The parallelism between 1 Cor. 11:23ff. and the Synoptic Lord's Supper tradition; between 1 Cor. 15:3ff. and Mark 10:45 par., the Synoptic burial tradition, Mark 16:1–8 par., and Luke 24:34; and between Rom. 4:25; 5:8–9; 8:32, and Mark 9:31; 10:33; 14:41 par. permits the supposition that Paul knew the main features of the passion narrative handed on in Jerusalem (and now incorporated into the gospels) just as well as he knew the interpretation, already common in the primitive church, of the death and resurrection of Jesus as an act of atonement.

The connection between Paul and the Jerusalem passion tradition is strengthened by the fact that the apostle by his apologetic, law-critical interpretation of Deut. 21:23 in Gal. 3:13 enters into the controversy, emanating from Jerusalem, between early Christians and Jews over the proper understanding of the death of Jesus (see the elaboration of thesis 3 above). On the basis of 1 Thess. 2:15, moreover, one can postulate that the apostle was acquainted with the critical early Christian talk about Jewish murder of the prophets, as it appears in Acts 7:52. 2 Corinthians 4:10ff.; 13:4, and Rom. 15:3–4 show finally that Paul must have also been acquainted with the conception of the death of Jesus as the Suffering Righteous One, in accord with Psalms 22 and 69, the conception that supported the earliest Synoptic account of the passion.—If one on this basis has sufficient reason to speak of a knowledge of the Jerusalem passion tradition also available to the apostle, one can go back to Jesus himself:

14. Jesus himself is not to be excluded from those who interpreted his death as an atonement; rather, the Lord's Supper texts unanimously show that at the last meal with his followers in Jerusalem he consecrated himself to die vicariously on their behalf.

As extremely difficult and controverted as the complex of questions is concerning the original form of the early Christian celebration of the Lord's Supper and of the so-called words of institution, just as little can the fundamental statements in Mark 14:17ff. par. and 1 Cor. 11:23 par. simply be designated historically as legendary. Rather one has to begin with the fact that at Jesus' farewell meal with his closest followers he consecrated himself to die vicariously for those who were his, and in so doing referred to the "covenant" of Exodus 24 and Jer. 31:31ff. that was to be newly established by God through the sacrifice of Jesus' life. One can say this because reference is made to Exod. 24:5–8 not only in Mark 14:24 par. but also in 1 Cor. 11:25 and Luke 22:20. The Son-of-man tradition in Mark 10:45 (compare with 1 Tim. 2:5–6), which points to the Lord's Supper context, making reference to Isa. 53:10ff. and, above all, to the Hebrew text of Isa. 43:4, confirms this connection.—Based on this a further inference is possible.

15. It can be seen not only from the Lord's Supper texts but also from Luke 13:31–33; Mark 9:31 par.; and 10:38, that in the course of his work Jesus considered his own violent end in Jerusalem. He did not shy away from this end, but without trying to escape it, obediently took it upon himself.

If one asks how under these circumstances Jesus understood his way toward death, one encounters a complex interpretive background. Having already seen the death of John the Baptist, there stood at his disposal for an interpretation of his way the Old Testament–Jewish traditions about the Suffering Righteous One, the Jewish martyr texts, the traditions about the fate of the prophets who died violently, the Servant Song of Isaiah 53, and the tradition about the martyr-Messiah in Zech. 12:10; 13:7. If we have viewed this correctly, it can be assumed that Jesus himself stood within and pondered those two traditions that were constitutive for Paul's theology of the cross, the atonement tradition and the tradition about the Suffering Righteous One.

16. According to Matt. 8:20 // Luke 9:58 and Matt. 10:38–39 // Luke 14:27 (and 17:33), Jesus summoned his disciples to follow him as the homeless Son of man threatened by death; moreover, according to Matt. 5:43ff. // Luke 6:27ff. and Mark 10:42ff. he made a self-surrendering love (of the enemy) their principal command.

If the subject under discussion is clear from the passages listed, Jesus' well-known word about crossbearing (Matt. 10:28 // Luke 14:27 // Mark 8:34 par. still needs a brief commentary. Mark 8:34 and parallels betray clear post-Easter reworking. While the phrase characteristic of Mark 8:34 par., *airein ton stauron*, is linked directly with Jesus' passion in Mark 15:20b, the expression *bastadzein ton stauron* that occurs in Luke 14:27 (and John 19:17) is actually an earlier technical term for hauling the cross(bar) to the place of execution. So Luke 14:27 also points to Jesus' crucifixion. If one does not want to begin with the all-too-easy assumption that Jesus foresaw his crucifixion by the Romans and under these auspices summoned his disciples to take up their crosses and follow him, one can ascribe the word about crossbearing to Jesus himself only if a plausible interpretation, traceable to Jesus himself, can be found for *lambanein ton stauron* in Matt. 10:38, a phrase that up to now has not been documented in other texts. Jesus' use of a zealotic formula (Martin Hengel) appears to me just as hard to imagine as what Erich Dinkler sees behind the saying, namely, Jesus taking recourse to a cultic sign that used the last letter of the Hebrew alphabet, the taw, written in old Hebrew script in the form of a cross. There only remains, then, the interpretation of the

saying proposed by Joachim Jeremias for Mark 8:34: "To agree to follow
Jesus means to venture on a life that is as hard as the last walk of a man condemned to death" (*New Testament Theology*, trans. J. Bowden [New York:
Charles Scribner's Sons, 1971], 242), especially since this interpretation can
be combined with the passages from the Temple Scroll from Qumran mentioned above (in connection with thesis 3). According to Col. 64:7-10, death
on the cross was deserved (in accord with Deut. 21:23) by a Jew who had done
evil against the people (Israel) or committed a crime worthy of death, fled to
the Gentiles, cursed the people, etc. If one understands Jesus' word about
taking up the cross with this as the starting point, then it is a call to discipleship of the one who saw himself caught in a deadly conflict with Israel's
officialdom because of his mission and who demanded of his disciples the
willingness to accompany him boldly on the way he thereby sketched out, thus
enduring Jesus' conflict with him, fully prepared to suffer and die. So understood, Mark 10:38 par. need not be denied the earthly Jesus. Rather one could
understand how, in the light of Jesus' actual death on the cross, it could have
gotten from this word to the other Synoptic versions of the same word,
directly connected with Jesus' passion.—But, however that may be, our entire
journey through theses 13—16 permits the conclusion, not insignificant historically and theologically:

**17. The principal features of Paul's theology of the cross can find confirmation
in what lies at the core of the Synoptic Jesus tradition; Paul proclaims what
Jesus himself sought and lived.**

If we go from this perception back to the question asked at the start about
Ernst Käsemann's concept of the theology of the cross, the following can be
seen at once: when Käsemann consciously puts the theology of the cross in
the context of the First Commandment, binding on Jesus and the community,
he puts the emphasis on a theological component that is really decisive for
Paul and Jesus. In tradition-historical terms, at issue is the tradition about the
life of the Suffering Righteous or justified One. To the degree, of course, in
which Käsemann, for the sake of this one component of the biblical theology
of the cross, reduces the atonement tradition to the idea of substitution, and
then in addition criticizes its content and speaks of it as an element of the tradition already surmounted by Paul, to that degree he distances himself from the
apostle as well as from the passion tradition and, in my view, also from Jesus
himself. It would therefore not be wise to continue such criticism because
otherwise not only does a historically distorted perspective arise but also the
Reformation's *sola fide propter Christum* is no longer clearly explicable.

The position that occasioned Käsemann's emphasis is, of course, still a critical problem in the church as it was in the past. It is a soteriology that precisely
with the aid of the christological idea of atonement operates on its own in the
church and that reduces ideas about discipleship and obedience to an optional
adiaphoron for Christians. In the light of this erroneous development, we need
to insist with Käsemann that in the New Testament Christ the reconciler is not
to be separated from Christ the Lord, and that neither Jesus himself, nor the

Jerusalem passion tradition, to say nothing of Paul, speaks of the sacrifice (of Jesus) on the cross on our behalf without also enlisting the community for discipleship under the cross. The principle stated in the second thesis of the Barmen Declaration, "As Jesus Christ is God's gift of the forgiveness of all our sins he also in the same seriousness is God's strong demand on our whole life," actually finds full confirmation in the New Testament. Therefore our concluding thesis is:

18. The theology of the cross, as defined by Paul and the Reformation, obligates us to constant theological criticism of all positions on faith and theology that try to evade the demand of Jesus Christ, who as the Risen One continues to be the one crucified for us and as such calls us to follow him.

BIBLIOGRAPHIC NOTES

*When I held a seminar on Paul's theology of the cross in summer semester 1975, E. Käsemann gave us the pleasure of discussing with us critically on July 5, 1975, the theses that the seminar produced. It is therefore natural to dedicate to him on his seventieth birthday this same set of theses in reworked form. In order not to exceed the limits of a contribution to a Festschrift, I have had to omit footnotes. But I would at least like to name the literature that was especially helpful to me in the formulation of the theses in this essay.

Of Käsemann's own works three deserve special mention: "Some Thoughts on the Theme, 'The Doctrine of Reconciliation in the New Testament,' " in *The Future of Our Religious Past. Essays in Honour of Rudolf Bultmann,* ed. J. M. Robinson, trans. C. E. Carlston and R. Scharlemann (New York: Harper & Row, 1971), 49–64; "Die Gegenwart des Gekreuzigten," in *Deutscher Ev. Kirchentag 1967* (Stuttgart: Kreuz Verlag, 1967), 424–37; "The Saving Significance of the Death of Jesus in Paul," in *Perspectives on Paul,* trans. M. Kohl (Philadelphia: Fortress Press, 1971), 32–59.

On the New Testament the following appear to me especially important at this time: E. Brandenburger, "*Stauros,* Kreuzigung Jesu und Kreuzestheologie," in *Wort und Dienst* N. F. 10 (1969): 17–43; H.-W. Kuhn, "Jesus als Gekreuzigter in der frühchristlichen Verkündigung bis zur Mitte des 2. Jahrhunderts," *ZTK* 72 (1975): 1–46; U. Luz, "Theologia crucis als Mitte der Theologie im Neuen Testament," *EvT* 34 (1974): 116–41; F.-J. Ortkemper, *Das Kreuz in der Verkündigung des Apostels Paulus,* 2d ed., SBS 24 (Stuttgart: Katholisches Bibelwerk, 1968); W. Schrage, "Leid, Kreuz und Eschaton. Die Peristasenkataloge als Merkmale paulinischer theologia crucis und Eschatologie," *EvT* 34 (1974): 141–75; and H. Schürmann, *Jesu ureigener Tod* (Freiburg: Herder, 1975).

The tradition about the Suffering Righteous One has been investigated especially by: D. Rössler, *Gesetz und Geschichte,* WMANT 3 (Neukirchen-Vluyn: Neukirchener Verlag, 1960), 88ff.; L. Ruppert, *Jesus als der leidende Gerechte?* SBS 59 (Stuttgart: Katholisches Bibelwerk, 1972); and O. H. Steck, *Israel und das gewaltsame Geschick der Propheten,* WMANT 23 (Neurkirchen-Vluyn: Neukirchener Verlag, 1967), esp. 252ff.

On the question of the understanding of crucifixion in Qumran compare: G. Jeremias, *Der Lehrer der Gerechtigkeit,* SUNT 2 (Göttingen: Vandenhoeck & Ruprecht, 1963), 127ff., and Y. Yadin, "Pesher Nahum (4QpNah) Reconsidered," *IEJ* 21 (1971): 1–12.

The present systematic theology discussion is shaped by E. Jüngel, "Vom Tod des lebendigen Gottes," in *Unterwegs zur Sache, BEvT* 61 (Munich: Kaiser, 1972), 105–25; idem, "Gott is Liebe. Zur Unterscheidung von Glaube und Liebe," in *Festschrift für Ernst Fuchs,* ed. G. Ebeling, E. Jüngel, and G. Schunack (Tübingen: Mohr, 1973), 193–202; and the three works by J. Moltmann, *The Crucified God,* trans. R. A. Wilson and J. Bowden (New York: Harper & Row, 1974); "Gesichtspunkte der Kreuzestheologie heute," *EvT* 33 (1973): 346–65; "Gedanken zur 'trinitarischen Geschichte Gottes,' " *EvT* 35 (1975): 208–23.

Overviews of the present (systematic theology) discussion are offered by H. G. Link, "Gegenwärtige Probleme einer Kreuzestheologie," *EvT* 33 (1973): 337–45; and H.-G. Koch, "Kreuzestod und Kreuzestheologie," *Herder Korrespondenz* 29 (1975): 147–56.

CHAPTER 10

On Pauline Christology*

I

In an inquiry about the decisive impulses and accents of Paul's Christology, two things must be kept in mind, the apostle's own particular experience of Christ and the fact that while Paul had to proclaim Christ very early, he was still not the first early Christian missionary. In the midst of Paul's persecution of the church and his militant commitment to the Mosaic law, Christ appeared to Paul the Pharisee in the glory of the Son of God (cf. Gal. 1:11–17). The very Lord for whose sake the Christians persecuted by Paul had abandoned the Jewish law in order to turn to Christ makes himself known to Paul as the one exalted and vindicated by God. He calls his earthly adversary to be an apostle and makes him recognize that it is not the way of the law but only faith in Christ that leads to salvation. Following this turning point in his life Paul proclaims Christ as the "end of the law" (Rom. 10:4). But how, in detail, Christ was to be proclaimed as the end of the law, as Lord of the community under his command, and as the trailblazer for the grace of God, this was decided for Paul not only in critical reflection on his own life of devotion to the law but also essentially by this, that the community which he first persecuted but later supported in its missionary activity already had a body of christological thought that was passed on to Paul and further developed by him. The actual key statements of the apostle's proclamation about Christ, in keeping with this whole set of circumstances, are critical of the law. But his christological thinking has as its basis the Christian missionary community's body of formulas and confessions that were handed on to Paul and that he used in his proclamation, as did other apostles and missionaries beside him. So, also and precisely in respect to Pauline christology, attention is to be given to tradition and interpretation.

At present one must, of course, guard against a twofold modern misjudgment in distinguishing between tradition and interpretation. The extent of Paul's use precisely of christological community tradition could lead to the assumption that Christology for the apostle was only a matter of tradition while his real interest lay only in the soteriological and anthropological consequences of this Christology. Such an understanding is corrected by continuous Pauline assertions such as Phil. 1:15–17; Gal. 1:11ff., 16; 3:1; 1 Cor. 1:30–31; 2:1–2; 2 Cor. 4:1–6; 5:16–21; Rom. 1:1ff., 16–17; 3:24–26; 5:1–11; 10:4, 9–10; etc. Christ is not only the presupposition for but also the controlling content of the Pauline gospel! But the other misunderstanding is also obvious; it acts as though what is characteristic of the Pauline proclamation of Christ is not also already there in the traditional phrases adopted by the apostle but only in those (few) interpretive comments that Paul interpolates into the traditional material. Speaking against this widely held understanding is the fact, which often seems so puzzling, that Paul, who knows very well how to evaluate the phenomenon of Christian tradition and determine its worth (cf. only 1 Cor. 11:23ff. or 1 Cor. 15:1ff.), never formally criticizes such traditions, but rather always lets them merge seamlessly into his own presentation. For an exegesis that is concerned about tradition history but concentrates on Paul, this means not only that it dare not simply single out the specifically Pauline interpretive phrases but that it must show how Paul affirms the content of the tradition about Christ quoted by him and on the basis of it proceeds to the proclamation of Jesus Christ as the end of the law.

Turning first to the christological tradition appropriated by the apostle through quotations and themes, we see that this is not only quite comprehensive but also highly variegated. There are in Paul not only formulas that speak of Christ wholly in Old Testament style as the bearer of the promise (Rom. 1:3–4); hymns in praise of Christ as the one who became incarnate, obediently went the way of death, and, in accord with Isa. 45:23, was exalted over all powers as Lord (Phil. 2:6–11); texts that speak of Christ as the embodiment of the preexistent wisdom through whom creation occurred (1 Cor. 8:6); and traditions that in confessional and formulaic summaries deal with the imminent coming of the Risen One to judge and save the world (1 Thess. 1:9–10; 4:15ff.; Phil. 3:20–21); but also a special abundance of material that speaks of the efficacy for salvation and the significance of the death and resurrection of Jesus (cf. only Rom. 3:25–26; 4:25; 5:8–9; 8:3–4; 10:9–10; 14:15; 1 Cor. 1:30; 8:11; 15:3–5; 2 Cor. 5:21; Gal. 1:4; 4:4–5, etc.). Common to all this diverse traditional material is its origin in Jewish-Christian congregations. Only there—and for the time of Paul's emergence and activity that specifically means in Jerusalem and Antioch—are the biblically saturated language and motifs of such traditions conceivable, and only there in the brief period of actual pre-Pauline Christianity could a body of christological statements arise that by recourse to the Old Testament and by reference to, but also criticism of, the tradition of Semitic and Greek-speaking Judaism, spoke of Christ as the creator of the world, the messianic redeemer and perfecter. So Paul rested upon the already markedly diverse Christology of the primitive community in Jerusalem and of the missionary community founded in Antioch by the

Stephen-circle. Indeed he is one of our most important transmitters of the christological materials in the New Testament that arose there.

To point to the fullness and diversity of the traditional material used by Paul is not, of course, meant to assert that the Christology we encounter in the apostle's letters is also disparate and disordered. The opposite is true. That is to say, in the Pauline letters there are three christological thought patterns that are related to one another and that in combination give Pauline theology as a whole a christological structure and contour. The first thought pattern speaks of the world-shaping and world-changing mission of Jesus as the messianic Son of God; this mission finds its true salvation-creating goal in the death and resurrection of Jesus the Messiah. The second pattern then speaks of the death and resurrection of Jesus as the eschatological consummation of that atonement and reconciliation which no longer creates only communion between God and his own people Israel but "peace" between God and all believers from among Jews and Gentiles. As the quantity of the quoted material already shows, the main accent in Paul's proclamation actually appears to be here. The third pattern, finally, speaks of the work that the Resurrected Crucified One as reconciler and Lord has to complete in God's name until the Parousia. By virtue of these three thought patterns the crucified and resurrected Christ appears in Paul in general as the end of the law for all believers, as Lord and revealer of the grace and will of God for all times, or, what is for Paul the same thing, as the embodiment and executor of the salvation-creating righteousness of God for Jews and Gentiles, that is, for the whole world.

II

If we try with desired brevity to pursue these thought patterns in greater detail, the following picture emerges. As the epistolary prescript of Romans, 1 Cor. 8:6, and Phil. 2:6ff., for example, show, Christ for Paul is no longer merely the Lord and redeemer who is installed as the Son of God by virtue of his resurrection, as he is for the part of Jewish Christianity that finds expression in the *maranatha* (Our Lord, come!) in 1 Cor. 16:23 and Rev. 22:20, in formulas like that in Acts 2:36, or the tradition in Rom. 1:3–4. Pauline Christology includes Jesus' preexistence from the start. Early Christians arrived at the idea of Jesus' preexistent status and work through an expansion along wisdom and messianic lines of the original christological traditions just mentioned. Already in the late stages of the Old Testament the preexistent creative wisdom of God (Prov. 8:22ff.; Wisd. of Sol. 7:21ff.; Ecclus. 24:1–22) was identified with the law (cf. Ecclus. 24:23ff.; Bar. 3:32—4:4). In the history of Old Testament–Jewish messianic expectation the Messiah of Isa. 11:1ff. appears as the bearer of wisdom (and preserver of righteousness) and, according to Ps. 2:7; 110:1ff., as the Son begotten by God, whose origin is from of old (Mic. 5:1). In Dan. 7:13ff. and the Enoch tradition this messianic expectation merges with the prophetic Son-of-man tradition and forms already in *1 Enoch* 48:2ff., 10; and 49:1–4, 61–62, a transcendent universal pattern of expectation that starts out from the preexistent giving of the Messiah's name and the cosmic function of the Son of man/Messiah himself. The nascent Christianity that comes from Jesus' claim to be the Son of man/Messiah enters into these Israelite streams of experience and interpretation; it follows them and also contrasts with them in its Christology. Since, according to the conviction of the first Christian generation, nothing more comprehensive and fundamental can be experienced and contemplated than God's freeing, life-reordering grace in Christ, one speaks of Christ in the style and by appropriation of the Old Testament–Jewish wisdom theology (cf. 1 Cor. 8:6; Col. 1:15–20, etc.) and also confesses him as the creator who before all time was with God and at work, as the messianic reconciler and Son of God sent into the world (cf. Gal. 4:4–5; John 3:16–17; Phil. 2:6–7; etc.). Paul willingly seizes the possibilities for thought and proclamation offered by this material and with its help and on the basis of his experience puts a stop to the claim of total supremacy put forward by the Mosaic law and by sin, the perverter of the law (Gal. 4:4; Rom. 8:3–4). The sending of the Son of God into the world inaugurates the new time of freedom from the law and from sin, because this incarnational sending into the world culminates in the obedient sacrifice of Jesus' life, that is, in his death on the cross. As is shown by the Christ-hymn adopted by Paul in Phil. 2:6–11, a hymn that follows Isaiah 53 and the proclamation of salvation found in Deutero-Isaiah, this idea was already there for Paul's use. Recent examinations of the style and structure of this famous text make it likely that the phrase in v. 8b, *thanatou de staurou*, "even death on a cross," long considered a Pauline interpolation, was already an original component of the hymn.

As far as Jesus' humanity and the meaning of the mission of the earthly Jesus are concerned, Paul stresses three things: Jesus appeared in Israel as a descendant of David and as Messiah, in order to fulfill for the chosen people of God the promises of the coming Son of God (Rom. 1:3; 9:5; 15:8; 2 Cor. 1:20). His existence was totally determined by the love that sacrificed itself for others in obedience to the will of God (Rom. 5:18–19; 14:15; 15:3, 8; 1 Cor. 8:11; Gal. 1:4; Phil 2:5ff.). By virtue of this obedience Jesus' life was sinless in character, that is, he possessed the faultlessness that qualified the Incarnate One to be the spotless sin offering for the guilt of the world (2 Cor. 5:21; Rom. 8:3).

So Paul had a totally clear-cut picture of Jesus' work and this picture should no longer be denied him on the basis of 2 Cor. 5:16. This passage is to be related to Paul's new knowledge of Jesus as a result of his call to be an apostle and has nothing to do with Paul's alleged disinterest in the earthly Jesus. As a persecutor of the Christian faith Paul had seen in Christ the lawless messianic pretender justly executed on the cross and had persecuted the community because they had confessed this person as Lord and Christ; now, as an apostle of Jesus Christ, he does not view Christ in this way any longer but confesses him as reconciler and Son of God.

If the sparse use of the Jesus tradition the apostle makes in his letters, something discussed again and again, is considered in this context, the following can be seen. First of all, one should consider the differences in genre between the preaching about Jesus in narrative form (Acts 10:34–43, for example), the gospel narrative as a whole, and the apostolic letters. The apostolic letter offered few possibilities for unfolding the narrative kerygma. The Lord's Supper tradition in 1 Cor. 11:23ff. and the tradition in 1 Cor. 15:3–5, 6–8 show that Paul knew the essential features of the passion narrative and of the Jerusalem tradition about the tomb and that in addition he possessed extensive reports of Jesus' resurrection and appearances. Texts and statements such as 1 Thess. 1:10; 4:15ff.; 1 Cor. 15:47, 50ff. appear to rest on the Synoptic Son-of-man tradition. The direct and indirect references to Jesus' words woven into Paul's parenesis (cf. 1 Cor. 7:10 with Mark 10:11–12; 1 Cor. 9:8 with Luke 10:7b // Matt. 10:10b; Gal. 5:14 and Rom. 13:8–10 with Mark 12:30–31 par.; 1 Cor. 4:12; 6:7; and Rom. 12:14, 17, 21 with Luke 6:27–28 par.; Rom. 14:14, 20 with Mark 7:15; 1 Cor. 13:2 with Mark 11:23, etc.), show in addition that the apostle presupposes knowledge of Q material and also of Markan traditions in his congregations and that in some cases he himself ascribes the highest authority to this material. If the apostle puts particular parenetic emphasis on the command to love your neighbor and your enemy, the command sealed by Jesus himself by his sacrificial death, and if he directs his principal christological attention to Jesus' death on the cross and his resurrection, the reason for this is that the saving significance of Jesus' mission was disclosed to him by the cross and resurrection and that he, who was always confronted with the mission proclamation of the Jerusalem apostles and Peter, who were particularly well versed in the Jesus tradition, for this reason also insisted on the particular significance of Jesus' atoning death. Thus Paul's eclecticism and reserved use of the Jesus tradition is understandable on the basis of his epistolary style, and, in addition, it has its own particular motivation and accent. However, this finding does not in my opinion make it necessary to call the Jesus tradition irrelevant for Pauline Christology. We should be restrained from making such a judgment also by considering that we know little about the apostle's actual method of preaching. In these sermons he certainly touched themes additional to and different from those expressed in the letters preserved for us.

According to Paul Christ became the Lord of the community and the designated ruler of the world because in obedience to God he died not any old death but precisely his sacrificial death on the cross. Jesus' mission arose from God's intention to save the world by the sacrifice of Jesus' life on the cross. God's saving decree, already comprehended before all time in Christ the Son, finds its soteriological climax in the mission and sacrifice of this Son, who adopted God's will as his own. The first christological thought pattern thus moves organically to the second.

III

Among the manifold interpretations that are part of early, post-Easter Christology the confessional statement that Christ died "for us" (cf. 1 Cor.

15:3 and the Lord's Supper formulas, Mark 14:22–25 par.; 1 Cor. 11:23–26) occupies a very special place and that for two reasons. First, in this statement the meaning and intention of Jesus of Nazareth's messianic work of reconciliation, culminating in the Passion, was pregnantly comprehended. Jesus had acted with the intention of establishing through his own work a new and enduring communion between God and the people of his time. This messianic claim, Jesus' provocative words, and his no less provocative symbolic acts, especially his table fellowship and the cleansing of the temple, had led logically to his death, and Jesus had not evaded this end, perhaps by trying to flee, but willingly taken it upon himself, true to his messianic mission.

But the christological talk about the death of Jesus "for us" is also highly significant for a second reason, because with the aid of this very formula, supported by Isaiah 53 and the sacrificial and atonement tradition of the Old Testament, the at first incomprehensible enigma of Jesus' death on the cross was penetrated and became comprehensible as an essential part of God's work through Jesus on behalf of humanity. Where at first only expressions of contrast were used, "You Jews crucified Jesus, but God raised him" (Acts 2:23; 10:39), there the *hyper hēmōn* ("for us") went decidedly further: God not only had turned the evil of Jesus' death into its opposite by the resurrection, but also had effected salvation already in the death of Jesus, precisely through the vicarious sacrifice of the life of his son. Thus Jesus' death is part of God's saving work and is indissolubly connected with the resurrection. God brings about atonement and salvation in Jesus' sacrificial death and ratifies this atonement by Jesus' resurrection.

As the Lord's Supper tradition and 1 Cor. 15:3ff. show, the above mentioned *hyper* formulas were formulated and handed on already in Jerusalem. In all probability it was then the Stephen-circle who, still in Jerusalem or a short time later in Antioch, shaped the tradition in Rom. 3:25–26a and took upon themselves the risk of speaking of Jesus' public installation as the *kappōret* = *hilastērion*, that is, as the place of God's revelation and of the atonement established once and for all by God, an installation that surpasses and renders obsolete all cultic atonement, making Jesus an antitype to the most significant Jewish atonement rite, the celebration of the Day of Atonement in accord with Leviticus 16. By these statements the Christian missionary congregation freed itself from the temple in Jerusalem and the Torah's cultic regulations observed in the temple.

Interestingly we now meet these very traditions again in Paul, not somewhere on the periphery, but at the heart of his proclamation about Christ. We can, in fact, say what led the apostle to give special emphasis to and to develop the saving significance of Jesus' death on the cross. If the other apostles, and especially Peter, wish to appeal to their encounters with the earthly Jesus and, correspondingly, wish to appear not only as witnesses of the Risen One but also as bearers and transmitters of the Jesus tradition, for Paul the world had turned upside down, for outside Damascus the one crucified under the sign of Deut. 21:22–23 let himself be known to Paul as the Risen One. This enabled

Paul to understand that his death was precisely not the deserved, accursed death of a blasphemer of God and lawbreaker, as Jesus' Jewish opponents, Paul at first included, had thought, but that, on the contrary, the curse of the law was taken away from sinners by God through the death of the guiltless Jesus. For this reason precisely the *hyper hēmōn*, and with it the tradition critical of cult and temple coming from the Stephen-circle, become for the apostle the foundation of his theology of justification. The atonement and reconciliation tradition is not, then, as has occasionally been thought, one traditional ingredient of Paul's Christology, which he also mentions along with many others, but rather the basis of his christologically based proclamation about justification.

On what basis can we infer this? Above all from the insight that Christian justification terminology was anchored in the very tradition context about which we are speaking, already before Paul and then especially in Paul himself. Already in an apparently pre-Pauline formula (from Jerusalem) based on Isaiah 53, it says of Christ in Rom. 4:25, "who was put to death [by God] for our trespasses/and raised [by God] for our justification." In a way of speaking that is strongly saturated by tradition and that calls to mind the messianic tradition of Jer. 23:5–6, the apostle says in 1 Cor. 1:30 that Christ has been made by God our wisdom, our righteousness and sanctification and redemption (cf. also 1 Cor. 6:11). In another traditional formulation, apparently woven by Paul into his letter as a quotation in 2 Cor. 5:21, we read that God "For our sake . . . made him to be [an offering for] sin [= an offering for the guilt of sin] who knew no sin, so that in him we might become the righteousness of God," that is, might attain the mode of existence of those who are righteous in God's sight. That the controverted phrase *hamartian epoiēsen* ("made sin") must be translated with the meaning we have given it is shown by the Septuagint translation of Lev. 4:21, 24; 5:12; 6:18; and Hos. 4:8, for example, where in each case the Hebrew *hattat* = "an offering for sin" is translated by *hamartia* ("sin"); *hamartia* is here shorthand for the full technical term that otherwise appears in the Septuagint: *to peri* (occasionally also *hyper*) *hamartias (dōron*, among others)—"the offering for sin." We encounter this very expression in Rom. 8:3, where it again designates Christ as the (sinless) sin offering put forward by God himself. The justification of the ungodly is thus made possible in that God, by putting forward Jesus to be himself a sin offering, creates that atonement by virtue of which sinners can be acquitted of the sins that both burden and rule them. It is the biblical idea of sacrifice and atonement that enables Paul to think theologically about justification through Christ. This idea of sacrifice and atonement, given a christological turn, together with the justification terminology, comes to the apostle from Jerusalem and Antioch. Paul by no means criticizes it but on the contrary uses it again and again. Besides Rom. 5:1–11, the famous passage Rom. 3:24–26 shows this especially clearly.

Here Paul has recourse to the tradition mentioned above which took shape in the Stephen-circle. He cites it in vv. 25–26a, thus for his part assuming that with God's public installation of Jesus as *kappōret* a once-and-for-all atonement was accomplished and in this way the ground was laid for the justification of sinners. Paul also shared with the Christians before him the view that this installation of Jesus was the eschatological demonstration, resulting in the forgiveness of sinners, of the salvation-creating righteousness of God. Yet Paul develops these traditional statements not only by the addition of *dia pisteōs* ("by faith") in v. 25 but also by the way he in Rom. 3:24–26 led up to the quotation of the tradition and then by this taking up and developing of the traditional terminology in v. 26b. Thereby he makes especially the following clear: The atonement effected by God in Christ can be appropriated only in faith, that is, in the thankful and also obedient acknowledgment of that saving work of God to which the sinner, fallen from the creative glory of God, can contribute absolutely nothing. Since this saving work of God in Christ is appropriated by faith and only thereby, the range of this saving event is extended to the borders of the world: no longer Israel alone as God's own people but all believers, Jews and Gentiles, are partakers in the salvation-creating righteousness of God. For God is and wants to be a God who shows his righteousness to all who believe in Jesus, by acquitting them of their guilt and thus making of them a new creation. Thus what the tradition in Rom. 3:25–26 envisions is construed universally by Paul. For him Christ is the reconciler of the world and not of Israel alone. God's righteousness opens in a salvation-creating manner beyond the borders of the chosen people of God to all believers. All people are incorporated as believers into the eschatological covenantal obligation that is reestablished by Jesus' atoning death. Its christological establishment is commemorated by the community in the celebration of the Lord's Supper, according to 1 Cor. 11:23. God is the God who has consigned the Gentiles and the Jews to disobedience in order to have mercy on all in the exercise of his righteousness in Christ (Rom. 11:32).

If the contrast with a piety of the law is already clearly spelled out in Rom. 3:21 and 5:20, the Pauline teaching about justification receives its real law-critical zenith in Rom. 8:3–4; 10:4; and Gal. 3:13–14. Paul knows from his own faith experience that the law does not save even the pious Jew devoted entirely to obeying the law and blamelessly righteous by Pharisaic standards (Phil. 3:6). Rather, it can make that person an enemy and opponent of God. Accordingly, his christological formulations in Galatians and Romans are similar in their criticism of the law. God sent his son as the incarnate, sinless offering for sin in order to do himself what the Mosaic law in its weakness did not succeed in doing, namely to judge sin and at the same time lead to true obedience to the will of God. Only and alone in the atonement offering of Christ, which God himself established, is sin atoned for and a new existence in the Spirit begun for believers, on the basis of which they are ready for and capable of full obedience. Only by virtue of the sacrifice of Christ is the entanglement in guilt broken and removed, entanglement the law was precisely incapable of removing. Rather, it was itself caught up in it and, in addition, still provokes it (Rom. 8:3–4). Or to use the language of Gal. 3:13–14:

since Christ took upon himself the accursed death of Deut. 21:22–23, this
curse was turned aside from those to whom it really applied, from sinners,
who paradoxically were held fast in their sin and involved in it more and more
deeply precisely through the law. In the substitutionary sacrifice of Jesus' life,
that is, by his death on the cross, the power over all sinners of the curse
emanating from the law, which led inevitably to death, was broken. The guiltless Son of God took over the fate of sinners—death—and precisely thereby
put the law, with its deadly claim of dominion, in its place.

We should be clear about how bold this line of thought is. If as we can say
with some certainty in the light of the Temple Scroll, Col. 64:6–13, that Jesus
was considered by his Jewish opponents, and probably also by the Pharisee
Paul, as one whose crucifixion was justified according to Deut 21:22–23 and
as the blasphemer and law-despiser cursed by God, Paul, the scribe-turned-
Christian, turned this very understanding back on the law itself. Instead of the
failure of Jesus before the inexorable and righteous law, Paul proclaimed the
smashing of the law's curse—and therewith of the law-oriented reality belong-
ing to the old aeon—in the death of Jesus, the Righteous One. No one had
dared to think this before Paul. But for Paul Christ really is the end of the
Mosaic law (Rom. 10:4), leading to salvation and righteousness for every
believer.

IV

Now, of course, there are certain problems inherent in a proclamation about
justification such as this one; especially the dimension and range of the atonement effected by God in Christ still need to be discussed. The tradition in
Rom. 3:25–26a related the atonement effected by the sacrifice of Jesus' life
expressly to the sins of the past. If the concept of new creation is connected
with the idea of justification, then something appears at first to be true here,
and not only of the pre-Pauline tradition, but, as 2 Cor. 5:17ff. shows, also
of Paul as well. In both cases the question is unavoidable how the existence
of the justified and newly created individual is described. As an existence in
the Spirit and therefore as sinless? Paul already knew that this was a fantasy
of the enthusiasts. As evidence reference can be made to his conflicts in
1 Corinthians as well as to Rom. 8:5–11. So are the justified, if they sin again,
subject again to the judgment? Does justification in general only blot out the
sins that were committed before baptism and incorporation into the community; and, according to Gal. 5:6, is what now matters for the justified following with all seriousness the will of God reestablished by Jesus in the form of
the love command; that is, is it deeds and evidences of love, by virtue of which
they then can be accounted righteous by Christ at the last judgment? Paul has
to this very day been interpreted in these varied ways. Yet anyone who makes
these thoughts, supported by Gal. 5:6; 1 Cor. 7:19; Phil. 2:12ff.; and Rom.
8:4ff.; 14:9ff., into an absolute for Paul would be guilty of a considerable one-
sidedness. This can be said with such great certainty because Paul develops

his teaching about justification precisely christologically, and Pauline Christology still has a third dimension that is also a consequence of the apostle's thinking about justification. It is concerned with the role and work of the Risen One.

Paul sees in Christ, the crucified and risen Son of God, the Lord, who is to finish the still incomplete work of God and that in a threefold sense. First, the Risen One is appointed and empowered to restore the whole universe to peace with God, and this goal is reached only when death will have definitively lost its power and effectiveness over the world (1 Cor. 15:25ff., 53ff.). Second, through Christ, the Risen One, when the call of the gospel has spread throughout the gentile world, Israel also, presently still hardened in unbelief, shall come to the salvation promised her by God. Therefore, in Rom. 11:25ff. Paul can describe the Parousia as the coming of the deliverer from Zion, as Israel's being brought home to peace with God, and the reality of the new covenantal obligation of Jer. 31:31ff. Finally, the Risen One, on his way to the subjection of the universe, is to uphold believers in their existence as justified sinners, he is to accompany and preserve them as Lord until the goal, God's new world, is actually attained (Rom. 8:12–39). Paul elaborates the character of this preservation especially in his theology of the cross. He does this on the basis of the twofold idea that in following their crucified Lord believers are doers of the true will of God established by this Lord in the form of love, and that the upholding and forgiving power of the Crucified Risen One is made strong precisely in the weak, suffering for Jesus' sake (2 Cor. 12:9–10).

Interestingly, these three aspects do not diverge in respect to the work of the Risen One but converge, depicting the Risen One from the day of his resurrection to the Parousia precisely as the messianic reconciler and Lord who is to lead the world to the state of perfect justification, that is, to the creation's eschatological peace. Also as the risen Lord working in the present and the future, Christ the Crucified and Risen One continues to be the justifier and reconciler he became in his sacrificial death, the one whom God publicly installed and on whom the community believes to its salvation.

The third thought pattern of Paul's Christology, which follows from the first and the second, makes Jesus the messianic agent of God's salvation-creating righteousness till judgment day. Besides 1 Thess. 5:9–10 and Rom. 5:8–11, the most telling evidence for this is Rom. 8:31ff. God sacrificed his son for believers and by the resurrection confirmed him in his office as reconciler, and now Christ, who was crucified and raised for us, is at work as advocate before God for those who are his against any accuser, especially at the last judgment. No power in heaven or on earth can separate believers from the peace and love that God opened to them in Christ. 1 Corinthians 3:15 says essentially the same thing.

Instead of a justification narrowly restricted to baptism, Paul proclaims justification through Christ as a process that controls the life of people and history in general right on through to judgment day. Just as Christ, by virtue of the sacrifice of his life on the cross, has become the Lord and reconciler, so also the new existence of the justified is an "existence in the process of coming into being" under the cross (Eberhard Jüngel) and in hope of completion.

V

Finally, two questions remain, first, how and why, according to Paul, Christ as reconciler and redeemer of believers is also able to be the world's judge, and second, whether the Christology of Paul can be summarized in a Pauline definition that comprehends both the whole of it and its central intention.

To the first question it can be said that Christ as justifier and reconciler not only can be judge of the world but actually must be if the salvation inaugurated in him really is what God has established eschatologically and finally. If God in Christ inaugurated the salvation of the world that can be acknowledged and appropriated only by faith, then refusing to believe means exclusion from salvation for time and eternity. Paul can proclaim Christ with such energy and boldness as the reconciler and Lord precisely because for him apart from the reconciliation and lordship of Christ temporal and eternal condemnation is already a reality and in the endtime will be seen as such. Passages such as 1 Cor. 4:5; 2 Cor. 5:10; and Rom. 2:16 distinguish Pauline Christology from a teaching about universal reconciliation that levels belief and unbelief and make it clear that other than by faith in Christ, the Lord and judge, the peace that is communion with God can be attained neither in time nor in eternity.

There remains the second question. Whoever wants to summarize the three patterns that cover Pauline Christology, the pattern of Jesus' mission, of his sacrifice on the cross, and of the fulfillment of God's work of reconciliation through the Risen One, and whoever also seeks a definition of this Christology's central intention, a definition that intends to grasp the justification-theological stress of the Christology in the death and resurrection of Jesus, that person must say, in my opinion, that for Paul Christ is the personification of God's salvation-creating righteousness. In the Old Testament and in Judaism the righteousness of God is the way God acts to set the world on the path to salvation. In the Messiah God directs his righteousness to his people (and the world)—cf. Isa. 11:1-10; Jer. 25:5ff. Also in Paul God is revealed in his Christ as the Righteous One who by pure grace inaugurates and carries through the salvation of the world alienated from him (1 Cor. 1:30). Accordingly, Christology is the real central theme of the Pauline gospel, in which the salvation that is realized in Christ, the Messiah crucified for us, that is, the righteousness of God, is revealed to all who believe (Rom. 1:1ff., 16-17).

One more thing appears worthy of consideration. We said that in the "for us" statements of the Jerusalem and the Antioch Christ tradition the work of Jesus as the messianic reconciler was comprehended in a particularly incisive way. But that tradition, delivered to Paul from Jerusalem and Antioch, also provides the basis for Pauline justification Christology. Pauline Christology is therefore no isolated or isolatable individual production but a proclamation-opus of the highest theological precision, an opus developed independently on the basis of very early kerygmatic Christ tradition. In Pauline Christology we definitely come to understand who Jesus was, why he lived and suffered. Jesus and Pauline Christology are, accordingly, no competing topics in biblical theology. Rather Jesus' work of reconciliation forms the basis for Pauline thought, and Pauline Christology teaches how to penetrate the work of Jesus right down to its soteriological core.

BIBLIOGRAPHIC NOTE

*This essay had been intended for the long-contemplated Festschrift for Nils A. Dahl, but (through no fault of mine) it could not appear there in the form I desired. Therefore I am now offering the lecture for discussion by publishing it in the *ZTK*. Since it is only an overview, I have omitted footnotes. My deliberations take up the perspective I expressed in my inaugural lecture at Erlangen, "The End of the Law. On the Origin and Beginnings of Pauline Theology" (chap. 8 in this volume), and they go together with three essays in which I have recently dealt with the question of Christology in the context of a biblical theology of the New Testament: "Jesus as Reconciler. Reflections on the Problem of the Portrayal of Jesus in the Context of a Biblical Theology of the New Testament," "Recent Exegesis on Romans 3:24–26," and "Eighteen Theses on Paul's Theology of the Cross" (chaps. 1, 6, and 9 in this volume).

In this overview, I build especially on the following literature (by way of agreement and criticism): J. Blank, *Paulus und Jesus* (Munich: Kösel-Verlag, 1968); G. Bornkamm, *Paul*, trans. D. M. Stalker (New York: Harper & Row, 1971), 109ff.; 248–49; R. Bultmann, "The Significance of the Historical Jesus for the Theology of Paul," in *Faith and Understanding*, vol. 1, ed. R. Funk, trans. L. P. Smith (New York: Harper & Row, 1969), 220–46; idem, *Theology of the New Testament*, trans. K. Grobel, 2 vols. (New York: Charles Scribner's Sons, 1951–55), 1:292ff.; H. Conzelmann, *An Outline of the Theology of the New Testament*, trans. J. Bowden (New York: Harper & Row, 1969), 199ff.; G. Delling, *Der Kreuzestod Jesu in der urchristlichen Verkündigung* (Göttingen: Vandenhoeck & Ruprecht, 1972), 9–45; G. Eichholz, *Die Theologie des Paulus im Umriss* (Neukirchen-Vluyn: Neukirchener Verlag, 1972), 101ff.; H. Gese, "The Atonement," "The Messiah," in *Essays on Biblical Theology*, trans. K. Crim (Minneapolis: Augsburg Pub. House, 1981), 93ff.; 141ff.; M. Hengel, *The Son of God*, trans. J. Bowden (Philadelphia: Fortress Press, 1976); O. Hofius, *Der Christushymnus Philipper 2:6–11* (Tübingen: Mohr, 1976); E. Käsemann, "The Saving Significance of the Death of Jesus in Paul," in *Perspectives on Paul*, trans. M. Kohl (Philadelphia: Fortress Press, 1971), 32–59; idem, "Some Thoughts on the Theme 'The Doctrine of Reconciliation in the New Testament' " in *The Future of Our Religious Past. Essays in Honour of Rudolf Bultmann*, ed. J. Robinson, trans. C. E. Carlston and R. Scharlemann (New York: Harper & Row, 1971), 49ff.; W. G. Kümmel, *The Theology of the New Testament According to Its Major Witnesses: Jesus—Paul—John*, trans. J. Steely (Nashville: Abingdon Press, 1973), 151–72; U. Luz, *Das Geschichtsverständnis des Paulus* (Munich: Kaiser, 1968) 139ff.; W. Schmithals, "Paulus und der 'historische Jesus,' " in *Jesus Christus in der Verkündigung der Kirche* (Neukirchen-Vluyn: Neukirchener Verlag, 1972), 36–59; W. Schrage, "Das Verständnis des Todes Jesu Christi im Neuen Testament," in *Das Kreuz Jesu Christi als Grund des Heils*, ed. F. Viering (Gütersloh: Gerd Mohn, 1967), 49–89, esp. 77f.; H. Schürmann, "Das Gesetz des Christus," in *Jesu Ureigener Tod* (Freiburg: Herder, 1975), 97–120; E. Schweizer,

"Zum religionsgeschichtlichen Hintergrund der 'Sendungsformel' Gal. 4:4f.; Rom. 8:3f.; John 3:16f.; 1 John 4:9," in *Beiträge zur Theologie des Neuen Testaments. Neutestamentliche Aufsätze, 1955–70* (Zürich: Zwingli-Verlag, 1970), 83–95; H. Thyen, *Studien zur Sündenvergebung* (Göttingen: Vandenhoeck & Ruprecht, 1970), 163ff.; U. Wilckens, "Christologie und Anthropologie im Zusammenhang der paulinischen Rechtfertigungslehre," *ZNW* 67 (1976): 64–82; idem, "Christus, der 'letzte Adam' und der Menschensohn," in *Jesus und der Menschensohn. Für A. Vögtle zur Vollendung des 65. Lebensjahres,* ed. R. Pesch and R. Schnackenburg (Freiburg: Herder, 1975), 387–403.

CHAPTER 11

"He is our Peace" (Eph. 2:14). On the Exegesis and Significance of Eph. 2:14–18

An essential part of the work in the Bible on traditions about peace and reconciliation is concentrated in Eph. 2:14–18. It is thus all the more painful to recognize that this very text is still hotly disputed in current exegesis. It is so hotly contested that the power of this New Testament tradition is scarcely introduced into the current Protestant debate about peace and reconciliation in the church and through the church in the world,[1] and really cannot yet be introduced by anyone who wants to be heard. That makes the attempt to gain clarity about our passage all the more necessary. It involves the following three groups of questions: On what traditions and concepts does the text depend? What is its literary form? What is the intention of the statements in the context of Ephesians and its original historical situation? Since we have Joachim Gnilka to thank for the most thorough recent commentary on Ephesians,[2] in which, moreover, precisely Eph. 2:14–18 is treated in very great detail, and since, in addition to what he has said in the commentary, he has devoted a separate treatise to this text,[3] it is appropriate to reconsider Eph. 2:14–18 particularly in dialogue with Gnilka.

I

If we wish to present the exegetical controversy about Eph. 2:14ff. as concisely as possible, we must speak about the conflict between two positions, a conflict Gnilka is concerned about overcoming. On one side stands the interpretation inspired especially by Heinrich Schlier and Ernst Käsemann.[4] Religion-historically this interpretation starts with gnostic cosmological thought, which it sees as pre-Christian, perhaps Jewish, and this Gnosticism's redeemer myth. Ephesians 2:14–18 in this view presupposes the thinking of this (Jewish) Gnosticism—especially in the idea of the earthly or heavenly wall (v. 14) that goes through the world dividing it into two spheres; in the concept that by coming to earth Christ has breached this wall (v. 14); and, finally, in the concept of the one new humanity created by Christ (v. 15)—and also makes this gnostic thought available for (critical) use in Christian proclamation about the reconciliation that comes through Christ's death. While Schlier of late wishes to distinguish only two stages of tradition in our text, namely, a gnosticizing Judaism that influenced the Phrygian Christian congregation addressed in Ephesians, and the text's polished hymnic statement by Paul himself in critical opposition to this influence,[5] those who follow Käsemann must separate at least three layers of tradition from one another, namely, the original gnostic conceptual pattern, then its incorporation into a Christ-liturgy that was at the disposal of the deutero-Pauline author of Ephesians, and third, the critical interpretation of this liturgical tradition by the letter's author himself.[6] While Käsemann himself gives only a rough description of the extent of the tradition,[7] Gottfried Schille,[8] Petr Pokorný,[9] and Jack T. Sanders,[10] among others, have tried to reconstruct, each in a very different way, the Christ-hymn underlying the text. But Reinhard Deichgräber has raised a philological objection to these attempts at reconstruction in his brilliant dissertation on "God-Hymns and Christ-hymns in early Christianity"[11] and stressed, by reference to the commentaries by Martin Dibelius—Heinrich Greeven[12] and Hans Conzelmann:[13] "Verses 14–18 are an explanation, partially formulated in lofty *prose,* of how it happened that through Christ's work of redemption those who were once far off may now belong to those near: the redeemer has taken away the wall of separation."[14] And yet, as will be shown directly, he has not gained acceptance for this criticism.

The counterposition against the "gnostic" interpretation of the text has been equally unable to gain acceptance. Before others Ernst Percy, in several works, rejected as erroneous the interpretation of (Colossians and) Ephesians from a gnostic thought world and instead proposed starting with Jewish conceptual perspectives,[15] specifically for Eph. 2:16 with the "concept of the ancestor who incorporates within himself all his offspring,"[16] and, for vv. 13–14, 17, with Isa. 57:19 and its Jewish interpretation.[17] The other ideas in the text, according to Percy, can be explained on the basis of Pauline tradition. Franz Mussner, in his habilitation thesis on "Christ, the universe, and the church,"[18] has developed this evaluation and tried to show, using a tradition-historical base considerably broader than Percy's, that for Eph. 2:13–18, "an Old Testament-rabbinic background is much more likely than a gnostic one."[19] Both authors are skeptical about the assumption of liturgical tradition in our text, with Mussner demanding, before a binding decision can be made, the development of a "precise methodology which makes it possible to distinguish tradition and redaction clearly."[20] How correct he is in making this demand will be seen directly.

But first we shall sketch Gnilka's attempt at a solution that combines both interpretive paths. From a history-of-religions perspective he finds himself obliged, with a view toward the work on this (portion of the) letter by Harald Hegermann,[21] Carsten Colpe,[22] and Eduard Schweizer,[23] to bid farewell "to the interesting theses of Schlier and Käsemann"[24] and to seek the thought background of Ephesians in the sphere of the Hellenistic synagogue.[25] One will agree to that just as readily as to Gnilka's thesis on the thoroughly deutero-Pauline character of the letter. Thus Gnilka evaluates positively the Jewish parallels offered by Percy, Mussner, and others to the law as a fence around Israel, to the interpretation of Scripture found in vv. 13 and 17, etc. Yet he would also like to acknowledge with appreciation the content of Schlier's interpretation and the hymnological investigations of Schille and his successors. The result is that Gnilka, despite Deichgräber's objection mentioned above, holds on to the thesis that in our text an originally cosmologically oriented Christian "hymn about peace and the redeemer" is interpreted critically by the letter's author, by reference to Christ's redemptive deed accomplished precisely on the cross. Conscious of the fact that in many respects the sketch remains hypothetical, Gnilka also tries to reconstruct from Eph. 2:14–17 a clearly structured hymn by separating hymnic tradition and redaction by the letter's author. With respect to the methology used in making such distinctions, Gnilka asserts that "in the process of discovering extant tradition," "theological considerations . . . without doubt [take] precedence over formal ones," but he expressly adds, "But when an idea is tied to an otherwise strange or rare concept which cannot or can only with difficulty be incorporated into a demonstrable outline,[26] formal considerations also deserve attention." By excluding the bracketed passages as redaction, he comes up with a nine-line hymn:

(14) *Autos (gar) estin (hē) eirēnē hymōn, ho poiēsas ta amphotera hen kai to mesotoichon (tou phragmou) lysas, tēn echthran, en tę sarki (autou). (15) (ton nomon tōn entolōn en dogmasin) katargēsas, hina (tous dyo) ktisę en autǫ (eis hena) kainon anthrōpon poiōn eirēnēn. (16) (kai apokatallaxē tous amphoterous en heni sōmati tǫ theǫ dia tou staurou), apokteinas tēn echthran en autǫ. (17) kai elthōn euengelisato eirēnēn (hymin) tois makran kai (eirēnēn) tois engys. (18) (hoti di autou echomen tēn prosagogēn hoi ampoteroi en heni pneumati pros ton patera).*

The hymn itself has the following wording and structure:[27]

> autos estin eirēnē hēmōn
> ho poiēsas ta amphotera hen
> kai to mesotoichon lysas
> tēn echthran en tę sarki katargēsas
> hina ktisę en hautǫ kainon anthrōpon
> poiōn eirēnē
> apokteinas ten echthran en hautǫ
> kai elthōn euengelisato eirēnēn
> [tois makran kai tois engys].

Gnilka's analysis of the text as a whole thus grows out of the critical combination of interpretations up to now in conflict. Unfortunately, it too is really unable to satisfy, since the criteria given by Gnilka for tradition criticism do not stand up, because he pays too little attention to the christological interpretation of Isa. 9:5–6; 52:7; and 57:19 carried out in Eph 2:13–18. Instead, his interpretation grows out of an exegetical perspective that actually develops the theses of a "gnostic" understanding of the text (which he acknowledged to be fundamentally untenable), rather than freeing itself from them.

II

It is a fundamental criterion of all exegesis that the interpretation must above all else be allowed to prove itself in the text itself. I therefore believe, in contrast to Gnilka, that precisely in tradition criticism and genre research, formal, that is, grammatical, philological, and literary-critical considerations, must have priority over theological and history-of-religions arguments. Otherwise our analysis proceeds from the start on uncertain, only hypothetically secure ground. The extreme delight "gnostic" investigation takes in concocting hypotheses about our very text sufficiently underscores this fact.[28]

Linguistically Gnilka finds the use of the neuter, *ta amphotera*, in v. 14 as a particularly striking criterion of traditional material. He notes further the "he" style, signaled by the *autos* introducing v. 14, and the numerous participial constructions in the text as characteristics of hymnic material and points out that there are some *hapax legomena* in the text of the hymn, namely *ta amphotera, to mesotoichon tou phragou* and *echthra*.[29] As certain as it is that the *autos* in v. 14 and the participial constructions *can* point to hymnic tradition,[30] the other evidence Gnilka offers is just as uncertain and ambivalent. In the New Testament, "The neuter is sometimes used with reference to persons if it is not the individuals but a general quality that is to be emphasized."[31] Since in the context of our verses, namely in vv. 11, 13 (cf. with v. 17), the groups of people reconciled by Christ are actually referred to in general terms frequently, as *akrobystia, peritomē,* and *hoi makran* or *engys (ontes)*, the neuter *ta amphotera* is grammatically correct, has linguistic parallels in 1 Cor. 1:27–28 and Heb. 7:7, and can no longer without further ado be claimed as a traditional element.

The results of word counts also argue against the assumption of hymnic tradition, if only they are studied fully enough. While *amphoteros* occurs only in vv. 2:14, 16, 18, and *echthra* also is attested in Ephesians only in vv. 2:14, 16, and *mesotoichon* in v. 14 is actually a *hapax legomenon* in the New Testament, there are among the parts of verses treated by Gnilka as redactional additions also expressions that are used in Ephesians only in our passage, namely *phragos* (v. 14), *nomos (tōn entolōn)* and *dogma* (v. 15), *apokatallassō* and *stauros* (v. 16). On the other hand, the text of what is called traditional material is filled with expressions that are used frequently in Ephesians and that in part are actually favorite terms in the letter: the letter uses *autos* emphatically, as in v. 14, several times: 4:11; 5:23. Because of its appearance in (1:2); 2:14, 15, 17 (twice); 4:3; 6:15, 23, *eirēnē* may really be considered one of the letter's favorite words. This is also true of formulations using *heis*: cf. 2:14, 15, 16, 18; 4:4, 5, 6. In addition to its use in 2:10, 15, *ktidzein* is also found in 3:9 and 4:24. The term *kainos anthropos* occurs again in 4:24; *euangelidzesthai* is found in 2:17 and 3:8. "Gospel of peace" is spoken of in 6:15 very much as it is in v. 17, and here as well as in 2:14–18, Isa. 52:7 is in the background. If the context of vv. 14–18, where the unique expressions cluster, is examined fully—*akrobystia* and *peritomē* are used in Ephesians only in 2:11, *atheos* in v. 12 is actually a *hapax legomenon* in the New Testament, as is *sympolitēs* in v. 19, *synoikodomein* in v. 22, etc.—it can be recognized that on the basis of word statistics the presence of a traditional passage in vv. 14–17 cannot be conclusively proven. Finally, since an overladen participial style is characteristic of Ephesians as a whole and not merely of 2:14ff., it must be concluded that on the basis of word usage, style, and grammar a pre-Pauline hymn is no more demonstrable than, say, a baptismal hymn in 2:19–22.[32]

Precisely because, like Gnilka, I am fully aware of the "ambiguity of the terminology" in Ephesians,[33] I nevertheless also find his arguments for the existence of a pre-Pauline redeemer-hymn in Eph. 2:14–17 on the basis of its content as minimally illuminating.—The fact that in vv. 14–18, "Christ himself *(autos)* appears as the one who effects pacification, redemption, and reconciliation" certainly does not mean that "therewith a perspective otherwise and widely characteristic of Ephesians [is] violated, according to which God is the initiator and worker of human redemption, the God who is at work in Christ."[34] Rather, as 5:2, 25–26 clearly show, this is a statement parallel to the other, actually used several times by the author of the letter.

The more clearly one sees that such parallel statements about the reconciliation effected by God and by Christ himself pervade all Paul's writings (just compare Gal. 1:4; 3:13 with 4:4–5 or Rom. 5:6 with 5:8–9; 3:25–26), the less one can designate the phrase about Christ achieving reconciliation as a mark of traditional material.

That one has to see an original cosmic wall of separation in *mesotoichon* which was identified with the "fence" of the law only redactionally by the author of Ephesians is indeed in keeping with interpretation of v. 14 begun primarily by Schlier, but not with the Hellenistic-Jewish comparative material quoted by Gnilka himself from the *Letter of Aristeas,* in which in sections 139 and 142 the law is *simultaneously* designated as an iron wall and as an enclosure surrounding Israel. Whoever begins with this material will find no justification for the gnostic interpretation of *mesotoichon* and particularly for the redactional differentiation between a wall in one place and the fence of the law in the other.[35] Rather, both refer to the law, and v. 15a continues this idea quite appropriately. But that does away with the concept of two cosmic spheres separated by an impenetrable wall, a concept that appeared to contradict Ephesians' picture of the world and to indicate traditional material. If we add that the neuter *ta amphotera* by no means designates cosmic regions but, in a grammatically correct way, designates specific groups of people, the cosmological argument for the gnostic interpretation becomes totally invalid. But that is also true of the evidence for Gnilka's attempt to distinguish originally speculative-cosmological thought in the hymn from personal thought about historical groups of people on the part of the letter's author who redacted the material. To refer *sarx,* mentioned in v. 14, to the incarnation on the basis of John 1:14 now appears to be more than risky, since in that case there is no longer any breaching of the cosmological wall left for the descending redeemer to do. Rather, *sarx* in v. 14 and certainly also *sōma* in v. 16 mean the crucified body of Christ given into death, which is also in clear termino-logical agreement with Col. 1:22 and the Pauline reconciliation tradition, according to Rom. 7:4 and 8:3.[36] The emphasis in v. 16 on reconciliation pre-cisely through the cross of Christ is, of course, extremely important theologi-cally, but there is, however, no longer any reason to ascribe this, on the analogy of the interpretive additions in Phil. 2:8 and Col. 1:20, only to the redactor and to charge the hymn with disregarding the cross.[37] Rather, v. 16a stems from the same letter writer who wrote vv. 14–18 as a whole. Finally, the conclusion of the hymn postulated by Gnilka shows the difficulties into which he gets with his reconstruction. In the last line of this hymn there is a reference to Isa. 57:19 and therewith, in the context of Eph. 2:11ff., a resumption of an exegetical thesis of the author's begun already in v. 13. But Gnilka, who, it's true, ascribes this concluding line to the hymn only with a question mark, hardly pays any attention to the reference to Scripture and wants to make the assumption that originally cosmic powers were designated by "far" and "near" in the hymn.[38] Unfortunately, however, this assumption has no support in the history of Jewish interpretation of Isa. 57:19,[39] and it only shows that Gnilka has not really recognized the exegetical context of vv. 13–18. But with this we have already reached the positive counterthesis to his analy-sis, which in my opinion is insufficiently grounded both philologically and tradition-critically and also with respect to the ideas in the passage.

III

Our counterthesis is that in vv. 13–18 the author offers a christological exegesis of Isa. 9:5–6; 52:7; and 57:19. In the context of vv. 11–22 this exegesis serves to express the reconciliation of Gentiles and Jews through Christ with God and each other in such a way that the miracle of the reception precisely of the Gen-tiles in the church and the nature of this church as the new people of God also becomes visible.

That an exegesis of Scripture is being carried on in our verses is a thesis already supported by Dibelius,[40] Percy,[41] Conzelmann,[42] Deichgräber,[43] and Mussner,[44] and if I am correct, not actually maintained consistently only in respect to vv. 14 and 17. It is supported by the following observations. As Gnilka himself, following Colpe, emphasized, the author of Ephesians shows himself in 1:22; 4:8ff.; and 5:31–32 to be thoroughly at home with Jewish interpretive methods, which he always uses in the service of his Christian faith.[45] From this perspective, then, it is not unusual that a christological exe-gesis of Scripture, its method inspired by the rabbis, also turns up in 2:13ff. On the basis of the catchword *eirēnē* it combines three passages of Scripture, Isa. 57:19 (vv. 13 and 17), Isa. 9:5–6 (v. 14) and Isa. 52:7 (v. 17). The way the passages are connected is thoroughly Jewish in form. The "peace" announced to the far and the near in Isa. 57:19 is brought about by the Messiah who is called the "prince of peace" (Isa. 9:5–6) and that in such a way that the Messiah, in accord with Isa. 52:7, appears as the proclaimer of peace for the far and the near. The combined reference of Isa. 57:7 and 9:5–6 to the Messiah as well as the messianic interpretation of Isa. 52:7 occur in Jewish texts.[46] Our letter writer is apparently aware of the possibility of a messianic interpretation of this kind, except that he now uses it christologically. For him "the far" and "the near" of Isa. 57:19 are the Gentiles and the Jews; the *eirēnē*, the salvation of God presented in Christ's atoning work; the Messiah referred to in Isa. 9:5–6 and 52:7 is Christ himself; and the fulfillment of the promise in Scripture is given by the work of creating peace and reconciliation through Christ, work that established the church out of Gentiles and Jews. One can grant that this exegesis fits just as well into vv. 11–22, which are saturated with Jewish-Christian material, as it does into the traditional material in the letter as a whole. And one is also able to assert that the content of this exegesis fits beautifully into the course of the argument in vv. 11–22, tracing the history of the promise.

Under these circumstances we can venture the following sketch of the sequence of ideas in vv. 11–22 and especially 14–18. Verses 11 and 12 refer back to the proclamation about justification in 2:1–10 and, using Jewish-Christian terminology, remind the gentile Christians, who are addressed in particular, of their former exclusion from the Israelite community and the salvation promised this community, salvation that has now come to the church as the true Israel. Verse 13 proclaims the wonderful change made possible and carried out by God in Christ's atoning death. In accord with the promise laid down in Scripture (Isa. 57:19), God, through Jesus' bloody death, procured salvation and forgiveness for the far, that is, the Gentiles (and for the near, that is, the Jews), and in this very way drew near to him through Christ those who were excluded by the law from attaining salvation. Verse 14a, linked to 13 by the causal connective "for,"[47] lays down the principle that is elaborated through v. 17 with the help of participial subordinate clauses. He, the Christ given up to death and, as 1:20 and 2:6 explain, raised by God and enthroned at God's right hand, is our peace. He is the Messiah promised in Isa. 9:5–6. Salvation, peace has been realized through him and brought to completion in him. That which, as Scripture says, is to come, which Israel expects only in the future, has in Christ already been fulfilled for the community. Christ has established a new inviolable communion between God and sinners from among the Gentiles and Jews who have experienced God's grace. How he established this communion and what it means is unfolded in vv. 14b, 15, and 16. In order to understand them we need to realize that the identification of Christ and peace, on the analogy of the Old Testament statement in Judg. 6:24, "The Lord is salvation" (= *yhwh šālôm*) is a dynamic way of speaking: Christ is the actualization of peace, and this peace remains tied to Jesus' fate and his person. But the peace itself is understood as reconciliation, that is, as the establishment of communion between God and humanity through Christ's atoning death, which God initiated and, in the resurrection, "ratified" as valid.[48] This interpretation of Jesus' death on the cross with the help of the Old Testament–Jewish concept of an atonement offering[49] was an early Christian intellectual and theological achievement of the first order since thereby

God's action on behalf of humanity in and through the death of Jesus became conceivable theologically and expressible kerygmatically. This interpretation was already there for Paul to use (cf. only Rom. 3:25–26 and 4:25); it was taken up by the apostle and made the basis of his law-critical theology of justification (cf., for example, Rom. 5:1ff.; 8:2–11, 31ff.; 2 Cor. 5:17ff., etc.); now here in Ephesians it is thought out and interpreted further in a way that rests on Paul but also goes beyond him ecclesiologically.

Verses 14b, 15, and 16 elucidate v. 14a in three statements: Christ has—first—abolished the law; he has—second—removed the hostility; he has—third—by virtue of the sacrifice he accomplished in the flesh, brought together and created anew Jews and Gentiles in the church. The gaze of the verses is thus fixed on the wonder of the bringing together of Gentiles and Jews to be the eschatological people of God, and the idea of reconciliation in vv. 14ff. is by no means restricted to what happens between an individual and his or her God but by definition includes the marvelous establishment of a new human community. The comprehensivenesss of this understanding of peace and reconciliation is actually the basic characteristic of our passage.[50] But it did not need to be wrested by the author, through criticism, from an idea of peace originally used in cosmological speculation. Rather, the author developed it directly from Scripture and Pauline statements about reconciliation, in critical confrontation with the law's power claim.

That the law is abolished, the law that in vv. 14, 15 is designated, in association with a Jewish-cosmological way of speaking, as a "wall of separation for fencing off" and then, in Christian terms, as "the law of commandments and ordinances," is best understood if we consider the following. For Judaism, the law revealed to it was not only a collection of commandments but also the basis for ordering its life and protection for its way of life. Protected by the law were a sphere of life and a mode of living from which the Gentiles were excluded insofar as they did not expressly convert to Judaism and desire circumcision. The law in this way acted as an extremely powerful wall of separation, both in theory and in practice, dividing Gentiles and Jews. In 3 Macc. 3:3, 4, with nearly literal reminiscenses of vv. 12, 14, it says: "The Jews, however, continued to maintain good will and unswerving loyalty toward the dynasty; (4) but because they worshiped God and conducted themselves by his law, they kept their separateness with respect to foods. For this reason they appeared hateful to some."[52] Generally, a very strained relationship between Jews and Gentiles in the cities of the Diaspora was the natural consequence of such religious separation. Our passage comes to speak, from a Christian perspective, extremely critically of the law that causes division in this sense. That is to say, to the understanding of the law as a dangerous wall of separation between Jews and Gentiles there is added the insight, worked out especially by Paul, that this law makes all people subject to it depend on themselves before God and forces them into high-handed self-assertion before God the judge (cf. Rom. 7:7–25; Gal. 3:19ff.). Therefore in our verses the torah is treated as a power that not only divides the world into hostile human groups but also bars the way to communion between God and humanity, sets up between God and the whole creation the hostility of the judgment, and feeds that hostility. Christ broke the threatening worldwide power of this law in that in his sacrificial death he brought the law to the end of its hostility-producing activity and thereby brought God to humanity and humanity to its creator once again. But now with the setting aside of the law the wall of separation formerly dividing Gentiles and Jews from one another is breached and the foundation laid in the church for a new human community between Jews and Gentiles, once bitter enemies. The new ecclesiastical way of life is now called "peace" or reconciliation and irrevocable communion with God.

The hostility mentioned twice in vv. 14 and 16 signifies, with a double-sidedness analogous to "peace," the confrontation prevailing between God and sinners and, according to early Christian perspective, encompassing the whole cosmos, on the one hand, and the situation of hatred and suspicion holding sway between the two parts of humanity, Jews and Gentiles,[54] on the other. But even this double hostility, kept alive and stabilized by the law, has been abolished by Christ through his bodily sacrifice on the cross,[55] which took away the law's power. As vv. 14b and 16 show, our passage wants to give an explicit interpretation of the cross of Jesus and its meaning as this is made evident in the resurrection. The meaning of the atoning death of Jesus on the cross is the removal of the (double) hostility. The removal of the hostility is accomplished in that Christ atones for the guilt of Gentiles and Jews and thereby makes possible a new communion, free from guilt and judgment, between God and the creation.

The meaning of the cross is the establishment of a new communion between God and humanity and the new creation, coming into being in such a "drawing near" to God, of the one new humanity out of Gentiles and Jews which serves God in freedom and gratitude. Primitive Christianity took up the idea, already understood quite concretely in Judaism, of new creation through the forgiveness of sin[56] and, as primarily 2 Cor. 5:17 shows, used it in the context of baptismal teaching. Coming from this tradition our text can describe in v. 15 the new creation from Gentiles and Jews as a result of the reconciliation established in the cross and resurrection. Then Eph. 4:24 again picks up the same idea parenetically.[57] The meaning of the cross with respect to creation is thus, to put it this time in Paul's own words, that in the church "There is neither Jew nor Greek, there is neither slave nor free, there is neither male nor female"; rather, "you are all one in Christ Jesus" (Gal. 3:28). Reconciliation reaches its goal in the creation of the new humanity that overcomes the ancient separation of Gentiles and Jews through life together in the community. Consequently, in contrast to the old world under the law, riddled with hostility, according to our letter the community as the body of Christ offers a new life, a sphere of new freedom as God's creation. With Ephesians' two-level way of thinking it is likely that *en heni sōmati* in v. 16 stresses not only the idea of the bodily sacrifice of Jesus on the cross but also the idea of the church established by this sacrifice, an association that lies very close at hand when we consider how Paul's body-of-Christ thinking was handed on and developed.[58]

Before the text explicitly draws the ecclesiological consequences for which it had already prepared the way in vv. 11ff., it points by way of summary in v. 17 to the christological fulfillment of Isa. 57:19 in the appearance of Jesus. That is what is meant by "he came" (cf. 1 Tim. 1:15).[59] In the appearance of Jesus, Israel's hope for the promised messianic evangelist and herald of peace is fulfilled, and this mission of Jesus, as the realization of the reconciliation of Jews and Gentiles, is the fulfillment of the promise of coming salvation expressed in Isa. 57:19. Thus the interpretations of Isa. 57:19 in v. 13 and Isa. 9:5-6 in v. 14 meet on a bridge provided in v. 17 by a christological understanding of Isa. 52:17. Verse 18 then confirms this by pointing to the access to the Father opened by the reconciliation that the Gentiles and Jews created anew by baptism have attained. The parallel to Rom. 5:1-2 is clear. Drawing upon vv. 11 and 12, vv. 19-22 then use this result once again ecclesiologically. The gentile Christians are no longer deprived of citizenship in (eschatological) Israel; rather, they are fellow members with Jewish Christians of the household of God. The church as temple, building, and dwelling place of God is held together by Jesus Christ as the keystone, but it is itself only in the process of coming into being. It is, that is to say, a missionary community created by Christ, intent on growing and being sustained; its foundation and life is called reconciliation and peace (cf. 4:1ff.; 6:15).

Thus it is, on the whole, completely possible to interpret our passage without borrowing later gnostic concepts and also without the difficult hypothesis of an underlying hymn, and an interpretation of this kind has the advantage of avoiding all difficulties of language and content into which Gnilka and his predecessors of necessity came.

IV

Gnilka correctly, but unfortunately still somewhat solitarily among present interpreters of our passage, pointed out that in Eph. 2:14-17 the main features of a New Testament theology of peace are given. According to Eph. 2:14ff. "peace" means God's new communion with humanity, established through Christ's atoning death, actualized by faith in the church as the body of Christ, and also the new communion between formerly hostile people who through the forgiveness of their guilt were set free for a new human encounter. Peace is here defined as a comprehensive reconciliation event connecting God and humanity and human beings to one another through Christ and personally represented in Christ. The parenesis in Ephesians 4—6 calls for testimony to the reality of this reconciliation in the life of the community and in this community's encounter with the world. Hence Gnilka is completely correct when he emphasizes that in our letter, and especially in Eph. 2:14ff., the church "comes in view as the intermediary that realizes in history the pacification of the world fundamentally accomplished by Christ."[60] His thesis gains importance the more clearly one sees that in Eph. 2:14ff. the lion's share of the work in the Bible on traditions about peace and reconciliation is assembled, because here converge the lines of Old Testament-Jewish tradition and of the work of

Jesus leading to reconciliation, as well as the fundamental experience of the
primitive community and the Pauline proclamation about justification and
reconciliation. Within the framework of this study, of course, all I can do is
mention that. But it is still important in our context to show how specific the
intention of the outlined proclamation about peace might originally have been.
Ephesians' tradition-saturated and theologically generalizing way of speaking
has led, at least in the more recent commentaries, to a failure to put with sufficient precision the question about the contemporary situation to which the
letter is addressed.[61] The well-known difficulties, arising from the textual tradition of v. 1:1, in locating the recipients of the letter and in characterizing the
letter with precision don't make any easier the question of the life situation
the letter was intended to address. And yet there are a few clear facts from
which to proceed. Our letter is directed in the years after 70 C.E. to the Christian congregation(s) in the cities in Asia Minor. Its major concern is to
impress upon the gentile Christians, who are again and again emphatically
addressed, that continuity with the salvation-historical beginnings of the community in Jewish Christianity continues to be of life-and-death importance to
them, because the miracle and nature of the community consists precisely in
the fact that in it the Gentiles together with the Jews have been called to
become a new people of God in which the promise of God is actualized. Ephesians expresses these theses in a time in which Jerusalem, until then for Jews
and Christians the real salvation-historical center and capital of the world, lay
in ruins, in which the remnant of the primitive community had apparently fled
to Pella, east of the Jordan, Jewish Christianity thus beginning to waste away,
and the congregations in Asia Minor were asking themselves with whom they
should align themselves spiritually. Precisely in view of Eph. 2:14ff. and the
hostility between Jews and Gentiles mentioned there, there is actually more
than can be said about conditions at that time. In the Diaspora in Asia Minor
and Egypt, despite the edicts of tolerance from Julius and Augustus Caesar
a hostile relationship had developed for decades between the Jews, who were
most numerous in the cities, and the native gentile population, a hostile relationship that was grounded primarily in the very different ways in which each
group led its religious life, hostility that was nurtured, in addition, by the Gentiles' envy of the privileges accorded the Jews from Rome—the free practice
of their religion, exemption from military service, etc., and that repeatedly
exploded into pogroms in the cities. Precisely in the time after 70 there was
a very marked increase in the Jewish aversion for the Gentiles, who had
robbed Israel of its temple and desecrated it.[62] From Alexandria comes our
most precise information about the disputes between the Jews and natives of
the city in the years 38–41 C.E.,[63] but with all necessary care we can take the
conditions there as a model of a situation and of a tense atmosphere such as
also prevailed in cities like Ephesus after 70 C.E. and could have exploded at
any time into persecutions of the Jews. Far from presenting only theological
instruction removed from life, our passage from Ephesians is aimed at the
world of ancient anti-Semitism and of Jewish contempt for Gentiles and *here*

proclaims that the former hostility between Jews and Gentiles has been over-come through Christ the reconciler. As the once strictly separated Jews and Gentiles lived together in the Christian community as reborn, united brothers and sisters and Ephesians actually specifically called on the gentile Christians to remain aware of their own dependence on their Jewish-Christian origins, there fell to the community, whether it liked it or not, the task and possibility of offering in its time a model of true reconciliation that overcame the ancient ethical and religious antagonisms. The Christian community established by reconciliation thereby presented to its time an answer, also of social interest to those around them, to late antiquity's universal longing for peace,[64] and it became its particular task to offer an alternative superior to the anti-Semitism and antipaganism around it by lives that showed what Christian reconciliation really looked like.

Precisely when we call to mind the circumstances to which Ephesians had to direct its witness, the significance and claim of the comprehensive christo-logical testimony to peace and reconciliation it directed to the community become provocatively clear. Hence, just as little as it is possible to reduce Christian talk about reconciliation to the religiously internalized relationship of the individual to God or to excuse the church from its task of making a gen-uine testimony on behalf of peace and reconciliation, just as clear must the significance precisely of our tradition be for a biblically based theology of reconciliation and the practice of peace.[65] Thus our text offers the present debate about peace and reconciliation a Christian force that needs to be seen and pondered anew and whose power to point the way is still to be exhausted.

A POSTSCRIPT

Only as I was proofreading this essay did I learn of the new edition of Klaus Wengst's dissertation on *Christologische Formeln und Lieder des Urchristen-tums* (Gütersloh: Mohn, 1972). On 181ff. Wengst analyzes Eph. 2:14–16 and in doing so also takes on Gnilka. Although he practices style criticism with more precision than Gnilka and ascribes all of vv. 17–18 to the author of the letter, I can see no real progress even in his suggested solution. Wengst would again like to find in Eph. 2:14–16 a gnosticizing hymn of the following kind: *autos estin hē eirēnē hēmōn; / hō poiēsas ta amphotera hen / kai to mesotoi-chon lysas, / hina tous dyo ktisę en hautǫ eis hena kainon anthropon, poiōn eirēnēn, / kai apokatallaxę tous amphoterous tǫ theǫ dia tou staurou, apok-teinas tēn echthran en hautǫ.*

He designates this text as a "reconciliation hymn" and proposes to find in it a "Gentile Christian adoption and development of the second part of a hymn for the enthroning of the agent of creation . . . , like the one in Col. 1:15–20" (p. 186). This hymn is supposed to have spoken originally, without a real soteriology and with only a minimal allusion to the cross of Christ, about the reconciliation of heavenly powers and humans on earth through the universal person Christ and about their attaining of peace with God. It was the author of Ephesians who first related it to the uniting of Jews and Gentiles in Christ and their reconciliation with God, as he expanded and reinterpreted the hymn text soteriologically and ecclesiologically.

This analysis offers nothing more than a new set of hypotheses: the history-of-religions starting point, Gnosticism, is, despite the allegedly indubitable "proofs by Dibelius and Schlier" (p. 185), speculatively chosen; Wengst does not deal with the Jewish material from the *Letter of Aristeas;* the interpretive context of vv. (12,) 13, 14, and 17–18 is torn apart once more; and the messianic exegesis of Isa. 57:19; 9:5–6; and 52:7 is not recognized. But this messianic exegesis emerges quite clearly even if our letter writer is supposed to have used only the text of the Septuagint. In Isa. 9:5 the name of the Messiah is *Megalēs boulēs angelos.* Of this messianic messenger of God's will—consider the parallelism between *angelos* and *euēngelisato* in Eph. 2:17—it is also said God will help him to achieve eternal sovereignty: *egō gar axō eirēnē epi tous archontas, eirēnē kai hygieian autǫ. (6) megale hē archē autou, kai tēs eirēnēs autou ouk estin horion epi ton thronon David.* . . . This reference to the prophecy of Nathan in 2 Sam. 7:12ff. fits excellently with Eph. 2:12 and makes the way of talking in vv. 18ff. (fellowship with God the "father," the church as God's "building") really comprehensible for the first time. Finally, the dative of advantage in the Septuagint, *eirēnē kai hygieian autǫ,* could, on the basis of Christian thinking about reconciliation, also be understood instrumentally and referred to the establishment of reconciliation and peace accomplished through the cross of Christ. If our passage is understood as Christian messianic exegesis, its cohesion and language become so readily comprehensible that I wish to hold to this understanding, also in opposition to Wengst.

NOTES

1. On this see H. Schmidt, *Frieden,* Themen der Theologie 3 (Stuttgart: Kreuz-Verlag, 1969), 145ff.; H. Hegermann, "Die Bedeutung des eschatologischen Friedens in Christus für den Weltfrieden heute nach dem Zeugnis des Neuen Testaments," in *Der Friedensdient der Christen. Beiträge zu einer Ethik des Friedens,* ed. W. Daniels-meyer (Gütersloh: Mohn, 1970), 17–39, esp. 27; P. Stuhlmacher, "Der Begriff des Friedens im Neuen Testament und seine Konsequenzen," in *Historische Beiträge zur Friedensforschung,* ed. W. Huber, Studien zur Friedensforschung 4 (Stuttgart: Klett; Munich: Kösel, 1970), 21–69, esp. 54ff.; E. Brandenburger, *Frieden im Neuen Testament* (Gütersloh: Mohn, 1973), 66–67.

2. J. Gnilka, *Der Epheserbrief,* HTKNT (Freiburg: Herder, 1971), henceforth abbreviated Gnilka, Comm. or just Comm.

3. J. Gnilka, "Christus unser Friede—ein Friedens-Erlöserlied in Eph. 2:14–17. Erwängungen zu einer neutestamentlichen Friedenstheologie," in *Die Zeit Jesu. Fest-schrift für H. Schlier,* ed. G. Bornkamm and K. Rahner (Freiburg: Herder, 1970), 190–207; henceforth cited as Gnilka, "Christus unser Friede," or just "Christus unser Friede."

4. Cf. H. Schlier, *Christus und die Kirche im Epheserbrief,* BHT 6 (Tübingen: Mohr, 1930), 18ff., and today especially *Der Brief an die Epheser,* 2d ed. (Düsseldorf: Patmos-Verlag, 1958), 118–45; E. Käsemann, *Leib und Leib Christi,* BHT 9 (Tübin-

gen: Mohr, 1933), 138ff., and especially, s. v. "Epheserbrief," *RGG* (3d ed.) 2:517–20; idem, "Epheser 2:17–22," in *Exegetische Versuche und Besinnungen (= EVB)*, 2 vols. (Göttingen: Vandenhoeck & Ruprecht, 1960–64), 1:280–83; idem, "Das Interpretationsproblem des Epheserbriefes," in *EVB* 2:253–61; idem, "The Theological Problem presented by the Motif of the Body of Christ," in *Pauline Perspectives* (Philadelphia: Fortress Press, 1969), 102–21, esp. 109–10.

5. Schlier, *Der Brief an die Epheser*, 123, n. 1.

6. Cf. *EVB* 1:280 and Käsemann's article "Epheserbrief," col. 518.

7. In *EVB* 1:280 Käsemann speaks of vv. 14–16 as a "reworked liturgical fragment," and in the article mentioned above in nn. 4 and 6, col. 519, says that a hymnic fragment underlies vv. 14–17.

8. G. Schille, *Frühchristliche Hymnen* (Berlin: Evangelische Verlagsanstalt, 1965), 24–31.

9. P. Pokorný, "Epheserbrief und gnostischer Mysterien," *ZNW* 53 (1962): 160–94, esp. 182ff.; cf. also Porkorný's study *Der Epheserbrief und die Gnosis* (Berlin: Evangelische Verlagsanstalt, 1965), 114–15.

10. J. T. Sanders, "Hymnic Elements in Ephesians 1—3," in *ZNW* 56 (1965): 214–32, esp. 216ff.

11. R. Deichgräber, *Gotteshymnus und Christushymnus in der frühen Christenheit*, SUNT 5 (Göttingen: Vandenhoeck & Ruprecht, 1967), 165–67.

12. M. Dibelius and H. Greeven, *An die Kolosser, Epheser, an Philemon*, 3d ed., HNT 12 (Tübingen: Mohr, 1953), 69 [= ET: Hermeneia, 1971].

13. H. Conzelmann, *Der Brief an die Epheser*, NTD 3 (Göttingen: Vandenhoeck & Ruprecht, 1968), 67ff.

14. Deichgräber, *Gotteshymnus*, 167, emphasis mine.

15. E. Percy, *Der Leib Christi (Sōma Christou) in den paulinischen Homologumena und Antilegomena* (Lund: Gleerup, 1942); *Die Probleme der Kolosser- und Epheserbriefe* (Lund: Gleerup, 1946), 278–88; "Zu den Problemen des Kolosser- und Epheserbriefes," *ZNW* 43 (1950/51): 178–94, esp. 187–88.

16. Percy, *Die Probleme der Kolosser- und Epheserbriefe*, 285, n. 38.

17. Ibid., 283.

18. F. Mussner, *Christus, das All und die Kirche*, Trierer Theologische Studien 5 (Trier: Paulinus-Verlag, 1955), 76ff.

19. Ibid., 96.

20. Ibid., 96, n. 96 (= p. 97).

21. H. Hegermann, *Die Vorstellung vom Schöpfungsmittler im hellenistischen Judentum und Urchristentum*, TU 82 (Berlin: Akademie-Verlag, 1961), 145–46.

22. C. Colpe, "Zur Leib-Christi-Vorstellung im Epheserbrief," in *Judentum, Urchristentum, Kirche. Festschrift for J. Jeremias*, ed. W. Eltester, Beihefte zur *ZNW* 26, 2d ed. (Berlin: Töpelmann, 1964), 172–87; cf. also Colpe's habilitation treatise, *Die religionsgeschichtliche Schule. Darstellung und Kritik ihres Bildes vom gnostischen Erlösermythus*, FRLANT 78 (Göttingen: Vandenhoeck & Ruprecht, 1961).

23. Cf. in addition to other works by E. Schweizer his essay, "Die Kirche als Leib Christi in den paulinischen Antilegomena," in *Neotestamentica* (Zürich: Zwingli-Verlag, 1963), 293–316.

24. Gnilka, Comm., 38, n. 3.

25. Ibid., 43–44.

26. Gnilka, "Christus unser Friede," 195; essentially the same in Comm., 147–48.

27. Printed with colometric divisions in "Christus unser Friede," 197–98 and Comm., 149.

28. D. Lührmann, in his essay "Rechtfertigung und Versöhnung," *ZTK* 67 (1970): 437–52, has added to the old hypotheses an, in my opinion, unfounded new one. He writes about Eph. 2:13–17: "It is based on cosmological concepts according to which

heaven and earth are separated from one another by a wall. These concepts are connected here with the understanding of the law as a 'fence.' But when the wall is identified with the law, heaven must be equated with Israel, earth (construed negatively) with the Gentiles. The salvation event succeeds in breaking through the wall of the law, so that the way to Israel is open to the Gentiles" (p. 447). On the question of genre research that in contrast to these speculations attempts once more to use methods that are more demonstrable, see my "Thesen zur Methodologie gegenwärtiger Exegese," *ZNW* 63 (1972): 18–26, esp. theses 6 and 7, and their further elaboration in my study "Zur Methoden- und Sachproblematik einer interkonfessionellen Auslegung des Neuen Testaments," *Evangelisch-Katholischer Kommentar zum Neuen Testament, Vorarbeiten* 4 (Zürich-Neukirchen: Neukirchener Verlag, 1972), 11–55, esp. 29ff., 35ff.

29. Gnilka, Comm., 139, 148, and "Christus unser Friede," 196.

30. Cf. Deichgräber, *Gotteshymnus,* 165–66; but see also his assertion on p. 167: "Every christological piece is not a Christ-hymn, not even when traces of hymnic terminology are in evidence."

31. BDF § 138.1 (p. 76); Gnilka, Comm., 139, n. 3 would like to grant this grammatical possibility only for the understanding of *ta amphotera* in the redaction of the hymn; by what right?

32. W. Nauck has wished to see such a baptismal hymn in Eph. 2:19–22; cf. his essay "Eph. 2:19–22—ein Tauflied?" *EvT* 13 (1953): 362–71. But Käsemann, in his meditation on Eph. 2:17–22 (see above, n. 4), has already argued against Nauck, saying the assumption of a baptismal hymn appears "undemonstrable by style criticism and inappropriate as far as content is concerned" (p. 282). In his commentary Schlier (see above, n. 4), ad loc., also regards Nauck's thesis as unproven, and Gnilka, like Käsemann, asserts that Nauck's interpretation can be "justified . . . neither from the structure nor the form. The style is fully that of the author" (Comm., 153). It is likely only fascination with the "gnostic" analysis of its background that has prevented an equally critical judgment with respect to Eph. 2:14ff.

33. Colpe, *Zur Leib-Christi-Vorstellung im Epheserbrief,* 186. The ambiguity shows itself in our passage in the comprehensive dimension of the idea of peace and animosity and in the ambiguity of the concept of the body in v. 16. Finally, it is to be kept in mind, as especially M. Hengel, *Judaism and Hellenism* (2 vols. [Philadelphia: Fortress Press, 1974], 1:171ff.), has emphasized, that for Hellenistic and rabbinic Judaism the Torah was an ontologically and cosmologically operative power. The new-creation and reconciliation ideas in our passage are thus antithetically opposed to an absolute cosmological-ontological claim by the law.

34. Gnilka, "Christus unser Friede," 194.

35. This is especially true in the light of the torah ontology mentioned in n. 33. If one considers that according to Jewish self-understanding the direct knowledge and possession of the law helps Jews achieve a way of life that distinguishes them from the Gentiles and does justice to the creator, then the statements concerning the law in the *Letter of Aristeas* appear in their true light: "(139) What need even to speak of other infatuated people, Egyptians and their like, who have put their reliance in wild beasts and most creeping creatures and animals, and worship these, and to these offer sacrifice, whether alive or dead?

(139) "When therefore our lawgiver, equipped by God for insight into all things, had surveyed each particular, he fenced us about with impregnable palisades and with walls of iron, to the end that we should mingle in no way with any of the other nations, remaining pure in body and in spirit, emancipated from vain opinions, revering the one and mighty God above the whole of creation. (140) Whence the priests who are the guides of the Egyptians . . . have named us 'men of God' *[anthrōpous theou],* a title applicable to none others but only to him who reveres the true God. . . . (142) And therefore, so that we should be polluted by none nor be infected with perversions by

associating with worthless persons, he has hedged us about on all sides with prescribed purifications *[pantothen hēmas periphraxen hagneiais]* in matters of food and drink and touch and hearing and sight." As the passage continues, this is explained ontologically and cosmologically, that is, to the effect that the individual laws are there to get the Israelites to stop to consider, in the fear of God and in righteousness, the creative power and wisdom of God that completely control people, right down to the members of their bodies, and, in addition, the course of the whole world, and from this also to draw the conclusion that "we are set apart from all men" *[dioti para pantas anthrōpous diestalmetha]*, § 151; the translation is that in *Aristeas to Philocrates (Letter of Aristeas)*, ed. and trans. Moses Hadas (New York: Harper & Brothers, 1951), 155ff. If one, in addition, considers Philo's ontological understanding of the torah, sketched by H. Fr. Weiss (*Untersuchungen zur Kosmologie des hellenistischen und palästinischen Judentums, TU* 97 [Berlin: Akademie-Verlag, 1966], 277ff.), it appears to be all the more impossible, indeed actually false, to assume in our passage only a subsequent identification of the "wall" and the "fence" of the law. In v. 12, indeed, it is said clearly enough that the Gentiles were once separated from the Jewish *politeia* (= *civitas*) constituted by the law, that is, by this very fence of the law that surrounds the *civitas* and keeps the Gentiles from the Jews. If one relates vv. 11–13 directly to v. 14ff., which is what needs to be done, the passage becomes entirely clear. On *politeia* in v. 12 see, in addition to Gnilka, Comm., ad loc., M. Hengel, "Die Synagoginschrift von Stobi," *ZNW* 57 (1966): 145–83, esp. 180–81, and H. I. Bell, *Jews and Christians in Egypt* (Oxford: Univ. Press, 1924), 13.

36. The connection also of Rom. 8:3 with the reconciliation tradition is assured by the fact that, in accord with the technical usage of the LXX, *kai peri hamartias* has to be translated "and as an offering for sin"; cf. E. Schweizer, "Zum religionsgeschichtlichen Hintergrund der 'Sendungsformel' Gal. 4:4f., Röm. 8:3f., Joh 3:16f., 1 Joh 4:9," in *Beiträge zur Theologie des Neuen Testaments, Neutestamentliche Aufsätze 1955–1970* (Zürich: Zwingli-Verlag, 1970), 94 (83–95). Gnilka, Comm., 141, n. 3, regards Col. 1:22 as "not a real parallel"; why not?

37. Thus Gnilka, "Christus unser Friede," 199; similarly also Schlier, *Der Brief an die Epheser,* 135. Whether Col. 1:20 actually is only an addendum to the hymn in Col. 1:15–20 cannot be discussed here; statistical evidence on word usage speaks against it.

38. Gnilka, "Christus unser Friede," 200; also Comm., 150.

39. In Jewish interpretation of Isa. 57:19 "the far" and "the near" designate sinners ready to repent and the righteous within Israel (so, for example in the targum ad loc. and in the passages listed in Str-B, 1:167, 215–16) or Gentiles and Jews on whom God bestows his salvation (cf. Str-B, 3:586: Dibelius-Greeven, *Kommentar,* on 2:14, among others. Beyond that it is quite common Jewish mission terminology to speak of "the far" *(rĕḥôqîm)* = the Gentiles and "the near" *(qĕrôbîm)* = the Jews. Since in the Jewish texts of which I am aware cosmological powers are never spoken of as far or near, and also since in the present text of v. 17 people alone are intended, it does not appear to me wise in interpreting Eph. 2:17 to break away from the linguistic usage common in the Jewish tradition.

40. Dibelius-Greeven, *Kommentar,* 69.

41. Percy, *Die Probleme der Kolosser- und Epheserbriefe,* 283.

42. Dibelius-Greeven, *Kommentar,* 68–69.

43. Deichgräber, *Gotteshymnus,* 167, n. 1.

44. Mussner, *Christus, das All und die Kirche,* 100ff.

45. Cf. Gnilka, Comm., 29, 96, 206ff., and Colpe, "Zur Leib-Christi-Vorstellung," 178ff., 182ff.

46. Cf. Str-B, 3:9ff., 587; Mussner, *Christus, das All und die Kirche,* 101; and P. Stuhlmacher, *Das paulinische Evangelium,* vol. 1: *Vorgeschichte,* FRLANT 95 (Göttingen: Vandenhoeck & Ruprecht, 1968), 148.

47. Cf. Deichgräber, *Gotteshymnus,* 166.

48. Since in the Pauline tradition and in Ephesians, as we have shown above, parallel expressions refer to reconciliation through the atonement offering that is either established by God or brought by Christ in voluntary, obedient self-surrender, we are also able to interpret our passage on the basis of this comprehensive thought, which always calls attention to God's initiative.

49. On this see G. von Rad, *Old Testament Theology,* trans. D. M. G. Stalker, 2 vols. (New York: Harper & Row, 1962–65), 1:262ff.; K. Koch, "Sühne und Sünden-vergebung um die Wende von der exilischen zur nachexilischen Zeit," *EvT* 26 (1966): 217–39, esp. 227ff.; E. Sjöberg, *Gott und die Sünder im palästinischen Judentum,* BWANT 79 (Stuttgart: W. Kohlhammer, 1939), 175ff.; E. Lohse, *Märtyrer und Got-tesknecht,* 2d ed., FRLANT 64 (Göttingen: Vandenhoeck & Ruprecht, 1963), 20–23, and frequently. Old Testament–Jewish tradition's main feature decisive for the New Testament and its understanding of Jesus' atoning death lay in this, that cultic atonement was considered to be established by God and that the sin offering and atonement offering is the medium graciously authorized by God to which human guilt may be transferred and in this way removed between God and the people.

50. Thus also Gnilka, Comm., 143, and E. Dinkler, s. v. "Friede," in *RAC* 8:464 (434–505): "What is special about the idea here is that *eirēnē* designates both the relationship of God to people, renewed through Christ, and that of people, that is, the near and the far, to one another; so Christ establishes peace between God and humanity as well as between one person and another."

51. On this see nn. 33 and 35.

52. (3) *hoi de Ioudaioi tēn men pros tous basileis eunoian kai pistin adiastrophon ēsan phylattontes, (4) sebomenoi de ton theon kai tǭ toutou nomǭ politeuomenoi chorismon epoioun epi tǭ kata tas trophas, di hēn aitian eniois apechtheis ephainonto.*

53. On the understanding of "hostility" as the opposition of the righteous God to the lawless, cf. Rom. 5:8ff.; Foerster, *TDNT* 2:812ff.; Str-B, 3:591–92.

54. On the hostility between Jews and Gentiles, cf. the quotation from 3 Macc. 3:3–4 in n. 52 and the contemporary materials given below in nn. 62 and 63.

55. With E. Schweizer, *TDNT* 7:137, 1077, I relate *en tē sarki autou,* v. 14, and *hen heni sōmati,* v. 16, primarily to the surrender of Jesus' life on the cross, without wishing to deny the parallelism of the second expression to 4:4; on this see nn. 33 and 57.

56. On the Jewish tradition see especially E. Sjöberg, "Wiedergeburt und Neu-schöpfung im palästinischen Judentum," *ST* 4 (1950): 44–85; Sjöberg, "Neuschöpfung in den Toten-Meer-Rollen," *ST* 8 (1954): 131–36; J. Jeremias, *Infant Baptism in the First Four Centuries,* trans. D. Cairns (London: SCM Press, 1960), 32–37. A comprehensive treatment of the New Testament and Pauline material is found in H. Schwantes, *Schöpfung der Endzeit* (Berlin: Evangelische Verlagsanstalt, 1963). I offer an experimental treatment of this material in my study, "Erwägungen zum ontologischen Charakter der *kainē ktisis* bei Paulus," *EvT* 27 (1967): 1–35, esp. 22ff.

57. The difference between our passage and Eph. 4:24, as Mussner, *Christus, das All und die Kirche,* 86, and Gnilka, Comm., 140, correctly stress, consists in this, that in Eph. 4:24 the new behavior of the baptized is looked at while Eph. 2:15 sketches how they attained their new ecclesiological existence. But both are parallel aspects of one and the same phenomenon, namely, the tangibly understood new creation through Christ's atoning death, in faith and through incorporation into the community by baptism.

58. In his treatise on "The Theological Problem presented by the Motif of the Body of Christ," 110ff., Käsemann is sharply critical of connecting the body on the cross, the eucharistic body of Christ, and the concept of the church. He wants to distinguish the ecclesiastical body, as "the earthly body of the risen and exalted Lord," from the "crucified body, which was Jesus' alone and in which no one can be incorporated. If

this distinction is overlooked . . . one arrives at an abstruse result from which only a mystical devotion to the Passion would fail to shrink" (p. 111f.). In my dissertation *Gerechtigkeit Gottes bei Paulus*, 2d ed., FRLANT 87 (Göttingen: Vandenhoeck & Ruprecht, 1966), 212ff., I also followed Käsemann extensively. Of course, in the light of the difficulties in which the gnostic interpretation has found itself and in the light of the fact that various traditions and concepts are admittedly bound together in Paul's body-of-Christ thinking, I believe I am now compelled to say that while originally the body of Jesus on the cross and the eucharistic element, on the one hand, and the concept of the community as a body and organism, on the other hand, arose from different realms of thought, they were, nevertheless, already consciously connected by the apostle under the designation *sōma Christou*. Therefore, I now wish to agree with G. Bornkamm's assertion, for example, that, according to Paul's understanding, "there could be no breaking of the connection between the body of Christ received in the sacrament and the church as the one body of Christ and, on the other hand, participation in the blood, that is, the death of Christ, and the 'new saving order' (the new covenant, 1 Cor. 11:25) manifesting itself in the church" (*Paul*, trans. D. M. G. Stalker [London: Hodder & Stoughton, 1969], 192–93). I hope I am in agreement with Gnilka, Comm., 99ff., on this also.

59. Precisely if a christological interpretation of the messenger of joy on Isa. 52:7 stands behind our verse, it is not advisable to restrict Jesus' activity as the evangelist of peace to his Easter activity.

60. Gnilka, "Christus unser Friede," 204.

61. Also in this respect Gnilka is concerned about making a new beginning in his commentary (pp. 45ff.). It is true that he doesn't get beyond the broadly conceived thesis, strongly oriented to the model provided in Colossians, that Ephesians presents the attempt, "in a time in which things were tending to come apart at the seams, a time of crisis, of religious individualism, of a loss of a sense of history . . . , to safeguard both God's salvation, which presented itself in historical form in the church, and concrete Christian responsibility." According to Gnilka, the theme that dominates our passage, the uniting of Gentiles and Jews in the one church, is to be integrated into and subordinated to this intention of the letter. I believe, in view of H. von Soden, *Der Brief an die Epheser*, HKNT 3:1 (Freiburg im Breisgau: Mohr, 1891), 82ff., and the sketch given by L. Goppelt, *Apostolic and Post-Apostolic Times*, trans. R. Guelich (London: Black, 1970), 117–35, that I am compelled to reverse the emphasis, to subordinate the themes in 4:14 to the topic of the unity of Jews and Gentiles in the church, and to say with Käsemann, "A Gentile Christian congregation that for the sake of orthodoxy has to set itself apart from false teaching (4:14) and threatens to lose its connection with Jewish-Christianity, needs instruction about the nature of the *una sancta*" (s. v. "Epheserbrief," *RGG* [3d ed.] 2:517).

62. Cf. Str-B, 3:139ff., 144ff.; 4.1:353ff. and E. Schürer, *Geschichte des jüdischen Volkes im Zeitalter Jesu Christi*, 4th ed., 3 vols. (Leipzig: Hinrichs, 1901–11), 3:126–27, 150ff.

63. Cf. the famous letter of the emperor Claudius to the Alexandrians in the year 41 c.e., which in col. 4, line 79ff., and col. 5, lines 1ff., reads: "and I tell you once for all that unless you put a stop to this ruinous and obstinate enmity *(an mē katapausētai tēn olethrion orgēn tautēn kat' allēlōn authadion)*, I shall be driven to show what a benevolent prince can do when turned to righteous indignation. Wherefore once again I conjure you that on the one hand the Alexandrians show themselves forbearing and kindly towards the Jews who for many years have dwelt in the same city, (col. 5) and dishonour none of the rites observed by them in the worship of their god, but allow them to observe their customs as in the time of the deified Augustus, which customs I also, after hearing both sides, have sanctioned; and on the other hand I explicitly order the Jews not to agitate for more privileges than they formerly possessed, and not

in future to send out a separate embassy as if they lived in a separate city, a thing unprecedented, and not to force their way into . . . (the) games . . . and not to bring in . . . (new) Jews . . . ; otherwise I will by all means take vengeance on them as fomenters of what is a general plague infecting the whole world. If desisting from these courses you consent to live with mutual forbearance and kindliness, I on my side will exercise a solicitude of very long standing for the city, as one which is bound to us by traditional friendship." (The translation is that found in *The New Testament Background: Selected Documents*, ed. C. K. Barrett, [New York: Harper & Row, Harper Torchbooks, 1957], 46; the Greek text and a commentary can be found in H. I. Bell, *Jews and Christians in Egypt* [see above, n. 35], 25, 36–37). To Christians who knew of such official proclamations precisely the parenesis in Ephesians 4 must also have seemed extremely relevant and close to life.

64. On the relationship between the Christian message about reconciliation and the longing for peace in antiquity, cf. now M. Hengel, *Victory over Violence. Jesus and the Revolutionists*, trans. D. Green, intro. R. Scroggs (Philadelphia: Fortress Press, 1973), 60ff.

65. Gnilka, Comm., 110, draws possible consequences when with an eye on our text he writes: "In the church God's work gets its chance in the world. In the church hostile human groups as reconciled with God have been reconciled with one another. That this happens in the church constitutes its responsibility to the world. It will maintain this advantage as long as it is responsible to the world on the basis of what happened to and in it. The church is to take this task seriously as a representative of Christ in the world. As such it is his body, it stands for Christ. In its being his body it actualized Christ's peace, which brought Jews and Gentiles together. Reconciliation, readiness for reconciliation, and action on behalf of reconciliation have to be its fundamental law. Nothing is more inimical to its Christ-established nature than disunity, strife, hatred. Not only is it to preserve the *eirēnē* in its own sphere but also actively to oppose evil." On the Protestant effort to regain this dimension of ecclesiastical peace activity, see the set of theses "Der Friedensdienst der Christen" and the significant paper by H. Fast, "Christologie und Friedensethik," both in *Der Friedensdienst der Christen* (see above, n. 1), 112–29 and 61–78.